Processor Architecture and Interfacing

Processor Architecture and Interfacing

Atul K Joshi
Assistant Professor
Department of Instrumentation and Control
Cummins College of Engineering, Pune

Swati Atul Joshi
Associate Professor
Department of Computer Science
Sinhgad College of Engineering, Pune

Hemlata M Jadhav
Associate Professor
Department of Information Technology
Sinhgad College of Engineering, Pune

Processor Architecture and Interfacing

Other Wiley Editorial Offices:
John Wiley & Sons, Inc. 111 River Street, Hoboken, NJ 07030, USA
Wiley-VCH Verlag GmbH, Pappellaee 3, D-69469 Weinheim, Germany
John Wiley & Sons Australia Ltd, 42 McDougall Street, Milton, Queensland 4064, Australia
John Wiley & Sons (Asia) Pte Ltd, 1 Fusionopolis Walk #07-01 Solaris, South Tower, Singapore 138628
John Wiley & Sons Canada Ltd, 22 Worcester Road, Etobicoke, Ontario, Canada, M9W 1L1

First Edition: 2014
ISBN: 978-81-265-4560-5
www.wileyindia.com

Printed at: *Bhushan Printline, Sahibabad*

Preface

The objectives of this book are to study the operation, performance, and applications of the microprocessor and microcontroller. This book mainly covers two chips:80386 microprocessor and 8051 micro controller. The prerequisites of this subject are – the fundamental knowledge of digital electronics regarding the logic circuit families, Boolean algebra, combinational and sequential logic circuits.

These devices are widely used for industrial and technological applications. Nowadays, it is found in almost every electronic gadget; from small devices to super computers. This has wide scope in data mining, analysis, processing, storage and computing for variety of applications. The latest technology is based upon the understanding of basic techniques so coverage of basics is important.

Coverage and Organization

First part of the book deals with the 80386 processor to establish the necessary base for studying microprocessor. **Chapter 1** throws light on 8086 assembly language programming, ALP tools: Assembler, linker, and loader. The structures of the debuggers, concepts of emulator and assembler directives are also covered in the chapter with supporting examples.

Chapter 2 introduces to the features and architecture of 80386 microprocessor, its register set and the information regarding the addressing modes, instruction set and format. Operation of the 80386 processor in real mode is essential to establish the processor in protected mode.

Chapter 3 gives introduction to the various pins available for 80386 and their usage. Memory organization and access mechanism via various bus cycles is covered in the same chapter.

Segmentation is an important feature of the 80386 processor which provides protection to the operating system and application programs. Address translation mechanism, supporting data structures and registers, their usage is covered in detailed fashion in **Chapter 4**.

Chapter 5 extends the protected mode and paging. All supporting registers, data structures required for linear to physical address translation are covered. Concept of the virtual memory and use of the TLB are the key mechanisms behind paging. Protection through privilege levels and mechanism for changing privilege level is explained in the same chapter.

Chapter 6 covers multitasking – concept, supportingregisters, data structures and mechanism to the required depth. It also covers the I/O permission bit map and its usage.

Further, **Chapter** 7 deals with working of 80386 in virtual mode for execution of 8086 based programs. How to enter and leave the virtual mode is also discussed in this chapter.

Interrupt processing methods in all three modes is in different fashion. All three mechanisms are discussed in **Chapter 8**. Comparison of all 3 modes – real, protected and virtual 8086 is done with all possible points. This chapter concludes with introduction to a new trend processor Core Duo by Intel.

Second part of the book deals with the micro controller 8051.

The concept of 8051 microcontroller, features of microcontrollers, functional comparison of microcontroller with microprocessor is discussed in the introduction of **Chapter 9**. It also covers the internal architecture and organization of the different sections of microcontroller like CPU timing, program and data memory, timer/counter, serial communication, interrupts, input and output section. It also focuses on the instruction format, set of instructions and CPU timing diagram.

Chapter 10 introduces the different methods for interfacing external memory to the 8051 microcontroller. It covers the hardware schemes for interfacing data memory, program memory and their combination. The examples on memory interfacing are also included in the chapter. It gives the idea of development of minimum system.

Chapter 11 commences with the different modes of timer/counters of the 8051 microcontroller. The setting of special function registers (SFRs) is discussed in the chapter. It covers the assembly language programs for generating delays using timer/counter. The timer/counter module of the 8051 can be used for various industrial applications which are also discussed in this chapter.

Microcontroller 8051 has capability of communicating with standard devices having serial communication port. **Chapter 12** introduces the communication module (UART) of the 8051 microcontroller. It shows comparison between parallel and serial, synchronous and asynchronous communication. It describes the differences in full and half duplex communication. The baud rate generation method is explained with an example. Chapter 12 also focuses on the connection of MAX 232 chip to interface 8051 microcontroller and computer with RS232 connector. Few programs are also included in this chapter.

The 8051 microcontroller has capability of handling external interrupts. **Chapter 13** introduces the SFRs for interrupt and structure of the interrupts. It compares polling versus interrupt. It covers the programming examples for handling external interrupts, timer interrupts and serial interrupts.

Knowing ins and outs of the 8051 microcontroller enables user to design an application specific embedded system. This needs to know about the interfacing techniques for external peripherals. **Chapter 14** deals with the interfacing of different peripheral devices like 7-segment LED displays, 7-segment decoders, key board, Analog to Digital Converter (ADC 0809), Digital to Analog Converter (DAC), uni-polar stepper motor etc. It also covers a sample design of an industrial product including the circuit schematic and the software.

We have tried to provide an overview of the processor architecture and interfacing. We hope that we have been able to achieve our goal of helping students and others working in this area to have an insight of this great technology.

Acknowledgements

We are thankful to Dr. Ajay Deshmukh, Dr. Ashok Gaikwad, Prof. Atul Rohankor and Prof. Pravin Futane for their constant support and encouragement.

We (Atul Joshi and Swati Joshi) are thankful to our friends and family members, especially our daughter Sayali for her co-operation and patience during the process.

I (Hemlata Jadhav) am very thankful to my family members, my husband Makarand and my kids Gautami and Gaurav for their moral support.

Atul Joshi
Swati Joshi
Hemlata Jadhav

Syllabus Map

Unit	Topic Covered in Chapter/Section
UNIT I – Introduction to Assembly Language Programming and 80386 Processors	
Introduction to assembly language programming	Chapter 1, Sections 1.1 and 1.2
ALP tools	Chapter 1, Section 1.3
Assembler	Chapter 1, Section 1.3.2
Linker	Chapter 1, Section 1.3.3
Loader	Chapter 1, Section 1.3.4
Debugger	Chapter 1, Section 1.3.5
Emulator concepts	Chapter 1, Section 1.3.6
Assembler directives	Chapter 1, Section 1.8.1
Far and near procedures	Chapter 1, Section 1.8.2
Macros	Chapter 1, Section 1.8.3
80386: Features and architecture	Chapter 2, Sections 2.1 and 2.2
Register set	Chapter 2, Section 2.3
80386 real mode segmentation	Chapter 2, Section 2.5
Instruction format	Chapter 2, Section 2.7
Addressing modes	Chapter 2, Section 2.8
Instruction set	Chapter 2, Section 2.9
UNIT II – 80386 Memory Segmentation	
Pin descriptions	Chapter 3, Sections 3.1 and 3.2
Bus cycles, and bus operations – non-pipelined and pipelined	Chapter 3, Section 3.4
Initialization and configuration	Chapter 3, Section 3.5
16/32 bit data transfer mechanism	Chapter 3, Section 3.3
Segmentation-support registers, related instructions	Chapter 4, Section 4.2
Descriptors	Chapter 4, Section 4.2.2
Memory management through segmentation	Chapter 4, Section 4.1
Logical to linear/physical address translation	Chapter 4, Sections 4.3 and 4.4
Protection in segmentation	Chapter 4, Section 4.5
Privileged instructions	Chapter 4, Section 4.6

UNIT III – Protected Mode	
Paging – support registers, descriptors	Chapter 5, Section 5.4
Linear to physical address translation	Chapter 5, Sections 5.4 and 5.5
Page level protection	Chapter 5, Section 5.6
Virtual memory	Chapter 5, Section 5.12
Entering into PM mode and returning back to RM mode	Chapter 5, Sections 5.13 and 5.14
Inter privilege level transfer using Call gates and confirming code segment	Chapter 5, Section 5.15
Multitasking – support registers, related descriptors	Chapter 6, Sections 6.1 and 6.3
Task switching	Chapter 6, Sections 6.4
I/O permission bit map	Chapter 6, Section 6.5

UNIT IV – Interrupts	
Virtual mode	Chapter 7, Section 7.1
Features	Chapter 7, Section 7.2
Address generation	Chapter 7, Section 7.4
Registers available	Chapter 7, Section 7.5
Entering and leaving V86 mode	Chapter 7, Sections 7.6 and 7.7
Real and protected mode interrupt structure – IVT	Chapter 8, Section 8.5
Types of exception and processing through IDT	Chapter 8, Section 8.6
Halt and shutdown	Chapter 3, Sections 3.3.5 and 3.3.6
Comparison of all three modes	Chapter 8, Section 8.9
Introduction to duo-core processor-features and block diagram	Chapter 8, Section 8.10

UNIT V – Microcontroller I	
Microcontroller 8051 architecture	Chapter 9, Sections 9.1 and 9.4
On-chip data memory and program memory organization	Chapter 9, Sections 9.5
Register set	Chapter 9, Section 9.5.1
Register bank	Chapter 9, Section 9.5.1
SFRs	Chapter 9, Section 9.5.2
Instruction format	Chapter 9, Section 9.11
Addressing modes	Chapter 9, Section 9.12
Instruction set	Chapter 9, Section 9.11
External data memory and program memory and its interfacing	Chapter 10
I/O ports programming	Chapter 9, Section 9.6

UNIT VI – Microcontroller II	
Interrupts structure and response	Chapter 13, Sections 13.1, 13.2, 13.3 and 13.4
Timers/counters and their programming	Chapter 11
Serial port and programming	Chapter 12
Interrupt programming	Chapter 13, Section 13.5
Design of minimum system using 8051 microcontroller for various applications	Chapter 14, Section 14.3

Contents

Chapter 2 80386 Processor 39

Unit III Protected Mode

Unit IV Interrupts

Chapter 7 Virtual Mode Operation 203

Chapter 8 Interrupt and Exception Processing 213

Unit V Microcontroller – I

Chapter 9 Microcontroller 8051 Architecture 241

About the Authors

Prof. Atul K. Joshi is currently working as an Assistant Professor in the Department of Instrumentation and Control at Cummins College of Engineering for Women, Karve Nagar, Pune. He has a master's degree in Instrumentation and Control Engineering from SRTMU, Vishnupuri, Nanded and has registered for PhD in the same university in the field of "Induced Acoustic Emission Testing".

He has received "best teacher award" for the year 2006–07 from the University of Pune. He has a patent in "**method and apparatus to study fracture mechanical properties of nails and its usage as a diagnostic tool**". He has published number of papers in international journals and 12 papers in international conferences and 10 papers in national conferences.

He has 5 years of industrial experience as application and development engineer in the field of metallurgical parameter testing machines, 19 years of teaching experience in the field of Instrumentation and Control. His fields of interest include micro controller based mechtronic systems, sensors and transducer designing, signal conditioning, digital techniques, electronic instrumentation, embedded system design, product development, etc. He has also worked for 5 years as member of Board of Studies in Instrumentation and Control at University of Pune.

Prof. Swati A. Joshi is an associate professor in the department of Computer Engineering at Sinhgad College of Engineering, Vadgaon, Pune. She has completed the masters in Electronics Engineering with specialization in Computers from Govt. College of Engineering, Pune. She has worked as a Development Engineer in Prime Machine Tools, Pune for 3 years. She is in teaching field since last 18 years.

She has taught various subjects in Computer Engineering, Information Technology – microprocessor interfacing techniques, microprocessor interfacing lab, computer organisation, microprocessor based systems, microprocessors and microcontrollers, hardware lab, advanced computer architecture, operating systems, distributed systems, computer networks for undergraduate students and emerging trends of computer architecture for post graduate students. She has completed a research project on wireless sensor networks with University of Pune. Currently she is working on data flow architectures and multicore architecture. She has also published 14 research papers international journals and conferences and 10 papers in national conferences.

Prof. Hemlata Makarand Jadhav is working as associate professor in the department of Information Technology at Sinhgad College of Engineering, Vadgaon, Pune. She has completed the masters in Electronics (Digital Systems) from Govt. College of Engineering, Pune. Currently she is pursuing her PhD in Electronics and Telecommunication in wireless communication domain at Sinhgad College of Engineering, Pune.

She has 14 years teaching experience in Information Technology and Computer Science and has taught various subjects of second year subjects such as principles of Communication Engineering, Analog and Digital Electronics, Digital Electronics and Microprocessor, Digital Electronics and Logic Design, Microprocessor Systems, Processor Architecture and Interfacing, Elements of Electronics Engineering, Analog Circuits and Signal Conditioning and Data Converters. Her area of interest is Wireless Communication.

UNIT I

Introduction to Assembly Language Programming and 80386 Processors

Introduction to Assembly Language Programming

LEARNING OBJECTIVES

After reading this chapter, you will be able to:

- Understand the significance and different aspects of assembly language programming.
- Get familiar with the different software such as assembler, linker, loader, debugger, emulator, which help the application programmer to assemble, execute and debug the assembly language programs.
- Understand the concept of assembler directives that direct the assembler to perform specific tasks.

1.1 Introduction

Manufacturers of processor chip design chip-specific instruction set. Instruction is nothing but a command given to the processor to perform a particular operation.

1. An instruction consists of two parts, an opcode and an operand. Opcode indicates what operation the particular instruction is going to perform. Opcode is unique for each instruction.
2. Operands are nothing but the factors on which the processor is going to perform the indented operation. Different kinds of possible operands are central processing unit (CPU) registers, memory, input/output (I/O) devices and immediate data.
3. The opcode of each instruction is decoded by an instruction decoder. Machine code is the code which a machine understands. CPU in a computer understands only the machine language.
4. The instructions written in the text form are called mnemonics.
5. Assembly language is nothing but machine code representation of an instruction written in short English statements, that is, mnemonics.

1.2 Significance of Assembly Language

Sometimes code written in assembly can be faster and smaller than compiler generated code. Assembly allows access to direct hardware features of the system that might be difficult or impossible to use from a higher level language.

1. Assembly language is beneficial to implement real-time applications where time is critical factor.
2. Learning the program in assembly helps one gain a deeper understanding of how computers work.
3. Learning the program in assembly helps one understand better how compilers and high level languages such as C work.

1.3 MS-DOS Programming Tools

To develop assembly language program, following programming tools are needed:

1. Editor.
2. Assembler.
3. Linker.
4. Loader.
5. Debugger.
6. Emulator.

All these tools will be discussed in the following subsections. Preparing a new program to run under MS-DOS is an iterative process with the following four basic steps:

1. Use of a text editor to create or modify an American Standard Code for Information Interchange (ASCII) source-code file.
2. Use of an assembler or high-level-language compiler (such as the Microsoft Macro Assembler or the Microsoft C Optimizing Compiler) to translate the source file into re-locatable object code.
3. Use of a linker to transform the re-locatable object code into an executable MS-DOS load module.
4. Use of a debugger to methodically test and debug the program.

Figure 1 shows the steps needed to execute assembly language program. Steps for creating an executable assembly language program are as follows:

1. Assemble.
2. Link.
3. Run.

Table 1 shows the steps to run the assembly language program.

Table 1 Steps to Run the Assembly Language Program

Step	*Input*	*Program*	*Output*
1. Edit	Usually keyboard	Editor	xyz.asm
2. Assemble	xyz.asm	MASM	xyz.obj
3. Link	xyz.obj	LINK	xyz.exe

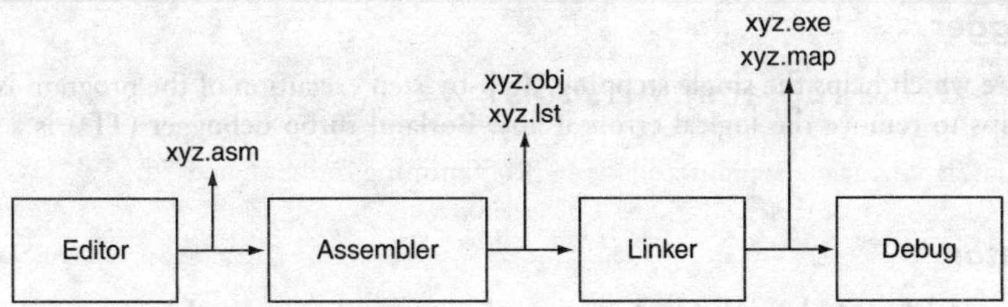

Figure 1 Steps to execute assembly language program.

1.3.1 Editor

Editor is a software. It provides the programmer the screen where he can type the assembly language program. There are different types of editors available such as WordStar, WordPad, Notepad, etc. The feature of editors are as follows:

1. Editor stores ASCII code of alphabets and numbers in random access memory.
2. The editor creates source file which is saved with the extension .asm.

1.3.2 Assembler

The source file created by an editor is further processed by an assembler. Assembler converts the assembly language program into respective machine (binary) codes. Two types of assemblers are available with IBM-PC: Microsoft micro assembler (MASM) and Borland turbo assembler (TASM).

Assembler determines the displacement of data items, offset of labels, etc. and puts this information into a symbol table. Two files are generated by an assembler: An object file and a list file. Object file is given the extension ".obj", which saves the binary codes of instructions and addresses of instructions. List file contains the assembly language statements, the binary codes for each instruction and offset of each instruction. Syntax errors are indicated by an assembler, but not the logical errors. Syntax errors are listed along with the line numbers.

1.3.3 Linker

It is a program which is used to link many small object files into a large object file. Normally for large-sized programs instead of writing a very big program, it is divided into smaller modules and then assembled. With this it becomes easy to test and debug the small modules.

Linker generates the link file which contains the binary codes for all the combined modules. It produces link map file which holds the address of all the linked files. Linker does not assign absolute addresses; it only assigns the relative addresses to the program starting from zero. It is re-locatable. Linker produces the link file with ".exe" extension.

1.3.4 Loader

It is a program which is used for assigning the specific address of the locations where the segments of the object code are to be loaded into the memory. IBM-PC provides a locator program called EXE2BIN. This program converts .EXE file to .BIN file.

1.3.5 Debugger

It is the software which helps the single stepping. Step-by-step execution of the program is possible with this; it also helps to remove the logical errors if any. Borland turbo debugger (TD) is a very powerful debugger.

1.3.6 Emulator

It is used to test and debug the hardware and software of an external system such as the microprocessor-based system. It is a combination of hardware and software. An emulator consists of a multi-wire cable that connects the host system to the external system. It allows the user to load the programs to be tested, and run the programs. It allows changing the contents of the registers and memory locations and also inserts the break points.

1.3.7 Extension File Type

The MS-DOS programming tools can create and process many different file types. These are as follows:

1. **.ASM:** Assembly language source file.
2. **.C:** C source file.
3. **.COM:** MS-DOS executable load module that does not require relocation at runtime.
4. **.EXE:** MS-DOS executable load module that requires relocation at runtime.
5. **.LST:** Program listing produced by the assembler that includes memory locations, machine code, the original program text and error messages.
6. **.MAP:** Listing of symbols and their locations within a load module; produced by the linker.
7. **.OBJ:** Re-locatable object code file produced by an assembler or compiler.

1.4 Processor 80386 Instructions: Basic Structure

The basic structure is as follows:

Label: Operator   Operand[s]   ; Comment

We discuss each entry in this structure as follows:

1. **Label:**
   - It is an optional alphanumeric string.
   - First character must be a–z, A–Z, ?, @, _ or $. No numeric digit is allowed.
   - Reserved words cannot be used as a label.
   - Maximum length of the characters in the label is 31.
2. **Operator:**
   - It is an assembly language instruction.
   - *Mnemonic:* It is a short name of an instruction for programmers.
   - Assembler translates mnemonic into hexadecimal opcode. For example, MOV is F8H.

3. **Operand:**
   - It can be of several different forms.
   - It is delineated by commas.
   - Possible operands are immediate data, register name, memory data and memory address.
4. **Comment:**
   - It is extremely useful in assembler language.
   - These fields are separated by white space (tab, blank, etc.).

1.4.1 80386 Instruction: Example

Consider

Label	Operator	Operand[s]	; Comment
up:	mov	ah, dl	; Copy contents of dl into ah

Here we have

Label	–	up:
Operator	–	mov
Operands	–	ah and dl
Comment	–	Alphanumeric string between semicolon and new line

They are not case sensitive and unlike other assemblers, destination operand is first.
In the above example **mov** is the *mnemonic* that the assembler translates into an opcode.

1.4.2 Introduction to Program Segments

A segment is an area of memory that includes up to 64 KB and begins an address evenly divisible by 16 (such an address ends in 0H). An assembly language program consists of following three segments:

1. **Code segment:** It holds the program code (instructions).
2. ***Data segment:*** It is used to store data (information) to be processed by the program.
3. **Stack segment:** It is used to store information temporarily.

1.5 Logical and Physical Address

The various addresses are discussed as follows:

1. Physical address is the 20-bit address that actually put on the address bus (in real mode of 80386). It has a range of 00000H–FFFFFH.
2. Offset address is a location within 64 KB segment range. It has a range of 0000H–FFFFH.
3. Logical address consists of segment address and offset address.

1.6 Commands Overview

The various commands are listed as follows:

1. To get help
   C:\Tasm /h
2. For Assembling
   C:\Tasm hello
   This causes TASM to create: HELLO.OBJ
3. Next step is to create executable file using the linker:
   C:\ Tlink hello
   This causes linker to create: HELLO.EXE
4. Next step is debugging
   C:\ Debug hello.exe
   Enter debug subcommands

1.7 Assembly Language Program Format

The general assembly language program format is as shown in Figs. 2(a) and (b).

```
.model small        ; allocates memory of 64 KB to DS and 64 KB to CS
.stack              ; optional field indicates start of stack segment
……
……
.data               ; indicates start of data segment
……
……                  ; data declaration
.code               ; indicates start of code segment
……
……                  ; program body
……
end                 ; last line of the code
```

(a)

```
Data segment
.....                    ; data declaration
.....
Data ends
Code segment
Assume cs: code, ds: data
.....
.....                    ; Program body
.....
Code ends
End                      ; last line of the code
```

(b)

Figure 2 (a) Program format-I and (b) Program format-II.

1.8 Assembler Directives, Far and Near Procedures, Macros

The concept of assembler directives, different types of procedures used and macros are discussed in the following sections.

1.8.1 Assembler Directives

Some of the features of assembler directives are as follows:

1. These are non-executable statements.
2. These statements are active only during assembly.
3. They direct the assembler to do a particular task but will not generate any machine code for it.

Different types of assembler directives are as follows:

1. **.code:** This directive indicates the beginning of the code segment.
2. **.data:** This directive indicates the beginning of the data segment. For example,

```
.data
msg1 db 4ah
msg2 dw 12d4h
temp db?                ; nothing is stored but a storage is assigned
```

3. **.stack[size]:** This directive indicates the beginning of the stack segment. The size of the stack is 1024 bytes by default, but this size can be modified. For example, stack 64h, which reserves 100 bytes for stack segment.
4. **.model:** This directive is used to allocate the memory of different sizes to different program segments. The memory models are selected depending upon the user's requirement. Different memory models are as shown in Table 2.

Table 2 Memory Models

Model	*No. of Code Segments (CS)*	*No. of Data Segments (DS)*
Small	One CS of size <= 64 KB	One DS of size <= 64 KB
Medium	CS may be of any number and size	One DS of size <= 64 KB
Compact	One CS of size <= 64 KB	DS may be of any number and size
Large	Any number and any size	Any number and any size
Huge	Any number and any size	Any number and any size
Tiny	It is used in .COM programs since they have their code, data and stack in only one 64 KB of memory segment	

It is to be noted that

- Small model is used for the student-level programs.
- In compact model, the assembler uses 32-bit addresses so the execution time for this model is more.
- Huge model consists of variables such as arrays which needs a larger space than 64 KB.

5. **Equate (EQU):** This directive assigns a symbolic name to a string or constant. Each time an assembler finds that name in the program, it replaces that name with the value assigned to that variable. For example,

    min equ 04h

6. **Define byte (db):** It defines the data variable of byte size. For example,

msg1	db	05h
(variable name)	(size of variable)	(initial value)

7. **Define word (dw):** It defines the data variable of word (two bytes) size. For example,

msg1	dw	12a5h
(variable name)	(size of variable)	(initial value)

8. **Define double word (dd):** It defines the data variable of double word (four bytes) size. For example,

msg1	dd	12345678h
(variable name)	(size of variable)	(initial value)

9. **Define quad word (dq):** It defines the data variable of quad word (four words) size. For example,

str1	dq	123456789abcdef0h
(variable name)	(size of variable)	(initial value)

10. **Define ten bytes (dt):** It defines the data variable of 10 bytes size.
11. **Originate (org):** With the help of this directive, location counter can be set to any value at any point in the program. The location counter is automatically set to 0000h when assembler reads the segment. For example,

    org 100h
12. **Assume:** What names are assigned to different logical segments are clear to assembler through this directive. For example,

    Assume segment register: segment name

    Assume cs: code, ds:data, ss:stack
13. **Offset:** The offset operator returns the distance of a label or variable from the beginning of its segment. The destination must be 16 bits. For example,

    mov cx, offset count

    Instead of this, we can write the instruction as

    lea cx, count
14. **Segment and ends:** The segment operator returns the segment part of a label or variable's address. It is used to indicate the start of a logical segment. Ends directive is used along with the segment directive. It indicates the end of respective segment. For example,

    data segment ; start of segment

    m1 db 02h

    data ends ; end of segment
15. **End:** It is placed at the end of a source-code. It indicates last line of a code. The assembler will not consider any statement written after end directive.
16. **DUP operator:** It only appears after a storage allocation directive (db, dw etc.). It is used to allocate the space for a table or an array. For example,

    M1 db 20 dup (?)
17. **The PTR operator:** It is used to assign specific type to a variable or to a label. For example,

```
INC [20h] ; is this byte/word/dword?
Or MOV [SI], 5;
-Is this byte 05?
```

```
-Is this word 0005?
-Or is it double word 00000005?
```

- Byte or word or doubleword?
- To clarify we use the PTR operator as

–INC BYTE PTR [20h]

–INC WORD PTR [20h]
–INC DWORD PTR [20h]
MOV byte ptr[SI], 5

MOV word ptr[SI], 5

18. Macro and endm: Macros are predefined functions which involve a group of instructions to perform a special task which can be used repeatedly. The endm directive is used along with the macro directive. The assembler directive endm indicates the end of a macro. For example, in order to print a string on the screen, INT 21H together with two more instructions can be used (three lines of code), which is as shown in example1. It does not make sense to rewrite them every time they are needed. In order to reduce the time to write the code and reduce the length of the code macros can be used. Macros allow a programmer to define the task (set of codes to perform a specific job) once only and invoke it whenever/wherever it is needed. For example,

```
Macro definition:
Name MACRO dummy1, dummy2, dummy3,…, dummyN
…
…
ENDM
```

Example 1

Write a macro called STRING which displays a string of text to the monitor.

Solution: The macro is written as follows:

```
STRING MACRO m1        ; start of macro
MOV AH, 09H            ; macro body
MOV DX, OFFSET m1
INT 21H
ENDM                   ; end of macro
```

Invoking a macro: You can invoke the above macro as follows:

```
                       ; from the data segment
STRING m1              ; Assembler will invoke the macro to perform
                         the defined function
```

19. Using MACROS in an assembly language program: The macros are defined outside the code segment of an assembly language program and can be invoked inside the code segment. There can be comments in macro definition.

20. **Proc and endp:** The start of procedure is indicated by this directive. The procedures are of two types: near and far. If the procedure is defined in the same segment, the near label must be used after the procedure. If the procedure is defined in another module, then far label must be used after the procedure. endp directive is used along with proc directive. It defines the end of the respective procedure. For example,

```
hex nearproc    ; start of procedure
.....
.....           ; body of procedure
hexendp         ; end of procedure
```

21. **Extrn:** The name or label that follows the extrn directive is present in the other module. For example,

```
extrnmypro : far
```

The above statement tells the assembler that the mypro is a label of far type and it is present in another module. The names or labels that are external in one module must be declared public with the public directive in the module where they are defined. For example,

```
proc
extrn sum: far
extrncnt : near
endp
```

22. **Public:** This directive indicates that the variable declared as public is referred by other module. For example,

```
public mypro
```

This makes mypro variable available to other module.

23. **Global:** This directive can be used instead of public or extrn directive. This directive is used to make the variable available to all the other modules. For example,

```
global arr
```

This makes the variable arr public so that it can be accessed from all other modules used. For example,

```
Global arr : word
```

It tells the assembler that variable arr is of word type which is present in another assembly module. It is of extrn type.

24. **Align:** This directive tells the assembler to align the next instruction on an address which corresponds to the given value. For example,

```
align number
```

This number should be 2, 4, …. (it should be a power of 2).

25. **Even:** This directive increments the location counter if needed, so that the next data item will be aligned on one of the even address. The advantage of this is that 80386 can read or write from memory in only one bus cycle if the word is at even address. For example,

```
even arr db 15 dup (0)
```

1.8.2 Procedure

When we want to make use of a group of instructions a number of times in a program then instead of rewriting the same group of instructions we can use either procedures or macros. Procedures are of two types, near and far.

1. We can write a group of instructions as a subroutine. The subroutine is nothing but a procedure and can be called using call and ret instructions. For making use of procedure, proc, near, far, public, extrn and endp assembler directives are necessary.
2. If the procedure is written in the same segment, it is called near procedure. If the procedure is written in the other segment than where the main program is written, it is called far procedure. For near procedure call instruction saves only the IP value on stack as contents of CS register remains unaltered, whereas for the far procedure contents of IP and CS both are pushed on the stack.

Table 3 shows the comparison of near and far procedure.

Table 3 Comparison of Near and Far Procedure

S. No.	*Near Procedure*	*Far Procedure*
1	It is declared in the same segment where the main program is stored.	It is declared in a different segment than the segment where the main program is stored.
2	While calling near procedure only the contents of IP are pushed on the stack and contents of CS remain unchanged.	When far procedure is called, the contents of IP and CS both are pushed on the stack.
3	Here less stack memory is required.	Here more stack memory is required.
4	It is also called intra-segment call.	It is also called inter-segment call.
5	Here near directive is used.	Here far directive is used.
6	Execution time required will be less.	Execution time required will be comparatively more.

1.8.3 Macros

When we want to make use of repetitive group of instructions, we can use macro. When this group of instructions is too short to be written as procedure, macro is a good option. Each time we call a macro in a program, the assembler will insert macro body in place of a call. The various features of macros are as follows:

1. With the help of macro, we can avoid writing repetitive code.
2. Macros execute faster; we will not need call and ret instruction.

3. Using macro the length of a program gets reduced but not the memory requirement.
4. The basic format of macro is as follows:

```
Macro name macro ; start of macro
.....
.....              ; macro body
Endm               ; end of macro
disp macro ; start of macro
   lea dx, m1
   mov ah, 09h
   int 21h                ;macro body
   Endm                   ;end of macro
```

Table 4 shows the comparison of macro and procedure.

Table 4 Comparison of Macro and Procedure

S. No.	*Macro*	*Procedure*
1	When an assembler finds call macro instruction in a program, it replaces the call macro instruction with corresponding macro body.	The processor branches to the procedure by making use of call instruction and can regain the control of the main program by use of ret instruction after executing the procedure.
2	Time taken to execute the macro is less.	Time taken to execute the procedure is more.
3	Macro does not require any latency period.	Procedure has a latency period as processor branches to another memory location and returns back.
4	Macro is used for small repetitive tasks.	Procedure is used for large repetitive tasks.
5	Using macro the length of the program reduces.	Making use of procedure does not reduce the length of the program.

1.9 Sample Assembly Language Programs

Program 1: Program to display a message (good.asm)

```
This program displays "Good Morning!"
.model small
.stack 100h
.data
```

```
Message db 0Ah, 0Dh, "Good Morning! $" ; newline + LF
.code
mov ax, @data           ; base address of data segment in ds
mov ds, ax
mov ah,09h
mov dx, offset message ; display msg (or LEA dx, message will do)
int 21h
mov ah,4Ch              ; halt the program and return
int 21h
end
```

Program 2: Program to display string

```
.MODEL SMALL            ; MEMORY ALLOCATION: DS <= 64KB, CS <= 64KB
.DATA
S1 DB "HELLO! $"
.CODE
MOV AX, @DATA           ; PUT BASE ADDRESS OF DATA SEGMENT IN DS
MOV DS, AX
LEA DX, S1              ; DISPLAY STRING S1
MOV AH, 09H
INT 21H
MOV AH, 4CH             ; RETURN CONTROL BACK TO DOS PROMPT
INT 21H
END ; LAST LINE OF CODE
```

Program 3: Program to display a string using macro

```
.MODEL SMALL            ; MEMORY ALLOCATION:.DS <= 64KB, CS <= 64KB
DISP MACRO              ; START OF MACRO
LEA DX, S1              ; DISPLAY STRING S1
MOV AH, 09H
INT 21H
ENDM ; END OF MACRO
.DATA
S1 DB 10, 13, "HELLO! $"
.CODE
MOV AX, @DATA           ; PUT BASE ADD OF DATA SEGMENT IN DS
MOV DS, AX
DISP                    ; MACRO BODY GETS INSERTED HERE
MOV AH, 4CH             ; RETURN CONTROL BACK TO DOS PROMPT
INT 21H
END                     ; LAST LINE OF CODE
```

Program 4: Program to display a string using near procedure

```
.MODEL SMALL              ; MEMORY ALLOCATION: DS <= 64KB, CS <= 64KB
.DATA
S1 DB 10,13, "HELLO! $"
.CODE
MOV AX, @DATA            ; PUT BASE ADDRESS OF DATA SEGMENT IN DS
MOV DS, AX
CALL MYPRO               ; MYPRO IS NEAR PROCEDURE NAME
MYPRO PROC NEAR
LEA DX, S1               ; DISPLAY STRING S1
MOV AH, 09H
INT 21H
RET
ENDP ; END OF PROCEDURE
MOV AH, 4CH                ; RETURN CONTROL BACK TO DOS PROMPT
INT 21H
END                        ; LAST LINE OF CODE
```

Program 5: Program to display a string using FAR procedure: MAIN PROGRAM (FILENAME1.ASM)

```
.MODEL SMALL            ; MEMORY ALLOCATION: DS <= 64KB, CS <= 64KB
.DATA
PUBLIC SI               ; S1 ISPUBLIC TO THIS PROGRAM
S1 DB 10, 13, "HELLO!$"
.CODE
MOV AX, @DATA           ; PUT BASE ADDRESS OF DATA SEGMENT IN DS
MOV DS, AX
EXTRN MYPRO:FAR         ; PROC IS EXTERNAL TO THIS PROGRAM
CALLMYPRO               ; MYPRO IS FAR PROCEDURE NAME
MOV AH, 4CH             ; RETURN CONTROL BACK TO DOS PROMPT
INT 21H                 ; LAST LINE OF CODE
END
```

Program 6: Program to display a string using FAR procedure: FAR PROCEDURE PROGRAM (FILENAME2.ASM)

```
.MODEL SMALL          ; MEMORY ALLOCATION: DS <= 64KB, CS <= 64KB
.DATA
EXTRN SI              ; S1 IS EXTERNAL TO THIS PRG S1 DB "HELLO! $"
.CODE
PUBLIC MYPRO          ; MYPRO IS NEAR PROCEDURE NAME
```

```
MYPRO PROC
LEA DX, S1              ; DISPLAY STRING S1
MOV AH, 09H
INT 21H
RET
ENDP                    ; END OF PROCEDURE
END                     ; LAST LINE OF CODE
```

Steps to execute far procedure program:

1. TASM FILENAME1.ASM
2. TASM FILENAME2.ASM
3. TLINK FILENAME1 + FILENAME2
4. FILENAME1

Example 2

Write a program to add two given numbers.

Solution: The program is as follows:

```
.MODEL SMALL
.STACK 64
.DATA
DATA1 DB 52h
DATA2 DB 29h
SUM DB ?
.CODE
MAIN PROC FAR
MOV AX, @ DATA          ; copy the data segment into the DS reg.
MOV DS, AX
MOV AL, DATA1
MOV BL, DATA2           ; or DATA1+1
ADD AL, BL
MOV SUM, AL
MOV AH, 4Ch
INT 21h
MAIN ENDP
END MAIN
```

Example 3

Write an assembly language program to add array elements.

Solution: The program is as follows:

```
.model small
.data
arr db 05h,02h,04h,0FFh ; array declaration
sum db ?                ; sum variable declaration
carry db ?              ; carry variable declaration
count db 04             ; counter
.code
mov ax, @data           ; physical initialisation of DS and ES
mov ds, ax
mov al,00h
lea si, arr             ; point to first element of array
up: add al,[si]         ; add with accumulator
jnc dn                  ; if carry is not produced jmp to dn
inc carry               ; else increment carry
dn: inc si              ; increment pointer
dec count               ; decrement counter
jnz up                  ; if counter not zero jmp to up
mov sum, al             ; store sum into sum variable
mov ah,4ch              ; terminate the code and safe exit to DOS
int 21h
end
```

```
------------------output---------------------------
C:\TASM>tasm arr.asm
Turbo Assembler Version 3.0 Copyright (c) 1988, 1991 Borland
International
Assembling file: arr.asm
Error messages: None
Warning messages: None
Passes: 1
Remaining memory: 461k
C:\TASM>tlink arr.obj
Turbo Link Version 2.0 Copyright (c) 1987, 1988 Borland International
Warning: no stack
C:\TASM>arr.exe
C:\TASM>
C:\TASM>debug arr.exe
-t
AX=0B53 BX=0000 CX=0027 DX=0000 SP=0000 BP=0000 SI=0000 DI=0000
DS=0B41 ES=0B41 SS=0B51 CS=0B51 IP=0003 NV UP EI PL NZ NA PO NC
0B51:0003 8ED8 MOV DS,AX
```

```
-t
AX=0B53 BX=0000 CX=0027 DX=0000 SP=0000 BP=0000 SI=0000 DI=0000
DS=0B53 ES=0B41 SS=0B51 CS=0B51 IP=0005 NV UP EI PL NZ NA PO NC
0B51:0005 B000 MOV AL,00
-d ds:0000
0B53:0000 05 02 04 FF 00 00 04 FF-FF FF FF FF FF FF FF FF ................
-d ds:0000
0B53:0000 05 02 04 FF 0A 01 00 FF-FF FF FF FF FF FF FF FF ................
```

Example 4

Write an assembly language program to convert BCD number to its equivalent HEX number.

Solution: The program is as follows:

```
.model small
;**************************DATA*******************************
.data
ans1 dw 0
h dw 10000
ans dw 0
divisor dw 10
menu db 10,13,'**********MENU**********',10,13,'$'
m1 db 10,13,'1.BCD to HEX Conversion',10,13,'$'
m2 db 10,13,'2.HEX to BCD Conversion',10,13,'$'
m3 db 10,13,'3.Exit',10,13,'$'
m0 db 10,13,' Enter Your Choice $'
op db ?
msgdb 10,13,'Enter the 5 digit BCD no.( <=65535 ) $',10,13
mg1 db 10,13,'Enter the 4 digit HEX no. $',10,13
new_linedb 10,13,'$' ; For new line
mg2 db 10,13,'the Equivalent HEX no. is = $'
mg3 db 10,13,'Invalid BCD number Enter again$',10,13
mg4 db 10,13,'Invalid HEX number Enter again$',10,13
default db 10,13,'Pls enter the valid choice$'
mg5 db 10,13,'the Equivalent BCD no. is = $'
;**************************MACRO******************************
mess macro m1
push ax
push dx
lea dx, m1
mov ah,09h
int 21h
```

```
pop dx
pop ax
endm
;***************************CODE*******************************
.code
main: mov ax, @data
mov ds, ax
up: mess new_line
mess menu
mess m1
mess m2
mess m3
mess new_line
mess m0
mov ah,01h
int 21h
mov op, al
case_1: cmp op,'1'
jne case_2
mess new_line
mess msg
call value_bcd
call disply
jmp up
case_2: cmp op,'2'
jne case_3
mess new_line
mess mg1
call value_hex
call disply1
jmp up
case_3: cmp op,'3'
je end1
mess default
jmp up
end1: mov ah, 4ch
int 21h
;**************************************************************
disply proc
mess new_line
```

```
mess mg2
mov ch,04h
mov cl,04h
up4 : rol ans1,CL
mov bx, ans1
and bx, 000Fh
mov dl, bl
call hex_asc
mov ah,02h
int 21h
dec ch
jnz up4
ret
disply endp
;***********************************************************
disply1 PROC
mess new_line
mess mg5
mov cl,05
mov bx,10000
up6: mov ax, ans
mov dx, 0000h
div bx
mov ans, dx
mov dl,al
call hex_asc
mov ah, 2
int 21h
mov ax, bx
mov dx, 0000h
div divisor
mov bx, ax
dec cl
jnz up6
ret
disply1 endp
;***********************************************************
value_hex proc
mov cl,04
mov ch,04
```

```
jmp up5
below1: mess mg4 ; Call to Macro
up5: mov ah, 01h ; input no.
int 21h
cmp al, '0'
jb d1
cmp al, '9'
jbe next
cmp al, 'A'
jb d1
cmp al, 'F'
jbe here
cmp al, 'a'
jb d1
cmp al, 'f'
ja d1
sub al, 57h
jmp d2
here : sub al, 37h
jmp d2
next : sub al, 30h
jmp d2
d1 : jmp below1
d2 : rol ans, cl
mov ah, 00
add ans, ax
dec ch
jnz up5
ret
value_hex endp
;*************************************************************
hex_asc proc
cmp dl, 09
jbe next1
add dl, 37h
jmp down1
next1: add dl, 30h
down1: ret
hex_asc endp
;************************PROCEDURE*************************
```

```
value_bcd proc
mov ans1,0
mov h,10000
mov ch,05h
jmp up3
mess new_line
below: mess mg3 ; Call to Macro
up3:
mov ah,01h ; input no.
int 21h
cmp al, '0' ; compare it with 0
jb below
cmp al, '9'
ja below
sub al, 30h ; ASSCI to hex conversion
store: mov ah,00h
mul h
add ans1,ax
down: mov ax, h
mov dx, 0
div divisor
mov h, ax
dec ch
jnz up3
ret
value_bcd ENDP
;******************************PROCEDURE END******************
end main
PROMPT MACRO MESSAGE ; Define macro with MESSAGE as a parameter
Push ax
mov ah, 09h
lea dx, message
int 21h
pop ax
endm
```

Example 5

Write an assembly language program to perform different operations on the string. Find length of the string, reverse the string, and find whether the string is palindrome or not.

Solution: The program is as follows:

```
.MODEL SMALL           ; select small model
.STACK 100
.DATA                  ; start data segment
 MES1  DB 10, 13, '1. ENTER THE STRING $'
 MES2  DB 10, 13, '2. CALCULATE THE LENGTH OF STRING $'
 MES3  DB 10, 13, '3. REVERSE THE STRING $'
 MES4  DB 10, 13, '4. PALINDROME $'
 MES5  DB 10, 13, '5. EXIT $'
 MES6  DB 10, 13, 'ENTER THE CHOICE : $'
 MES7  DB 10, 13, 'ENTER CORRECT CHOICE : $'
MES8 DB 10, 13,'$'
MES9 DB 10, 13, 'FAILED : STRING IS MISSING - PLEASE ENTER THE
STRING$'
MES10 DB 10, 13, 'STRING LENGTH IN DECIMAL IS : $'
MES11 DB 10, 13, 'STRING IS NOT PALINDROME $'
MES12 DB 10, 13, 'STRING IS PALINDROME $'
 FLAG DB 0
MES13 DB 10,13, 'ENTER THE STRING: $'
MES14 DB 10,13, 'THE STRING IS : $'
BUFF   DB 80
       DB 0
       DB 80 DUP (0)
COUNTER1     DW 0
COUNTER2     DW 0
NUMBER DW ?                 ; define NUMBER
 .CODE                      ; start code segment
 START:MOV AX, @DATA        ; [Initialize
      MOV DS, AX            ; data segment]
BEGIN: PROMPT MES8          ; Display MES8
PROMPT MES8                 ; Display MES8
PROMPT MES1                 ; Display MES1
      PROMPT MES2           ; Display MES2
      PROMPT MES3           ; Display MES3
      PROMPT MES4           ; Display MES4
      PROMPT MES5           ; Display MES5
      PROMPT MES6           ; Display MES6
AGAIN: MOV AH, 01           ; [READ
      INT 21H               ; OPTION]
PROMPT MES8                 ; Display MES8
```

```
CMP AL, '5'              ; [If choice is 5
 JZ LAST                 ; exit]
      CMP AL, '1'        ; [If choice is 1
JNZ NEXT1
      CALL E_STR         ; Enter the string
PROMPT MES8
PROMPT MES14
CALL D_STR               ; Display the string
      JMP BEGIN          ; exit
NEXT1: CMP AL, '2'       ; If choice is 2
JNZ NEXT2
CALL L_STR               ; Calculate the length of the string
      JMP BEGIN          ; exit]
NEXT2: CMP AL, '3'       ; [If choice is 3
JNZ NEXT3
CALL R_STR               ; Reverse the string
      JMP BEGIN          ; exit]
NEXT3: CMP AL, '4'       ; [If choice is 4
JNZ NEXT4
CALL P_STR               ; Palindrome of the string
      JMP BEGIN          ; exit]
NEXT4: PROMPT MES7       ; Display MES7
JMP AGAIN
 LAST: MOV AH, 4CH       ; Return to DOS
      INT 21H
E_STR PROC NEAR
PROMPT MES13             ; Display message MES13
MOV AH, 0AH
LEA DX, BUFF             ; I/P the string.
INT 21H
      MOV FLAG, 1
 RET
 ENDP
L_STR PROC NEAR
CMP FLAG, 0
JNZ SKIP
PROMPT MES9
RET
SKIP:  MOV AL, BUFF+1
 PROMPT MES10
```

```
    CALL D_HEX
    RET
    ENDP
R_STR PROC NEAR
CMP FLAG, 0
JNZ SKIP1
PROMPT MES9
RET
SKIP1: CALL DR_STR
    RET
    ENDP
P_STR PROC NEAR
    LEA BX, BUFF+2              ; Get starting address of string
    MOV CH, 00H
    MOV CL, BUFF+1
    MOV DI, CX
    DEC DI
    SAR CL, 1
    MOV SI, 00H
BACK4: MOV AL, [BX + DI]; Get the right most character
    MOV AH, [BX + SI]           ; Get the left most character
    CMP AL, AH                  ; Check for palindrome
JNZ LAST2                       ; If not exit
    DEC DI                      ; Decrement end pointer
    INC SI                      ; Increment starting pointer
    DEC CL                      ; Decrement counter
JNZ BACK4                       ; If count not = 0, repeat
    PROMPT MES12                ; Display message 12
    RET
LAST2: PROMPT MES11             ; Display message 11
    RET
    ENDP
D_STR PROC NEAR
        LEA   BX, BUFF
        MOV   CH, 00H           ; [Take character
MOV CL, BUFF +1                 ; count in
MOV DI, 00                      ; DI]
BACK: MOV DL, [BX+DI+2] ; Point to the start
                                ; character and read it
```

```
        MOV   AH, 02H
        INT   21H           ; Display the character
        INC DI              ; Decrement count
  LOOP BACK                 ; Repeat until count is 0
   RET
   ENDP
  DR_STR PROC NEAR
        LEA   BX, BUFF
        MOV   CH, 00H       ; [Take character
  MOV CL, BUFF+1            ; count in
  MOV DI, CX                ; DI]
  BACK3: MOV DL, [BX+DI+1]; Point to the start
                            ; character and read it
        MOV   AH, 02H
        INT   21H           ; Display the character
  DEC DI                    ; Decrement count
  JNZ BACK3                 ; Repeat until count is 0
  RET
   ENDP
  D_HEX PROC NEAR
        MOV AH, 00H         ; Clear AH
        AAM                 ; Convert to BCD
  ADD AX, 3030H             ; Convert to ASCII
  MOV BX, AX                ; Save result
  MOV DL, BH                ; Load first digit (MSD)
        MOV AH, 02          ; Load function number
        INT 21H             ; Display first digit (MSD)
  MOV DL, BL                ; Load second digit (LSD)
        INT 21H             ; Display second digit (LSD)
        RET
        ENDP
  END
```

Summary

- Assembly language is nothing but machine code representation of instructions written in short English statements, that is, mnemonics.
- Assembly language allows access to direct hardware features of the system that might be difficult or impossible to use from a higher level language.

- Assembly language is beneficial to implement real-time applications where time is a critical factor.
- Learning the program in assembly language helps one gain a deeper understanding of how computers work.
- To develop assembly language program following programming tools are needed:
  - **Editor:** Editor is software which provides programmer the screen where he can type the assembly language program. Different types of editors are WordStar, WordPad and Notepad.
  - **Assembler:** Assembler converts the assembly language program into respective machine (binary) codes. Two types of assembler are available with IBM-PC: Microsoft Micro Assembler (MASM) and Borland Turbo Assembler (TASM).
  - **Linker:** Linker is a program which is used to link many small object files into a large object file.
  - **Loader:** Loader is a program which is used for assigning the specific address of the locations where the segments of the object code are to be loaded into the memory. IBM-PC provides a locator program called EXE2BIN.
  - **Debugger:** Debugger is software which helps the single stepping. Borland turbo debugger (TD) is a very powerful debugger.
  - **Emulator:** Emulator is used to test and debug the hardware and software of an external system such as microprocessor based system.
  - Assembler directives are non-executable statements. These statements are active only during assembly.
- A group of instructions is called subroutine. The subroutine which is nothing but a procedure can be called using call and ret instructions. For making use of procedure, proc, near, far, public, extrn and endp assembler directives are necessary.
- If the procedure is written in the same segment, it is called near procedure.
- If the procedure is written in the other segment than where the main program is written, it is called far procedure.

Multiple-Choice Questions

1. Which is right syntax of creating an ASM file?

   (a) C:filename.asm

   (b) C:\filename.asm

   (c) C:\tasm\edit filename.asm

   (d) C:\edit filename.asm

2. What is the extension of ALP program?

   (a) .asm

   (b) .obj

   (c) .Exe

   (d) .txt

3. Which is a right syntax for assemble a file?
   (a) C:\Tasm\tasm filename.asm
   (b) C:\tasm.asm
   (c) C:\tasm\tasm filename.obj
   (d) C:\tasm\td filename.exe
4. Which keyword is used to debug a file?
   (a) Tasm
   (b) Td
   (c) Tlink
   (d) Debug
5. How to debug a file?
   (a) filename.exe
   (b) Td filename.exe
   (c) td filename.obj
   (d) debug filename.asm
6. How to create. obj file?
   (a) Tasm filename.asm
   (b) Tlink filename.obj
   (c) Td filename.exe
   (d) filename.obj
7. How to create executable file?
   (a) Tlink filename.obj
   (b) Td filename.exe
   (c) Tasm filename.obj
   (d) Filename.exe
8. Which is a right step to execute a ALP Program?
   (a) Tasm filename.asm, Tlink filename.obj, filename.exe
   (b) Tlink filename.obj, Tasm filename.asm, filename.exe
   (c) Tasm filename.obj, filename, Td filename.asm
   (d) Tasm filename.asm, Tlink filename.exe, filename
9. How to create Macro?
   (a) macro, ____, end
   (b) macro macroname, ____, endm
   (c) macro macroname, ____, end
   (d) macro , ____, endm

10. How to create a procedure?
(a) proc, ____, end
(b) proc, ____, endm
(c) proc procedure name, ____, endp
(d) proc procedure name, ____, end

11. How to call a procedure?
(a) Call procedure name
(b) procedure name
(c) Proc procedure
(d) Procedure call

12. How to call a macro?
(a) call macro
(b) call macro macroname
(c) macroname
(d) call macroname

13. What is a function of db?
(a) defined byte
(b) defined bit
(c) distinguish byte
(d) different bit

14. What is the full form of LEA?
(a) load effective address
(b) least effective address
(c) lost entered address
(d) none of these

15. Which function of INT 21H is used for acceptance of number or digit?
(a) 09h
(b) 02h
(c) 4ch
(d) 01h

16. Which function of INT 21H is used to display a digit?
(a) 09h
(b) 02h
(c) 4ch
(d) 01h

17. Which function of INT 21H is used to display string?

(a) 09h

(b) 02h

(c) 4ch

(d) 01h

18. How can one declare an array?

(a) a1 db 20h dup()

(b) db 20h dup(?)

(c) a1 20h

(d) a1 dup(0)

19. Size of AX register is

(a) 8 bit

(b) 16 bit

(c) 8 byte

(d) 16 byte

20. AX register is divided into two ____ parts.

(a) 8 bit

(b) 16 bit

(c) 8 byte

(d) 16 byte

21. What is the meaning of INC BX?

(a) increment BX

(b) decrement BX

(c) Interrupt BX

(d) increment BH

22. What is the meaning of JNZ A1?

(a) if result is not equal to zero then jump to A1

(b) if result is equal to zero then jump to AL

(c) if carry then jump to label A1

23. Which of the following sequence you must follow to write ALP program?

(a) .model small
.data
.code
.stack

(b) .model small
.stack
.data
.code

(c) .model
.code
.data
.init

(d) .init
.model small
.data
.end

24. Which function of INT 21H is used to accept the string?

(a) 09h
(b) 02h
(c) 0Ah
(d) 01h

25. Which of the following is an example of index addressing mode?

(a) mov al, 05h
(b) mov si, [1000h]
(c) mov al, bh
(d) int 21h

26. Specify addressing modes for the given instruction: add ax, bx.

(a) immediate
(b) register
(c) index
(d) based

27. Which assembler directive is used in far procedure?

(a) end
(b) extrn
(c) .data
(d) assume

28. Which assembler directive is used in procedure?

(a) short
(b) .code
(c) near
(d) assume

29. Which assembler directive is used in far procedure?

(a) public

(b) ends

(c) end

(d) assume

30. Which assembler directive is used in near procedure?

(a) proc

(b) global

(c) .data

(d) assume

31. What size memory is allocated to DS and CS using small memory model?

(a) 64 KB, 1 MB

(b) 64 KB, 64 KB

(c) 1 MB, 64 KB

(d) 1 MB, 1 MB

32. What is DD in 80386?

(a) Instruction

(b) prefix

(c) assembler directive

(d) label

33. What size memory is allocated in tiny memory model?

(a) Less than or equal to 64 KB

(b) 1 GB

(c) 1 MB

(d) 4 GB

34. Operator 10h dup (0) allocates memory of how many bytes?

(a) 10

(b) 16

(c) 15

(d) 0

35. What is a function of dd?

(a) define data

(b) define double word

(c) distinguish double byte

(d) different double word

36. What is a function of DT?

(a) define trap
(b) define test
(c) distinguish ten bytes of data
(d) define ten bytes of data

37. Amongst given which are non-executable statements?

(a) assume
(b) mov ah, 09h
(c) lea si, arr
(d) int 21h

38. Amongst given which are non-executable statements?

(a) ror al,cl
(b) mov ah,09h
(c) .code
(d) int 21h

39. In far procedure contents of which register gets modified?

(a) only CS
(b) only IP
(c) CS and IP both
(d) none of these

40. In near procedure contents of which register gets modified?

(a) only CS
(b) only IP
(c) CS and IP both
(d) none of these

41. TASM software creates which files?

(a) .asm and .obj
(b) .obj and .lst
(c) .exe and .map
(d) .lst and .map

42. TLINK software creates which files?

(a) .asm and .obj
(b) .obj and .lst
(c) .exe and .map
(d) .lst and .map

43. Amongst given software who makes out the syntax errors?

(a) TLINK

(b) TD

(c) TASM

(d) EDITOR

44. Which software converts the assembly language program to machine language?

(a) Debugger

(b) Linker

(c) Assembler

(d) Editor

45. Which software converts the high-level language program to machine language?

(a) Compiler

(b) Linker

(c) Assembler

(d) Editor

46. Along with macro which other assembler directive is must?

(a) end

(b) endm

(c) endp

(d) ends

47. Along with proc which other assembler directive is must?

(a) end

(b) endm

(c) endp

(d) ends

48. Before endp assembler directive which instruction is must?

(a) mul

(b) ret

(c) imul

(d) div

49. In the instruction mov ax, @data, @ sign indicates which address of data segment?

(a) Base address

(b) Offset address

(c) Physical address

(d) Effective address

50. Along with segment assembler directive which other assembler directive is required?

(a) end

(b) endp

(c) endm

(d) ends

Review Questions

1. What do you mean by assembler directives? Explain following assembler directives: DB, MACRO, EXTRN, PUBLIC.
2. Explain any four programming tools needed to write an assembly language program.
3. Write notes on PUBLIC & EXTRN assembler directives.
4. Compare following:
   - Near and Far procedure
   - Macro and Procedure
5. How can one generate .asm, .obj, .lst and.exe? Give their significance.
6. Write a program in TASM assembly language to convert a two digit BCD number into HEX.
7. Write a program in assembly language to convert string of characters from uppercase to lowercase. Accept the string of 8 characters from user.
8. Write a program in assembly language to multiply two 16-bit hex numbers stored in data segment. Store your result in data segment. Write comment for each of your instruction.

Answers

Multiple-Choice Questions

1. (c)
2. (a)
3. (a)
4. (b)
5. (b)
6. (b)
7. (d)
8. (a)
9. (b)
10. (c)
11. (a)
12. (c)
13. (a)
14. (a)
15. (d)
16. (b)
17. (a)
18. (a)
19. (b)
20. (a)
21. (a)
22. (a)
23. (b)
24. (c)

25. (b)
26. (b)
27. (b)
28. (c)
29. (a)
30. (a)
31. (b)
32. (c)
33. (a)
34. (b)
35. (b)
36. (d)
37. (a)
38. (c)
39. (c)
40. (b)
41. (b)
42. (c)
43. (c)
44. (c)
45. (a)
46. (b)
47. (c)
48. (b)
49. (a)
50. (d)

2 80386 Processor

LEARNING OBJECTIVES

After reading this chapter, you will be able to:

- Understand the detailed architecture of a 32-bit 80386 processor.
- Understand the programmers' model of real mode.
- Evaluate the performance of different operating modes of the processor like real and protected mode.
- Understand the different addressing modes of the processor.
- Get familiar with the instruction format and the instruction set needed to write an assembly language program.

2.1 Features of 80386

It is a 32-bit microprocessor. Its arithmetic and logical unit (ALU) is 32 bit, which allows to process 32-bit data at a time. Its address bus is also 32-bit wide. Therefore, it can access 4 GB, that is, (2^{32}) physical memory. It can also address 64 TB, that is, (2^{46}) of virtual memory.

1. It uses 8-, 16- and 32-bit data types.
2. It has a pipelined architecture.
3. It is compatible with 8086, 8088, 80186 and 80286 architectures.
4. It can operate in real mode, protected mode or virtual 8086 mode.
5. Real address mode has compatibility with 8086.
6. Protected mode offers enhanced system level features such as memory management, multitasking and protection.
7. Virtual 86 mode provides 8086 real-mode compatibility while being operated in protected mode.
8. 80386 provides on-chip address translation caches.
9. 80386 operates at 20, 25 and 33 MHz clock.
10. 80386 has 132 pin grid array package.
11. This processor has integrated memory management unit.
12. This processor has operational on-chip PG.

2.2 Architecture of 80386

Upon power-up or reset 80386 processor operates in real mode. In this mode, 80386 can access all 8086 registers along with 80386 32-bit registers. The main purpose of the real mode is to initialize 80386 in protected mode.

1. The architecture of 80386 is made of six functional units:
   - Bus interface unit (BIU).
   - Code pre-fetch unit.
   - Instruction decode unit (IDU).
   - Execution unit (EU).
   - Segmentation unit (SU).
   - Paging unit (PU).
2. All these units of 80386 operate in parallel. This parallel operation is called pipelined processing.

Figure 1 shows the architecture of 80386. These six units are completely independent of each other and they share the work of the CPU. This speeds up the processing speed of the CPU. All these six units are discussed in the following subsections.

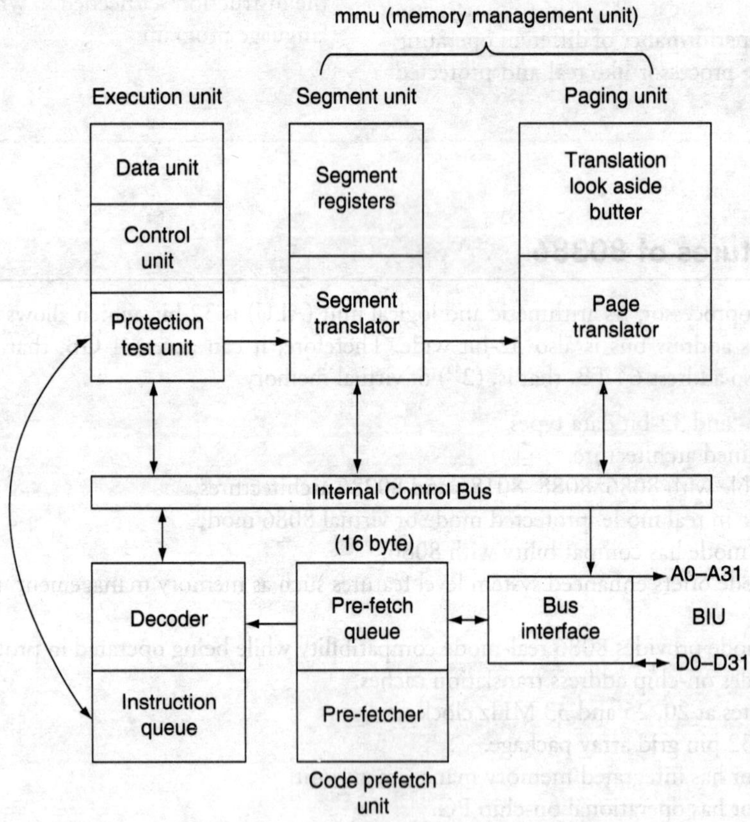

Figure 1 Architecture of 80386 processor.

2.2.1 Bus Interface Unit

It is responsible for interfacing the microprocessor with external memory and input/output (I/O) devices. It provides 32-bit bi-directional data bus and 32-bit address bus. It accepts internal request for fetching the instruction and transferring data from the code pre-fetch unit. BIU then generates the address, data and control signals for the current bus cycles. It also reads and writes data to and from memory and I/O devices. Address relocation facility is provided by it.

2.2.2 Code Pre-Fetch Unit

The code pre-fetch unit fetches instructions from the memory when BIU is not executing bus cycles. The pre-fetched instruction is stored in 16 byte pre-fetch queue. The bytes within the queue are stored in a first-in-first-out (FIFO) register set which is known as pre-fetched queue. The behavior of pre-fetch queue in jump and call instruction is discussed below.

1. Fetching operation will not be initialized by BIU until there are four empty bytes in its queue.
2. Whenever the jump and call instructions appear in the program, the whole queue is flushed out and the queue is made empty. Then, the queue is reloaded with new instruction bytes corresponding to new locations of jump and call instruction.
3. The size of the longest instruction in the instruction set of 80386 is 16-bytes long. Hence, with the queue of the size of 16 bytes, it is possible to pre-fetch even the longest instruction in the instruction set.

2.2.3 Instruction Decode Unit

It takes an instruction from 16 byte pre-fetch queue and converts it into the micro-code which is then stored in the instruction queue.

2.2.4 Execution Unit

It executes each instruction received from an instruction decoded queue. EU consists of the control unit, the data unit and the protection test unit.

2.2.5 Control Unit

It is used to perform control function of an instruction and effective address calculation.

2.2.6 Data Unit

This unit performs operations requested by the control unit. It consists of 32-bit ALU, 8 general-purpose registers and 64-bit barrel shifter (multi-bit shift in one clock).

2.2.7 Protection Test Unit

It performs checks for segmentation violations.

2.2.8 Segmentation Unit

It translates the logical address into the linear address (32 bit) at the request of EU. Translated linear address is then given to the paging unit (PU). There are six segment registers present in this unit.

2.2.9 Paging Unit

When paging mechanism is enabled, it translates the linear address to the physical address. If not enabled, the physical address is identical to the linear address. It gives the physical address to the BIU for memory or I/O access.

2.3 80386 Register Set

The 80386 register set can be categorized according to their usage as follows:

1. General-purpose registers.
2. Segment registers.
3. Index registers, Pointer and Base registers.
4. Flag registers.
5. System address registers.
6. Control registers.
7. Debug registers.

These registers will be discussed in the following subsections. Figure 2 shows the register set of 80386.

2.3.1 General-Purpose Registers

The 80386 consists of eight general-purpose registers which are 32-bit registers – EAX, EBX, ECX, EDX, EBP, ESP, ESI and EDI. They are used for the temporary storage of frequently used data. These registers are used for holding the source or destination operands of arithmetic and logical operations.

The advantage of storing the data in the internal register is that during the program execution, the data can be accessed much faster. The low-order word of each of these eight registers has a separate name. This feature is useful for handling 16-bit data items and for compatibility with 8086 and 80286 processors.

The word registers are named AX, BX, CX, DX, BP, SP, SI and DI. Each byte of 16-bit registers has a separate name such as AH, BH (high bytes), AL, BL (low bytes) which can be used as separate 8-bit registers for holding characters and other 8-bit data items.

The general-purpose registers perform their intended functions which are described as follows:

1. **AX (accumulator):** The result of arithmetic and logical operations is held by an accumulator.
2. **BX (base):** It holds the base (offset) address of data located in the memory. It also holds the base address of table used by translate instruction.
3. **CX (count):** It is used for holding the shift count for certain instructions like shift and rotate. It is also used in the LOOP instructions.
4. **DX (data):** It holds the upper-word of product after 16- or 32-bit multiplication. The upper-word of dividend is also held by it. The I/O port address is held by it in case of indirect I/O addressing.

2.3.2 Segment Registers

80386 have 1 MB address space in the real mode. The entire memory cannot be accessed at a time; hence, the memory is chopped into six memory blocks which are called segments. Each segment is of 64 KB size independent memory block. These segments can be accessed by 16-bit registers. They are listed as follows:

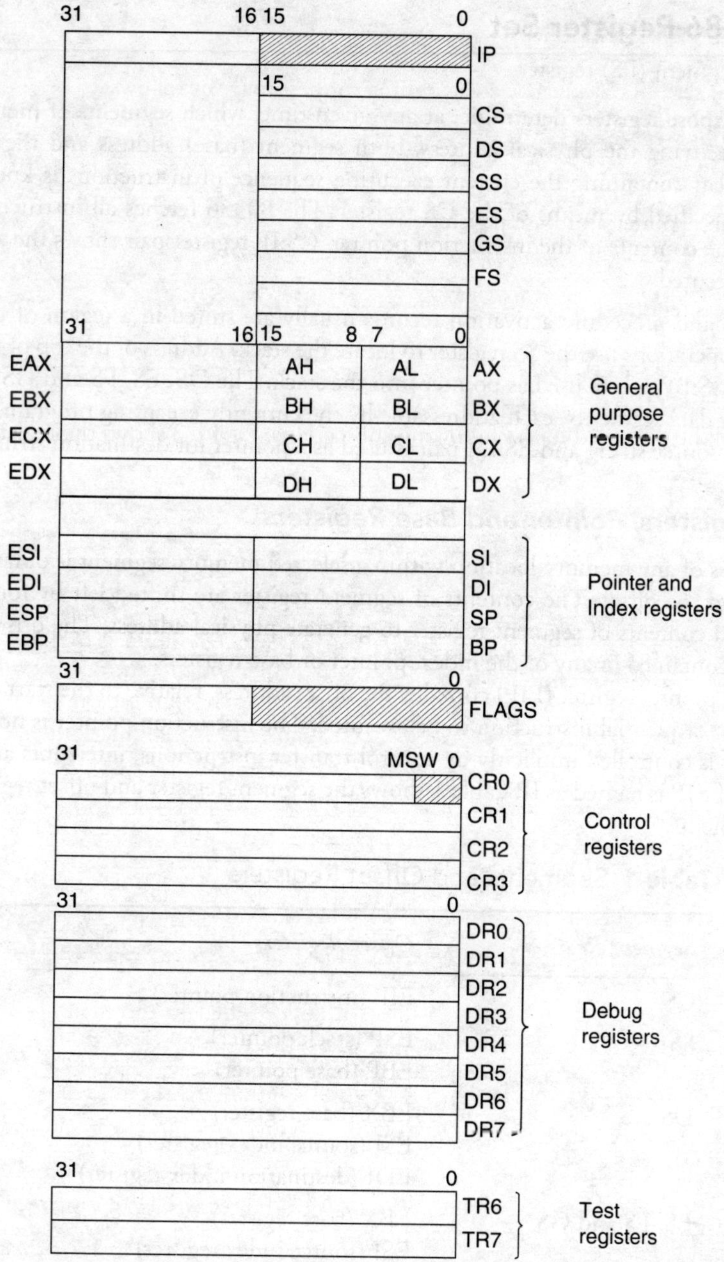

Figure 2 Real mode register set of 80386.

1. Code segment (CS) register.
2. Stack segment (SS) register.
3. Data segment (DS) register.
4. Extra segment (ES) register.

5. General data segment (GS) register.
6. General data segment (FS) register.

These six special-purpose registers determine, at any given time, which segments of memory are currently addressable. For specifying the physical address, both segment (base) address and the offset address are required. The segment containing the current executing sequence of instructions is known as the *current code segment*; it is specified by means of the CS register. The 80386 fetches all instructions from this CS using as an offset, the contents of the instruction pointer. CS:IP register pair shows the address of the next instruction to be executed.

Subroutine calls and procedure activation records usually are stored in a region of the memory called stack. All the stack operations use the SS register to locate the stack. Address of the top of the stack is held by SS:SP register pair. SS:BP pair is used as pointer into the stack. The DS, ES, FS and GS registers allow the specification of four data segments, each addressable by the currently executing program. The DS:SI pair is used as a pointer to source string and ES:DI pair is used as a pointer for destination string.

2.3.3 Index Registers, Pointer and Base Registers

The physical address of any memory location within a selected memory segment is obtained by adding the segment address and the offset. The contents of segment register are shifted left by four and the offset is added to the shifted contents of segment register to generate physical address. The offset used to calculate physical address is contained in any of the index, pointer or base registers.

The instruction pointer register (EIP) contains the offset address, relative to the start of the current code segment, of the next sequential instruction to be executed. The instruction pointer is not directly visible to the programmer; it is controlled implicitly by control-transfer instructions, interrupts and exceptions. The low-order 16 bits of EIP is named as IP. Table 1 shows the segment register and offset registers used with the corresponding segments.

Table 1 Segments and Offset Registers

Segment Register	*Offset Registers*
CS	EIP (instruction pointer)
SS	ESP (stack pointer) EBP (base pointer)
DS	EBX (base register) ESI (source index register) EDI (destination index register)
ES, FS and GS	EBX (base register) ESI (source index register)

2.3.4 Flag Register

Flag register is shown in Fig. 3. It is a 32-bit register and termed as EFLAG. The low-order 16 bits of EFLAGS is named FLAGS. It is useful when executing 8086 and 80286 codes, because this part of EFLAGS is identical to the FLAGS register of 8086 and 80286. The flags are divided into three groups: The status (conditional) flags, the control flags and the systems flags. The systems flags are discussed in detail in Chapter 5.

In 80386 real mode, nine flags are present out of which six are status (or conditional) flags and three are control flags. They are as follows:

1. **Status flags:**
   - **Carry flag (CF):** Carry generated after performing any arithmetic or logical operation sets this flag.
   - **Parity flag (PF):** Even parity of last operation sets this data.
   - **Auxiliary carry flag (ACF):** It is used in BCD arithmetic. It is set when carry is generated from lower to upper nibble of a data.
   - **Sign flag (SF):** It saves sign bit of last operation.
   - **Overflow flag (OF):** Error generated after performing arithmetic operation on signed numbers sets this flag.
   - **Zero flag (ZF):** This flag gets set if last operation results into zero value.
2. **Control flags:** To control certain operation of the processor, these flags are used.
   - **Trap flag (TF):** It is set for single stepping operation.
   - **Interrupt flag (IF):** If IF = 1, the INTR pin is enabled and if IF = 0, the INTR pin is disabled. The state of this flag is controlled by STI and CLI instructions.
   - **Direction flag (DF):** This flag is used in string operations. When set, it is used for auto-decrementing SI and DI value by one and resetting will result into auto-increment operation.
3. **System flags (active in protection mode only):** These flags reflect the current status of the machine. They are normally used by the operating system.
   - **Input output privilege level (IOPL):** It is a 2-bit flag. It is used when 80386 executes the I/O related instructions. It holds privilege level from 0 to 3 at which the code is running.
   - **Resume flag:** This bit is used to selectively mask some exceptions while the code is debugged.
   - **Virtual mode flag (VMF):** Setting this flag will cause 80386 to enter into virtual mode.
   - **Nested task flag (NTF):** It is used in protected mode. When one task involves other, this flag is set.

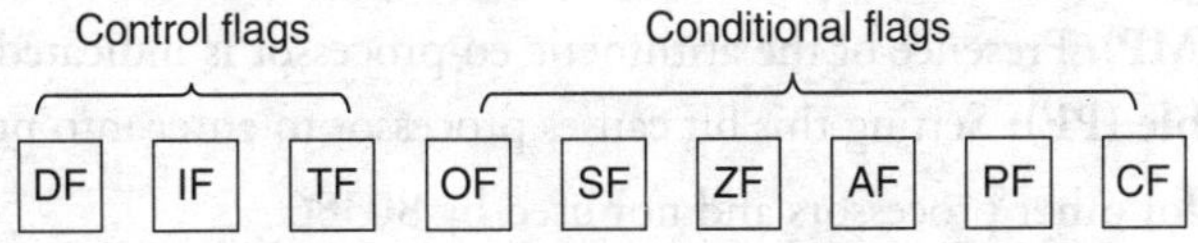

Figure 3 Real mode flag register.

2.3.5 System Address Registers

There are four system address registers: TR (task register), IDTR (interrupt descriptor table register), GDTR (global descriptor table register) and LDTR (local descriptor table register). These registers are used in protected mode. These registers are discussed in detail in Chapter 5.

2.4 Special 80386 Registers

80386 consists of a set of special-purpose registers as control registers, test registers and debug registers.

2.4.1 Control Registers

There are four control registers – CR0, CR1, CR2 and CR3. These registers are shown in Fig. 4 and are discussed as follows:

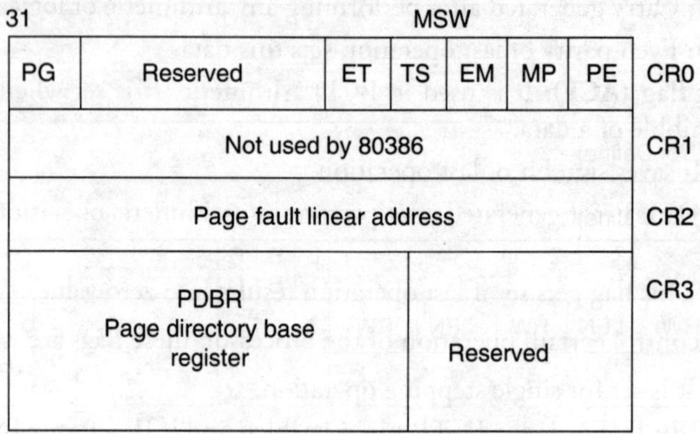

Figure 4 Control registers.

1. **CR0**: It contains six status bits. Its holds the machine status word (MSW). The six control bits are as follows:
   - **Paging (PG):** Setting this bit enables the PG mechanism where the linear address is converted to the physical address.
   - **Extension type (ET):** When ET = 0, processor selects 80287 co-processor and when ET = 1, processor selects 80387 co-processor.
   - **Task switched (TS):** At every task switching processor sets this bit. The processor never clears this bit but the user has to clear this bit.
   - **Emulate co-processor (EM):** Whenever the processor fetches the floating point instruction, setting this bit indicates an exception 11, that is, device not available.
   - **Math present (MP):** Presence of the arithmetic co-processor is indicated by this bit.
   - **Protection enable (PE):** Setting this bit causes processor to enter into protected mode.
2. **CR1:** It is reserved for other processors and not used by 80386.
3. **CR2:** It is a read-only register. It holds the page fault linear address.
4. **CR3:** This register holds the base address of the page directory. It is also known as page directory base register (PDBR).

2.4.2 Debug Registers

Figure 5 shows the set of debug registers. To control the debug features, eight debug registers from DR0 to DR7 are used. They are discussed as follows:

1. **DR0–DR3**:
   - They contain 32-bit linear breakpoint addresses.
   - These addresses are continuously compared with the addresses generated by the program. After a match is found, the processor will cause type1 interrupt to occur if directed by the debug registers DR6 and DR7.

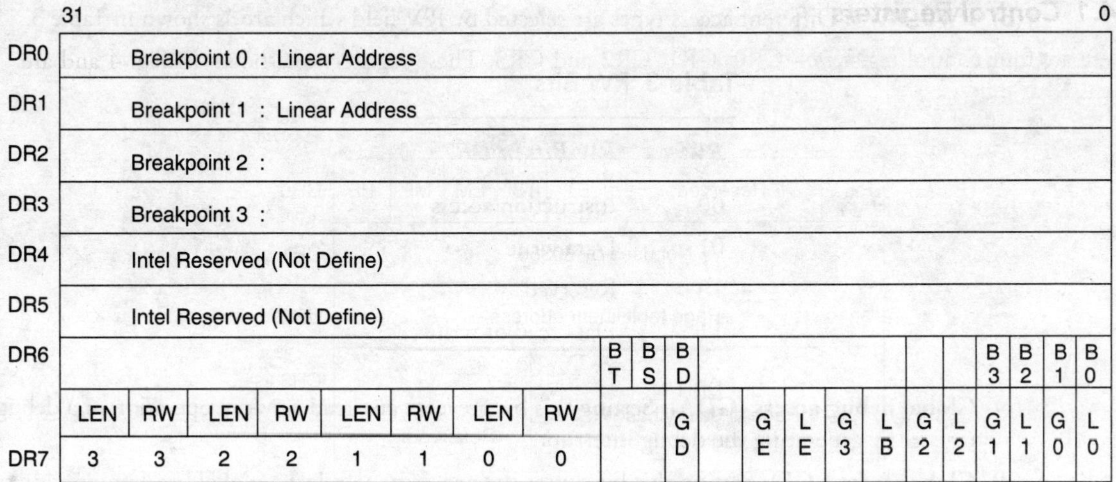

Figure 5 Debug registers.

2. **DR4–DR5:** They are reserved by the Intel.
3. **DR6:**
   - It is called debug status register. These bits are never cleared by the processor and so these must be manually cleared. Exception 1, that is, last debug fault is indicated by this bit.
   - The control bits in DR6 and DR7 are as follows:
     (a) **B0–B3:** It indicates debug interrupt has been caused by which breakpoint addresses.
     (b) **BD (break for debug register access):** Setting this bit indicates that debug interrupt has been caused by making an attempt to read the debug register with GDA bit set.
     (c) **BS (break for single step):** Setting this bit indicates that the debug interrupt has been caused by the TF bit in the flag register.
     (d) **BT (break for task switch):** Setting this bit indicates that the debug interrupt has been caused by a task switch.
4. **DR7:**
   - It allows us to control the operation of four linear address breakpoints. The set of four fields controls each break point.
     (a) **LEN0–LEN3 (breakpoint length):** These bits define the size of access of the breakpoint. Different combinations of LEN bits are as shown in Table 2.

Table 2 LEN Bits

LEN	*LEN Bits in DR7*
00	1 byte
01	1 word (2 bytes)
10	Reserved
11	1 double word (4 bytes)

(b) RW0–RW3: Different access types are selected by RW field which are as shown in Table 3.

Table 3 RW Bits

RW	*RW Bits in DR7*
00	Instruction access
01	Data write
10	Reserved
11	Data read or write

(c) Global debug access (GDA): Setting this bit prevents any read or write operation of a debug register by generating the debug interrupt.

(d) Global exact (GE): Setting this bit causes the processor to select a global breakpoint address for any of the four breakpoint address registers.

(e) Local exact (LE): Setting this bit causes the processor to select a local breakpoint address for any of the four breakpoint address registers.

2.4.3 Test Registers

There are two test registers, TR6 and TR7. They are used to test the translation look-aside buffer (TLB). TR6 holds tag field (linear address) of the TLB and TR7 holds the physical address of the TLB. Figure 6 shows the structure of TR6 and TR7. The following bits are found in TR6 and TR7:

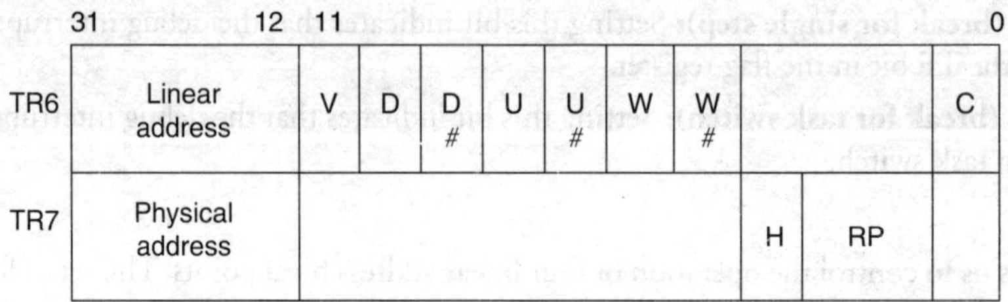

Figure 6 Test registers.

1. **C:** It is the command bit. When $C = 1$, it indicates immediate look up for TLB and when $C = 0$, it indicates a write to TLB.
2. **W:** It indicates that the area accessed by TLB entry is writable.
3. **W#:** It indicates that the area accessed by TLB entry is not writable.
4. **U:** It indicates that bit is a user bit.
5. **U#:** It indicates that bit is not a user bit.

6. **D:** It indicates that the entry in TLB is invalid or dirty.
7. **D#:** It indicates that the entry in TLB is not dirty.
8. **V:** It indicates that the entry in TLB is valid entry.
9. **Linear address:** Bits 12–31 of the TR6 serve as the upper 20 bits of linear address to be used for TLB reference.
10. **Replacement pointer (RP):** It selects the block of TLB to be written.
11. **Pointer location (H):** When $H = 1$, RP field indicates which cache set to write to and when $H = 0$, the cache set is determined with an internal algorithm.
12. **Physical address:** It contains the physical address to be written into TLB.

2.5 80386 Real-Mode Memory Segmentation

In real mode, the lower 20 address bits, that is, A0–A19, are active and the address bus size is 20-bit wide. In this mode, 80386 can directly access up to 1 MB of external memory, that is, 2^{20} = 1 MB.

A 1-MB address space is divided into memory segments of 64 KB size. The respective segment registers hold the starting address (base address) of a particular segment. Segment base address is a multiple of 4_H (4-bit shift left). There are six such segments possible which are CS, SS, DS, ES, FS and GS. Hence, only six 64 KB (384 KB) can be active at a time.

In real mode, paging mechanism is not enabled. So in real mode, linear address is same as the physical address. In real mode, only SI and DI can be used as index registers and the two base registers used are BX and BP. Scaling is not supported in this mode.

As all the segments can be accessed by the programmer, the segments can be set as contiguous, adjacent, disjoint or even overlapping. Figure 7 shows the memory segmentation in real mode.

Since the information stored in the segments does not require the whole 64 KB of the memory, the segments can be overlapped. So, a program can be stored anywhere in the memory; such program is known as re-locatable program. The segmentation of the memory allows both the program and the data to be relocated.

2.6 Data Types Used in Real Mode

The following data types are used in the real mode:

1. **Fundamental data format:** Byte, word, double word.
2. **Integer:** Unsigned: Byte, word, double word; signed: byte, word, double word.
3. **BCD (binary-coded decimal) numbers:** Packed, unpacked.
4. American Standard Code for Information Interchange (ASCII).

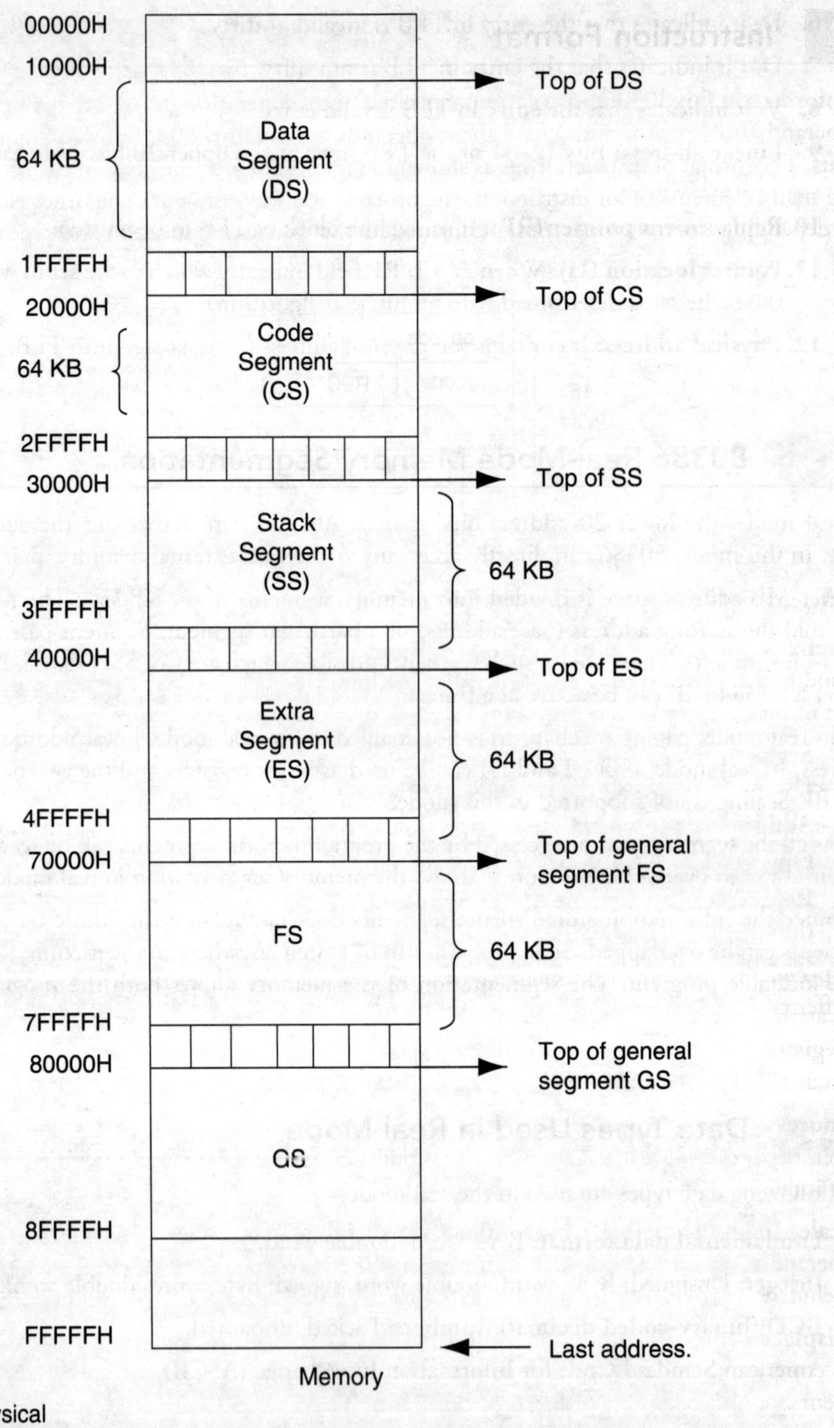

Figure 7 Real-mode memory segmentation.

2.7 Instruction Format

The information in 80386 instructions specifies what operation is to be performed and on whom (the operands) to perform and where these operands are present. 80386 instructions are made of several elements. The format of instructions is as shown in Fig. 8; the different fields of instructions are also shown. Among many elements of an instruction, the op-code is always present. The other elements are present or absent depending upon the operation performed by the instruction location and type of the operands.

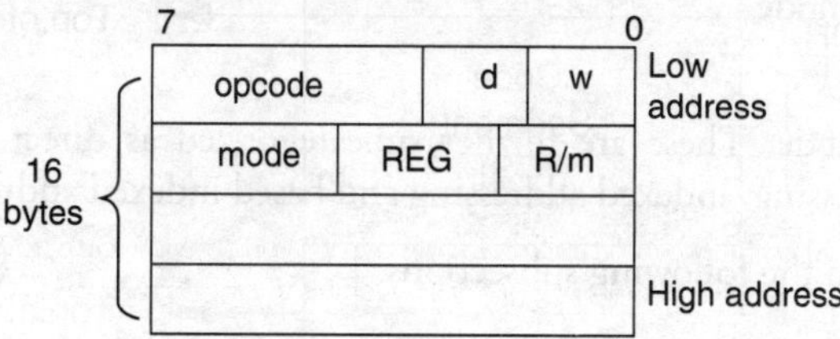

Figure 8 Instruction format of 80386.

The different bytes present in an instruction are as follows:

1. **Prefixes:** Prefixes are nothing but one or more bytes which can be appended before an instruction that modify the operation of the instruction. The following types of prefixes are available in the instruction set of processor 80386:
   - **Segment override:** It helps the processor to alter the segment register present in an instruction. Using this processor can override the default segment-register of the respective instruction.
   - **Address size:** It switches between 32-bit and 16-bit address generation.
   - **Operand size:** Operands can be of 32 bit or 16 bit in size.
   - **Repeat:** It is used before the string instruction to cause the instruction to act on each element of the string.
2. **Op-code:** It specifies the operation performed by the instruction. Some operations have several different op-codes, each specifying a different variant of the operation.
3. **Register specifier:** An instruction may specify one or two register operands. Register specifiers may occur either in the same byte as the op-code or in the same byte as the addressing mode specifier.
4. **Addressing-mode specifier:** It indicates whether an operand present in an instruction is a register or memory location; if it is a memory location, then it specifies whether a displacement, a base register, an index register and scaling is to be used.
5. **Scale, index, base (SIB) byte:** Whenever the addressing mode specifier indicates that one of the operand in an instruction is an index register then to compute the address of an operand, SIB byte is included in the instruction to encode the base register, the index register and a scaling factor.
6. **Displacement:** Whenever the addressing-mode specifier indicates that the displacement is used to compute the address of an operand, the displacement is encoded in the instruction. A displacement is a signed integer of 8, 16 or of 32 bits. The eight bit form is used in the common case when the displacement is sufficiently small. The sign of the displacement is also taken into account by the processor.

2.8 Addressing Modes of 80386

Before discussing the instruction set, it is necessary to know how 80386 accesses different possible operands present in the instruction in different ways.

Addressing mode is a method of specifying an operand within the instruction. There are different types of operands possible like data within the instruction, registers, memory or I/O ports. The addressing modes of 80386 are as follows:

1. Immediate addressing mode.
2. Register addressing mode.
3. Memory addressing mode: These are further subcategorized as direct addressing, register indirect addressing, based addressing, indexed addressing and based indexed addressing modes.

These modes are discussed in the following subsections.

2.8.1 Immediate Addressing Mode

In this addressing mode, an operand is a part of an instruction. The operand is immediately available within the instruction only. Here, immediate operand is nothing but constant data available in an instruction. Operand can be of 8 bits, 16 bits or 32 bits in length. For example, MOV AL, 15H.

2.8.2 Register Addressing Mode

In this addressing mode, both the source and the destination operands are registers only. Operands can be accessed in byte, word or double word sizes.

1. Byte size operands are AL, AH, BL, BH, CL, CH, DL and DH.
2. Word size operands are AX, BX, CX, DX, SP, BP, SI, DI, CS, DS, SS, ES, FS and GS.
3. Double word size operands are EAX, EBX, ECX, EDX, ESP, EBP, ESI and EDI.

For example, MOV AX, BX.

2.8.3 Memory Addressing Mode

In this addressing mode, the memory operand must be transferred to and from the CPU over the bus. Whenever the execution unit needs to read or write a memory operand, it must pass an offset value to BIU.

2.8.3.1 Effective Address

It is also termed as an offset address. It is an unsigned 32-bit number that indicates the operand's distance in bytes from the start of the segment in which it resides. The effective address is calculated by adding any of the following four combinations:

1. **Displacement:** 8- or 32-bit immediate data following the instruction.
2. **Base:** The contents of any general-purpose register can be used as base.
3. **Index:** The contents of any general-purpose register (except ESP) can be used as an index register.
4. **Scale:** The contents of index register can be multiplied (scaled) by a factor of 1, 2, 4 or 8. This mode is efficient for accessing arrays and structures.

Thus, we can write

Effective address (EA) = Base register + (Index register * Scaling factor) + Displacement

Once EA is known, physical address (PA) can be calculated as follows (see Fig. 9):

1. **Physical address = Segment base:** EA.
2. **Segment base address (SBA):** The starting location of the segment.
3. **EA:** The offset of the operand from the beginning of the segment of memory.

EA = Base + Index * (Scale) + Displacement

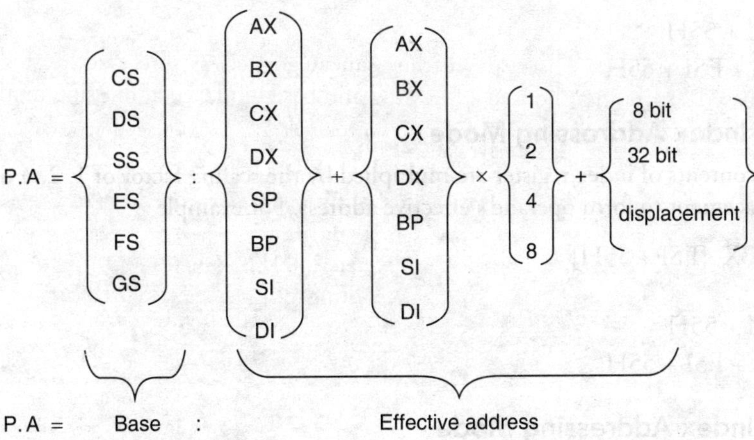

Figure 9 Addressing modes (physical address generation).

2.8.3.2 Direct Addressing Mode

In this mode, the effective address is nothing but 8-, 16- or 32-bit displacement from the current value of the data segment register, which is directly available in the instruction itself. For example,

MOV CX, [4326H]

Here,

EA = 4326 H

PA = DS + 4326 H

2.8.3.3 Register Indirect Addressing Mode

In this mode, operands effective address is present either in base register or index register. For example

MOV ECX, [EAX]

Here,

EA = EAX

PA = DS + EAX

2.8.3.4 Based Addressing Mode

In this mode, operands effective address is formed by adding the contents of base register to displacement. For example

MOV EDI, [EAX + 89H]

Here,

EA = EAX + 89HPA = DS + EAX + 89H

2.8.3.5 Index Addressing Mode

In this mode, the operands effective address is formed by adding the contents of index register to displacement. For example

MOV EBX, [ESI + 55H]

Here,

EA = ESI + 55H
PA = DS + ESI + 55H

2.8.3.6 Scaled Index Addressing Mode

In this mode, the contents of index register are multiplied by the scaling factor of 1, 2, 4 or 8 which is then added to the displacement to form operand's effective address. For example

MOV EBX, [ESI + 55H]

Here,

EA = ESI + 55H
PA = DS + ESI + 55H

2.8.3.7 Based Index Addressing Mode

In this mode, operands effective address is formed by adding the contents of base register to index register. For example

MOV EBX, [ESI][EBX]

Here,

EA = ESI + EBX
PA = DS + ESI + EBX

2.9 Instruction Set

The instruction set of 80386 is divided into a number of groups based on operations performed by the instructions. The different groups are as follows:

1. Data transfer group.
2. Arithmetic group.
3. Bit manipulation group.
4. String instruction group.
5. Program transfer instruction group.
6. Program control instruction group.

We will discuss these separately.

2.9.1 Data Transfer Group

Data transfer instructions are discussed below. Table 4 shows the format of MOV instruction and Table 5 shows the possible operands for MOV instruction.

Table 4 Data Transfer Instruction – MOV

Mnemonic	*Meaning*	*Format*	*Operation*	*Flags Affected*
MOV	Move	MOV D,S	(S) moved to (D)	None

Table 5 Possible Operands of MOV Instruction

Destination	*Source*
Memory	Accumulator
Accumulator	Memory
Register	Register
Register	Memory
Memory	Register
Register 16	Segment register
Memory	Immediate
Segment register	Register 16
Register	Immediate
Segment register	Memory 16
Memory	Segment register

Movement of data is not possible for the following pair of source and destination operands:

1. Memory – memory.
2. Immediate – segment register.
3. Segment register – segment register.

For cxamplc

X: MOV EAX, EBX

Table 6 shows the format of exchange instruction. Table 7 shows the possible operands of exchange instruction.

Table 6 Data Transfer Instruction – XCHG

Mnemonic	*Meaning*	*Format*	*Operation*	*Flags Affected*
XCHG	Exchange	XCHG	(S) moved to (D)	None

Table 7 Possible Operands of XCHG Instruction

Destination	*Source*
Accumulator	Register 16
Register	Register
Register	Memory
Memory	Register

The example of exchange instruction is

XCHG [1234h], BX

Exchange of data is not possible between memory locations and even between segment registers. Table 8 shows the format of LEA, LDS, LES instructions. The equivalent instruction for LEA SI DATA is MOV SI Offset DATA. Table 9 shows the format of translate instruction.

Table 8 Data Transfer Instructions – LEA, LDS, LES

Mnemonic	*Meaning*	*Format*	*Operation*	*Flags Affected*
LEA	Load effective address	LEA Reg16, EA	EA to (Reg16)	None
LDS	Load register and DS	LDS Reg16, MEM32	(MEM32) to (Reg16) (Mem32+2) to (DS)	None
LES	Load register and ES	LES Reg16, MEM32	(MEM32) to (Reg16) (Mem32 + 2) to (DS)	None

Table 9 The XLAT Instruction

Mnemonic	*Meaning*	*Format*	*Operation*	*Flags Affected*
XLAT	Translate	XLAT	((AL) + (BX) + (DS)0) to (AL)	None

For example, assume (DS) = 0300H, (BX) = 0100H and (AL) = 0DH. XLAT replaces contents of AL by contents of memory location with

$$PA = (DS)0 + (BX) + (AL) = 03000H + 0100H + 0DH = 0310DH$$

Thus, (0310DH) is moved to (AL).

2.9.2 Arithmetic Group

This group consists of addition, subtraction and comparison instructions. Table 10 shows the format of ADD, ADC, INC, AAA and DAA instructions.

Table 10 Arithmetic Instructions: ADD, ADC, INC, AAA, DAA

Mnemonic	*Meaning*	*Format*	*Operation*	*Flags Affected*
ADD	Addition	ADD D,S	(S) + (D) to (D) carry to (CF)	ALL
ADC	Add with carry	ADC D,S	(S) + (D) + (CF) to (D) carry to (CF)	ALL
INC	Increment by One	INC D	(D) + 1 to (D)	ALL but CY
AAA	ASCII adjust for addition	AAA	If the sum is >9, AH is incremented by 1	AF, CF
DAA	Decimal adjust for addition	DAA	Adjust AL for decimal Packed BCD	ALL

An example of ADD instruction is shown below.

1. ADD AX, 2: This instruction adds 2 to the AX register and result is saved into AX register.
2. ADC AX, 2: This instruction adds 2 to the AX register along with the contents of carry flag and result is saved into AX register.
3. INC BX ; This instruction increments the contents of BX register by 1.
   INC WORD PTR [BX]
4. ASCII CODE 0–9 = 30–39h
   MOV AX, 38H ; (ASCII code for number 8)
   ADD AL, 39H ; (ASCII code for number 9) AL=71h
   AAA ; used for addition AH=01, AL=07
   ADD AX, 3030H ; answer to ASCII 0107 AX=3137
5. AL contains 25 (packed BCD)
   BL contains 56 (packed BCD)
   ADD AL, BL ; The result in AL = 7BH
   DAA; After performing this operation the result in AL = 81

```
  25
+ 56
------
  81
```

Table 11 shows the format of SUB, SBB, DEC, AAS, DAS and NEG instructions.

Table 11 Arithmetic Instructions – SUB, SBB, DEC, AAS, DAS, NEG

Mnemonic	*Meaning*	*Format*	*Operation*	*Flags Affected*
SUB	Subtract	SUB D,S	(D) - (S) to (D) Borrow to (CF).	ALL
SBB	Subtract with Borrow	SBB D,S	(D) - (S) - (CF) to (D).	ALL

(Continued)

Table 11 (Continued)

Mnemonic	*Meaning*	*Format*	*Operation*	*Flags Affected*
DEC	Decrement by one	DEC D	(D) - 1 to (D).	All but CF
NEG	Negate	NEG D		All
DAS	Decimal adjust for subtraction	DAS	Convert the result in AL to packed decimal format.	All
AAS	ASCII adjust For subtraction	AAS	(AL) difference (AH) decrement by one if borrowed.	CY, ACF

For example

1. DAS
MOV BL, 28H
MOV AL, 83H
SUB AL, BL; AL = 5BH.

2. DAS; adjust as AL = 55H
MOV AX, 38H
SUB AL, 39H; AX = 00FF
AAS; AX = FF09 ten's complement of -1 (Borrow one from AH)
OR AL, 30H; AL=39.

Tables 12 and 13 show the format of multiplication and division instructions, respectively.

Table 12 Multiplication Instructions

Multiplication (MUL or IMUL)	*Multiplicand*	*Operand (Multiplier)*	*Result*
Byte*Byte	AL	Register or memory	AX
Word*Word	AX	Register or memory	DX:AX
Dword*Dword	EAX	Register or memory	EAX:EDX

Table 13 Division Instructions

Division (DIV or IDIV)	*Dividend*	*Operand (Divisor)*	*Quotient: Remainder*
Word/Byte	AX	Register or memory	AL:AH
Dword/Word	DX:AX	Register or memory	AX:DX
Qword/Dword	EDX: EAX	Register or memory	EAX:EDX

Examples for multiplication and division are as follows:

1. Assume that each instruction starts from these values:

   AL = 85H, BL = 35H, AH = 0H

   MUL BL → AL . BL = 85H * 35H = 1B89H → AX = 1B89H

   IMUL BL → AL . BL = 2'S AL * BL = 2'S (85H) * 35H

   = 7BH * 35H = 1977H → 2's comp → E689H → AX.

   DIV BL → =AX/BL = 0085H/35H= 02 (85-02*35=1B) → AH = 1B, AL = 02

   IDIV BL → =AX/BL = 0085H/35H= 02 (85-02*35=1B) → AH = 1B, AL = 02

2. AX = F000H, BX= 9015H, DX= 0000H

   MUL BX = F000H * 9015H : DX= 8713 and AX = B000

   IMUL BX = 2'S(F000H) * 2'S(9015H) = 1000 * 6FEB : DX= 06FE and AX = B000

Table 14 shows the format of logical instructions and Table 15 shows the possible operands for logical instructions.

Table 14 Logical Instructions

Mnemonic	*Meaning*	*Format*	*Operation*	*Flags Affected*
AND	Logical AND	AND D,S	(S) · (D) → (D)	OF, SF, ZF, PF, CF, AF undefined.
OR	Logical inclusive OR	OR D,S	(S)+(D) → (D)	OF, SF, ZF, PF, CF, AF undefined.
XOR	Logical exclusive OR	XOR D,S	(S) (D) → (D)	OF, SF, ZF, PF, CF AF undefined.
NOT	logical NOT	NOT D	¯(D) → (D)	None.

Table 15 Possible Operands of Logical Instructions

Destination	*Source*
Register	Memory
Memory	Register
Register	Immediate
Memory	Immediate
Accumulator	Immediate
Register	Register

The logical instructions are discussed in detail as follow:

1. **AND**
   - This instruction uses any addressing mode except memory-to-memory and segment registers.
   - It is especially used in clearing certain bits (masking).
     xxxx xxxx AND 0000 1111 = 0000 xxxx
     (Clear the first four bits)
   - Examples:

     AND BL, 0FH

     AND AL, 345H
2. **OR**
   - It is used in setting certain bits
     xxxx xxxx OR 0000 1111 = xxxx 1111
     (Set the upper four bits).
3. **XOR**
   - This instruction is used in inverting bits.
     xxxx xxxx XOR 0000 1111 = xxxxx'x'x'x'
   - Example: Clear bits 0 and 1, set bits 6 and 7, invert bit 5 of register CL:
     AND CL, OFCH ; 1111 1100B
     OR CL, 0C0H ; 1100 0000B
     XOR CL, 020H ; 0010 0000B

2.9.3 Shift and Rotate Instructions

The instructions are as follows:

1. **SHLSAL**: Shift logical left/Shift arithmetic left.
2. **SHR**: Shift logical right.
3. **SAR**: Shift arithmetic right.
4. **ROL**: Rotate left.
5. **ROR**: Rotate right.
6. **RCL**: Rotate left through carry.
7. **RCR**: Rotate right through carry.

2.9.4 Logical Vs. Arithmetic Shifts

The difference between the logical and arithmetic shift operation is discussed as follows:

1. A logical shift fills the newly created bit position with zero.
2. An arithmetic shift fills the newly created bit position with a copy of the number's sign bit.

Table 16 shows the format of logical and arithmetic shift instructions.

Table 16 Logical and Arithmetic Shift Instructions

Mnemonic	*Meaning*	*Format*	*Operation*	*Flags Affected*
SAL/SHL	Shift arithmetic left/shift logical left.	Count	Shift the (D) left by the number of bit positions equal to count and fill the vacated bits positions on the right with zero.	CF, PF, SF, ZF AF undefined OF undefined if count ≠ 1.
SHR	Shift logical right.	SHR D, Count	Shift the (D) right by the number of bit positions equal to count and fill the vacated bits positions on the left with zeros.	CF, PF, SF, ZF AF undefined OF undefined if count ≠ 1.
SAR	Shift arithmetic right.	SAR D, Count	Shift the (D) right by the number of bit positions equal to count and fill the vacated bits positions on the left with the original most significant bit.	CF, PF, SF, ZF AF undefined OF undefined if count ≠ 1.

Table 17 shows the possible operands for shift instructions.

Table 17 Allowed Operands of Shift Instructions

Destination	*Count*
Register	1
Register	CL
Memory	1
Memory	CL

2.9.5 SHL Instruction

The SHL instruction performs a logical left shift on the destination operand, filling the lowest bit with zero.

2.9.6 Operand Types

The operand types are as follows:

1. SHL *reg,imm8.*
2. SHL *mem,imm8.*
3. SHL *reg*,CL.
4. SHL *mem*,CL.

2.9.7 Fast Multiplication

One can improve the multiplication operation speed using shift instructions in the following manner:

```
mov dl,5
shl dl,1
```

Shifting left 1 bit multiplies a number by 2

```
mov dl,5
shl dl,2 ; DL = 20
```

Shifting left *n* bits multiplies the operand by 2*n*

For example, 5 * 22 = 20.

Multiply AX by 10

```
SHL AX, 1
MOV BX, AX
MOV CL, 2
SHL AX, CL
ADD AX, BX.
```

2.9.8 SHR Instruction

The SHR instruction performs a logical right shift on the destination operand. The highest bit position is filled with a zero.

```
MOV DL, 80
SHR DL, 1; DL = 40
SHR DL, 2; DL = 10.
```

Shifting right *n* bits divides the operand by 2*n*.

2.9.9 SAR Instruction

SAR performs a right arithmetic shift on the destination operand. An arithmetic shift preserves the number's sign.

```
MOV DL, 80
SAR DL, 1; DL = 40
SAR DL, 2; DL = 10
```

Table 18 shows the format of rotate instructions.

Table 18 Rotate Instructions

Mnemonic	*Meaning*	*Format*	*Operation*	*Flags Affected*
ROR	Rotate right	ROR D, Count	Rotate the (D) right by the number of bit positions equal to Count. Each bit shifted out from the rightmost bit goes back into the leftmost bit position.	CF OF undefined if count ≠ 1.
RCL	Rotate left through carry	RCL D, Count	Same as ROL except carry is attached to (D) for rotation.	CF OF undefined if count ≠ 1.
RCR	Rotate right through carry	RCR D, Count	Same as ROR except carry is attached to (D) for rotation.	CF OF undefined if count ≠ 1.

2.9.10 ROL Instruction

ROL (rotate) shifts each bit to the left. The highest bit is copied into both the CF and the lowest bit. No bits are lost.

MOV Al, 11110000b
ROL Al, 1; AL = 11100001b
MOV Dl, 3Fh
ROL Dl, 4; DL = F3h

2.9.11 ROR Instruction

ROR (rotate right) shifts each bit to the right. The lowest bit is copied into both the CF and the highest bit. No bits are lost.

MOV AL, 11110000b
ROR AL, 1; AL = 01111000b
MOV DL, 3Fh
ROR DL, 4; DL = F3h

2.9.12 RCL Instruction

RCL (rotate carry left) shifts each bit to the left. It copies CF to the least significant bit and copies the most significant bit to CF.

CLC; CF = 0
MOV BL, 88H; CF,BL = 0 10001000b
RCL BL,1; CF,BL = 1 00010000b
RCL BL,1; CF,BL = 0 00100001b

2.9.13 RCR Instruction

RCR (rotate carry right) shifts each bit to the right. It copies CF to the most significant bit and copies the least significant bit to CF.

STC; CF = 1
MOV AH,10H; CF,AH = 00010000 1
RCR AH,1; CF,AH = 10001000 0

Table 19 shows the possible operands for rotate instructions and Table 20 shows the format of flag control instructions.

Table 19 Allowed Operands of Rotate Instructions

Destination	*Count*
Register	1
Register	CL
Memory	1
Memory	CL

Table 20 Flag Control Instructions

Mnemonic	*Meaning*	*Operation*	*Flags Affected*
CLC	Clear carry flag.	(CF) = 0	CF
STC	Set carry flag.	(CF) = 1	CF
CMC	Complement carry flag.	(CF) = 1's complement of (CF).	CF
CLD	Clear direction flag.	(DF) = 0 SI and DI will be auto-incremented while string instructions are executed.	DF
STD	Set DF.	(DF) = 1 SI and DI will be auto-decremented while string instructions are executed.	DF
CLI	Clear interrupt flag.	IF = 0.	IF
STI	Set interrupt flag.	(IF) = 1.	IF

Table 21 shows the format of compare instruction and Table 22 shows the possible operands for compare instructions.

Table 21 Compare Instruction – CMP

Mnemonic	*Meaning*	*Format*	*Operation*	*Flags Affected*
CMP	Compare	CMP D,S	(D) – (S) is used in setting or resetting the flags	CF, AF, OF, PF, SF, ZF

Now

(D) = (S) ; ZF=0

(D) > (S) ; ZF=0, CF=0

(D) < (S) ; ZF=0, CF=1.

Table 22 Allowed Operands of Compare Instruction

Destination	*Count*
Register	Register
Register	Memory
Memory	Register
Register	Immediate
Memory	Immediate
Accumulator	Immediate

2.9.14 String

It is an array of bytes or words located in memory. Some supported string operations are as follows:

1. Copy (move, load)
2. Search (scan)
3. Store
4. Compare

2.9.15 String Instruction Basics

String instructions are discussed below.

1. Source DS:SI, Destination ES:DI.
   - You must ensure DS and ES are correct.
   - You must ensure SI and DI are offsets into DS and ES, respectively.
2. DF (0 = Up, 1 = Down).
   - CLD – Increment addresses (left to right).
   - STD – Decrement addresses (right to left).

Table 23 shows the possible prefixes for string instructions and Table 24 shows the format of string instructions.

Table 23 String Instruction Prefixes

Prefix	*Used with*	*Meaning*
REP	MOVS STOS	Repeat while not end of string. CX ≠ 0.
REPE/REPZ	CMPS SCAS	Repeat while not end of string and strings are equal. CX ≠ 0 and ZF = 1.
REPNE/REPNZ	CMPS SCAS	Repeat while not end of string and strings are not equal. CX ≠ 0 and ZF = 0.

Table 24 String Instructions

Mnemonic	*Meaning*	*Format*	*Operation*	*Flags Affected*
MOVS	Move string DS:SI to ES:DI	MOVSB/ MOVSW	((ES)0+(DI)) to ((DS)0+(SI)) (SI) = (SI) + 1 or 2 (DI) = (DI)+ 1 or 2	None
CMPS	Compare string DS:SI to ES:DI	CMPSB/ CMPSW	((DS)0+(SI)) minus ((ES)0+(DI)) (SI) = (SI) + 1 or 2 (DI) = (DI) + 1 or 2	All set flags as per status flags.

(Continued)

Table 24 (Continued)

Mnemonic	*Meaning*	*Format*	*Operation*	*Flags Affected*
SCAS	Scan string AX – ES:DI	SCASB/ SCASW	Set flags as per (AL or AX) – ((ES)0 + (DI)) (DI) = (DI) + 1 or 2	
LODS	Load string DS:SI to AX	LODSB/ LODSW	(AL or AX) to [(DS)0 + (SI)] (SI) = (SI) + 1 or 2	
STOS	Store string ES:DI to AX	STOSB/ STOSW	[(ES)0 + (DI)] to (AL or A) } 1 or 2 (DI) = (DI) + 1 or 2	

2.10 Branch Group of Instructions

Branch instructions provide lot of convenience to the programmer to perform operations selectively, repetitively, etc. The following are the types:

1. Conditional jumps.
2. Unconditional jumps.
3. Iteration instructions.
4. CALL instructions.
5. Return instructions.

2.10.1 Subroutine and Subroutine Handling Instructions

A subroutine is a special segment of program that can be called for execution from any point in a program. An assembly language subroutine is also referred to as a 'procedure'. Whenever the subroutine is needed, a single instruction is inserted in to the main body of the program to call subroutine. To branch a subroutine, the value in the IP or CS and IP must be modified. After execution, the user can return the control to the instruction that immediately follows the call instruction, that is, the original value of IP or CS and IP must be preserved. Execution of the instruction causes the contents of IP to be saved on the stack. This time (SP) = (SP) – 2. A new 16-bit (near - proc, mem 16, reg 16, that is, intra segment) value which is specified by the instructions operand is loaded into IP.

Examples: CALL 1234H, CALL BX, CALL [BX].

2.10.2 Inter Segment

The concept of inter segment call is discussed below.

1. At starting CS and IP are placed in a stack.
2. The address of subroutine is loaded into CS and IP which is provided by the operand.
3. After execution, original CS and IP values are placed as it is.

Table 25 shows the format of Call instruction.

Table 25 CALL Instruction

Mnemonic	*Meaning*	*Format*	*Operation*	*Flags Affected*
CALL	Subroutine call	CALL operand	Execution continues from the address of the subroutine specified by the operand. Information required to return back to the main program such as IP and CS are saved on the stack.	None

2.10.3 Operands

The possible operands of Call instruction are mentioned below.

1. Near-proc
2. Far-proc
3. Memptr 16
4. Regptr 16
5. Memptr 32

2.10.4 Return

Every subroutine must end by executing an instruction that returns control to the main program. This is return (RET) instruction. By execution, the values of IP or IP and CS that were saved in the stack are to be returned back to their corresponding registers. This time (SP) = (SP) + 2. Table 26 shows the format of return instruction.

Table 26 Return Instruction

Mnemonic	*Meaning*	*Format*	*Operation*	*Flags Affected*
RET	Return	RET or RET operand	Return to the main program by restoring IP (and CS for far-proc). If operand is present, it is added to the contents of SP.	None

2.10.5 Loop Instructions

These instructions are used to repeat a set of instructions several times.

1. **Format:** LOOP short-Label.
2. **Operation:** (CX) = (CX) – 1.

Jump is initialized to location defined by short label if CX ≠ 0. Otherwise, execute next sequential instruction. Instruction LOOP works with respect to the contents of CX. CX must be pre-loaded with a count that represents the number of times the loop is to be repeated. Whenever the loop is executed, contents at CX are first decremented then checked to determine if they are equal to zero.

1. If CX = 0, loop is complete and the instruction following loop is executed.
2. If CX ≠ 0, content returns to the instruction at the label specified in the loop instruction.

General format: LOOP r8; r8 is 8-bit signed value.

1. It is a 2-byte instruction.
2. Used for backward jump only.
3. Maximum distance for backward jump is only 128 bytes.
4. LOOP AGAIN is almost same as DEC CX, JNZ AGAIN.5. LOOP instruction does not affect any flags.

Table 27 shows the format of loop instructions.

Table 27 Loop Instructions

Mnemonic	*Meaning*	*Format*	*Operation*
LOOP	Loop	Loop short-label	(CX) = (CX) – 1, Jump to location given by short-label if CX ≠ 0
LOOPE/ LOOPZ	Loop while equal/ loop while zero	LOOPE/ LOOPZ short-label	(CX) = (CX) – 1, Jump to location given by short-label if CX ≠ 0 and ZF = 1
LOOPNE/ LOOPNZ	Loop while not equal/loop while not zero	LOOPNE/ LOOPNZ short-label	(CX) = (CX) – 1, Jump to location given by short-label if CX ≠ 0 and ZF = 0

2.10.6 Control Flow and Jump Instructions

JMP: Unconditional jump. The syntax of the instruction is JMP operand.

2.10.6.1 Unconditional Jump Instructions

Unconditional jump instructions can be a near or far jump.

1. **Near jump or intra segment jump (jump within the segment):**
    - It is limited to the address within the current segment.
    - It is achieved by modifying value in IP.
2. **Far jump or inter segment jump (jump to a different segment):**
    - It permits jumps from one code segment (CS) to another.
    - It is achieved by modifying CS and IP.

2.10.6.2 Possible Operands

The possible operands are as follows:

1. Short label.
2. Near label.t
3. Far label.
4. Memptr 16.
5. Regptr 16.
6. Memptr 32.

2.10.6.3 Conditional Jump

Conditional jump instructions in 8086 are just 2-bytes long. 1-byte op-code is followed by 1-byte signed displacement (range of –128 to + 127). Types of conditional jump instructions are as follows:

1. Jumps based on a single flag.
2. Jumps based on more than one flag.

2.10.6.4 Conditional Jump Instructions

Conditional jump instructions are discussed as follows:

1. **Mnemonic:** Jcc.
2. **Meaning:** Conditional jump.
3. **Format:** Jcc operand.
4. **Operation:** If condition is true jump to the address specified by operand. Otherwise the next instruction is executed.
5. **Flags affected:** None.

Table 28 shows the format of conditional jump instructions.

Table 28 Conditional Jump Instructions

Mnemonic	*Meaning*	*Condition*
JA	Above	CF = 0 and ZF = 0
JB	Above or equal	CF = 0 JB below CF = 1
JBE	Below or equal	CF = 1 or ZF = 1
JC	Carry	CF = 1
JCXZ	CX register is zero	(CF or ZF) = 0
JE	Equal	ZF = 1
JG	Greater	ZF = 0 and SF = OF
JGE	Greater or equal	SF = OF

(Continued)

Table 28 (Continued)

Mnemonic	*Meaning*	*Condition*
JL	Less	(SF XOR OF) = 1
JLE	Less or equal	((SF XOR OF) or ZF) = 1
JNA	Not above	CF = 1 or ZF = 1
JNAE	Not above nor equal	CF = 1
JNB	Not below	CF = 0
JNBE	Not below nor equal	CF = 0 and ZF = 0
JNC	Not carry	CF = 0
JNE	Not equal	ZF = 0
JNL	Not less	SF = OF
JNG	Not greater	((SF XOR OF) or ZF)=1
JNLE	Not less nor equal	ZF = 0 and SF = OF
JNO	Not overflow	OF = 0
JNP	Not parity	PF = 0
JNZ	Not zero	ZF = 0
JNS	Not sign	SF = 0
JO	Overflow	OF = 1
JP	Parity	PF = 1
JPE	Parity even	PF = 1
JPO	Parity odd	PF = 0
JS	Sign	SF = 1
JZ	Zero	ZF = 1

2.10.6.5 Jumps Based on a Single Flag

Jump instructions which are based on single flag are discussed below.

1. JZ r8; jump if zero flag set to 1 (jump if result is zero).
2. JNZ r8; jump if zero flag is not set (Z flag = 0, that is, result is non-zero).
3. JS r8; jump if sign flag set to 1 (result is negative).
4. JNS r8; jump if not sign (result is positive).
5. JC r8; jump if carry flag set to 1.
6. JNC r8; jump if no carry.
7. JP r8; jump if parity flag set to 1 (parity is even).
8. JNP r8; jump if no parity (parity is odd).

9. JO r8; jump if overflow flag set to 1 (result is wrong).
10. JNO r8; jump if no overflow (result is correct).
11. There is no jump based on ACF.
12. JZ r8; JE (jump if equal) also means same.
13. JNZ r8; JNE (jump if not equal) also means same.
14. JC r8; JB (jump if below) and JNAE (jump if not above or equal) also mean same.
15. JNC r8; JAE (jump if above or equal) and JNB (jump if not above) also mean same.
16. JZ, JNZ, JC and JNC used after arithmetic operation.
17. JE, JNE, JB, JNAE, JAE and JNB are used after a compare operation.
18. JP r8; JPE (jump if parity even) also means the same.
19. JNP r8; JPO (jump if parity odd) also means the same.

Examples for JE or JZ Instruction

1. Example for forward jump

CMP SI, DI

JE SAME

Should be <=127 bytes

ADD CX, DX; executed if Z = 0: (if SI not equal to DI):

SAME: SUB BX, AX; executed if Z = 1: (if SI = DI).

2. Example for backward jump

BACK: SUB BX, AX; executed if Z = 1 Should be <= 128 bytes: (if SI = DI): CMP SI, DI

JE BACK

ADD CX, DX executed if Z = 0

(if SI not equal to DI).

Similarly other conditional jump instructions can be elaborated.

3. Jumping beyond –128 to +127?

Requirement: (What if >127 Bytes)	**Then do this:**
CMP SI, DI	CMP SI, DI
JE SAME	JNE NEXT
ADD CX, DX	JMP SAME
--- ---	NEXT: ADD CX, DX
--- ---	--- ---
--- ---	--- ---
--- ---	--- ---
SAME: SUB BX, AX	SAME: SUB BX, AX

Range for JMP (unconditional jump) can be +, -2^{15} = +, –32 K

2.10.4.6 Terms Used in Comparison

Following terms are used in comparison instruction.

1. Above and below used for comparing unsigned numbers.
2. Greater than and less than used with signed numbers.
3. All the Intel microprocessors use this convention.

   95H is above 65H: Unsigned comparison – True
   95H is less than 65H: Signed comparison – True
   95H is negative, 65H is positive
   65H is below 95H: Unsigned comparison – True
   65H is greater than 95H: Signed comparison – True

2.10.6.7 Jump on Multiple Flags

Conditional jumps based on more than one flag are used after a CMP (compare) instruction.

1. **JBE (jump if below or equal) or JNA (jump if not above)**

   : *Jump if* Cy = 1 OR Z = 1: Below OR Equal
   : *No jump if* Cy = 0 AND Z = 0: Surely above

   For example, CMP BX, CX

   JBE BX_BE

2. **JNBE (jump if not below or equal) or JA (jump if above): Below or equal above**

   : *Jump if* Cy = 0 AND Z = 0
   No jump if Cy = 1 OR Z = 1: Surely Above
   For example, CMP BX, CX
   JA BX

3. **JLE (jump if less than or equal) or JNG (jump if not greater than)**

   Jump if S = 1 AND V = 0: (surely negative)
   OR S = 0 AND V = 1
   (wrong answer positive!)
   OR Z – 1 (equal)
   that is, S XOR V = 1 or Z = 1
   No jump if S = 0 AND V = 0: (surely positive)
   OR OR (S = 1 AND V = 1)
   (wrong answer negative!)
   AND Z = 0 (not equal)
   that is, S XOR V = 0 AND Z = 0

4. **JNLE jump if not (less than or equal) or JG (jump if greater than)**

   Jump if S = 0 AND V = 0

(surely positive)
OR (S = 1 AND V = 1)
(wrong answer negative!)
AND Z = 0 (not equal)
that is, S XOR V = 0 AND Z = 0
No jump if S = 1 AND V = 0
(surely negative)
OR (S = 0 AND V = 1)
(wrong answer positive!)
OR Z = 1 (equal)
that is, S XOR V = 1 OR Z = 1

5. **JL (jump if less than) or JNGE (jump if not (greater than or equal))**
Jump if S = 1 AND V = 0
(surely negative)
OR (S = 0 AND V = 1)
(wrong answer positive!)
that is, S XOR V = 1
When S = 1, result cannot be 0
No jump if S = 0 AND V = 0
(surely positive)
OR (S = 1 AND V = 1)
(wrong answer negative!)
that is, S XOR V = 0
When S = 0, result can be 0

6. **JNL (jump if not less than) or JGE (jump if greater than or equal)**
Jump if S = 0 AND V = 0
(surely positive)
OR (S = 1 AND V = 1)
(wrong answer negative!)
that is, S XOR V = 0
When S = 0, result can be 0
No jump if S = 1 AND V = 0
(surely negative)
OR (S = 0 AND V = 1)
(wrong answer positive!)
that is, S XOR V = 1
When S = 1, result cannot be 0

The features of various jumps are as follows:

1. **Near jump:**
   - **Direct jump (common):**

     (a) Short jump: 2 bytes

     EB r8

     range +, – 2^7

     (b) Long jump: 3 bytes

     E9 r16

     range +, – 2^{15}
   - **Indirect jump (uncommon):**

     2 or more bytes
     Starting with FFH
     Range: complete segment
   - 3 Near jump and 2 far jump instructions have the same mnemonic JMP but different opcodes.
2. **Short jump:**
   - 2 byte.
   - (EB r8).
   - Instruction range: –128 to +127 bytes.
3. **Backward jump:**
   - Assembler knows the quantum of jump.
   - Generates short jump code if <=128 bytes is the required jump.
   - Generates code for long jump if >128 bytes is the required jump.
4. **Forward jump:**
   - Assembler does not know jump quantum in pass 1.
   - Assembler reserves 3 bytes for the forward jump instruction.
   - If jump distance turns out to be >128 bytes, the instruction is coded as E9 r16 (E9H = Long jump code).
   - If jump distance becomes <=128 bytes, the instruction is coded as EB r8 followed by code for NOP (E8H = Short jump code).

2.10.7 Short Assembler Directives

Assembler generates only 2 byte short jump code for forward jump if the SHORT assembler directive is used. For example

```
JMP SHORT SAME
      :
      :
SAME: MOV CX, DX
```

Programmer should ensure that the jump distance is <=127 bytes.

The features of various jumps are as follows:

1. **Long jump:**
   - 3-byte.
   - (E9 r16).
   - Instruction range: –32768 to +32767 bytes.
   - Long jump can cover entire 64 KB of CS.
   - Jump can handle it as jump quantum is <=32767.

   For example,

   CS:8000H JMP FRWD

   :

   :

   FRWD = CS:FFFFH

   It can cover entire 64 KB of CS. Long jump can handle it as jump quantum is <=32768.

2. **Intra segment indirect:**
   - Near indirect jump is uncommon.
   - *Instruction length*: 2 or more bytes.
   - *Range*: Complete segment.

   For example,

   (a) JMP DX

   If DX = 1234H, branches to CS:1234H

   1234H is not signed relative displacement

   (b) JMP wordptr 2000H[BX]

   BX1234H DS:3234H5678H branches to

   DS:3236HAB22H CS:5678H.

3. **Far jump:**
   - **Direct jump (common):**

     (a) 5 bytes EA.

     (b) 2 byte offset.

     (c) 2 byte segment.

     (d) *Range*: anywhere.
   - **Indirect jump (uncommon):**

     (a) 2 or more bytes.

     (b) Starting with FFH.

     (c) *Range*: anywhere.

4. **Inter segment direct jump:**
   - It is also called far direct jump.
   - It is the common inter segment jump scheme.

- It is a 5 byte instruction.
- 1 byte op-code (EAH).
- 2 byte offset value.
- 2 byte segment value.

For example,

JMP Far ptr LOC

5. **Inter segment indirect jump:**
   - Instruction length depends on the way jump location is specified.
   - It can be a minimum of 2 bytes. For example

     JMP DWORD PTR 2000H[BX]
   - It is also called far indirect jump.
   - It is not commonly used.
   - Instruction length is a minimum of 2 bytes.
   - It depends on the way jump location is specified. For example

     JMP DWORD PTR 2000H[BX]

     BX 1234H branches to

     ABCDH:5678H

     DS:3234H 5678H It is a 4-byte instruction

     DS:3236H ABCDH

2.10.8 Machine Control Instructions

1. **HLT instruction – HALT processing:**
   - The HLT instruction will cause 80386 to stop fetching and executing instructions. 80386 will enter a halt state.
   - The only way to get processor out of the halt state is with an interrupt signal on the INTR pin or an interrupt signal on NMI pin or a reset signal on the RESET input.
2. **NOP instruction:**
   - This instruction simply takes up three clock cycles and does no processing. After this, it will execute the next instruction.
   - This instruction is normally used to provide delays in between instructions.
3. **ESC instruction:**
   - Whenever this instruction executes, the microprocessor does NOP or access a data from memory for co-processor.
   - This instruction passes the information to 80387 math processor. Six bits of ESC instruction provide the op-code to co-processor.
   - When 80386 fetches instruction bytes, co-processor also picks up these bytes and puts in its queue. The co-processor will treat normal 80386 instructions as NOP.
   - Floating-point instructions are executed by 80387 and during this 80386 will be in WAIT.

4. **LOCK instruction:**
   - This is a prefix to an instruction. This prefix makes sure that during execution of the instruction, control of system bus is not taken by other microprocessor.
   - In the multiprocessor systems, individual microprocessors are connected together by a system bus. This is to share the common resources.
   - Each processor will take control of this bus only when it needs to use common resource. The lock prefix will ensure that in the middle of an instruction, system bus is not taken by other processors.
   - This is achieved by hardware signal "LOCK" available on one of the CPU pin. This signal will be made active during this instruction and it is used by the bus control logic to prevent others from taking the bus.
   - Once this instruction is completed, lock signal becomes inactive and the microprocessors can take the system bus.
5. **WAIT instruction:**
   - This instruction takes 80386 to an idle condition. The CPU will not do any processing during this. It will continue to be in idle state until TEST pin of 80386 becomes low or an interrupt signal is received on INTR or NMI. On valid interrupt, ISR is executed and processor enters the idle state again.

Summary

- 80386 processor is a 32-bit processor.
- It operates in three different modes: real, protected and virtual 8086 mode.
- Its address bus width is 20-bit wide in real mode while all 32 bits of address bus are activated in protected mode.
- Real mode is superfast 8086 processor, wherein 80386 can have the compatibility with processors like 8086.
- The architecture of 80386 is divided into six functional units that perform different tasks parallel. The modules are:
  - Bus Interface Unit (BIU).
  - Code fetch unit.
  - Instruction decode unit (IDU).
  - Execution unit (EU).
  - Segmentation unit (SU).
  - Paging unit (PU).
- Upon power-up or reset, 80386 operates in real mode. In this mode, 80386 can access all 8086 registers along with 80386 32-bit registers.
- The main purpose of real mode is to initialize 80386 in the protected mode.
- The information in 80386 instructions specifies the operation to be performed, the operand types to be manipulated and where these operands are present.

- 80386 instructions are made of various elements.
- Addressing mode is a method of specifying an operand within the instruction. There are different types of operands possible like data within the instruction, registers, memory or I/O ports.
- The addressing modes of 80386 are as given as follows:
  - Immediate addressing mode.
  - Register addressing mode.
  - Memory addressing mode.
- Instruction set of 80386 is divided into number of groups, based on operations performed by the instructions. The different groups are as the follows:
  - Data transfer group.
  - Arithmetic group.
  - Bit manipulation group.
  - String instruction group.
  - Program transfer instruction group.
  - Program control instruction group.

Multiple-Choice Questions

1. How many segment registers are present in 80386?
   (a) 4
   (b) 6
   (c) 7
   (d) 8
2. For source string which is the default register pair used to hold the physical address?
   (a) CS:IP
   (b) SS:SP
   (c) DS:SI
   (d) ES:DI
3. For destination string which is the default register pair used to hold the physical address?
   (a) CS:IP
   (b) SS:SP
   (c) DS:SI
   (d) ES:DI
4. If CS holds the base address then which register can hold the offset address?
   (a) BP
   (b) SP

(c) IP

(d) SI

5. What is the size of logical address in 80386?

(a) 8 bit

(b) 16 bit

(c) 20 bit

(d) 32 bit

6. What is the size of linear address in 80386?

(a) 8 bit

(b) 16 bit

(c) 20 bit

(d) 32 bit

7. What is the size of physical address in 80386 real mode?

(a) 8 bit

(b) 16 bit

(c) 20 bit

(d) 32 bit

8. What is the power supply requirement of 80386 µp?

(a) –5V DC

(b) +5V DC

(c) –10V DC

(d) +10V DC

9. What is the size of instruction queue in 80386?

(a) 4 bytes

(b) 6 bytes

(c) 8 bytes

(d) 16 bytes

10. Which flag is used in string instructions?

(a) TF

(b) IF

(c) DF

(d) OF

11. TEST instruction is equivalent to
(a) CMP
(b) XOR
(c) AND
(d) MUL

12. The result of MUL BL instruction gets saved in 80386 at
(a) DX: AX
(b) AX: DX
(c) DX
(d) AX

13. Which register is used by LOOP instruction?
(a) AX
(b) BX
(c) CX
(d) DX

14. The result of MUL BX instruction gets saved in 80386 at
(a) DX: AX
(b) AX: DX
(c) DH: AL
(d) AL: AH

15. The result of DIV instruction, quotient: remainder gets saved in 80386 at
(a) DX: AX
(b) AX: DX
(c) DH: AL
(d) AL: AH

16. What is 80386?
(a) Processor
(b) Assembler
(c) Emulator
(d) Micro controller

17. 80386 is _____ processor.
(a) 8 bit
(b) 16 bit
(c) 20 bit
(d) 32 bit

18. Why is 80386 called as 32-bit microprocessor?
    (a) Its data bus is 32-bit wide
    (b) Its address bus is 32-bit wide
    (c) Its data bus is 16-bit wide
    (d) Its address bus is 20-bit wide
19. What is the size of data bus for 80386 processor in real mode?
    (a) 8 bit
    (b) 16 bit
    (c) 20 bit
    (d) 32 bit
20. What is the size of address bus for 80386 processor in real mode?
    (a) 8 bit
    (b) 16 bit
    (c) 20 bit
    (d) 32 bit
21. In 80386 which unit calculates the physical address in real mode?
    (a) Decode unit
    (b) Pre-fetch unit
    (c) execution unit
    (d) BIU
22. The result of DIV BL instruction, quotient:remainder gets saved in 80386 at
    (a) DX: AX
    (b) AX: DX
    (c) DH: AL
    (d) AL: AH
23. What is the maximum memory accessing capacity of processor 80386 in real mode?
    (a) 1 MB
    (b) 64 KB
    (c) 4 GB
    (d) 64 TB
24. Which flag is present in 80386 real mode?
    (a) AC
    (b) VM
    (c) NT
    (d) IOPL

25. What is the maximum memory accessing capacity of 80386 processor in virtual 86 mode?

(a) 1 MB

(b) 64 KB

(c) 4 GB

(d) 64 TB

26. What is the size of IP register in case of real mode?

(a) 8 bit

(b) 16 bit

(c) 20 bit

(d) 32 bit

27. What is the size of flag register in case of real mode?

(a) 8 bit

(b) 16 bit

(c) 20 bit

(d) 32 bit

28. How many debug registers are present in 80386?

(a) 2

(b) 4

(c) 6

(d) 8

29. Which flag is absent in 80386 real mode?

(a) AC

(b) OF

(c) NT

(d) PF

30. Amongst given which is the example of control register?

(a) AC

(b) CY

(c) OF

(d) DF

31. Amongst given which is the example of control register?

(a) AC

(b) CY

(c) IF

(d) ZF

32. Amongst given which is the example of control flag register?
(a) TF
(b) CY
(c) PF
(d) SF

33. Amongst given which is the example of conditional flag register?
(a) AC
(b) IF
(c) TF
(d) DF

34. Amongst given which is the example of conditional flag register?
(a) DF
(b) IF
(c) TF
(d) ZF

35. Amongst given which is the example of conditional flag register?
(a) DF
(b) IOPL
(c) PF
(d) NT

36. Amongst given which is the example of conditional flag register?
(a) DF
(b) IOPL
(c) CF
(d) NT

37. Amongst given which is the example of conditional flag register?
(a) DF
(b) IOPL
(c) SF
(d) RF

38. Amongst given which is the example of system flag register?
(a) DF
(b) IOPL
(c) CF
(d) SF

39. Amongst given which is the example of system flag register?
(a) DF
(b) ZF
(c) CF
(d) NT

40. Amongst given which is the example of system flag register?
(a) RF
(b) IOPL
(c) CF
(d) ZF

41. Amongst given which is the example of system flag register?
(a) DF
(b) OF
(c) VM
(d) SF

42. In real mode how much memory is allotted to I/O address?
(a) 64 KB
(b) 1 MB
(c) 2 MB
(d) 1 GB

43. Amongst given which addressing mode is not supported by the real mode?
(a) Index
(b) Register
(c) Scaling
(d) Immediate

44. In real mode which registers can be used as index registers?
(a) SI & DI
(b) BX & SI
(c) DI & AX
(d) CX & SI

45. In real mode which registers can be used as base registers?
(a) SI & DI
(b) BX & BP

(c) BX & AX

(d) BP & SI

46. The pre-fetch queue in 80386 is of which type register?

(a) FILO

(b) LIFO

(c) FIFO

(d) PIPO

47. The protection test unit is present in which functional unit of 80386?

(a) BIU

(b) Decode unit

(c) Paging unit

(d) Execution unit

48. What is the size of general data segment register FS?

(a) 8 bit

(b) 16 bit

(c) 20 bit

(d) 32 bit

49. What is the size of general data segment register GS?

(a) 16 bit

(b) 8 bit

(c) 20 bit

(d) 32 bit

50. What is the result of execution of an instruction SAR AL, 01H, if contents of register AL before execution were 10001000?

(a) 10001000

(b) 00001000

(c) 11000100

(d) 10001001

51. What is the result of execution of an instruction SHR AL, 01H, if contents of register AL before execution were 10001000?

(a) 10001000

(b) 01000100

(c) 11000100

(d) 10001001

52. What is the result of execution of an instruction SAL AL, 01H, if contents of register AL before execution were 10001001?
   (a) 00010010
   (b) 00010011
   (c) 11000100
   (d) 10001001

53. What is the result of execution of an instruction SHL AL, 01H, if contents of register AL before execution were 10001000?
   (a) 00010010
   (b) 00010011
   (c) 11000100
   (d) 10001001

Review Questions

1. Draw and explain functional architecture diagram of 80386.
2. Draw and explain the register set of 80386.
3. With the help of suitable examples explain any four indirect memory addressing modes of 80386.
4. Explain the flag register of processor 80386.
5. Draw and explain the function of all control registers (CR0 – CR3) of processor 80386.
6. Draw & explain 80386 real mode programmers model?
7. Write features of 80386. Draw real mode register set of 80386 and explain their function?
8. How to convert Logical address to physical address in real mode of 80386? Explain with example.
9. Give difference between 8086 and 80386.
10. What is MSW (Machine Status Word) in 80386? Draw its format.
11. Explain the following addressing modes of 80386:
    (a) Direct addressing
    (b) Immediate addressing
    (c) Register indirect addressing
    (d) Base register addressing
    (e) Index addressing
12. State and explain any five memory addressing modes of 80386 with example showing physical address generation.
13. Explain any 3 string instructions. What is the use of REP prefix while using string instructions?

14. Explain following instructions of 80386: JMP and INT n.
15. State the syntax and mention operations carried out by 80386 microprocessor to execute the following instructions:
    (a) XLAT
    (b) CWD
    (c) LOOP
    (d) REP
16. What is LOOP instruction? Write a small assembly program to demonstrate LOOP instruction?
17. What is REPNZ instruction? With the help of small program demonstrate REPNZ instruction.
18. Explain the following instructions with an example:
    (a) XCHG
    (b) TEST
    (c) LOOP
    (d) ROR

Answers

Multiple-Choice Questions

1. (b)	**14.** (a)	**27.** (b)
2. (c)	**15.** (b)	**28.** (d)
3. (d)	**16.** (a)	**29.** (c)
4. (c)	**17.** (d)	**30.** (d)
5. (b)	**18.** (a)	**31.** (c)
6. (d)	**19.** (d)	**32.** (a)
7. (c)	**20.** (c)	**33.** (a)
8. (b)	**21.** (d)	**34.** (d)
9. (d)	**22.** (d)	**35.** (c)
10. (c)	**23.** (a)	**36.** (c)
11. (c)	**24.** (a)	**37.** (c)
12. (d)	**25.** (d)	**38.** (b)
13. (c)	**26.** (b)	**39.** (d)

40. (a)
41. (c)
42. (a)
43. (c)
44. (a)
45. (b)
46. (c)
47. (d)
48. (b)
49. (a)
50. (c)
51. (b)
52. (a)
53. (a)

UNIT II

80386 Memory Segmentation

3 Bus Cycles and Memory Interfacing

LEARNING OBJECTIVES

After reading this chapter you will be able to:

- Understand the various hardware pins and signals that are used to operate the 80386 processor as a complete microprocessor-based system.
- Understand various types of bus cycle generation required to access memory.
- Discuss 16- and 32-bit memory interfacing and related issues.

3.1 Introduction

The 80386 chip is packaged in a 132-pin grid array form as shown in Fig. 1 and draws approximately 400 mA, which is less power than even the 8086 requires. The 80386 has a smaller power requirement because it is made of CMOS (complementary metal oxide semiconductor) semiconductor materials. The CMOS design enables devices to consume extremely low levels of power and high packaging density.

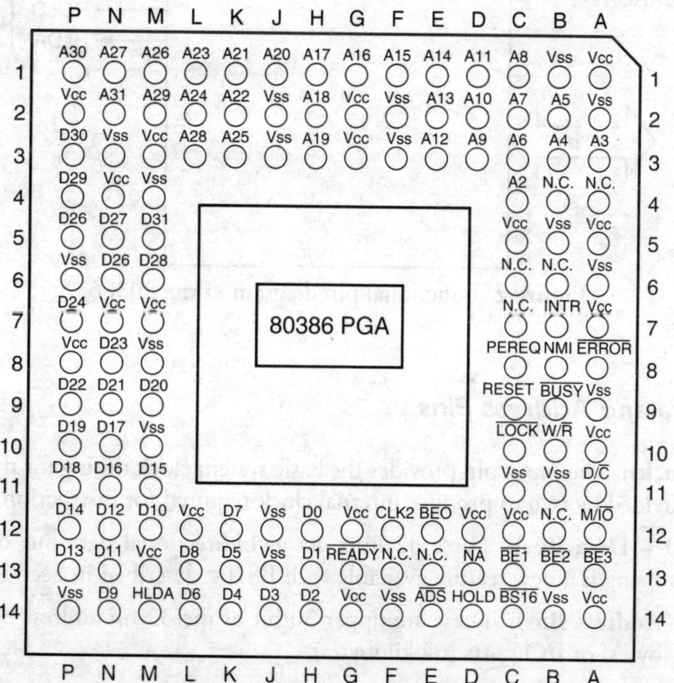

Figure 1 80386 processor pin diagram.

3.2 Functionality of Pins

Though, the processor is packaged as pin grid array, for easy understanding, we study the diagram according to the pin functionality rather than sequential pin numbers as shown in Fig. 2.

The '#' symbol used in description indicates an active low signal, whereas I indicates input signal and O indicates output signal.

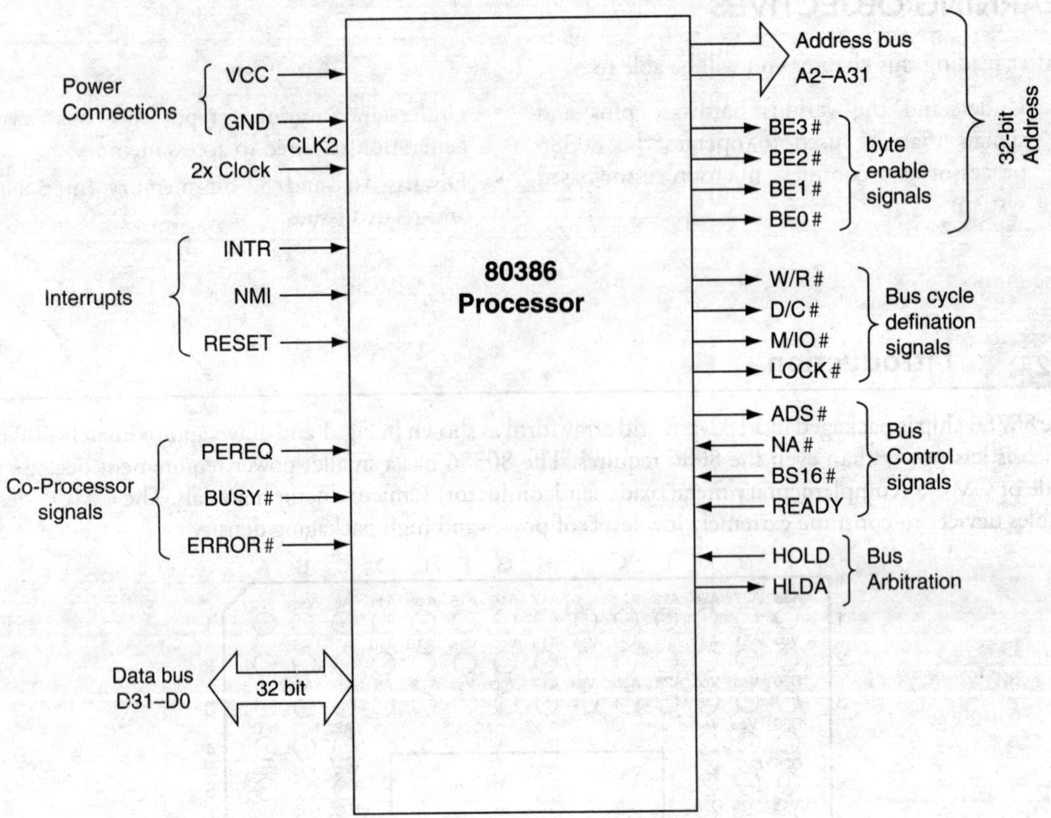

Figure 2 Functional pin diagram of the 80386.

3.2.1 Clock, Data and Address Pins

1. **CLK2# (I – Clock):** The input pin provides the basic system clock timing for the operation of 80386. It is internally divided by two to produce internal clock required for instruction execution.
2. **D31–D0# (I/O – Data Bus):** These 32 lines act as bidirectional data bus during different access cycles. Data bus sizing is a new feature available with BS16# described in Section 3.2.3.
3. **A31–A2# (O – Address Bus):** These are upper 30 bit of the 32-bit address bus addressing physical memory (4 Gigabytes) or I/O ports (64 kilobytes).

4. **BE0#–BE3# (O – Byte Enable):** The 32-bit data bus is supported by 80386 and the memory system of the 80386 processor can be viewed as a 4-byte wide memory access mechanism (4 banks). The 4 byte enable lines BE0# to BE3#, are used for enabling these 4 banks. Using these 4 enable signal lines, the CPU may transfer 1 byte, 2 bytes, 3 bytes or 4 bytes of data simultaneously. Data bus signals are used with respect to byte enable signals as shown in Table 1.

Table 1 Byte Enable Signals Usage

Byte Enable Signal	*Data Bus*
BE0#	D7–D0
BE1#	D15–D8
BE2#	D23–D16
BE3#	D31–D24

The number of byte enables activated tells the physical size of the operand being fetched.

3.2.2 Bus Cycle Definition Signals

1. **W/R# (O – Write/Read):** A low signal on the pin indicates Read cycle whereas a high signal indicates a write cycle.
2. **D/C# (O – Data/Control):** This pin distinguishes data cycles, either memory or I/O, from control cycles which may be either of interrupt acknowledge, halt, or instruction fetching.
3. **M/IO#(O – Memory/I/O):** A high signal indicates that the current cycle is memory access cycle and a low signal indicates it is an Input / output device access.
4. **LOCK# (O – Lock):** Assertion of the pin indicates the other system bus masters requesting for bus that the current cycle is not to be interrupted. For example, Interrupt Acknowledge cycle and Misaligned Transfer cycles.

3.2.3 Bus Control Signals

The bus control signals allow external logic to control the bus cycle.

1. **ADS# (O – Address Status):** The address status output pin indicates that the address bus and bus cycle definition pins (W/R#, D/C#, M/IO#, BE0# to BE3#) are carrying the respective valid values. The 80386 processor does not have any ALE signals. Therefore, this signal is used for latching the address to external latches.
2. **READY# (I – Transfer Acknowledge):** The ready signal indicates to the CPU that the previous bus cycle has been terminated and the bus is ready for the next cycle. The signal is used to insert WAIT states in a bus cycle and is useful for interfacing of slow devices with CPU.

3. **BS16# (I – Bus Size):** The bus size – 16 input pins allow the interfacing of 16-bit devices with the 32-bit wide 80386 processor data bus. Successive 16-bit bus cycles may be executed to read a 32 bit data from a peripheral. Status "low" indicates 16-bit data bus (D0–D15 and BE0#, BE#1) and status high indicates use of 32-bit data bus (D0–D31 and BE0#–BE3#).
4. **NA16# (I – Next Address):** The pin is used to request address pipelining for fore coming bus cycle. This signal provides sufficient time to slower memory devices to adjust with processor speed.

3.2.4 Bus Arbitration Signals

1. **HOLD (I – Bus Hold Request):** The bus hold input pin enables the other bus masters to gain control of the system bus if it is asserted. If RESET is asserted HOLD is not recognized since RESET has high priority. HOLD is synchronous with clock and level sensitive.
2. **HLDA (O – Hold Acknowledge):** This signal indicates that a valid bus hold request has been received and the bus has been relinquished by the CPU.

3.2.5 Co-Processor Interfacing Signals

1. **BUSY# (I – Co-processor Busy):** The signal is generated by co-processor, and it indicates to the CPU that the co-processor is still executing instructions of the allocated task. This signal is sampled (read by main processor) when the 80386 processor comes across any co-processor instruction like FLD, FSTP, etc. FINIT can be executed when BUSY# is asserted.

   BUSY# is asynchronous with clock and level sensitive pin. Additionally, when BUSY# is low and RESET is going from high to low, the processor performs an internal self test. If BUSY# is high, the self test is skipped.
2. **ERROR# (I – Error):** The signal is generated when co-processor indicates to the CPU that it has encountered an error while executing previous instruction. This pin is automatically read by main processor. This is an asynchronous and level sensitive signal.
3. **PEREQ (I – Processor Extension Request):** This is also generated by co-processor requesting the CPU to fetch a data word on behalf of the co-processor. PEREQ is also an asynchronous and level sensitive signal with clk2.

3.2.6 Interrupt Control Signals

1. **INTR (I – Interrupt Request):** This pin may be activated by external device. In response, the processor suspends execution of the current program and executes an interrupt acknowledge function. This interrupt pin is a maskable interrupt, that can be masked using the IF bit of the E-flags register.
2. **NMI (I – Non-Maskable Interrupt Request):** A valid request signal at the non-maskable interrupt request input pin internally generates a non-maskable interrupt of type2. Processor response action is similar as above.
3. **RESET (I – Reset):** A high at this input pin suspends the current operation and restart the execution from the starting location. RESET signal is asynchronous with clock signal.

3.2.7 Power Supply Pins

1. **V_{CC} (I – System Power):** These are system power supply lines. The 80386 requires a 5V DC supply input at two different physical pins.
2. **V_{SS} (I – System Ground):** Two return lines for the power supply.
3. **N/C (No Connection):** Pins are expected to be left open while connecting the 80386 processor in the circuit.

3.2.8 Generation of A0 and A1

As it is clear that the address pins are only 30 (A2–A31) rather than 32, A0 and A1 pins are physically absent. A0 and A1 are given in the form of BE0#–BE3#. One or more byte enable signals are activated to dynamically generate A0 and A1. Figures 3(a) and 3(b) show how the A0 and A1 are derived from byte enable signals. At the same time processor does the automatic duplication of data for achieving optimum write performance on 16 bit buses. Table 2 shows the status of address bus during the generation.

Table 2 A0, A1 Generation via Byte Enable Signals

A31…A2					*BE3#*	*BE2#*	*BE1#*	*BE0#*
A31	Physical Base Address							
	……	A2	A1	A0				
A31	0	A2	0	0	X	X	X	0
A31	Physical Base Address							
		A2	A1	A0				
A31	0	A2	0	1	X	X	0	0
A31	0	A2	1	0	X	0	1	0
A31	0	A2	1	1	0	1	1	0

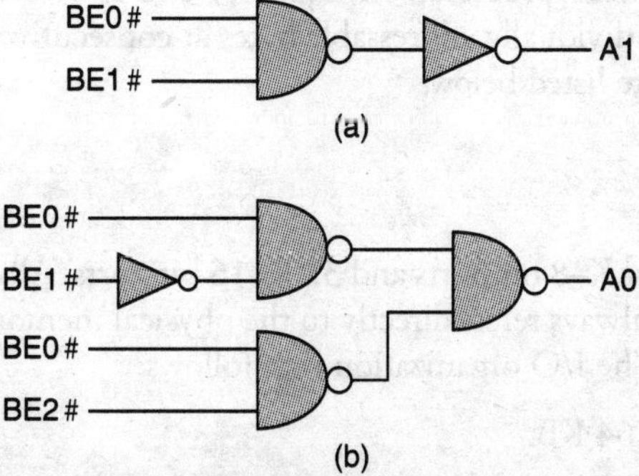

Figure 3 (a) A0 generation hardware logic. (b) A1 generation hardware logic.

3.2.9 Generation of BHE and BLE for Accessing 16-Bit Memories

For 16 bit accesses, three signals are required to be generated to form complete address on the address bus as shown in Figs. 4(a), 4(b) and 4(c). To generate these signals for 16-bit access, A0/ BLE# is asserted, when D0–D7 of 16-bit bus is active. BHE# is asserted when D8–D15 of 16-bit bus is active. A1 remains low for all even words and remains high for all odd words.

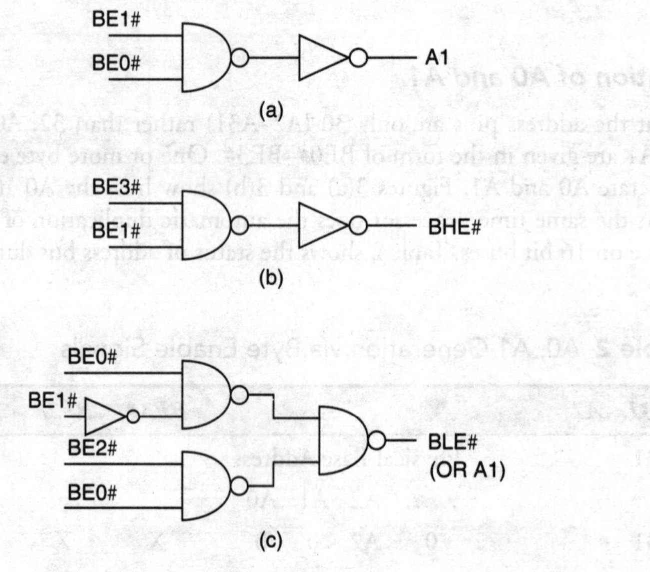

Figure 4 (a) A1 generation hardware logic. (b) BHE# generation hardware logic. (c) A0/BLE# generation hardware logic.

3.3 16/32-Bit Data Transfer Mechanism

Before understanding the data transfer mechanism it would be appropriate to understand the I/O and memory organization for the 80386 processor. All memory and I/O locations are 32-bit (double word) wide. Each double word has 4 individually addressable bytes at consecutive locations. Key points about the memory and I/O organization are listed below.

3.3.1 I/O Organization

The 80386 I/O space contains 64 K–8 bit ports and 32 K–16 bit ports. All I/O instructions bypass segmentation and paging units. So I/O always refers directly to the physical memory. The M/IO# pin distinguishes between the memory and I/O. The I/O organization is as follows:

1. Total I/O space available is 64 KB.
2. The addresses range from 0000 H to FFFF H as shown in Fig. 5.
3. Additionally the co-processor uses I/O 8000 00F8H to 8000 00FFH, beyond the address range of programmed I/O.

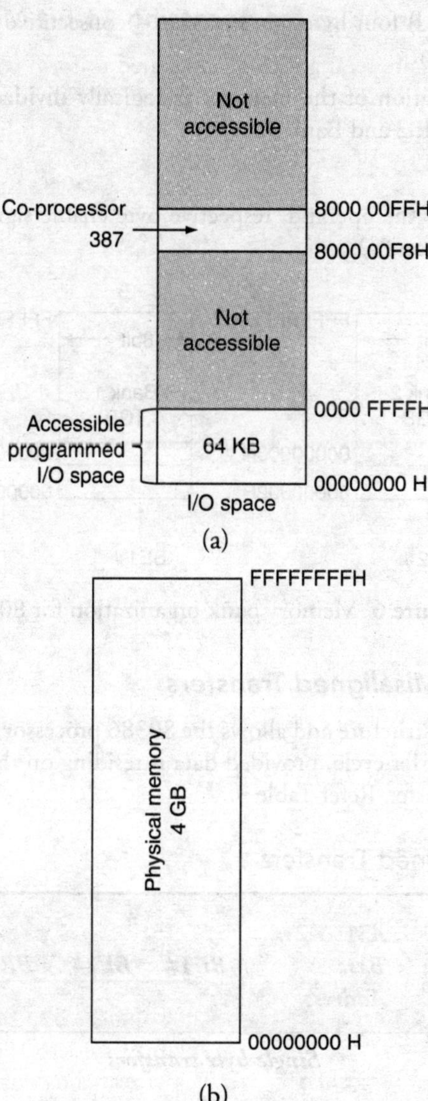

Figure 5 (a) I/O organization and (b) physical memory.

3.3.2 Memory Organization

The memory of the 80386 processor is divided into 4 memory banks. Concept of different address spaces for the memory is discussed in Chapter 4. The memory organization is as follows:

1. Total memory address space available is 2^{32} means 4 GB physical memory which can store 8/16/32 bit size data items. Every location is a byte wide.
2. The addresses range from 00000000 H to FFFFFFFF H as shown in Fig. 5.
3. For 16-bit data (word) lower byte is stored at the lower address and higher byte at the higher address in 2 consecutive locations. The lower byte address is treated as the address of the word.

4. For 32-bit data (double word) four bytes are stored in 4 consecutive locations with the lowest byte at the lowest location and so on.
5. Figure 6 shows the organization of the memory as logically divided into four, 8-bit wide memory banks- Bank 0, Bank 1, Bank 2 and Bank 3.
6. Each bank is of 1 GB size.
7. Depending upon the size of the operand, respective byte enable signals are activated to generate A0 and A1, as discussed in Section 3.2.8.

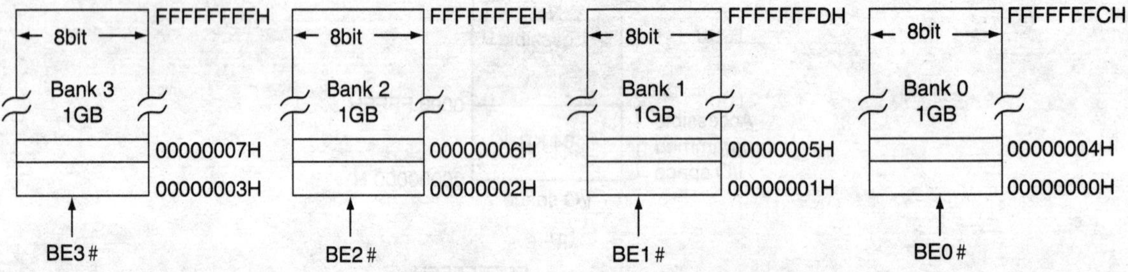

Figure 6 Memory bank organization for 80386.

3.3.3 Good Aligned and Misaligned Transfers

This separates the memory bank structure and allows the 80386 processor to access data in 8, 16 and 32 bit quantities with one memory transfer cycle, provided data is residing on the address which is multiple of 4. This is called an aligned data transfer. Refer Table 3.

Table 3 Aligned Transfers

Required Destination Address	*A31– A2 Base Address*	*BE3#*	*BE2#*	*BE1#*	*BE0#*
		Single byte transfers			
1000	1000	1	1	1	0
1001	1000	1	1	0	1
1002	1000	1	0	1	1
1003	1000	0	1	1	1
1004	1004	1	1	1	0
1005	1004	1	1	0	1

(Continued)

Table 3 (Continued)

Required Destination Address	*A31– A2 Base Address*	*BE3#*	*BE2#*	*BE1#*	*BE0#*
	Word (two bytes) transfers				
1000	1000	1	1	0	0
1001	1000	1	0	0	1
1002	1000	0	0	1	1
1003	Refer Table 4				
1004	1000	1	1	0	0
	Double word (four bytes) transfers				
1000	1000	0	0	0	0
1001	Refer Table 4				
1002	Refer Table 4				
1003	Refer Table 4				
1004	1004	0	0	0	0
1005	Refer Table 4				

If we want to write two consecutive bytes (a word) in memory it can be written using an instruction

MOV WORD PTR DS: [1000H], 5678H

The lower byte "78" is written to the address 1000 and the upper byte to the address 1001. This can happen with four consecutive bytes in a very much similar fashion. The processor uses an instruction as

MOV DWORD PTR DS: [1000H], 56781234H

This would write four bytes to four different byte addresses in a single cycle. The question is, how the processor understands that it has to write to addresses 1000, 1001, 1002, and 1003? Which address is actually generated on address bus?

To distinguish between these four addresses the processor drives one or more byte enable pins. If the desired data is at base address 1000 H, BE0# will be activated. For 1001 H, BE1# will be driven and so on. But here a strong assumption is that data being transferred is an aligned address and does not cross an address that is a multiple of four. Four bytes data transfer at the address 1000 H is aligned but the same data at an address starting from 1001 H or 1002 H is not aligned because it implicitly refers to addresses 1004 H or 1005 H and cross the 4 byte boundary. In this case 1004 H or 1005 H becomes a new multiple of 4. Such types of transfers are referred as unaligned or misaligned transfers.

Table 4 Misaligned Transfers

Required Destination Address	*A31– A2 Base Address*	*BE3#*	*BE2#*	*BE1#*	*BE0#*
	Word (two bytes) transfers				
1003	1004	1	1	1	0
	1000	0	1	1	1
	Double word (four bytes) transfers				
1001	1004	1	1	1	0
	1000	1	0	0	0
1002	1004	1	1	0	0
	1000	0	0	1	1
1003	1004	1	0	0	0
	1000	0	1	1	1
1005	1008	1	1	1	0
	1007	0	0	0	1

When misaligned type of data transfers are requested, processor splits it into two different transfer cycles. First it transfers the higher addressed portion of the data and then it transfers the lower addressed portion. Let us see the previous example once again. If a word is to be written at address 1003 H, the processors performs a "single byte write for higher byte of the data" to 1004 H (address = 1004 H, BE0# – Active) followed by again a "single byte write of the lower byte of the data" to 1003 H (address 1000 H, BE3# – Active). Since two bus cycles are conducted, time required is twice as that of good aligned transfer. The -process is software transparent so the effect is observed during program execution only. Table 4 illustrates the example.

3.3.4 Interfacing 16- and 32-Bit Memories

Now we know that, the 80386 processor memory is accessible in 8, 16 and 32 bit quantities. 32 Bit memories are organized as arrays of physical double words (4 bytes). Physical double words begin at addresses evenly divisible by 4. The double words are addressable by physical address lines A31–A2. Memories that are

32-bit wide require external logic for generating A1, A0 and BE3#–BE0# for selection of respective memory banks. BS16 # is totally deactivated since the operand size is 32 bit.

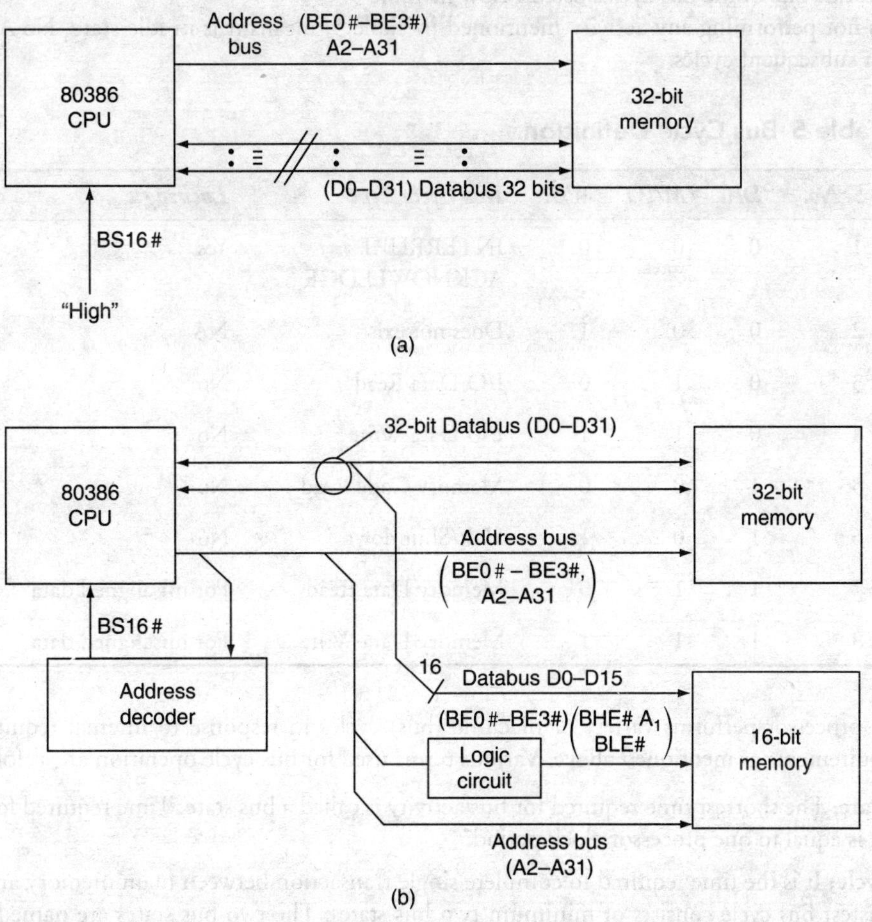

Figure 7 (a) 32-bit memory interfacing. (b) 16-, 32-bit memory interfacing.

16-bit memories are organized as arrays of physical words (2 bytes). Physical words begin at addresses evenly divisible by 2. The words are addressable by physical address lines A31–A2, A1, A0, BHE#, and BLE#. A0 and A1 can be decoded from the byte enables according to Table 2. BLE# and BHE# can be decoded from the byte enables according to the logic shown in Fig. 4. The logic circuit block shown in Fig. 7 contains encoding logic to generate A0, A1, BHE# and BLE#.

3.4 Bus Cycles and Bus Operations

All data transfers occur as a result of a basic mechanism one or more bus cycles. The 80386's address and data buses are interpreted and controlled via several other concerned control signals. The definition of each bus cycle is given by M/IO#, D/C#, W/R#, LOCK#. At the same time, a valid bus address is present on the byte enable signals and address bus. Bus status signal ADS# indicates the validity if the bus definition and start of the new bus cycle. The 32-bit address bus, 32-bit data bus and all associated control signals are referred as "the bus". The 80386 processor supports a number of different types of bus cycles. When active, the bus performs one of the bus cycles listed below in Table 5.

If bus is not performing any activity mentioned in Table 5, means it is in idle state. No ADS# will be activated for subsequent cycles.

Table 5 Bus Cycle Definition

S. No.	*D/C*	*M/IO*	*W/R*	*Bus Cycle Type*	*Locking*
1	0	0	0	INTERRUPT ACKNOWLEDGE	Yes
2	0	0	1	Does not exist	NA
3	0	1	0	I/O Data Read	No
4	0	1	1	I/O Data Write	No
5	1	0	0	Memory Code Read	No
6	1	0	1	Halt/Shut down	No
7	1	1	0	Memory Data Read	For misaligned data
8	1	1	1	Memory Data Write	For misaligned data

The 80386 processor performs variety of machine (bus) cycles in response to intemal requirements and external requirements as mentioned above. Various terms used for bus cycle operation are as follows:

1. **Bus state:** The shortest time required for bus activity is called a bus state. Time required for a bus state period is equal to one processor clock period.
2. **Bus cycle:** It is the time required to complete single transaction between main memory and the CPU. The fastest bus cycle consists of minimum two bus states. The two bus states are named T1 and T2 respectively.
3. **Wait states, Tw:** If memories are slower then additional bus states (T2) are required called as – WAIT states.
4. **Idle state, Ti: If** processor is not performing any of the 7 cycles mentioned in Table 5 then, the processor enters in idle state.
5. For data transfer operation bus cycles are either Read cycle or Write cycle.
6. **Significance of NA#:** The time for which address will be available to the device depends upon whether the signal NA# (Next Address #) is in active or non-active state. This pin is polled by the Processor during each bus cycle to decide whether next cycle will be address pipelined or not. Activation of this signal provides memory address required for the next cycle in advance to the memory device. This feature of **address pipelining** is discussed in detail in Section 3.4.3
7. **Significance of BS16#:** Data bus width (16 bits/32 bits) is also dynamically selectable via BS16# pin. This pin is polled by the processor at the end of each bus cycle (T2). A low (active state) on this indicates that the operand width is 16 bits. A high (inactive state) indicates 32-bit wide operand transaction. This feature is also called as **dynamic bus sizing**.

Once NA# is sampled asserted, the processor 80386 processor dedicates itself to the highest priority bus request that is pending internally. It cannot perform any more 16-bit transfers. Thereafter, the current bus size remains 32 bits. Therefore, if NA# is sampled low within a bus cycle, BS16# must be negated thereafter in that bus cycle or else, do not assert NA# during bus cycles which must have BS16# driven active.

3.4.1 Read Cycle

During Read cycle data is transferred from an external memory/device to the 80386 processor. Here we discuss the simplest fast Read cycle without address pipelining. Steps taken by the 80386 processor during conduction of the read cycle are as follows (refer Fig. 8):

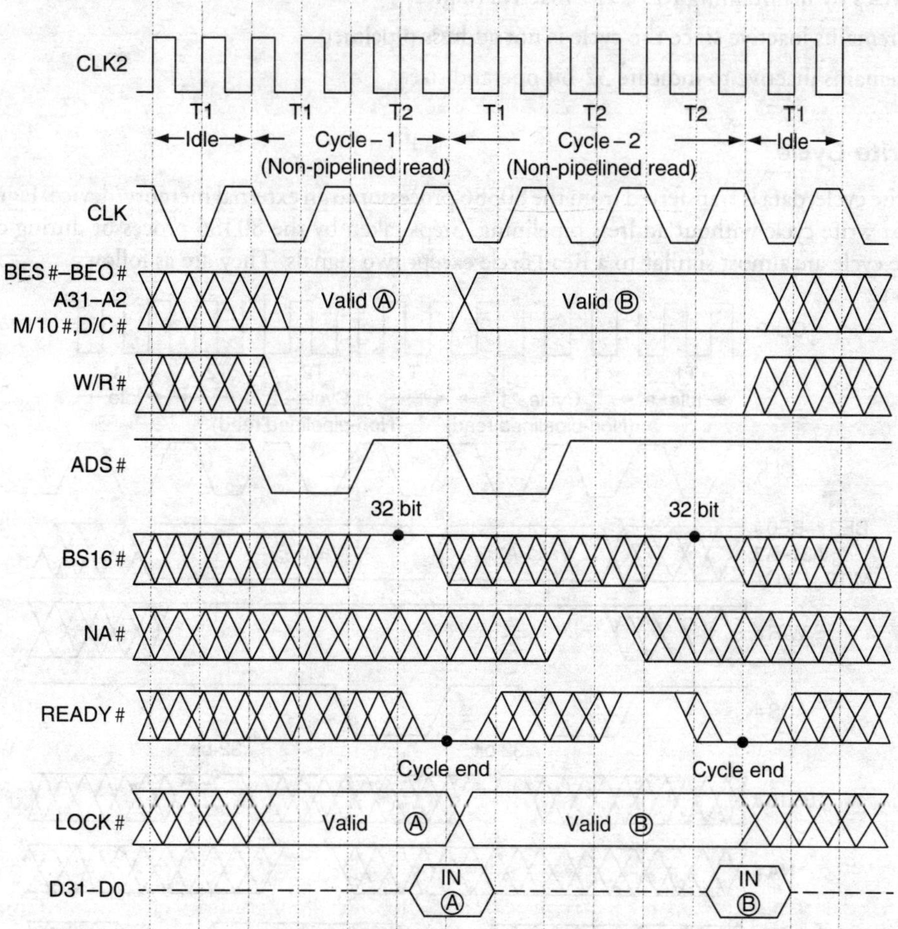

Figure 8 Non-pipelined read bus cycle.

1. The 80386 processor initiates a cycle by asserting the address status signal – ADS# in the first state (T1). The ADS# output indicates that a valid bus cycle definition and address is available on the cycle definition pins and the address bus.
2. W/R# is asserted low by the processor at the same time that of ADS# is asserted. This indicates to memory that a Read cycle is in progress.

3. READY# is returned (active low) by the external system (memory system) in the second clock (T2) of the bus cycle for a *zero wait state transfer*. READY# indicates that the external system has presented/accepted valid data on the data pins in response to a read/write request. Assertion of the READY# signal indicates the end of the current cycle.
4. The data will be available on the data bus (D0–D31) as soon as READY# is active (low). Assertion of READY# indicates that the data has been accepted by the processor.
5. If the system is not ready to drive or accept data, wait states can be added to these cycles by not returning READY# to the processor at the end of the second clock (T2). READY# must be driven inactive (high) at the end of the second clock. Any number of wait states can be added to the processor bus cycles by maintaining READY# inactive (high).
6. NA# remains inactive since the cycle is not address pipelined.
7. BS# remains inactive to indicate 32-bit operand size.

3.4.2 Write Cycle

During Write cycle, data is transferred from the 80386 processor to an external memory/device. Figure 9 shows simplest fast write cycle without address pipelining. Steps taken by the 80386 processor during conduction of the write cycle are almost similar to a Read cycle except two signals. They are as follows:

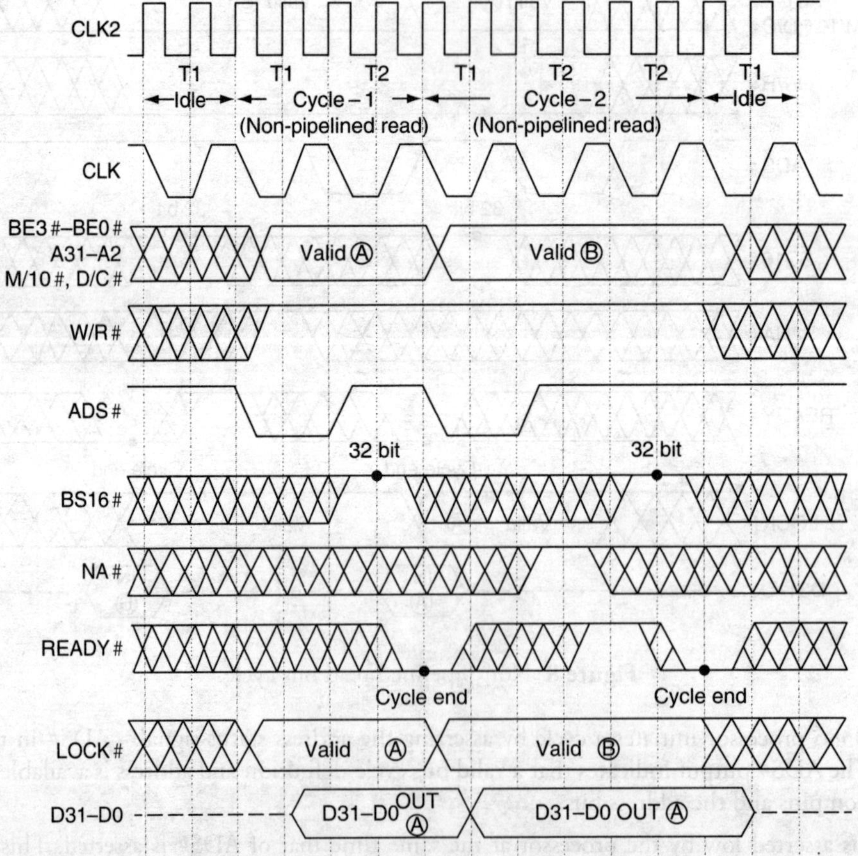

Figure 9 Non-pipelined write bus cycle.

1. The 80386 processor initiates a cycle by asserting the address status signal – ADS# in the first state (T1). The ADS# output indicates that a valid bus cycle definition and address is available on the cycle definition pins and the address bus.
2. W/R# is asserted high by the processor at the same time that of ADS# is asserted. This indicates to memory that a Write Cycle is in progress.
3. READY# is returned (active low) by the external system (memory system) in the second clock (T2) of the bus cycle for a zero waits state transfer. READY# indicates that the external system has presented/ accepted valid data on the data pins in response to a read/write request. Assertion of the READY# signal indicates the end of the current cycle.
4. Data to be written is readily available on data bus (D0–D31) and when READY# is asserted it indicates that the data has been written to the memory.
5. If the system is not ready to drive or accept data, wait states can be added to these cycles by not returning READY# to the processor at the end of the second clock (T2). READY# must be driven inactive (high) at the end of the second clock. Any number of wait states can be added to the processor bus cycles by maintaining READY# inactive (high).
6. NA# remains inactive since the cycle is not address pipelined.
7. BS# remains inactive to indicate 32-bit operand size.

3.4.3 Address Pipelining

Address pipelining is a feature which requests the bus cycle definition signal and address of the next operand in advance during execution of the current cycle. So this generates intentional pending bus cycle before the current bus cycle is completed. When a bus cycle is in execution state and current address has been valid (with active ADS#) at least for an entire bus state then NA# is activated (low) to initiate address pipelining for next cycle. Figure 10 shows the sampling low of NA# signal for the first time at the end of T2 during cycle 2. This extends T2 as T2P in the same cycle as third T state. Here P indicates next cycle as pipelined cycle. NA# is required to be sampled low at the end of every cycle's T2 to continue with address pipelining facility. Otherwise, no further effect remains for subsequent cycles.

NA# is activated low by external memory control system to interface slower memories with faster CPU. This pipelining does not improve the performance of the processor but helps to bridge up speed gap between slower peripherals and faster CPU.

This feature is supported only for 32 bit operands. In other words during address pipelining, dynamic bus sizing is not possible. BS16# is required to be inactive when NA# is active. Those are complementary features.

Any cycle followed by idle bus state is always non pipelined cycle. This indicates that, before address pipelining processor must execute at least one non pipelined read or write cycle.

Since address pipelining capability is limited to only one bus cycle ahead. If address pipelining is already active for pre fetching next address, one more new request is not accepted by the 80386 processor. So the processor inserts one more T state called T21. Refer cycle 4 in Fig. 10.

The fastest path to initiate and maintain address pipelining can be shown as follows with reference to Fig. 10:

Ti, Ti, Ti....| T1- T2- T2p | T1P-T2P
Idle states | Non pipelined Cycle | Pipelined Cycle

Ti, Ti, Ti,.. | T1- T2- T2P | T1P-T2P | T1P-T2P | T1P-T21-T21....
Idle states | Non pipelined Cycle | Pipelined Cycle | Pipelined cycle| Not possible to pipeline

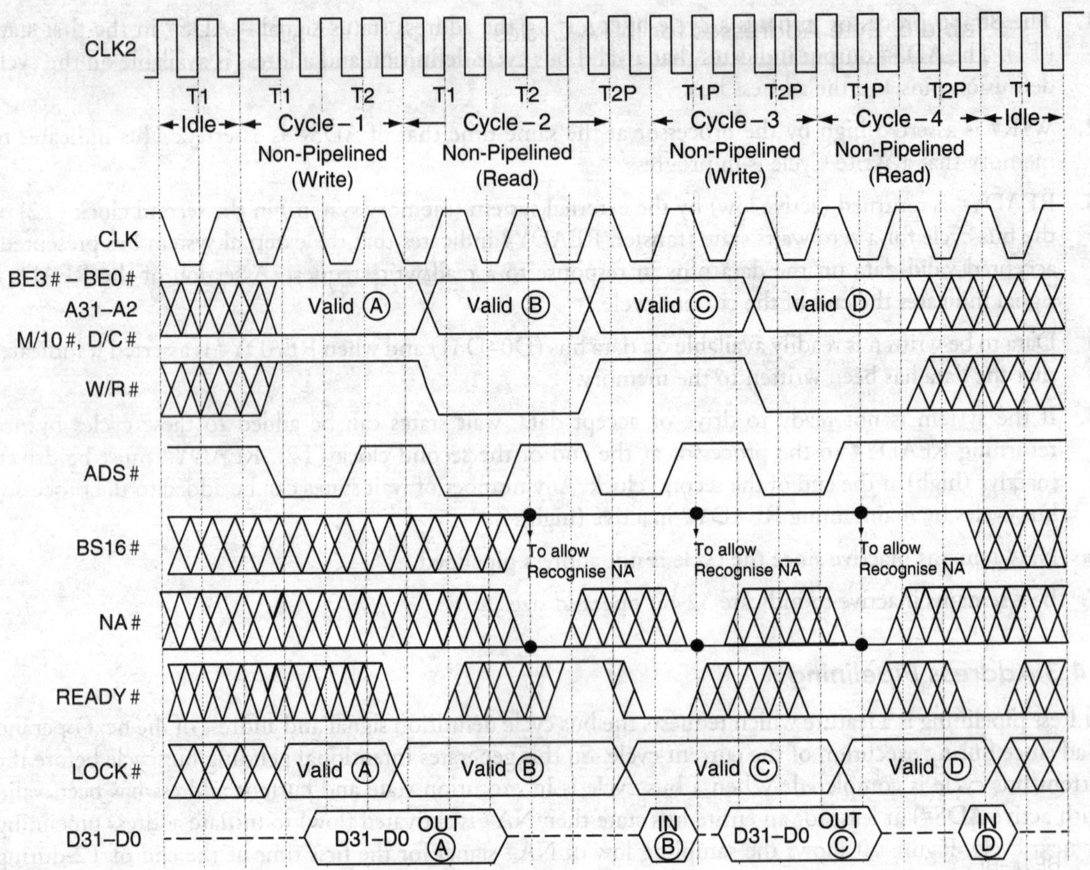

Figure 10 Address pipelined cycles.

3.4.4 Interrupt Acknowledge (INTA) Cycles

Interrupt request are sent to INTR pin by the external device. In response to occurrence of interrupt, the 80386 processor drives two interrupt acknowledge cycles. For INTA cycles bus definition signals define the type of bus activity. This is very much similar to read cycles. Each cycle is terminated after assertion (a low on pin) of READY# signal by the requesting device. A high on an address line A2 indicates the first INTA cycle and zero on A2 indicates second cycle. Byte addresses driven by the processor during first and second cycle are shown in Table 6. Steps taken by the 80386 processor during conduction of the INTA cycles are as follows (refer Fig. 11):

1. The LOCK# signal is asserted low from the beginning of first INTA cycle to the end of second INTA cycle to indicate that those two cycles must not be interrupted. Four idle states Ti are inserted between first and second INTA cycles. This is required because as per CPU design time taken from the end of first INTA to the Next INTA should be within 160 nanoseconds.

2. The data bus (D0–D31) is in floating state till the end of second cycle. So data read operation is not performed till the end of second INTA cycle. The processor reads an external interrupt vector (address) on lower 8 bits of the data bus (D0–D7). This vector indicates specific interrupt number between 0–255 which is requesting service.

Table 6 Byte Addresses for INTA Cycles

	A31…A2					*BE3#*	*BE2#*	*BE1#*	*BE0#*
	Physical Base Address								
	A31	……	**A2**	A1	A0				
1st INTA cycle Address 04H	A31	0	**1**	0	0	1	1	1	0
2nd INTA cycle Address 00H	A31	0	**0**	0	0	1	1	1	0

3. The program control is transferred to the vector number in IVT to fetch address of the respective ISR.
4. NA# does not have effect during first INTA cycle. If NA# is asserted during second INTA cycle, immediate next cycle will be address pipelined.

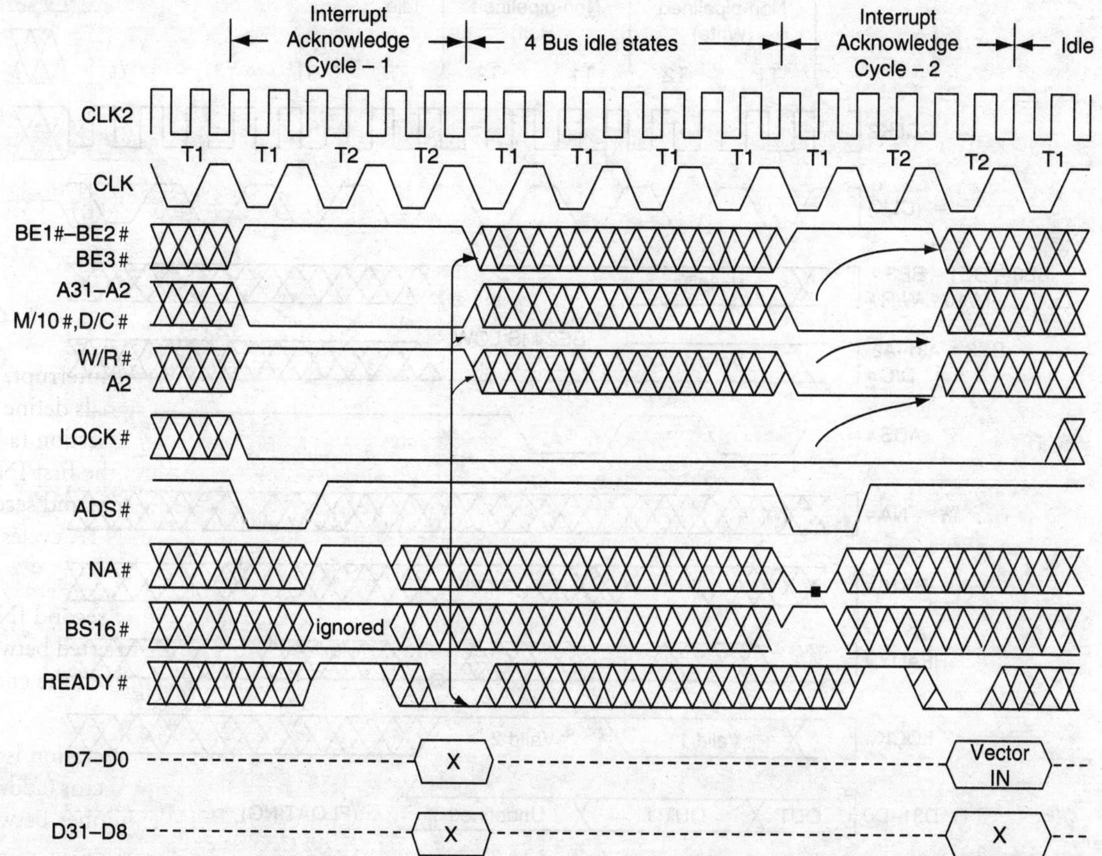

Figure 11 Interrupt acknowledge (INTA) cycles.

3.4.5 Halt Indication Cycle

As a result of HALT instruction execution, the 80386 processor halts. Bus definition for halt cycle is shown in Table 5. Byte address is 02 H as shown in Table 7. To resume execution after HALT either INTR or NMI or RESET is required to be activated. Figure 12 shows the halt indication cycle.

Table 7 Byte Address for Halt and Shutdown

	A31…A2					*BE3#*	*BE2#*	*BE1#*	*BE0#*
	A31	Physical Base Address							
		……	**A2**	**A1**	**A0**				
Byte Address for Halt 02H	A31	0	0	**1**	0	1	0	1	1
Byte Address for Shutdown 00H	A31	0	0	**0**	0	1	1	1	0

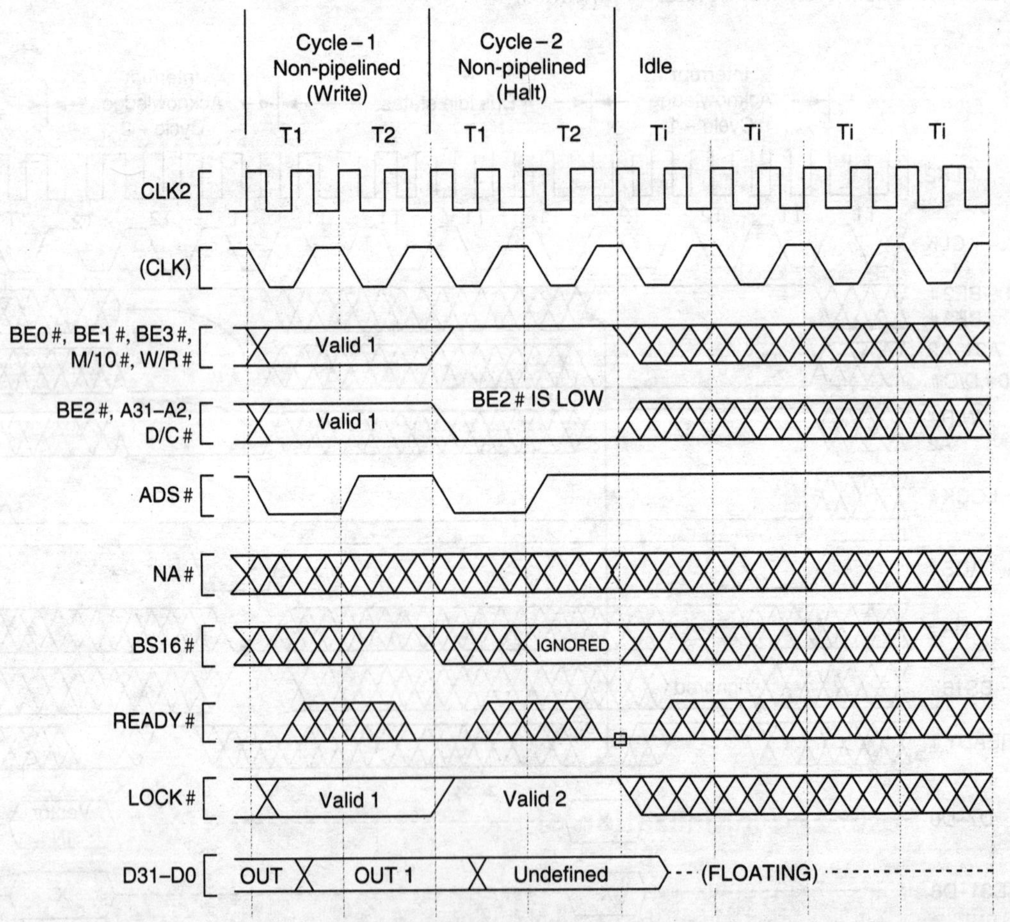

Figure 12 Halt indication cycle.

3.4.6 Shutdown Indication Cycle

As a result of processing double fault the 80386 processor executes shut down indication cycle and actually shuts down at the end of the cycle. Consider a situation when a double fault would occur: It is when an interrupt is triggered but the segment in which the interrupt handler (ISR) resides is invalid. As double faults can only happen due to kernel bugs, they are rarely caused by user space programs in protected mode. Bus definition for shutdown cycle is shown in Table 7. Byte address is 00 H as shown in Table 7.

The data bus (D0–D31) carries undefined data during the shutdown cycle and the cycle is acknowledged by assertion of a low on READY# pin. To resume execution after HALT either NMI or RESET is required to be activated. Figure 13 shows shutdown activity during cycle 2.

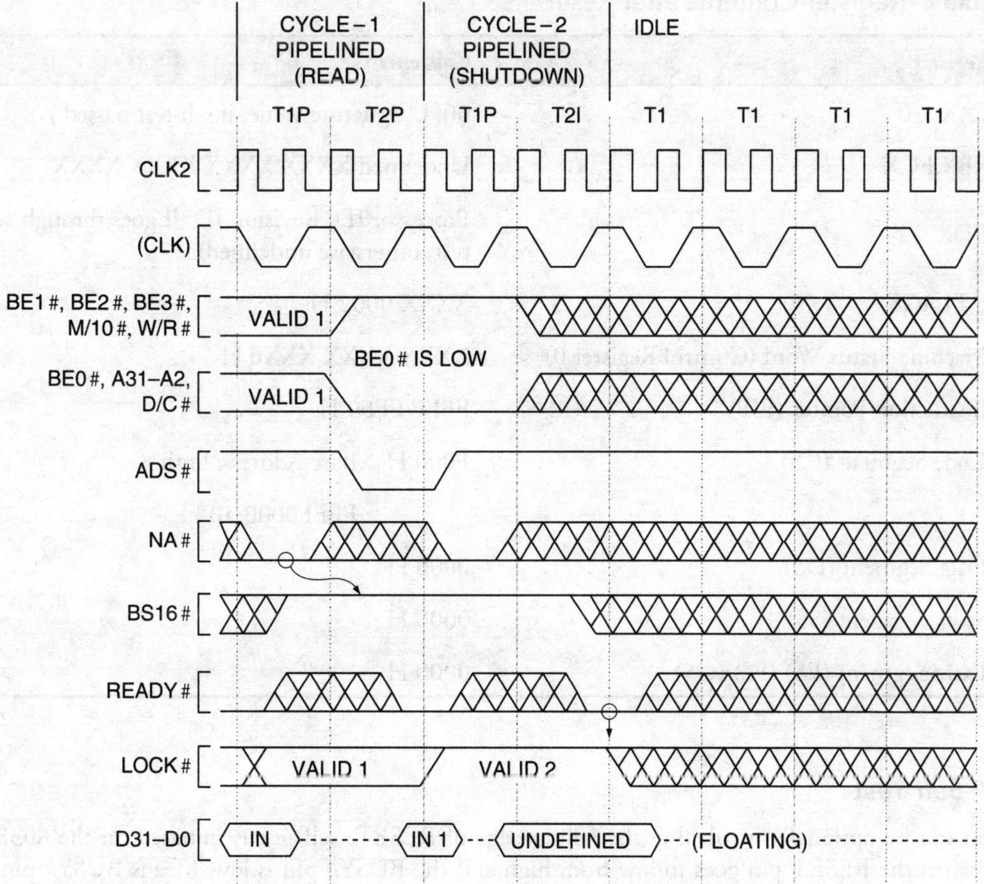

Figure 13 Shutdown indication cycle.

3.5 Reset and Initialization of the 80386 Processor

Reset is the highest priority input signal. Whenever the processor receives an active high on RESET pin then it terminates its all execution, processes as well as any local bus activity currently going on. For this, reset should remain active (high) for at least 15 CLK2 periods otherwise, it may not be recognized by the processor.

When reset becomes again low (inactive) after at least 350 to 450 CLK2 pulses, the processor 80386 starts instruction execution near the top of the physical memory from the address FFFFFFF0 H. After activation of the RESET pin the processor enters in real mode with a FAR jump. When processor executes first far (inter segment) call/jump instruction, status of higher address lines A20–A31 become low. So that processor can execute instructions from a code segment that resides in the lower 1 Megabyte of the physical memory. Therefore, the system designer is allowed to use a ROM at the top of physical memory to take care of resets and reinitialize the system. All the internal caches (Translation look aside buffer and segment descriptor cache) are invalidated upon RESET. Various registers initial contents are as shown in Table 8.

Table 8 Register Contents after Reset

Register	*Contents*
EAX	00H (signature value, if self test passed.)
EBX,ECX	Undefined XXXX XXXX XXXX XXXX
EDX	Processor ID, Revision ID (if goes through self test, otherwise undefined).
E FLAGS	XXXX 0002 H
Machine Status Word (Control Register 0)	XXXX XXXX XXX0 H
Instruction Pointer (EIP)	FFFF FFF0 H
Code Segment (CS)	F000 H Base Address: limit FFFF0000: 0FFF
Data Segment (DS)	0000 H
Stack Segment (SS)	0000 H
Extra Segment (ES) (FS) (GS)	0000 H

3.5.1 Self Test

Self test can be optionally invoked at the falling edge of RESET. Self test is initiated on the 80386 processor when the RESET pin goes to low from high and the BUSY# pin is low. Means BUSY# pin is also required to be checked at the same time. The 80386 processor can perform self test to check its internal functionality of control ROM, RAM, PLA, etc. 50% part of the 80386 processor is tested during self test. The self test takes approximately 2^{19} clock cycles, i.e., approximately 26 milliseconds for a clock of 20 MHz. The outcome of the self test is reflected in the EAX register. Zero value in EAX indicates all checks passed whereas, non-zero value indicates a faulty processor. EDX register always holds component and stepping identifier (refer Table 8).

Summary

- This chapter started with pin configuration and functions of various pins available on the 80386 processor.
- It clears the concept of memory banks and usage of associated bank enable signals required to generate A0/BLE, A1, and BHE so that it enables to interface both 16-and 32-bit memories.
- Various types of bus cycles are required to be conducted for the operation of the 80386 processor.
- Address pipelining technique for interfacing slower memories is discussed in detail.
- When processor RESET is activated, it can conduct self test to check correct functioning of the chip.
- It also gives the processor id and stepping id of the processor.

Multiple-Choice Questions

1. The 80386 processor is packaged in

(a) 140 Pin Grid Array

(b) 132 Pin DIP

(c) 132 Pin Grid Array

(d) 140 Pin QFP

2. The CMOS design enables devices to consume extremely

(a) high power with high packaging density

(b) low power with low packaging density

(c) high power with low packaging density

(d) low power with high packaging density

3. For 80386 DX clock frequency is internally divided by ______ to produce internal clock required for instruction execution

(a) 2

(b) 4

(c) 8

(d) 12

4. How many address pins are available for 80386 processor?

(a) 32

(b) 30

(c) 31

(d) 28

5. Which among the following pins indicates the start of new bus cycle?
   (a) NA#
   (b) ADS#
   (c) BS16#
   (d) READY#
6. Which among the following pin indicates the end of the current bus cycle?
   (a) NA#
   (b) ADS#
   (c) BS16#
   (d) READY#
7. Which among the following set represent the co-processor signals?
   (a) BUSY#, ERROR# , PEREQ
   (b) INTR , NMI, RESET
   (c) HOLD, HLDA
   (d) None of Above
8. All bus definition signals are
   (a) unidirectional Input signals for the 80386 processor
   (b) unidirectional output signals for the 80386 processor
   (c) bidirectional signals for the 80386 processor
   (d) None of above
9. The 80386 processor has _____ number of memory banks.
   (a) 2
   (b) 4
   (c) 8
   (d) 12
10. For the 80386 processor _____ number Vcc and _____ ground pins are available.
    (a) 1, 1
    (b) 2, 2
    (c) 1, 2
    (d) 2, 1
11. Total I/O space available for The 80386 processor is
    (a) 64 KB
    (b) 64 MB

(c) 1GB

(d) 4 GB

12. Total memory space available for The 80386 processor is

(a) 64 KB

(b) 64 MB

(c) 1GB

(d) 4 GB

13. For transferring 16 bit data at the unaligned addresses the 80386 processor conducts _____ number of memory cycles.

(a) 1

(b) 2

(c) 3

(d) 4

14. For transferring 32 bit data at the unaligned addresses the 80386 processor conducts _____ number of memory cycles.

(a) 1

(b) 2

(c) 3

(d) 4

15. To interface slower memories following signal plays important role.

(a) NA#

(b) ADS#

(c) BS16#

(d) READY#

16. Address pipelining helps

(a) to improve speed of memory

(b) to interface slower memories.

(c) to improve processor performance speed

(d) to improve overall system performance

17. Activation of BS# 16 indicates the operand size equals to

(a) 8 bits

(b) 16 bits

(c) 32 bits

(d) 64 bits

18. In response to occurrence of interrupt is the 80386 processor drives _____ interrupt acknowledge cycle(s).

(a) 1

(b) 2

(c) 3

(d) 4

19. For writing a word at the address 1003 H the address on the address pins is during first cycle is _____ and then

(a) 1003 H, 1004 H

(b) 1003 H, 1004 H

(c) 1000 H, 1004 H

(d) 1004 H, 1000 H

20. Upon reset the 80386 processor's EIP points to the address _____ H.

(a) 0000 0000

(b) FFFF FFFF

(c) FFFF FFF0

(d) FFFF000

21. Upon reset, the 80386 processor's, except _____ register every segment register contains a value 0.

(a) CS

(b) DS

(c) ES

(d) FS

(e) GS

22. Upon reset, the 80386 processor's, EAX register contains

(a) Processor id

(b) Revision id

(c) Signature value

(d) None of above

23. Upon reset, the 80386 processor's, EDX register contains

(a) Processor id

(b) Processor id and revision id

(c) Signature value

(d) None of above

24. Upon reset, the 80386 processor conducts self test when

(a) RESET is low and BUSY is low

(b) RESET is going low and BUSY is low

(c) RESET is going high and BUSY is low

(d) RESET is going low and BUSY is high

25. The frequency applied to the pin CLK2 is internally divided by _____ by the 80386 processor.

(a) 1

(b) 2

(c) 3

(d) 4

26. Interrupt pin is a maskable interrupt, that can be masked using the _____ of the EFLAGS register.

(a) IF bit

(b) DF bit

(c) TF bit

(d) None of the given

27. The co-processor uses I/O address range of

(a) F000000F H to F80000FFH

(b) 8000008FH to 800000FFH

(c) 800000F8H to 800000FFH

(d) None of the given

28. During Address pipelined cycles _____ signal is activated to indicate address pipelining.

(a) BS16#

(b) NA#

(c) LOCK #

(d) None of the given

29. During Address pipelined cycles _____ signal cannot be is activated at all.

(a) BS16#

(b) NA#

(c) LOCK #

(d) None of the given

30. During non pipeline read which signal indicates that it is non pipelined cycle?

(a) BS16#

(b) NA#

(c) LOCK #

(d) None of the given

31. Which of the signals cannot be active at the same time ?

(a) BE1#–BE0#

(b) BS 16#–NA#

(c) LOCK #–NA#

(d) None of the given

32. During _____ bus cycle the processor reads an external interrupt vector (address) on lower 8 bits of the data bus (D0–D7) .

(a) Read

(b) Write

(c) Halt

(d) Interrupt acknowledge

33. During HALT indication bus cycle the byte address is

(a) 0

(b) 1

(c) 2

(d) 4

34. During Shutdown indication bus cycle the byte address is

(a) 0

(b) 1

(c) 2

(d) 4

35. During INTA cycles _____ signal is activated to indicate that two consecutive cycles are not to be interrupted.

(a) BS16#

(b) NA#

(c) LOCK#

(d) None of the given

36. Address pipelining feature is supported only for _____ bit operands.

(a) 8

(b) 16

(c) 32

(d) 64

37. BS# remains inactive for _____ bit operands.

(a) 8

(b) 16

(c) 32

(d) 64

38. During write cycle data to be written is readily available on data bus (D0–D31) and when _____ is asserted.

(a) BS16#

(b) NA#

(c) LOCK #

(d) READY#

39. Address signal A1 is generated using _____ and _____.

(a) BE1#, BE0#

(b) BE1# , BE2#

(c) BE1# , BE3#

(d) BE2# , BE0#

40. Address signal A0/BLE# is generated using _____, _____ and _____.

(a) BE0#, BE1#, BE3#

(b) BE0#, BE1#, BE2#

(c) BE1#, BE2#, BE3#

(d) BE0#, BE2#, BE3#

41. Address signal BHE# is generated using _____, _____ and _____.

(a) BE1#, BE0#

(b) BE1#, BE2#

(c) BE1#, BE3#

(d) BE2#, BE0#

42. When _____ is High the self test is skipped.

(a) BS16#

(b) BUSY#

(c) LOCK #

(d) READY#

43. Which among the following set represent the Bus arbitration signals ?

(a) BUSY#, ERROR# , PEREQ

(b) INTR , NMI, RESET

(c) HOLD, HLDA

(d) M/IO# , D/C#, W/R#

44. Which among the following set represent the Bus cycle definition signals ?

(a) BUSY#, ERROR#, PEREQ

(b) INTR , NMI, RESET

(c) HOLD, HLDA

(d) M/IO#, D/C#, W/R#, lock#

45. Which among the following set represent the Bus cycle definition signals ?

(a) ADS#, NA#, BS16#, READY

(b) INTR, NMI, RESET

(c) HOLD, HLDA

(d) M/IO#, D/C#, W/R#, LOCK#

46. During 16-bit or 32-bit misaligned transfers _____ is asserted conduct two uninterrupted cycles.

(a) BS16#

(b) BUSY#

(c) LOCK#

(d) READY#

47. _____ is generated by co processor requesting the CPU to fetch a data word on behalf of the coprocessor.

(a) ERROR#

(b) BUSY#

(c) PEREQ

(d) READY#

48. The ERROR # signal is generated by _____ indicates to the CPU that it has encountered an error while executing previous instruction.

(a) the co-processor

(b) an Instruction

(c) the Memory

(d) an Interrupt

49. The BUSY# signal is generated by _____.

(a) the CPU

(b) the co-processor

(c) the Memory

(d) an Interrupt

50. Due to misaligned data, number of cycles required to fetch the data are _____ as that of aligned data.

(a) same

(b) double

(c) half

(d) None of the given

51. Dynamic bus sizing feature uses following signal.

(a) BS16#

(b) NA#

(c) LOCK#

(d) None of the given

Review Questions

1. Explain the significance of the following signals of the 80386 system:

   (a) BE0#–BE3#

   (b) PREQ

   (c) BS16#

   (d) NA#

   (e) ERROR#

   (f) READY

   Also explain the interdependency of (a)–(d).

2. What is the use of ADS# and NA# pins of the 80386 processor?
3. What is the function of BE0# to BE3# signals? Explain with respect to aligned and misaligned access.
4. How are A0, A1 and BHE , BLE generated? Explain with logic diagram.
5. How can 80386 access data from memory as a word 16-bit or a double word 32-bit? Explain with suitable diagram.
6. How is memory of the 80386 processor organized? Explain how misaligned transfers are handled by the 80386 processor.
7. What are the signals related with co-processor? Explain.
8. Draw the timing diagram of the 80386 processor with address pipelining. What conditions need to be satisfied for transition to address pipelining?
9. Explain with suitable control signals, the timing diagram of a non-pipelined Read followed by a pipelined Write.
10. Explain with suitable control signals, the timing diagram of a non-pipelined Write cycle of the 80386 processor.
11. What is the difference between Halt and shutdown?
12. What is a misaligned data transfer in 80386? How does it do a double word write at 1003 H?
13. Explain the RESET activity and self test of the 80386 processor.
14. What is the significance of the contents of EAX, EDX, EIP and CS on RESET?

Answers

Multiple-Choice Questions

1. (c)
2. (d)
3. (a)
4. (b)
5. (b)
6. (d)
7. (a)
8. (b)
9. (b)
10. (b)
11. (a)
12. (d)
13. (b)
14. (b)
15. (a)
16. (b)
17. (b)
18. (b)
19. (d)
20. (c)
21. (a)
22. (c)
23. (b)
24. (b)
25. (b)
26. (a)
27. (c)
28. (b)
29. (a)
30. (b)
31. (b)
32. (d)
33. (c)
34. (a)
35. (c)
36. (c)
37. (c)
38. (d)
39. (a)
40. (b)
41. (c)
42. (b)
43. (c)
44. (d)
45. (a)
46. (c)
47. (c)
48. (a)
49. (b)
50. (b)
51. (a)

4 Segmentation

LEARNING OBJECTIVES

After reading this chapter, you will be able to:

- Understand the concepts of segmentation and hence memory management through segmentation. This process is considerably complex than the 8086 addressing mechanism and segmentation.
- Use variable length segments rather than 64 KB.
- Discuss how the protection is provided by means of segmentation using four privilege levels and special instructions used for achieving protection.

4.1 Memory Management through Segmentation

All the capabilities of 80386 processor are exploited in protected mode only. So the memory accessing mechanism is advanced and provides full support for protection, multitasking and sophisticated memory management.

The memory management facilities of the 80386 processor in protected mode can be divided into two parts: Segmentation and paging. *Paging is optional whereas segmentation cannot be made off.* So segmentation is a method of memory management. Primarily, segmentation is used to manage the 80386 processor's main memory in a secured way. So it can be said that it is one of the method of implementing primary memory protection. Segmentation divides the primary memory into segments or sections. Segmentation provides a mechanism of isolating individual code, data, and stack modules so that multiple programs (or tasks) can run on the same processor without interfering with one another. It also provides isolation between operating system and application programs. Each program can be assigned its own set of segments. The processor then decides the boundaries between these segments. This process is implemented via strong hardware support providing the design of the system with a high degree of integrity.

For Understanding concept of segmentation more clearly consider four terms related with addresses used by the 80386 processor as follows (refer Fig. 1):

1. **Logical address**: Logical address is the address generated by the processor. A logical address is comprised of a 16-bit segment selector and a 32-bit offset. The segment selector recognizes the segment from which the byte is to be fetched and the offset tells the exact location of the byte within the segment relative to the base address of the segment. One of the segment register contents are copied to the selector portion and an offset is formed by the combination of the addressing components (base, index, displacement and scale factor).

2. **Effective address**: Effective address is the address of the operand supplied with the instruction. (Refer "addressing modes of 80386 processor".) It is calculated by various combinations of four factors as – displacement, base, index and scaling factor. Displacement and base are added with product of index and scaling factor which may be 1, 2, 4 or 8. This summation gives the effective address of the operand which is fed to segmentation unit along with selector contents.
3. **Linear address**: Segmentation unit receives logical address as the input and translates it to 32-bit linear address. This translation process is nothing but the memory segmentation. If the paging unit is not enabled then this 32-bit linear address directly corresponds to the physical address.
4. **Physical address**: The address available on the address bus is the physical address. As said above, if paging is disabled then linear address is same as the physical address, that is, the linear address goes out on the processor's address bus. If paging is "ON" then a second level of address translation takes place to convert the linear address into a physical address.

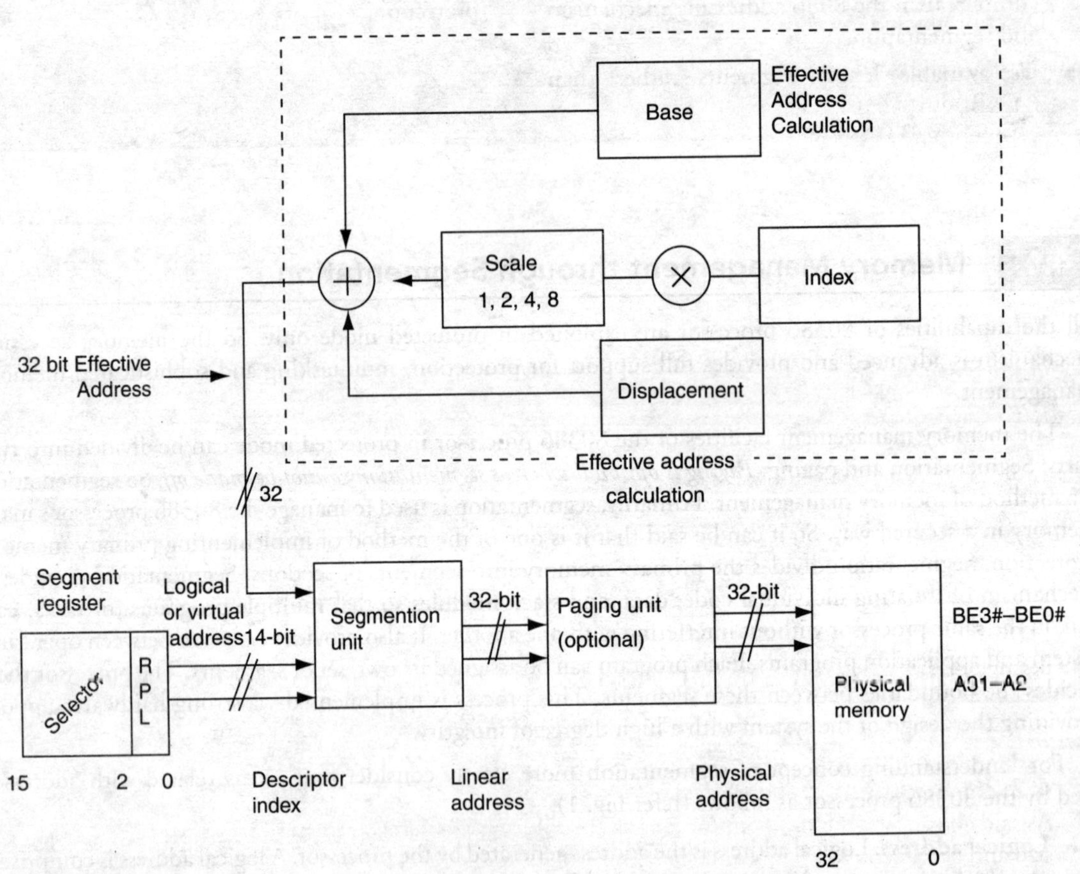

Figure 1 Relationship between address spaces.

This chapter focuses on the generation of linear address i.e. segmentation process. So here we discuss terms special system registers and data structures related with segmentation.

4.2 Supporting Registers and Data Structures

In this section, we discuss various terms, special system registers and data structures related to segmentation.

4.2.1 Segments

Segments are portions of memory and need not be of fixed size of 64 KB. Segments are variable in length may be from 1 byte to 4 GB. A system programmer can define base address and size of the segment, purpose (code, data, stack) and attributes (read/write, protection level, etc.) of the segment.

Base address may be chosen any arbitrary value from 32 bit linear address space (2^{32} = 4 GB) which is loaded in segment register and then in selector. A segment is described by a special data structure called segment descriptor.

4.2.2 Descriptors

Descriptors can be classified as system descriptors and segment descriptors.

1. **System descriptors**: As the name suggests, system descriptors are used by the operating system for various activities like defining area occupied by system tables, changing privilege levels or switching to another task, etc.
2. **Segment descriptors**: They define memory areas used by the application programs. All descriptors are of size 8 bytes.

Detailed classification is given in Table 1.

Table 1 Descriptor Types

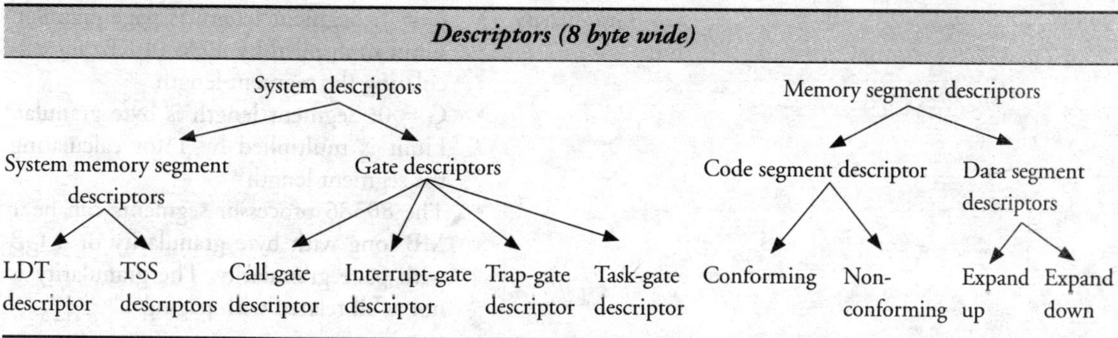

4.2.2.1 Segment Descriptors

As said above, a segment descriptor tells all the information about the memory segment such as base address, size and access control rights and status information of the respective segment. Some additional properties of descriptors are given as follows:

1. Exactly one descriptor must be created for each segment.
2. Segment descriptors are typically created by compilers, linkers, loaders, or the operating system or executive, but not by any application programs.

3. Figure 2 shows the general format of the segment descriptor. "S bit" and "type field" decides the type of the descriptor. Significance of each field in the descriptor is discussed in Table 2.
4. The Access right byte is responsible for controlling access to the protected mode memory segment.
5. Table 3 interprets the specific bits in the access rights byte in the code and data segment descriptors.

63 ··· 56	55	54	53	52	51 ··· 48	47	46, 45	44	43 ··· 41	40	39 ··· 15	··· 0
Segment base 31—24	G	D/B	0	AVL	Segment limit 19–16	P	DPL	S	Type	A	Segment base 23–0	Segment limit 15–0

(Access right byte: bits 47–40)

Figure 2 Segment descriptor format [S (bit-44 = 1)].

Table 2 Details of Segment Descriptor

Offset	*No. of Bits*	*Field*	*Significance*
(D0–D15)(D48–D51)	20	Segment limit	Specifies the length of the segment.
(D16–D39)(D63–D56)	32	Segment base	Base address of the segment in linear address space.
D55	1	G – Granularity bit	• G = 1: Segment length is page granular. Limit multiplied by 4096 (4 KB) for calculating the segment length. • G = 0: Segment length is byte granular. Limit is multiplied by 1 for calculating the segment length. • The 80386 processor segments can be 1 MB long with byte granularity or 4 GB with page granularity. The granularity is not at all related with paging
D54	1	D/B – Default operation size	• Applicable only for in code segment descriptors. • The D bit indicates the default length for operands and effective addresses. • If D = 1, then 32-bit operands and 32-bit addressing modes are assumed. • If D = 0, then 16-bit operands and 16-bit addressing modes are assumed.

(Continued)

Table 2 (Continued)

Offset	*No. of Bits*	*Field*	*Significance*
		B bit for stack segment	• B bit controls the size of the stack pointer register. • If B = 1, then stack related instructions (PUSHes, POPs, and CALLs) use the 32-bit ESP register for stack references. • If B = 0, stack related instructions (PUSHes, POPs, and CALLs) use the 16-bit SP register.
D53	1	Set to 0	• Bit must be zero (0) for compatibility with future processors.
D52	1	AVL – Available	• User defined field for user or OS.
D47–D40	8	ARB – Access right byte	• For memory segment descriptors, ARB specifies access rights as protection level, readability etc. Refer Table 3.

Table 3 Access Right Byte (D47–D40) Significance for Code and Data Segments

Bit Position in ARB	*Field and Name*	*Significance*
7	P– Present	• P = 1: Segment is mapped into physical memory. • P = 0: No mapping to physical memory exits, base and limit fields are not used.
5–6	DPL – Descriptors privilege level	• 2 bits specifies segment's privilege level used for privilege validations.
4	S – Segment descriptor	• S = 0: System segment descriptor or gate descriptor. • S = 1: Code or data/stack segment descriptor.
For Data Segment S = 1, E = 0		
3	E – Executable	• E = 0: Descriptor for data segment.
2	ED – Expansion Direction	• ED = 0: Expand up segment, offsets must be <= limit, i.e., data segment. • ED = 1: Expand up segment, offsets must be >= limit, i.e., stack segment.
1	W – Writeable	• W = 0: Read only data segment. • W = 1: Read/write data segment.

(Continued)

Table 3 (Continued)

Bit Position in ARB	*Field and Name*	*Significance*
For Data Segment S = 1, E = 1		
3	E – Executable	• E = 1: Descriptor for code segment.
2	C – Conforming	• C = 1: Code segment may only be executed when code. • CPL>= DPL and CPL remains unchanged.
1	R – Readable	• R = 0: Code segment may not be read. • R = 1: Code segment may be read.
0	A – Accessed	• A = 0: The code segment has not been accessed yet. • A = 1: The code segment selector has been loaded into segment register at least once.

4.2.2.2 System Descriptors

The S field in the descriptor format when set to zero indicates the system descriptor. Further, type field tells the exact category of the descriptor. Figure 3 shows the general format of the system descriptor and Table 4 gives the type field value and classification of the system descriptor. Bits D54–D52 are permanently set to zero. Call gates are used to change privilege levels. Task gates are used to perform a task switch, and interrupt and trap gates are used to specify interrupt service routines.

Formats and usage of the gate descriptors are discussed as and when required.

63 ------------ 56	55	54	53	52	51---- 48	47	46 45	44	43 ------------ 40	39 -------- 16	15 ---------- 0
Segment base 31—24	G	0	0	0	Segment Limit 19–16	P	DPL	0	Type	Segment base 23–0	Segment Limit 15–0

Figure 3 System descriptor format [S(bit-44 = 0)].

Table 4 System Descriptor Types

Type Field Bits	*Descriptor Type*
0	Invalid
1	Available 16-bit TSS
2	LDT
3	Busy 16-bit TSS
4	16-bit call gate

(Continued)

Table 4 (Continued)

Type Field Bits	*Descriptor Type*
5	Task gate
6	16-bit interrupt gate
7	16-bit trap gate
8	Invalid
9	Available 80386 32-bit TSS
A	Undefined (Reserved)
B	Busy 80386 32-bit TSS
C	80386 32-bit call gate
D	Undefined (Reserved)
E	80386 32-bit interrupt gate
F	80386 32-bit trap gate

4.2.3 Descriptor Tables

Descriptors are stored as set of elements in tables called as descriptor tables. Descriptor tables occupy consecutive locations in the main memory. Each element is of size 64 bits. Descriptor tables are also called as system tables. Three different types of descriptor tables are as follows:

1. Global descriptor table (GDT).
2. Local descriptor table (LDT).
3. Interrupt descriptor table (IDT).

The base addresses of these tables are stored in special registers. These registers are named GDTR, IDTR, LDTR respectively. The use of these registers is discussed in Section 4.2.4.

4.2.3.1 Global Descriptor Table (GDT)

As the name indicates global descriptor table can be used by any of the task present in the system. There can be an LDT within GDT. Some of the features of GDT are as follows:

1. Every 80386-processor-based system contains only one GDT.
2. GDT is the main, general purpose variable length table.
3. Length of GDT can be any size between 8 bytes and 64 Kilobytes.

4. Each table can hold up to maximum 8192 number of descriptors of 8 byte each.
5. The Global Descriptor Table (GDT) contains descriptors which may be available to all of the tasks in a system.
6. The GDT can contain any type of segment descriptor excluding interrupt and trap gate descriptors.
7. GDT also may contain descriptors for segments which are common to all tasks.
8. Typically, the GDT contains code, data segments descriptors used by the operating systems. In addition, it also contains task state segments and LDT descriptors.
9. The very first descriptor in the Global Descriptor Table always contains the null selector containing a null pointer value.

4.2.3.2 Local Descriptor Table (LDT)

Local descriptor tables are private tables used by individual tasks only. They are mainly used for storing concerned code/data descriptors. We can say that LDTs are extensions of GDT. Some of the features of LDT are as follows:

1. Multiple LDTs can exist depending upon number of tasks currently present in the multitasking system. Each task may have a separate private LDT. Still LDT is optional part.
2. LDTs contain descriptors which are related to a given task.
3. The LDT can contain code, data, stack, task gate, and call gate descriptors, but not the LDT Descriptors.
4. LDTs facilitate a mechanism for isolating and protecting a task's code and data segments from the operating system and other tasks.
5. A segment cannot be accessed at all by a task if its segment descriptor is not present in either the current LDT or the GDT. This allows global data to be shared among tasks and provide isolation too.

4.2.3.3 Interrupt Descriptor Table (IDT)

Interrupt descriptor tables are referred when an exception or interrupt is raised. The 8-byte descriptors in the IDT are used to store the addresses of the Interrupt service routines. Some of the features of IDT are as follows:

1. The IDT contains the descriptors, which maintain a list of the locations of interrupt service routines.
2. It can hold a maximum of 256 ISR descriptors.
3. The IDT can contain only task gates, interrupt gates, and trap gates.
4. The IDT should be a minimum of 256 bytes in length that holds the descriptors for the 32 Intel reserved interrupts.
5. Every interrupt used by a system has an entry in the IDT which can be referenced by means of INT instructions, external interrupt vectors, or exceptions.

4.2.4 Descriptor Table Registers

Since, system tables described before are nothing but arrays, so to point to the array we need base address of the respective table. Those base addresses are stored in special dedicated system registers called as descriptor table registers. Three descriptor table registers are available to point to the base of the each table GDT, LDT and IDT respectively. Figure 4 shows the format of each register.

Special instructions can be executed only at privilege level 0 to load and store contents to the descriptor table registers. Such privileged instructions are discussed in Section 4.6.

4.2.4.1 Global Descriptor Table Register (GDTR)

As the name suggests, GDTR is used to point to the base of the GDT. As shown in Fig. 4, the GDTR is 48 -bits long having two fields: The 32-bit linear base address and 16-bit limit of the GDT. The 32-bit linear base address of the GDT is the linear address of the first byte of the first descriptor. The limit field tells the length of the table minus one.

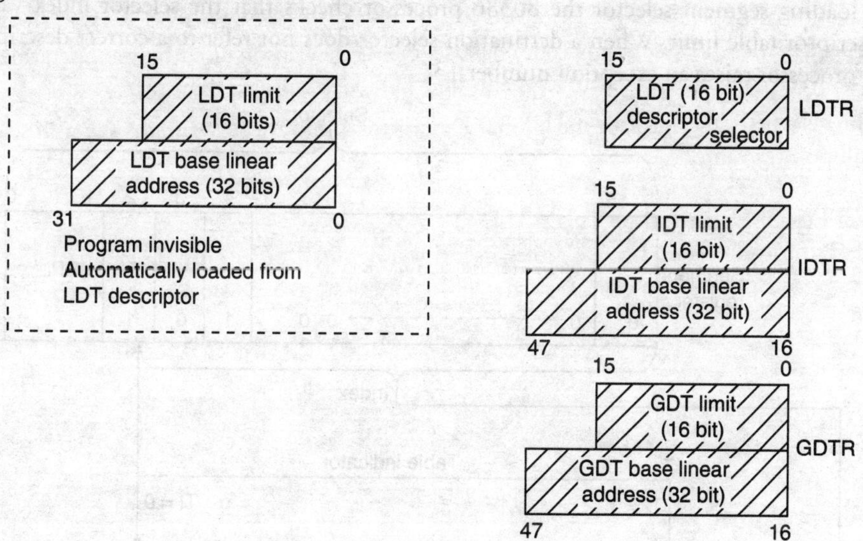

Figure 4 GDTR, LDTR and IDTR structures.

4.2.4.2 Interrupt Descriptor Table Register (IDTR)

Obviously, IDTR is used to point to the base of the IDT. As shown in Fig. 4, the IDTR is also 48-bit long having two fields: The 32-bit linear base address and 16-bit limit of the IDT. The 32-bit linear base address of the IDT is the linear address of the first byte of the first descriptor. The limit field tells the length of the table minus one.

4.2.4.3 Local Descriptor Table Register

LDTR is having slightly different function. It does not point to the base of the LDT. It holds the 16-bit selector for the LDT descriptor. A programmer-invisible segment descriptor register is associated with LDTR which is automatically loaded from LDT descriptor. Refer Fig. 4

4.2.5 Segment Selectors

Six different segment registers (16 bit) hold segment selector values indicating the currently addressable memory segments. Segment registers are discussed in Chapter 2. For example, the selector in CS indicates the current code segment; the selector in SS indicates the current stack segment; the selectors in DS, ES, FS and GS indicate the current data segments. Unlike 8086 processor the selector does not point to the base of the target segment. Rather selector helps to select one of the descriptor from either of the descriptor table. The upper 13 bits of a selector are used as an index into the descriptor table. Some additional properties of the selector are discussed as follows:

1. A selector in protected mode has three fields: Local or Global Descriptor Table Indicator (TI), Descriptor Entry Index (Index), and Requestor (the selector's) Privilege Level (RPL) as shown in Fig. 5.
2. The TI bit selects one of two memory-based tables of descriptors. When TI = 0, Global descriptor table is selected to access memory. TI = 1 selects the local descriptor table.

3. The index field (13 bits, $2^{13} = 8192$) selects one of the 8K descriptors from the appropriate descriptor table.
4. The RPL field (2 bits) allows the checking of the selector's privilege levels against descriptors Privilege level for protection checking.
5. While loading segment selector the 80386 processor checks that the selector index value is within the descriptor table limit. When a destination selector does not refer to a correct descriptor type, the 80386 processor raises an exception number 13.

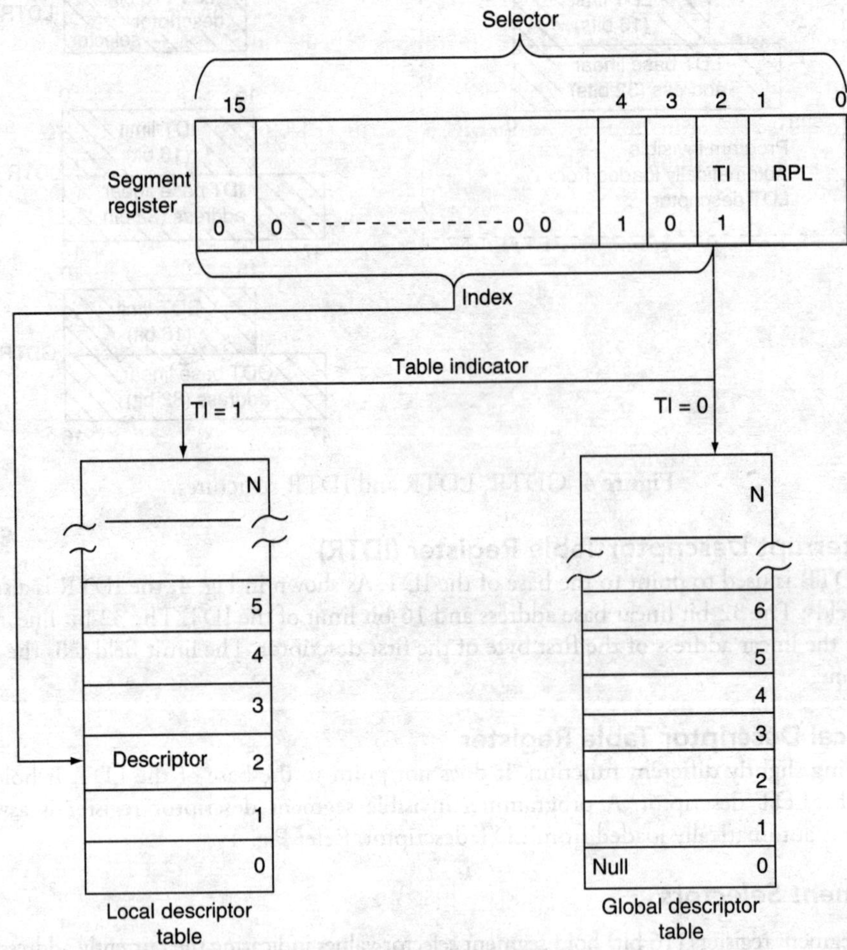

Figure 5 Use of selector for descriptor selection.

4.3 Steps For Logical To Linear/Physical Address Translation when TI = 0

Figure 6 shows the whole process of translating logical address to linear address with the help of components required for segmentation. Here, consider the case (D2 bit of the selector) TI = 0. This suggests that the MMU has to access the GDT.

The steps are as follows:

1. The 80386 processor generates 32-bit logical address which has two components as – selector and offset.
2. One of the six segment register contents are loaded as selector part of the logical address.
3. When TI bit of the selector is found 0 then the MMU starts accessing global descriptor table to reach to the target byte from the destination segment.
4. GDTR supplies the 32-bit base address of the Global descriptor table, which is added with the 13 bit index portion of the selector.
5. Step number 4 gives the exact address of the descriptor of the destination segment in the GDT.
6. Descriptor of the destination segment in turn supplies the base address of the destination segment.
7. Necessary privilege checks are done by comparing RPL from selector, current privilege level (CPL) and destination segment descriptor's privilege level (DPL). Access is allowed only if the RPL is numerically same or greater than the DPL value contained in the descriptor. If selector has numerically lower privilege level then memory access violation exception number 13 is generated.
8. When privilege checks are passed, the base address of the segment is added with offset portion of the logical address.
9. This value after addition is nothing but the linear address of the target location in the destination segment.
10. If paging is off then this 32-bit linear address is treated as 32-bit physical address and the target location is accessed.
11. If paging is on then linear address is fed to the paging unit for second level translation.

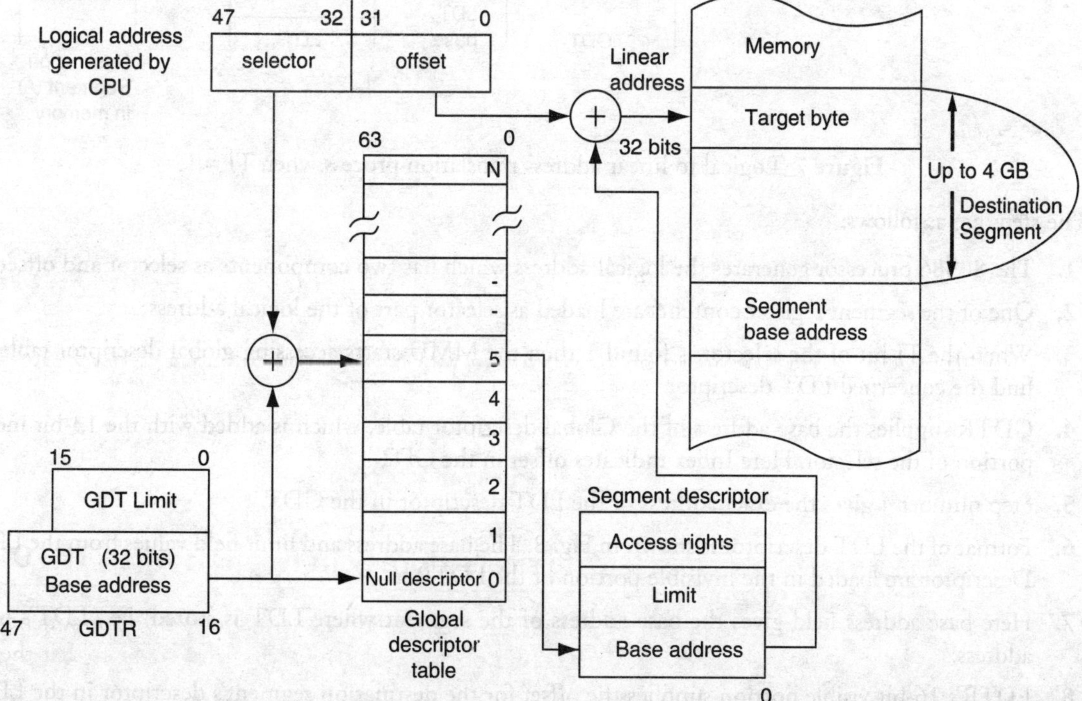

Figure 6 Logical to linear address translation process when TI = 0.

4.4 Steps For Logical To Linear/Physical Address Translation when TI = 1

Figure 7 shows the whole process of translating logical address to linear address with the help of components required for segmentation. Here consider the case (D2 bit of selector) TI = 1. This suggests that the destination segment's descriptor is in the LDT.

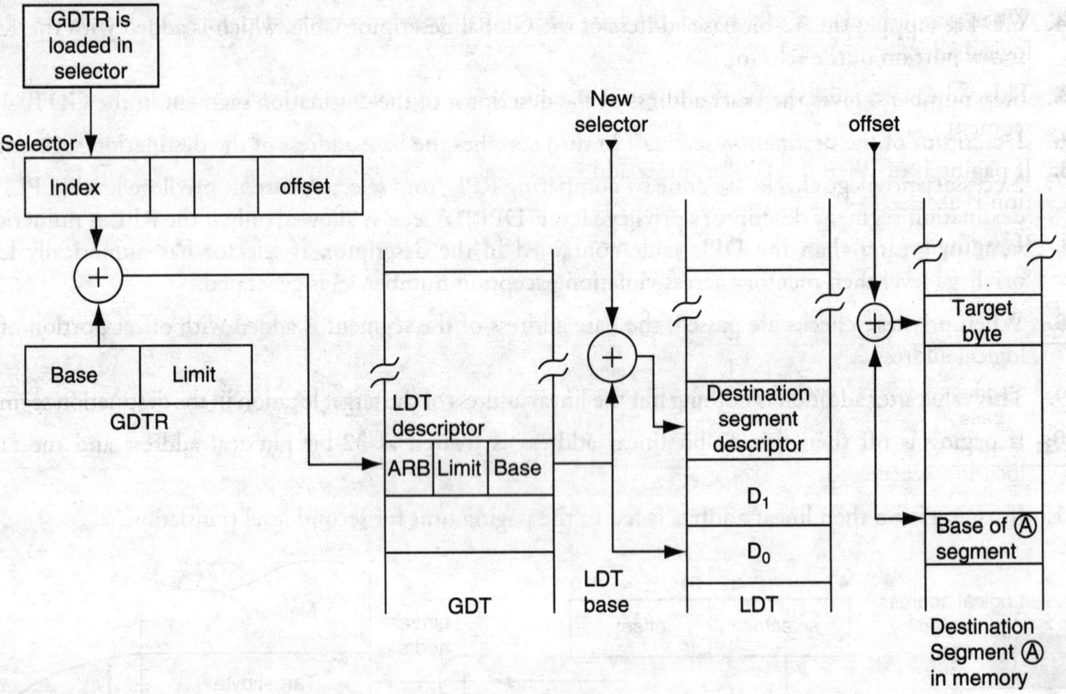

Figure 7 Logical to linear address translation process when TI = 1.

The steps are as follows:

1. The 80386 processor generates the logical address which has two components as selector and offset.
2. One of the segment register contents are loaded as selector part of the logical address.
3. When the TI bit of the selector is found 1 then the MMU starts accessing global descriptor table to find the concerned LDT descriptor.
4. GDTR supplies the base address of the Global descriptor table, which is added with the 13-bit index portion of the selector. Here Index indicates offset in the GDT.
5. Step number 4 gives the exact address of the LDT descriptor in the GDT.
6. Format of the LDT descriptor is shown in Fig. 8. The base address and limit field values from the LDT Descriptor are loaded in the invisible portion of the LDTR.
7. Here base address field gives the base address of the segment where LDT is stored, i.e., LDT's base address.
8. LDTR's 16-bit visible portion supplies the offset for the destination segment's descriptor in the LDT. Summation of the offset and base address of the local descriptor table, gives the exact address of the descriptor of the destination segment in the LDT.

9. Descriptor of the destination segment in turn supplies the base address of the destination segment.
10. Necessary privilege checks are done by comparing RPL from selector, current privilege level (CPL) and destination segment descriptor's privilege level (DPL). Access is allowed only if the RPL is same or greater than the DPL value contained in the descriptor. If selector has lower privilege level then memory access violation exception number 13, general protection fault is generated.
11. When privilege checks are passed, the base address of the segment is added with offset portion of the logical address.
12. This value after addition is nothing but the linear address of the target location in the destination segment.
13. If paging is off then this 32-bit linear address is treated as 32-bit physical address and the target location is accessed.
14. If paging is on then linear address is fed to the paging unit for second level translation.

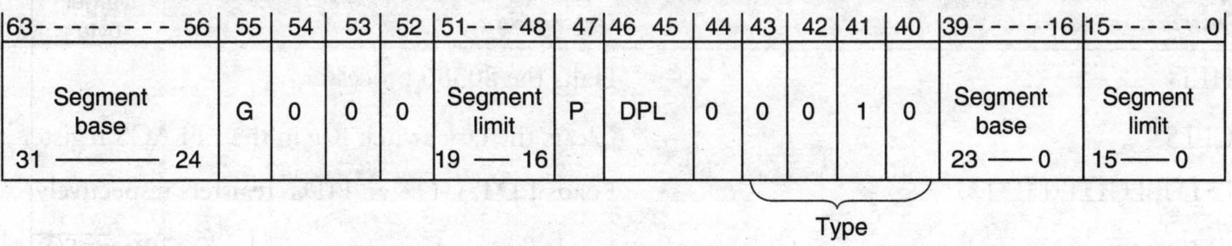

Figure 8 LDT descriptor.

4.5 Protection in Segmentation

Basically, segmentation is meant for providing isolation and protection for different task as well operating system by means of sophisticated memory management. DPL field of the segment descriptor plays important role for protection. The Descriptor Privilege Level (DPL) is a two-bit field which specifies the protection level 0–3 associated with a segment. Privilege level 0 is the most protected whereas, level 3 is least protected. The 80386 processor controls access to both data and code between levels of a task. Certain rules are required to be followed for inter segment and inter privilege accesses. Those rules are as follows:

1. Data stored in a segment having privilege level *p* can be accessed only by the code executing at a privilege level at least as privileged as *p*.
2. A code segment/procedure having privilege level *p* can only be given call by a task executing at the same or a lesser privilege level than *p*. (Refer Fig. 2 for points 3 to 6.)
3. Whenever a new code segment selector is to be loaded in CS the 80386 processor checks the type field of the descriptor to ensure that it is a code segment.
4. Executable bit is also checked.
5. The processor also checks the destination code segment is marked present.

6. The new value of EIP must be within the limits of the new code segment.
7. Gates provide a mechanism of indirection between the source and destination of the control transfer. This indirection allows the processor to automatically perform protection checks. It also allows controlling entry points to the operating system.

4.6 Privileged Instructions

Privileged instructions are the special instructions which affect the segmentation and protection mechanisms upon execution. Such instructions alter the Interrupt flag or perform I/O operation. A total of 19 privileged instructions are available for execution for the 80386 processor. To execute any privileged instruction the code must be at privilege level zero. These instructions are used to access special system registers like GDTR, LDTR, IDTR, control registers, debug registers and test registers. List of such instructions is given in Table 5.

Table 5 Privileged Instructions

Instruction	*Description*
HLT	Halts the 80386 processor
CLTS	Clears the task switch flag in the EFLAGS register
LLDT, LGDT, LIDT	Loads LDT, GDT and IDT registers respectively
LMSW	Loads the machine status word, i.e., CR0
LTR	Loads the task register
MOV reg, CRx/MOV CRx, reg	Moves to/from control register number x
MOV reg, DRx/MOV DRx, reg	Moves to/from Debug register number x
MOV reg, TRx/MOV TRx, reg	Moves to/from test register number x

In addition to this, there are some instructions that control I/O access or control Interrupts activation. For execution of those instructions privilege level is not required to be zero. Instead, those instructions can be executed if the current privilege level CPL is numerically less than or equal to IOPL field in the EFLAGS register. So, those are also called as IOPL sensitive instructions. Here, if IOPL is set to 3, then any program can access I/O devices and if IOPL is 0, then only code segments having privilege level zero can access I/O devices. IOPL sensitive Instructions are listed in Table 6.

Table 6 IOPL Sensitive Instructions

Instruction	*Description*
CLI	Clears the interrupt flag from EFLAGS register to disable interrupts
STI	Sets the interrupt flag from EFLAGS register to enable interrupts
IN, INS	Reads data from I/O port
OUT, OUTS	Writes data to I/O port

Summary

- Segmentation provides the basis of protection.
- The flexibility of the having variable segment length modularizes the data and programs and also provides the isolation.
- The 32-bit logical address generated by the processor is primarily used to locate the destination segment descriptor and then used to locate the actual destination segment and target location.
- Outcome of the segmentation unit is the 32-bit linear address which may be mapped on physical memory if paging is disabled.

Multiple-Choice Questions

1. The segmentation in 80386 facilitates

(a) Protection

(b) Isolation and memory management

(c) Memory management with multitasking

(d) All of the above

2. Which of the following statements is true?

(a) Paging is compulsory and segmentation is optional

(b) Segmentation and paging both are optional

(c) Segmentation and paging both are compulsory

(d) Segmentation is compulsory and paging is optional

3. Segmentation translates

(a) Logical address to physical address

(b) Linear address to physical address

(c) Logical address to linear address

(d) Logical address to absolute address

4. An Effective address is calculated by using

(a) Base 32

(b) Index and scale

(c) Displacement

(d) All of the above

5. Paging unit translates

(a) Logical address to physical address

(b) Linear address to physical address

(c) Logical address to linear address

(d) Logical address to absolute address

6. For the 80386 processor, segment size is

(a) Fixed to 64 KB

(b) Fixed to 4 GB

(c) Not fixed

(d) None of the above

7. The 800386 processor can address up to _____ memory.

(a) 64 KB

(b) 4 GB

(c) 1 MB

(d) None of the above

8. There can be _____ descriptor(s) per segment.

(a) 1

(b) 2

(c) 0

(d) 4

9. A descriptor size is _____ bytes.

(a) 2

(b) 4

(c) 6

(d) 8

10. Size of GDTR is _____ bits.

(a) 16

(b) 32

(c) 48

(d) 64

11. Size of IDTR is _____ bits.

(a) 16

(b) 32

(c) 48

(d) 64

12. Size of LDTR is _____ bits.

(a) 16

(b) 32

(c) 48

(d) 64

13. Type 2 system descriptor is

(a) An LDT descriptor

(b) A TSS descriptor

(c) A call gate descriptor

(d) None of the above

14. Which of the following statement is false?

(a) Global descript table can store any type of descriptor

(b) Descriptor table can store code, data, stack, call gate, task gate descriptors

(c) Interrupt descriptor table can store ode and data segment descriptors

(d) None of the above

15. Length of the GDT is

(a) Fixed

(b) 64 KB

(c) Between 8 bytes to 64 KB

(d) 8 KB

16. Selector value is copied from

(a) Segment register

(b) Descriptor

(c) Descriptor table register

(d) Descriptor cache

17. In segmentation process when TI = 1, the selector's Index part points to the

(a) Target segment descriptor

(b) Interrupt gate descriptor

(c) LDT descriptors

(d) None of the above

18. In segmentation process when TI = 1, then destination segment descriptor is fetched from

(a) GDT

(b) LDT

(c) IDT

(d) None of the above

19. In segmentation process when TI = 0 , then destination segment descriptor is fetched from

(a) GDT

(b) LDT

(c) IDT

(d) None of the above

20. If paging is off then 32 bit linear address is treated as

(a) Logical address

(b) Linear address

(c) Physical address

(d) Absolute address

21. During segmentation, access to the segment is allowed only if the selector's RPL is _____ the DPL value contained in the descriptor

(a) Privilege wise same or greater than

(b) Numerically same or greater than

(c) Privilege wise same or less than

(d) Numerically same or less than

22. During execution of an IOPL sensitive instruction, if IOPL is set to 3 then any program

(a) Can access I/O devices

(b) Cannot access I/O devices

(c) Can access some of the I/O devices

(d) None of the above

23. During execution of an IOPL sensitive instruction, if IOPL is 0 then only code segments having privilege level _____ can access I/O devices.

(a) 0

(b) 1

(c) 2

(d) 3

24. Segment descriptors are created by

(a) Compilers

(b) Linkers and loaders

(c) System but not by application programs

(d) All of the above

25. If granularity G bit of a descriptor is = 1 and limit field consists of a value 2KB then size of the segment is

(a) 2 KB

(b) 4 KB

(c) 8 KB

(d) 16 KB

Review Questions

1. Draw and explain how 80386 microprocessor translates logical address into linear address. Draw the required data structures also.
2. What are the privileged and IOPL sensitive instructions of 80386 processor? Explain the significance of each instruction in short.
3. The GDTR, IDTR are 48 bits with base address and limits specified, but the LDTR is only 16 bit How does then this access memory? Explain with neat diagram.
4. What is logical address Physical address and linear address in the 80386 processor?
5. What are the privilege checks made if a code, data or stack segment is accessed?
6. How the segment registers are different in protected mode from real mode?
7. Draw the general segment descriptor format. Explain how granularity G bit affects the LIMIT field.
8. How protection is provided at segmentation level in the 80386 processor?
9. What is LDT descriptor? Describe its use in protected mode.
10. How one can define segment size 4 GB for the 80386 processor Explain.
11. With the help of descriptor format explain the different field used to provide protection to a segment.
12. Which system descriptors can be placed in GDT?
13. What is the difference between a system descriptor and non system descriptor? How to distinguish between them?
14. What are selectors? Explain their use in segmentation process for 80386 processor.
15. Explain following instructions: SGDT, LLDT, LGDT, SLDT.
16. What is granularity bit? Where it is found? What happens if it is set?

Answers

Multiple-Choice Questions

1. (d)	**7.** (b)	**13.** (a)
2. (d)	**8.** (a)	**14.** (c)
3. (c)	**9.** (d)	**15.** (c)
4. (d)	**10.** (c)	**16.** (a)
5. (b)	**11.** (c)	**17.** (c)
6. (c)	**12.** (a)	**18.** (b)

19. (a)

20. (c)

21. (b)

22. (a)

23. (a)

24. (d)

25. (c)

UNIT III

Protected Mode

5 Protected Mode

LEARNING OBJECTIVES

After reading this chapter, you will be able to:

- Understand how the performance of processor 80386 gets enhanced in the protected mode.
- Study the mechanism needed for the processor to switch form protected to real mode and viceversa.
- Study the enhanced instructions of protected mode.
- Understand the need of protection and how to achieve it.
- Understand the concept of inter-privilege level transfer using call gates and conforming code segment.

5.1 Features of Protected Mode

Protected mode is a powerful and complex mode. Memory addressing capacity of this mode is 4 GB. In this mode, active address lines are A0 to A31. This mode provides advance features like on-chip support for operating system functions such as memory management, protection and multitasking.

1. Paging is available only in the protection mode. Demand paging creates virtual environment of 64 TB.
2. **Instruction set:** In addition to real-mode instruction set, protected-mode system control instruction set is also available in the protection mode. These instructions either apply only to the protection mode operation or are used in real mode to prepare 80386 for the entry into protection mode.
3. **Address translation:** It is different in real and protected mode.
4. Multitasking.

5.2 Protected Mode Registers

Protected mode has all registers in the architecture with the changed functionality of segment registers. Different registers used in protection mode are categorized as follows:

1. General-purpose registers.
2. Segment registers.
3. Index, pointer and base registers.
4. Flag registers.

5. System address registers.
6. Control registers.
7. Debug registers.

Register set of 80386 is shown in Fig. 1.

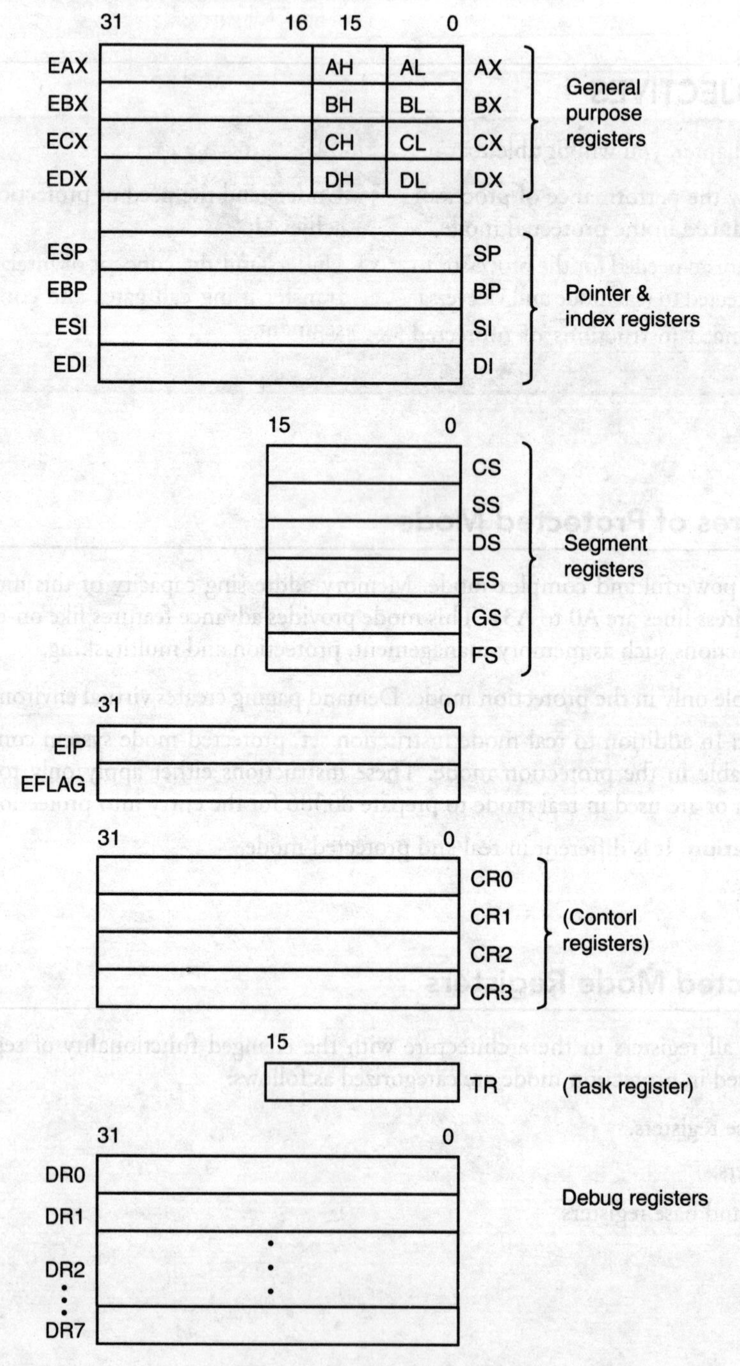

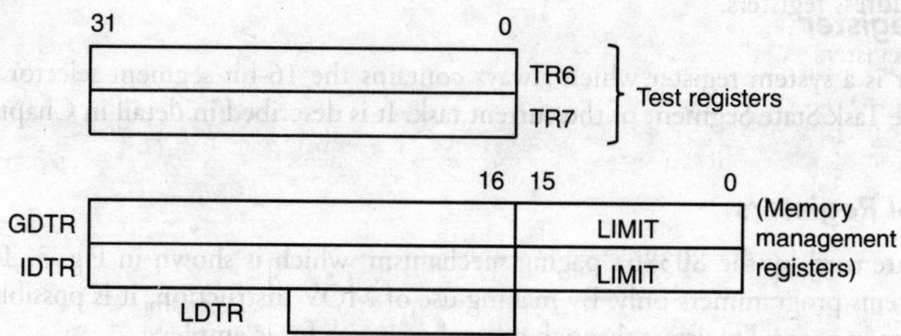

Figure 1 Protected mode register set.

5.2.1 Flag Register

Flag register is shown in Fig. 2.

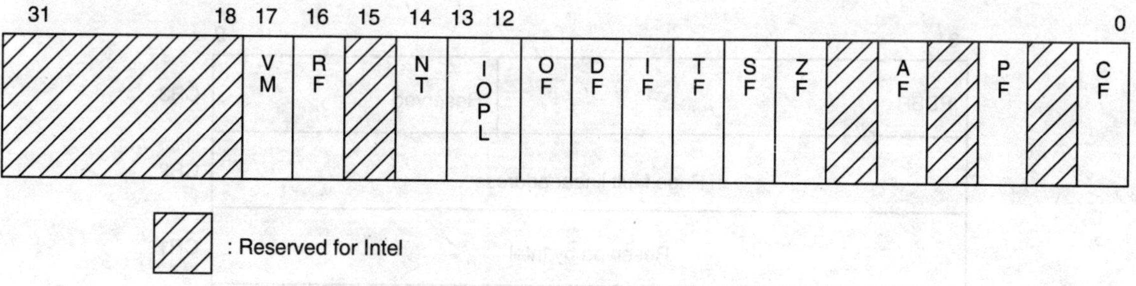

Figure 2 Protected mode flag register.

Three categories of flags are as follows:

1. **Status flags (6):** CF, PF, ACF, ZF, SF, OF
2. **Control flags (3):** TF, IF, DF
3. **System flags (4):** IOPL, NT, RF, VM

Status and control flags are already discussed in Chapter 2. A new set of four flags known as system flags is discussed as follows:

1. **Input output privilege level (IOPL) flags:** For protected mode operations, it indicates the privilege level, 0 to 3, at which your code must be running in order to execute any I/O-related instructions.
2. **Nested task (NT) flag:** When set, it indicates that one system task has invoked another through a CALL instruction as opposed to a JMP instruction. NT influences the operation of the IRET instruction. For multitasking, this flag can be manipulated to the user's advantage.
3. **Resume flag (RF):** It is related to debug registers DR6 and DR7. By setting this, the user can selectively mask some exceptions while he is debugging the code. This flag temporarily disables debug exceptions so that an instruction can be restarted after a debug exception without immediately causing another debug exception.
4. **Virtual 8086 mode flag (VM):** When it is set, the 80386 processor is basically converted into a high-speed 8086 processor. This flag indicates that the task is executing an 8086 program.

5.2.2 *Task Register*

The task register is a system register which always contains the 16-bit segment selector and the segment descriptor for the Task State Segment of the current task. It is described in detail in Chapter 6.

5.2.3 *Control Registers*

These registers are used by the 80386's paging mechanism, which is shown in Fig. 3. These registers are accessible to systems programmers only. By making use of MOV instruction, it is possible to load from or store in some data in control registers through general registers; for example:

```
MOV EDX, CR0
MOV CR2, EAX
```

Four control registers are CR0, CR1, CR2 and CR3, out of which CR1 is left undefined by Intel. The other three are discussed as in the following subsections.

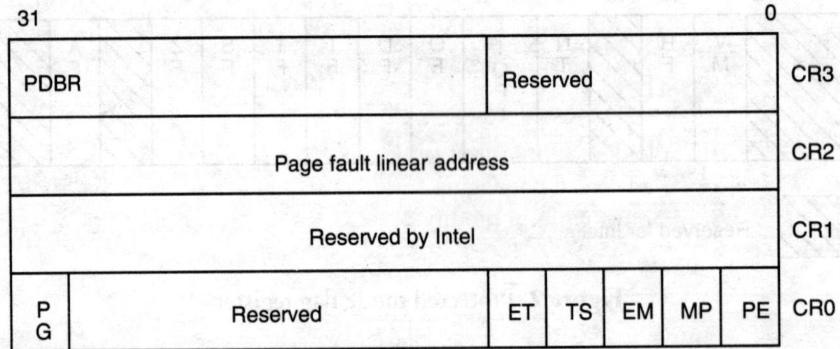

Figure 3 Control registers.

5.2.3.1 CR0

CR0 contains system control flags, which control or indicate conditions that apply to the system as a whole. The details of CR0 are shown in Fig. 4 and are explained as follows:

1. **MSW:** Machine status word
2. **Protection enable (PE):** Setting PE causes the processor to begin executing the instructions in protected mode. Resetting PE returns to real-address mode.

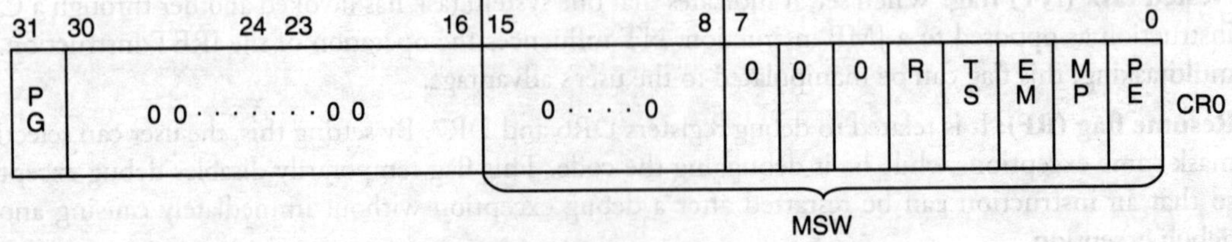

Figure 4 Structure of CR0.

3. **Math present (MP):** If set, assumes that real floating point hardware is attached to it.
4. **Emulate co-processor (EM):** When this bit is set, 80386 will generate an exception 11 (device not available) whenever it fetches a floating point instruction. This exception handler can be used to emulate floating-point hardware in software.
5. **Task switched (TS):** The processor sets this bit automatically every time it performs a task switch. This bit has to be cleared by the programmer.
6. **Extension type (ET):** It indicates the type of coprocessor present in the system (80287 or 80387).
7. **Paging (PG):** When set enables paging and if reset disables paging in MMU.

5.2.3.2 CR2 and CR3

CR2 is used when PG bit is set. CR2 is a read-only register which is used to handle page faults and the processor stores the last 32-bit address that caused page fault.

CR3 is used when PG bit is set. The processor can locate the page table directory for the current task using this register.

5.3 Debug Registers

Through these registers, a whole new approach of program debugging is implemented. These registers are shown in Fig. 5. They provide advanced debugging features to the processor like data breakpoints and the ability to set instruction breakpoints without modifying code segments.

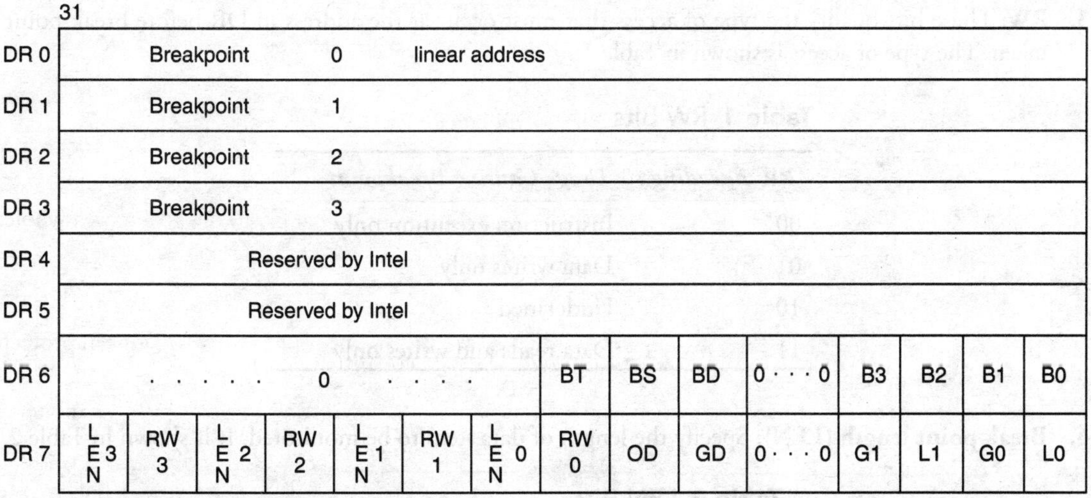

Register (bit 31 …)	Contents
DR 0	Breakpoint 0 linear address
DR 1	Breakpoint 1
DR 2	Breakpoint 2
DR 3	Breakpoint 3
DR 4	Reserved by Intel
DR 5	Reserved by Intel

DR 6	. . . . . . 0								BT	BS	BD	0 · · · 0	B3	B2	B1	B0
DR 7	LEN 3	RW 3	LEN 2	RW 2	LEN 1	RW 1	LEN 0	RW 0	OD	GD	0 · · · 0	G1	L1	G0	L0	

Figure 5 Debug registers.

5.3.1 DR0 to DR3

These registers hold up to four linear address breakpoints. The addresses in registers are compared with processors' address generation logic on every instruction and if match is found, an **exception 1** (debug fault) is generated. The debug address registers are effective whether or not paging is enabled.

5.3.2 Debug Status Register (DR6)

Debug register 6 is also called as debug status register. The 80386 processor sets the appropriate bits in this register which provides information of the probable causes for the last debug fault. The processor never clears these bits. Programmer must clear these bits. The status bits are as follows:

1. **B0:** The processor sets this bit when it references the linear address contained in DR0, modified by the conditions set by LEN0, RW0, L0, G0, LE and GE fields in DR7. B1 to B3 are applied similarly to DR1 to DR3, respectively.
2. **Break for debug register access (BD):** This bit is set if the Exception 1 handler is invoked by the illegal reference to one of the debug registers (due to GD bit = 1 in DR7).
3. **Break for single step(BS):** If TF is set.
4. **Break for task switch (BT):** These bits are never cleared by processor.

5.3.3 Debug Control Register (DR7)

Debug register 7 is also called as debug control register. Programmer can configure the debug operation of the four linear address breakpoints by programming bits in this register. Each breakpoint is controlled by a set of four fields. These are as follows:

1. **L0 (Local enable 0):** When this bit is set the breakpoint address in DR0 is monitored as long as the 80386 is running the current task. When the task switch occurs, this bit is cleared by the processor and must be re-enabled under program control.
2. **G0:** As long as this bit is set 386 monitors the linear address in DR0 all the times, regardless of task.
3. **RW:** These bits qualify the type of access that must occur at the address in DR before break point is taken. The type of access is shown in Table 1.

Table 1 RW Bits

RW Encoding	*Usage Causing Breakpoint*
00	Instruction execution only
01	Data writes only
10	Undefined
11	Data reads and writes only

4. **Break point length (LEN):** Specify the length of data item to be monitored. It is shown in Table 2.

Table 2 LEN Bits

LEN	*LEN Bits in Register DR7*
00	1 byte
01	2 bytes, word aligned
10	Reserved
11	4 bytes, double word aligned

5. **Local exact (LE):** If set, the processor slows execution so that data breakpoints are reported on the instruction that causes them. Only for current task.
6. **Global exact (GE):** The processor clears LE at a task switch but does not clear GE.
7. **Global debug access (GD):** Once this bit is set the processor will deny all further access to any of the debug register.

5.3.4 Test Registers

There are two test registers TR6 and TR7. The test registers are used to perform confidence checking on the paging MMU's translation look aside buffer (TLB). By writing into this register, one can write directly into 80386 TLB or perform a mock TLB lookup. TR6 is a test command register and TR7 is a test data register and are shown in Fig. 6.

31											0	
Linear address	V	D	D #	U	U #	W	W #	0	0 0	0	C	TR6
Physical address	0	0	0	0	0	0	0	P L	R E P	0	0	TR7

0 : Indicates Intel reserved (Do not define)

Figure 6 Structure of TR6 and TR7.

5.3.4.1 TR6

Test register 6 is the TLB testing command register. By writing into this register, it is possible to either initiate a write into the 80386's TLB or to perform TLB lookups. TR6 is divided into different fields as follows:

1. **C (Command):** When this bit is cleared, a write to the TLB is performed. If it is set, processor performs TLB lookup.
2. **Linear address:** This is the tag field of the TLB. On a TLB write, a TLB entry is allocated to this linear address and the rest of that TLB entry is set as per the value of TR7 and the value just written into TR6.
3. **V:** The valid bit for this TLB entry. All valid bits can also be cleared by writing to CR3.
4. **D, D#:** The dirty bit for/from the TLB entry.
5. **U, U#:** The user bit for/from the TLB entry.
6. **W, W#:** The writable bit for/from the TLB entry.

5.3.4.2 TR7

Test register 7 is the data testing register of the TLB. When a program is performing write operations, the entry to be stored is contained in this register, along with cache set information. TR7 is divided into different fields as follows:

1. **Physical address:** This is the data field of the TLB. On a write to the TLB, the TLB entry allocated to the linear address in TR6 is set to this value.

2. **Replacement pointer (REP):** This field indicates which set of TLB's four way set associative cache to write to.
3. **PL:** On a TLB write, PL=1 causes the REP field of TR7 to select which of the four associative blocks of the TLB is to be written, but PL=0 allows the internal pointer in the paging unit to select which TLB block is written.

5.4 Linear to Physical Address Translation

The memory management unit is made up of the segmentation unit and the paging unit. The task of memory management unit is to convert the logical addresses to physical addresses. Figure 7 shows the logical to physical address translation and is explained as follows:

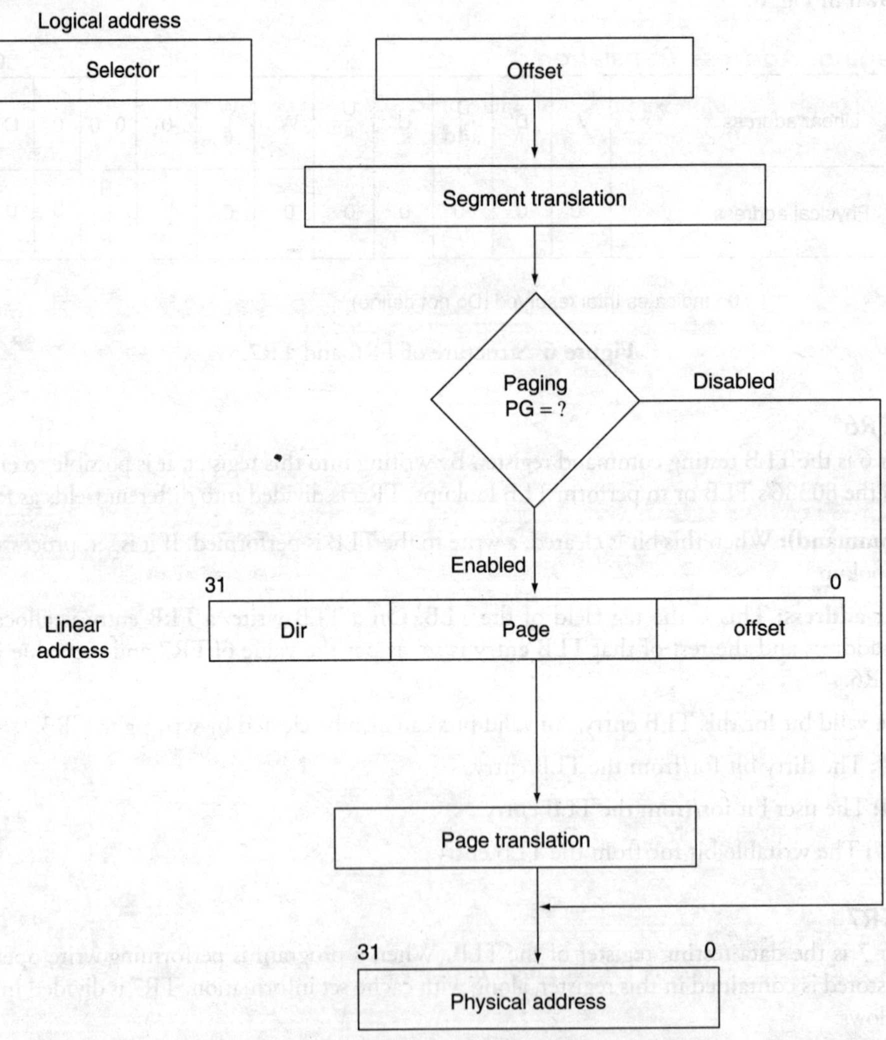

Figure 7 The logical to physical address translation.

1. The processor has three address fields: logical, linear and physical. In Chapter 3, we have seen the segment translation in detail, where the process of converting logical to linear address is called segment translation (here paging mechanism is disabled). The linear address itself is called physical address.
2. But if the paging mechanism is enabled then the linear address is transformed to physical address. This process is called paging translation. Thus, the logical address is converted to physical address.

5.4.1 Paging Memory Management

It is divided into two parts segmentation and paging. In segmentation, 4 GB of physical memory is organized into segments that can be of any size from 1 byte to 4 GB. While in paging 1,048,496 pages are present in which each page is of 4 KB (4096 bytes) long.

5.4.2 Paging: Address Translation

It is the second phase of address translation. Here processor converts the linear address that is generated by the segment address translation to the physical address. When paging is activated (PG = 1), the physical address space consists of 1,048,496 pages. Each page is of 4096 bytes. Figure 8 shows the physical address space organization in paging.

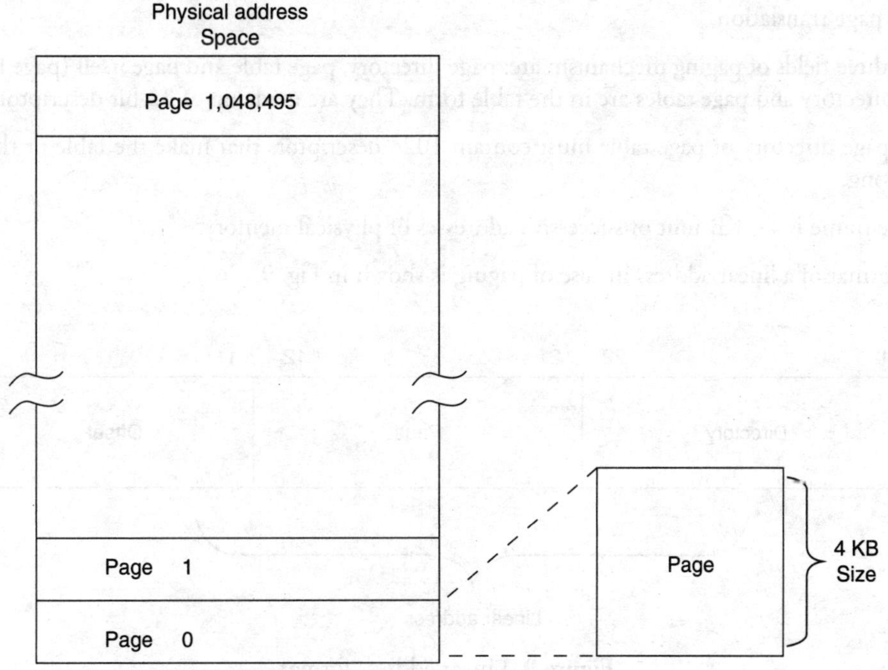

Figure 8 Organization of physical address space in paging.

The difference between segmentation and paging is shown in Table 3.

Table 3 Segmentation and Paging

S. No.	*Segmentation*	*Paging*
1	The 4 GB physical address space is organized into segments, where the segment size varies from 1 byte to 4 GB.	The 4 GB physical address space consists of 1,048,496 pages, where the size of page is fixed of 4KB.
2	More efficient use of memory with less segmentation.	Less efficient use of memory with more fragmentation.
3	Memory management software is not simplified.	Memory management software is simplified.

The processes used in paging mechanism are listed as follows:

1. The creation of unused section of memory is called "fragmentation". In paging process, the fixed size of the page gives fragmentation.
2. The linear address produced by the segment translation process is not valid in the case of paging (i.e., PG = 1). Therefore, it has to be given the second translation. This second translation mechanism is called page translation.
3. Basic three fields of paging mechanism are: page directory, page table and page itself (page frame). The page directory and page tables are in the table form. They are made up of 32-bit descriptors.
4. Each page directory or page table must contain 1024 descriptors that make the table or the directory 4KB long.
5. A page frame is a 4 KB-unit of successive addresses of physical memory.
6. The format of a linear address in case of paging is shown in Fig. 9.

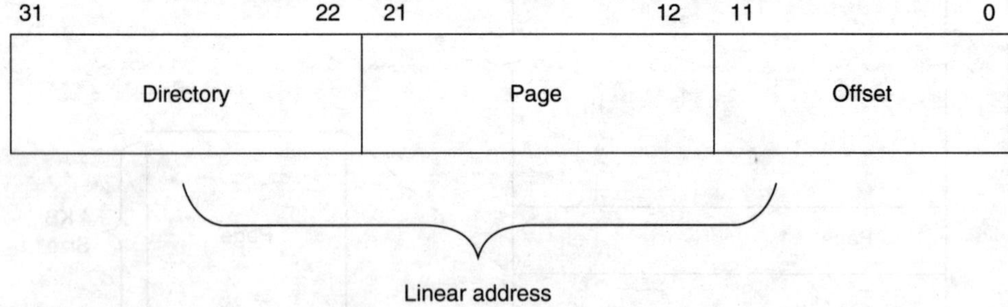

Figure 9 Linear address format.

7. The linear to physical address translation is shown in Fig. 10.
8. Three fields of linear address format are:

- 10-bit directory field.
- 10-bit page field.
- 12-bit offset field.

9. Directory field is used as an index to the page directory.

10. Page field is used as an index to the page table.

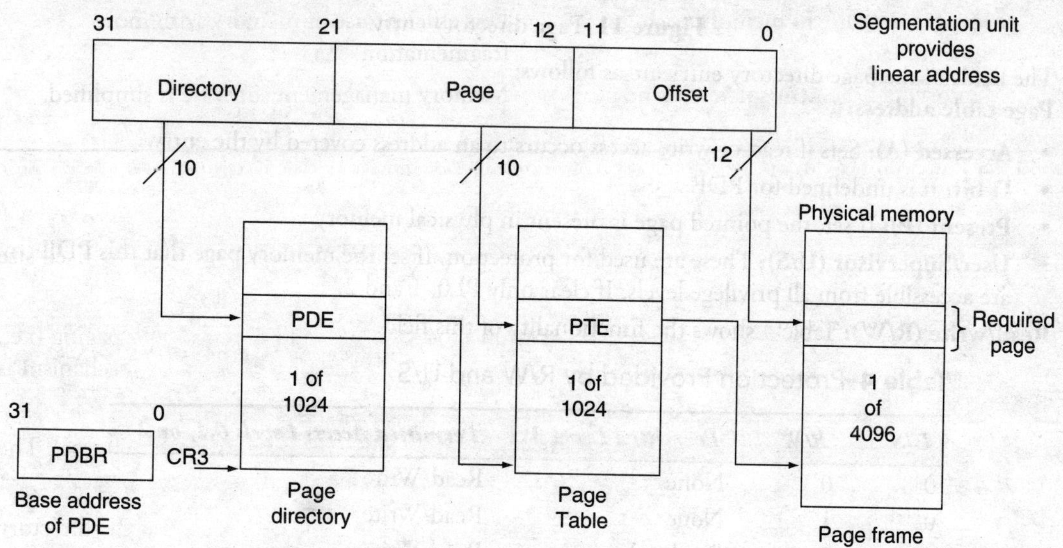

Figure 10 Linear to physical address translation.

11. Offset field selects one of the 4096 bytes of the memory from the page frame.

12. The base address of the current page directory is held by the control register CR3 which is called as the page directory base register (PDBR).

13. The base address of the page table is held by page directory entry.

14. The base address of the page frame is held by page table entry.

15. Offset address of the page directory is held by bits 22 to 31and that of page table is held by bits 12 to 21.

16. Bits 0 to 11 are used as an offset address holder of the page.

17. Paging can be enabled or disabled with the help of the most significant bit (PG bit) in control register CR0.

18. TLB is used to enhance the speed of paging.

5.4.3 Page Directory Entry

Page directory is 4 KB long and allows up to 1024 page directory entries. Each page directory entry contains the address of the next level of tables, page tables and information about the page table. The format of page directory entry (PDE) is shown in Fig. 11.

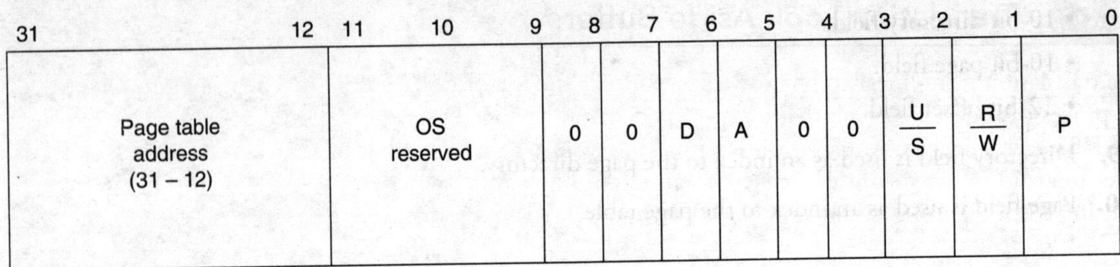

Figure 11 Page directory entry.

The fields of the page directory entry are as follows:

1. **Page table address:**
   - **Accessed (A):** Sets if read or write access occurs to an address covered by the entry.
   - **D bit:** It is undefined for PDE.
   - **Present (P):** If set, the pointed page is present in physical memory.
   - **User/Supervisor (U/S):** These are used for protection. If set the memory page that this PDE covers are accessible from all privilege levels. If clear only PL0, 1 and 2.
2. **Read/write (R/W):** Table 4 shows the functionality of this field.

Table 4 Protection Provided by R/W and U/S

U/S	*R/W*	*Permitted Level 3*	*Permitted Access Levels 0,1, or 2*
0	0	None	Read/Write
0	1	None	Read/Write
1	0	Read only	Read/Write
1	1	Read/Write	Read/Write

5.4.4 Page Table Entry

The page table is 4 KB long and allows up to 1024 page table entries. Each page table entry (PTE) contains the address of the page frame and the information about the page frame. The format of page table entry is shown in Fig. 12.

31 – 12	11 –									0
Page Fram Address (31 12)	AVAIL	0	0	D	A	0	0	U/S	R/W	P

P : Present
R/W : Read/ Write
U/S : User/ Supervisor
AVAIL : Available for systems programmer use
0 : Indicates reserved by Intel

Figure 12 Page table entry.

5.5 Translation Look Aside Buffers

The translation from linear to physical address needs the use of PDE and PTE. The paging mechanism of the processor is designed such that it supports demand paging. The size of page directory and page table is of 4 KB. Access to them would be difficult in conditions where every time an address require translation. In order to avoid this, a small cache called "Translation Look aside Buffer" is used. Paging can be speeded up by using TLB. Figure 13 shows how the TLB supports paging mechanism.

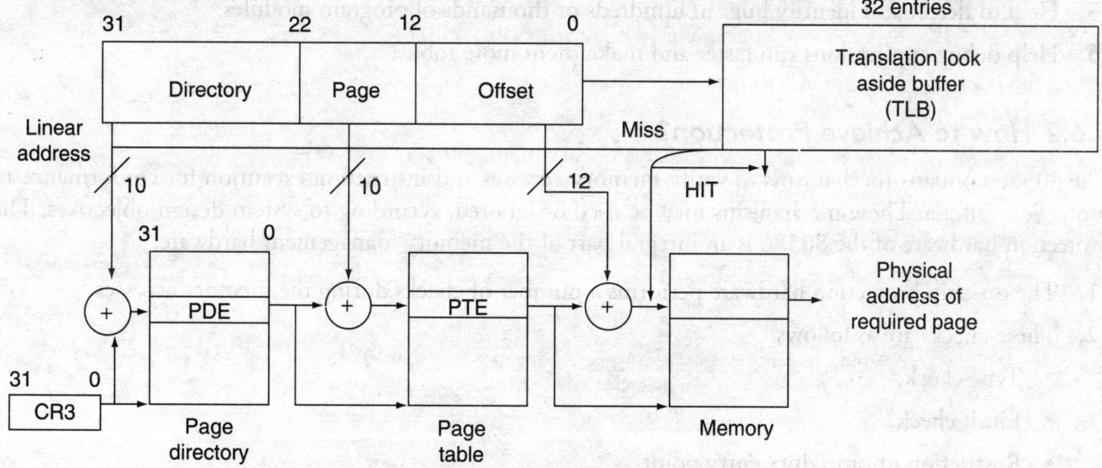

Figure 13 Page translation using TLB.

1. The TLB cache holds the recent 32 entries of page tables.
2. Therefore 128 KB of paged memory is directly accessible. That is, the operands from the current pages can be accessed without referring the new entries from the page tables. This improves the system performance during address translation.
3. If an operand is not in one of the current pages, then the processor has to access the page directory and page table entries stored in RAM. The operating system takes care of loading the new translation into the TLB.
4. Before loading the TLB with the new translation, the previous contents of the TLB are to be invalidated.
5. The hit rate is about 98%, that is, processor will only have to access two-level page structure on 2% of all memory accesses.

5.6 Page-Level Protection

The protection mechanism is divided into two parts:

1. Memory management.
2. Privilege protection.

The memory management unit helps in tracing programmer's errors, that is, illegal addresses etc; while privilege protection mechanism helps up in catching errors that are more subtle.

5.6.1 Need of Protection

The purpose of the protection features of the 80386 is to

1. Prevent users from interfering each other.
2. Prevent program bugs from damaging data.
3. Prevent malicious attempts to compromise system integrity.
4. Prevent accidental damage to data.
5. Help to detect and identify bugs in hundreds or thousands of program modules.
6. Help debug applications run faster and make them more robust.

5.6.2 How to Achieve Protection?

The 80386 contains mechanisms to verify memory accesses and instruction execution for conformance to protection criteria. These mechanisms may be used or ignored, according to system design objectives. The protection hardware of the 80386 is an integral part of the memory management hardware.

1. The on-chip protection hardware performs a number of checks during the memory accesses.
2. These checks are as follows:
    - Type check.
    - Limit check.
    - Restriction of procedure entry point.
    - Restriction of addressable domain.
    - Restriction of instruction set.
3. The checks during the memory access can also be performed by privilege protection.

5.7 Protection Rings

The four possible privilege levels for each task are shown in Fig. 14. Levels 0, 1, 2 and 3 shown using concentric circles are called protection model of the 80386 processor. Here level 0 is the most privilege level and level 3 is the least privileged level. The features of these levels are discussed as follows:

1. The kernel consists of application independent software. It provides microprocessor oriented functions such as I/O control, task sequencing and memory management. Therefore, this software is kept at the most privilege level (level 0).
2. The system services such as file processing are kept at level 1.
3. Level 2 is used to implement custom routines to support special purpose system operations.
4. The least privilege level (level 3), is the level s at which user programs are run.
5. The privilege levels are used to isolate system level software from the user's program.
6. Tasks at a level can use programs from the higher privilege levels but cannot change the contents of these routines in any way. Therefore application programs are allowed to use the system routines in any way without affecting their integrity. For example, an application program running at PL = 3 may call an operating system routine at PL = 1.

7. The protection also puts the restriction on the instruction set. For example, the system control instructions can only be executed in the code segment at PL = 0.

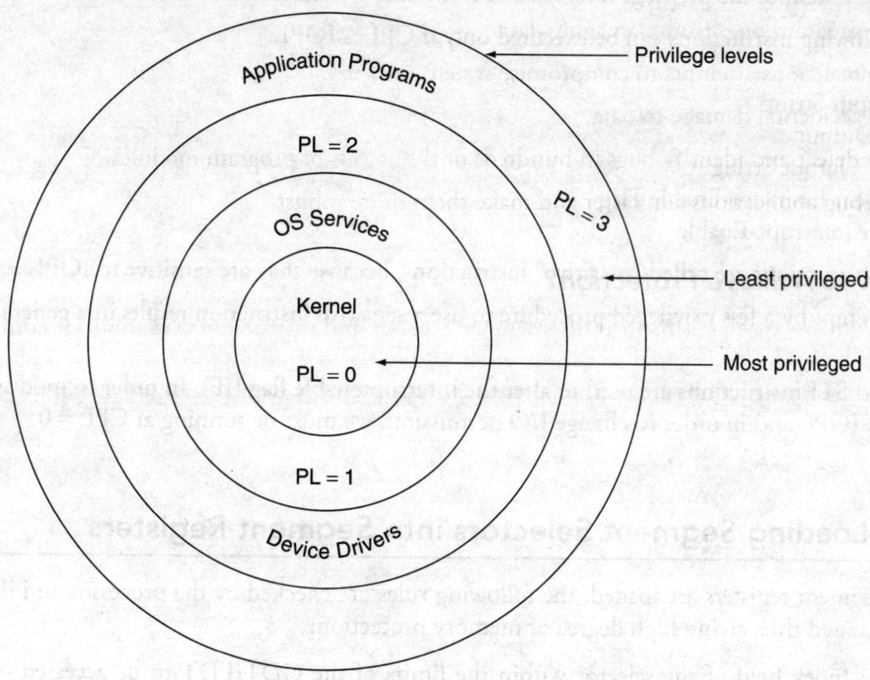

Figure 14 Protection rings of 80386.

5.8 Privileged Instructions

Instructions that deal with the interrupt flag or perform peripheral I/O, and affect the segmentation and paging are known as privileged instructions. Instructions that affect segmentation and paging must be executed only when current privilege level (CPL) is 0. Following are the examples of the instructions which can be used only if descriptor privilege level (DPL) of code segment is 0:

HLT
CLTS
LLDT
LGDT
LIDT
LTR
LMSW
MOV CRn, REG OR MOV REG, CRn
MOV DRn, REG OR MOV REG, DRn
INVLPG
WBINVD

1. An attempt made to execute these instructions with CPL greater than 0 results in general protection fault.
2. The IOPL defines the privilege level needed to execute I/O-related instructions.
3. The following instructions can be executed only if CPL ≤ IOPL:
   IN: Input
   INS: Input String
   OUT: Output
   OUTS: Output String
   CLI: Clear Interrupt-Enable Flag
   STI: Set Interrupt-Enable
4. These instructions are called "sensitive" instructions, because they are sensitive to IOPL.
5. Any attempt by a less privileged procedure to use a sensitive instruction results in a general protection exception.
6. CLI and STI instructions are used to alter the interruptenable flag (IF). In order to modify the IF bit, CPL<= IOPL and in order to change I/O permission, we must be running at CPL = 0.

5.9 Loading Segment Selectors into Segment Registers

Whenever segment registers are loaded, the following rules are checked by the processor and if violated an exception is raised thus giving high degree of memory protection:

1. **Rule 1:** Index field of the selector within the limits of the GDT/LDT to be accessed – else raise a general protection fault exception.
2. **Rule 2:** The selector references the correct descriptor table.
3. **Rule 3:** The descriptor is of the correct type.
4. Loading a selector into DS, ES, FS or GS that point to a non-readable segment results in an exception.
5. For loading into SS, the segment pointed to should be readable and writable.
6. For loading into CS, the segment should be executable type.
7. **Rule 4:** The selector uses the correct privilege level. This will be discussed later in detail.

   - All segment registers except CS may be loaded using MOV, LDS, LES, LFS, LGS and LSS.
   - The CS is loaded using a JMP or a CALL instruction.

5.10 Privilege Protection

Continuous checking is done by the processor on whether the application is privileged enough to perform either of the following operations. The possible operations are:

1. Type 1: Execute certain instructions.
2. Type 2: Reference data other than its own.
3. Type 3: Transfer control to code other than its own.

To manage this, every segment has a privilege level called DPL bits 45, 46.

5.10.1 Privilege Level – DPL, CPL, RPL

The different privilege levels are described as follows:

1. **DPL:** The privilege level is defined in the segment descriptor, DPL field. (The descriptor has no privilege level assigned to it.)
2. Privilege levels apply to entire segments.
3. **CPL:** At the given point, the processors privilege level is determined by the DPL of the code segment from which it is currently fetching and executing code, this is referred as CPL.
4. **RPL:** Requestors privilege level (segment selector) (RPL) is the two least significant bits in the segment selector.

5.10.2 The Least Privilege Principle

At ring 0, you can do whatever you want. Can we put some limit on it, such that we only use the least privilege that is needed? We can drop the privilege temporarily.

5.10.3 How to Achieve the Least Privilege Principle: RPL?

Normally RPL is usually less than or equal to CPL. When RPL is equal to zero, the RPL will have no effect.

5.10.3 Type 1: Execute Certain Instructions

Privileged instructions are the instructions that modify the interrupt flag, alter segmentation, perform peripheral I/O or affect the protection mechanism.

1. Segmentation and protection based (HLT, CLTS, LGDT, LIDT, LLDT, LTR, moving data to control, debug and test registers).
2. Interrupt flag based and peripheral I/O based (CLI, STI, IN, INS, OUT, OUTS).

First type of privileged instructions can be executed only when CPL = 0, that is, these instructions can be in code segment with DPL = 0.

5.10.4 I/O Instructions

The I/O based privileged instructions are executed only if CPL <= IOPL in EFLAGS register. To add to the security, the POPF/POPFD instructions which load values into the EFLAGS shall not touch the IOPL bit or IF bit if CPL > 0.

5.10.5 Type 2: Referring Data Other Than its Own

This type is used with applications in a multi-tasking environment share data. Programs are not allowed to read or write data items that have a higher privilege level; however, applications can use data at the same or lower privilege level. With stack segments, it is more restrictive. (CPL=DPL of stack Descriptor.) This is achieved by two ways:

1. Whenever selector is loaded in data segment register, CPU checks if max(RPL,CPL) <= DPL (RPL may weaken your privilege level) and if not true then 80386 rejects the selector immediately.
2. When selector makes a memory reference, 80386 checks whether the type of access you are requesting (read or write) is allowed for that segment.

5.10.6 Privilege Check for Data

Control transfer privilege level checks for data are shown in Fig. 15.

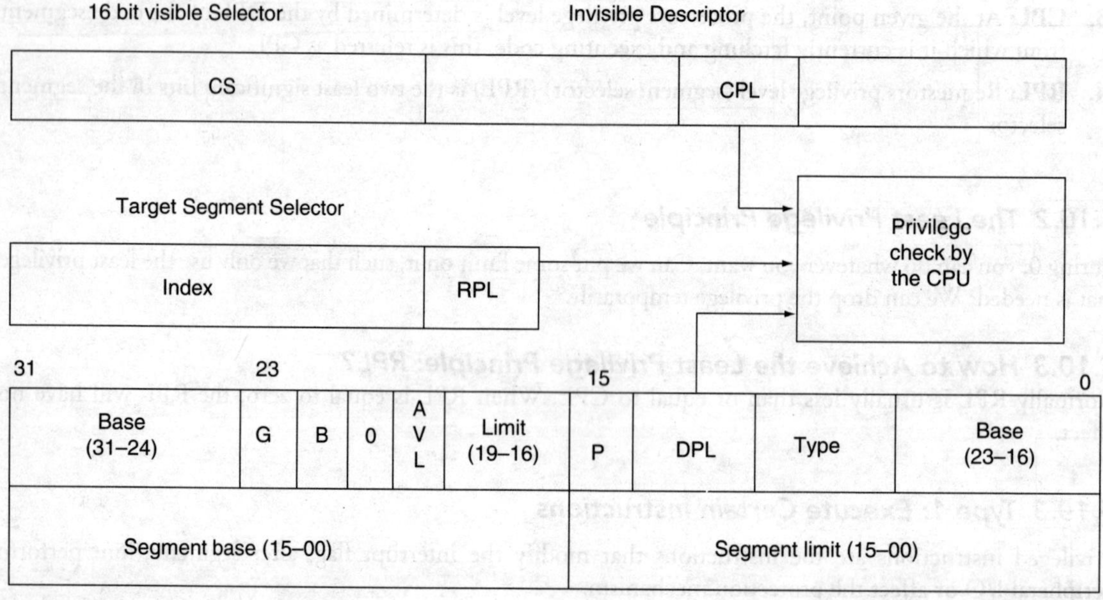

Figure 15 Control transfer privilege level checks for data.

Examples of accessing data segments from various privilege levels are shown in Fig. 16.

5.10.7 Type 3: Transfer Control to Code Other Than its Own

This type of operation performs following tasks:

1. Essentially load a new selector into the CS register.
2. Many programs in multitasking share pieces of code such as run time libraries.
3. Programs are not allowed to CALL or JMP to code segment:
   - That has different privilege level.
   - Another segment must be a code segment (executable permission) and marked present.
4. To move between code segments requires inter-segment JMP, CALL or RET instruction.

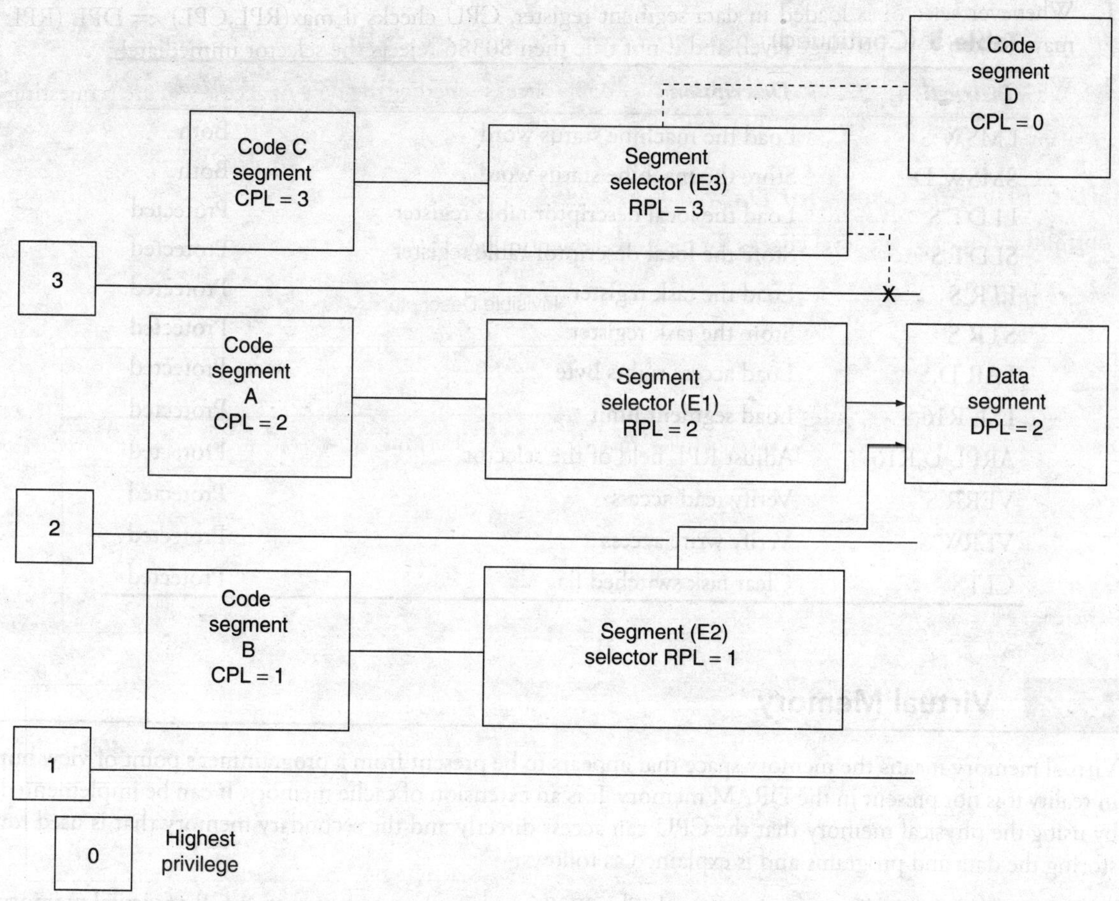

Figure 16 Accessing data segments from various privilege levels.

5.11 Protected Mode System Control Instructions

All the instructions available in the real mode are executed by the processor in protection mode also; rather the instruction set is enhanced with a number of additional instructions. These instructions are used only in the protected mode or used in the real mode so that processor can switch from real to protected mode. Such instructions are called "system control instructions". The protected mode instructions are given in Table 5.

Table 5 System Control Instructions

Instruction	*Description*	*Mode*
LGDT S	Load the global descriptor table register	Both
SGDT D	Store the global descriptor table register	Both
LIDT S	Load the interrupt descriptor table register	Both
SIDT D	Store the interrupt descriptor table register	Both

(Continued)

Table 5 (Continued)

Instruction	*Description*	*Mode*
LMSW S	Load the machine status word	Both
SMSW D	Store the machine status word	Both
LLDT S	Load the local descriptor table register	Protected
SLDT S	Store the local descriptor table register	Protected
LTR S	Load the task register	Protected
STR S	Store the task register	Protected
LAR D,S	Load access rights byte	Protected
LSL R16,S	Load segment limit	Protected
ARPL D,R16	Adjust RPL field of the selector	Protected
VERR S	Verify read access	Protected
VERW S	Verify write access	Protected
CLTS	Clear task switched flag	Protected

5.12 Virtual Memory

Virtual memory means the memory space that appears to be present from a programmer's point of view but in reality it is not present in the DRAM memory. It is an extension of cache memory. It can be implemented by using the physical memory that the CPU can access directly and the secondary memory that is used for storing the data and programs and is explained as follows:

1. Per task, the virtual memory is assigned. The 80386 processor can access up to 1 GB of virtual memory per task.
2. This memory adds hard disk drive to the memory hierarchy.
3. The code segment or data segment required for the execution at any particular instant are read from the secondary memory into the physical memory. After this, the next segment is also fetched from the secondary memory and the result is stored from the primary memory to secondary memory.
4. The process continues till the whole program is executed. The programmer feels that he is getting the full utilization of the memory. Such type of memory is called as *virtual memory.*

5.13 Entering into Protected Mode

The 80386 begins its execution in real mode immediately after reset signal. To enter into protected mode it must set the PE bit of control register CR0. The following sequence is used by the processor before entering to protected mode:

1. The GDT, LDT and IDT need to be maintained. At least one of these tables should be defined.

2. Once the protected mode is enabled, the next instruction should be a JMP to reload CS which will point to valid code segment selector.
3. Now the processor operates in protected mode.

5.14 Returning Back to Real Mode (Leaving Protected Mode)

Processor can return back to real mode without turning off the power or resetting the system just by clearing the PE bit of CR0. But before returning to the real mode, we must check that all the values used by the processor should be legal real mode values. The following sequence is used by the processor for returning to real mode:

1. In case paging is enabled, it should be disabled by clearing the PG bit in CR0.
2. To clear paging cache control register, CR3 should be cleared.
3. Make use of segment descriptor containing the following values
4. Initialise segment registers as required by real mode.
5. Clear PE bit.
6. Flush the instruction queue by executing a far JMP to real mode code. This puts appropriate values in the access rights of CS register.
7. Load the base and limit of the real mode IDT using LIDT instruction.
8. With this processor enters into the real mode.

5.15 Inter Privilege Level Transfer using Call Gates and Conforming Code Segment (Changing Privilege levels)

If a task cannot access a segment with a more privileged (numerically less) DPL, how can user programs access the operating system kernel, BIOS, or utility procedures in segments which have more privileged DPLs? For this, there are two ways to access a procedure located in a segment which has a higher privilege level. They are as follows:

1. Using conforming code segment.
2. Using a special segment descriptor called call gate.

5.15.1 Conforming Code Segment

Conforming code segments confirms with the privilege level of the calling code. So if a control transfer happens from segment S to a confirming segment T, the privilege of T would be the privilege of S.

1. Privilege check for control transfer without using a gate.
2. Policy:
   - CPL = DPL of code segment.
   - CPL > DPL (allowed if the conforming bit is 1, but when the conforming bit is 0, this is not allowed).
   - CPL = 2 can invoke DPL = 1.

- CPL = 2 cannot invoke code with DPL = 3.
- You can transfer control across or up not down.

3. Why cannot we access code with a higher DPL (i.e., lower privilege)? It is easy to jump (lower the CPL) to the code with higher DPL, but it is difficult to return back, because on returning, we jump from a lower privileged ring to a higher privileged ring. This violates the mandatory access control policy.
4. Why cannot we jump to code with a lower DPL (i.e., higher privilege)?
   - For security reasons, we cannot do this.
   - However, we definitely need this. For example, we want to access device driver code, which should be in segments with a higher privilege.

Figure 17 shows the examples of accessing conforming and non-conforming code segments from various privilege levels.

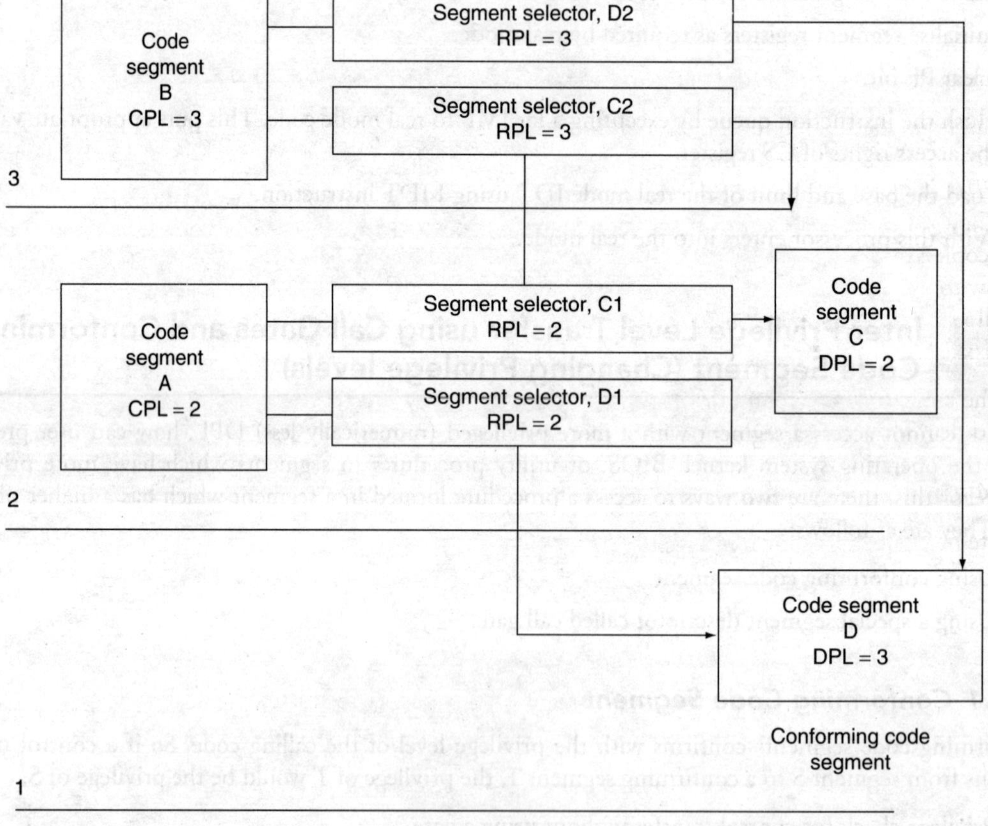

Figure 17 Examples of accessing conforming and non-conforming code segments from various privilege levels.

5.15.2 Call Gates

Call gate acts as an interface layer between code segments at different privilege levels. It provides the only means to alter the current privilege level. It defines the entry points to other privilege levels. Call gate must be invoked using a CALL Instruction. It occupies a slot in the descriptor tables. They are defined like segment descriptors but do not describe a memory segment.

5.15.3 Call Gate Descriptor

It is defined by a system descriptor (S = 0) in GDT which is used by the JMP or CALL. It is 64-bit descriptor in GDT. Call gate descriptor is shown in Fig. 18.

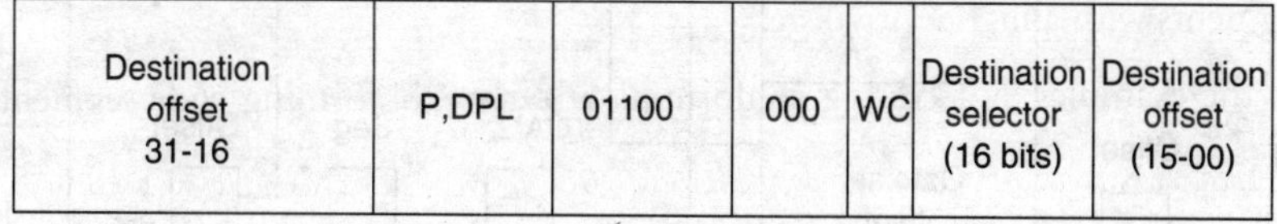

Figure 18 Call gate descriptor.

Call gate descriptor contains the following information:

1. *Destination selector*: Code segment to be accessed through segment descriptor.
2. *Destination offset*: Entry point for a procedure in the specified code segment.
3. *DPL* (Call gate PL): Privilege level required for a caller trying to access the procedure.
4. *WC (Word Parameter Count)*: If a stack switch occurs, it specifies the number of optional parameters to be copied between stacks.
5. How to use call gates?
   Call xxxxxx.
   xxxxxx specifies the call gate entry in the GDT.

From the table, the entry point of the procedure will be obtained. DPL of the gate descriptor allows the CPU to decide whether the invocator can enter the gate.

5.15.4 Call Gate Mechanism

Call gate mechanism is shown in Fig. 19.

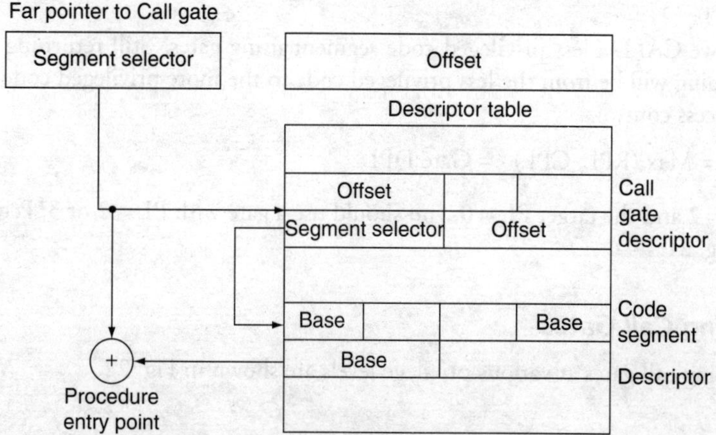

Figure 19 Call gate mechanism.

5.15.5 Call Gate Accessibility

Calling higher privileged code to access the call gate is shown in Fig. 20.

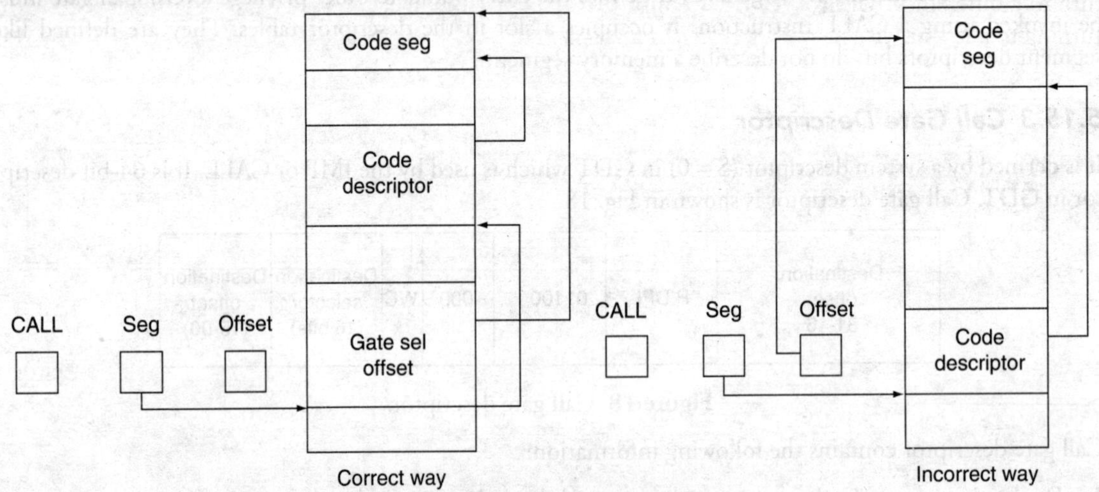

Figure 20 Call gate accessibility.

5.16 Access Control Policy for Call Gates

During the process of access the validity of control transfer is checked using four different privilege levels the CPL, RPL of the selector used to specify the call gate, DPL of the gate descriptor and DPL of the descriptor of the target executable segment. Privilege requirements to use a call gate are as follows:

1. CPL ≤ DPL of the call gate.
2. **For CALL**: DPL of the target code segment ≤ CPL (Only calls to the more privileged code segment are allowed).
3. Why cannot we CALL a less privileged code segment using gates? Still returning will be a problem, because returning will be from the less privileged code to the more privileged code, and it violates the mandatory access control.
4. Target DPL <= Max (RPL, CPL) <= Gate DPL

For example CPL = 2 and the target PL = 0, you should use a gate with PL = 2 or 3. Privilege check via call gate is shown in Fig. 21.

5.16.1 Accessing Call Gates

Examples of accessing call gates at various privilege levels are shown in Fig. 22.

5.16.2 Returning from a Called Procedure

The RET instruction can be used to perform a near return, a far return at the same privilege level, and a far return to a different privilege level. A far return that requires a privilege-level change is only allowed when returning to a less privileged level.

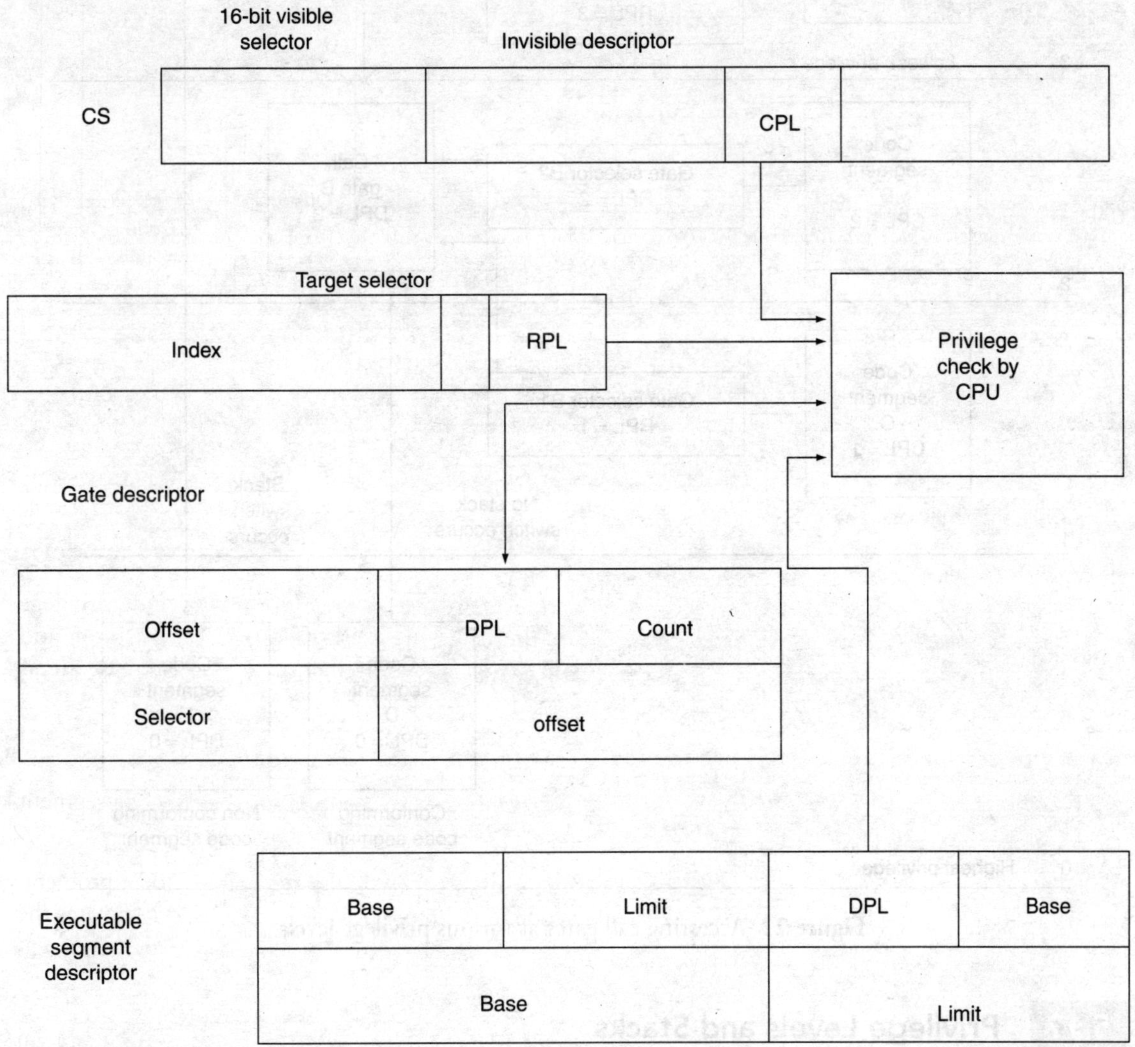

Figure 21 Privilege check via call gate.

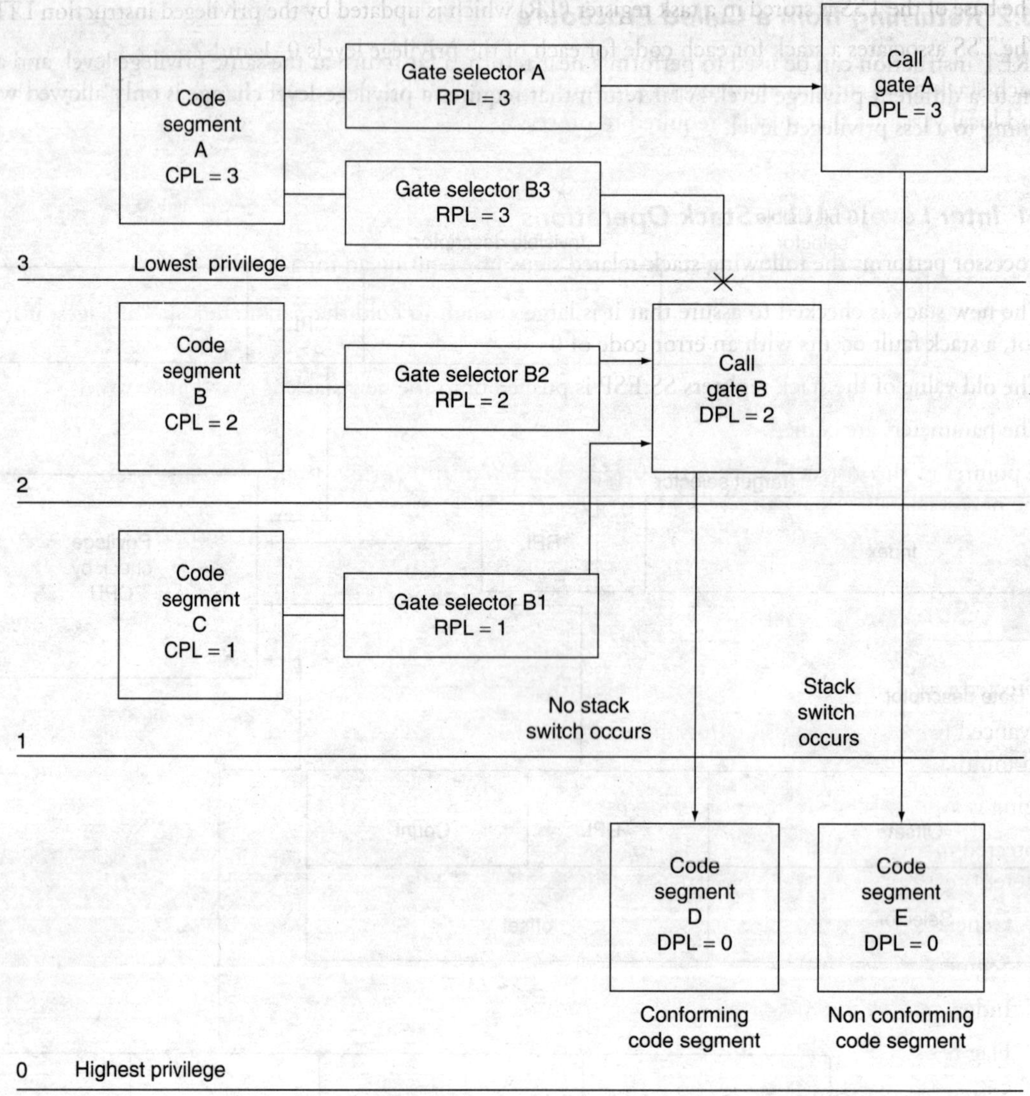

Figure 22 Accessing call gates at various privilege levels.

5.17 Privilege Levels and Stacks

The change in privilege level changes the address domain of the program. The 80386 also changes stacks in case of change in privilege level.

1. To maintain system integrity, each privilege level has a separate stack.
2. The stack PL = CPL always.
3. When changing the CPL, the processor automatically changes the stack.
4. This is done using the task state segment (TSS).

5. The base of the TSS is stored in a task register (TR) which is updated by the privileged instruction LTR.
6. The TSS associates a stack for each code for each of the privilege levels 0, 1 and 2.
7. Each stack must contain enough space to hold the old SS:ESP, the return address, and all parameters and local variables that may be required to process a call.

5.17.1 Inter-Level CALL – Stack Operations

The processor performs the following stack-related steps in executing an inter-level CALL:

1. The new stack is checked to assure that it is large enough to hold the parameters and linkages; if it is not, a stack fault occurs with an error code of 0.
2. The old value of the stack registers SS:ESP is pushed onto the new stack as two double words.
3. The parameters are copied.
4. A pointer to the instruction after the CALL instruction (the former value of CS:EIP) is pushed onto the new stack. The final value of SS:ESP points to this return pointer on the new stack.

Summary

- Protected mode of processor 80386 is a powerful and complex mode.
- Advanced features, that is, on chip support for OS functions such as memory management, protection and multitasking is available only in the protected mode.
- Paging is available only in the protection mode. Demand paging creates virtual environment of 64 TB.
- Protected mode has all registers in the architecture with changed functionality of segment registers. The different registers used in the protection mode are categorized as follows:
    - General-purpose registers.
    - Segment registers.
    - Index, pointer and base registers.
    - Flag registers.
    - System address registers.
    - Control registers.
    - Debug registers.
- In the real mode, memory segment size is fixed as 64 KB. But in the protected mode, size of the memory segment is variable, that is, from 1 Byte to 4 GB.
- The 80386 memory management uses segment selectors and segment descriptors tables for address translation.
- The memory management unit is made up of the segmentation unit and paging unit. The task of memory management unit is to convert the logical addresses to physical addresses. The processor has three address fields: logical, linear and physical.

- The protection mechanism is divided into two parts: Memory management and privilege protection. The memory management unit helps in tracing programmer's errors, that is, illegal addresses etc. While privilege protection mechanism helps in catching errors that are more subtle.
- Instructions that deal with the interrupt flag or perform peripheral I/O, affect the segmentation and paging are known as privileged instructions. Instructions that affect segmentation and paging must be executed only when CPL is 0. Some of the examples of privilege instructions are: HLT, CLTS, LLDT etc.
- Virtual memory means the memory space that appears to be present from a programmer's point of view but in reality it is not present in the DRAM memory.
- The virtual memory is assigned as per task. The 80386 processor can access up to 1 GB of virtual memory per task. This memory adds hard disk drive to the memory hierarchy.
- Control transfer from a code of some PL to another code with a different PL is possible using conforming code segments or a special segment descriptor called call gates.

Multiple-Choice Questions

1. What is the size of IP register in protected mode?

(a) 32 bit

(b) 16 bit

(c) 8 bit

(d) 20 bit

2. What is the size of segment descriptors in 80386?

(a) 48 bit

(b) 64 bit

(c) 8 bit

(d) 20 bit

3. Amongst given which is the non-system segment descriptor?

(a) TSS

(b) Stack

(c) LDT

(d) Gate

4. Amongst given which is the system segment descriptor?

(a) Code

(b) Stack

(c) Data

(d) Gate

5. What is the size of segment in protected mode of 80386?

(a) 64 KB

(b) 1 Byte to 4 GB

(c) 1 MB

(d) 64 TB

6. In which mode of processor paging feature is available?

(a) Real

(b) Protected

(c) VM86

(d) Virtual

7. Amongst the given which is a privilege instruction?

(a) CLTS

(b) TEST

(c) XOR

(d) STD

8. Amongst the given which is not a privilege instruction?

(a) CLTS

(b) TEST

(c) HLT

(d) LLDT

9. Amongst the given which is a privilege instruction?

(a) LMSW

(b) TEST

(c) AND

(d) STD

10. Amongst the given which is not a privilege instruction?

(a) CLTS

(b) XOR

(c) HLT

(d) LTR

11. Amongst the given which is a privilege instruction?

(a) AAA

(b) OR

(c) OUTS

(d) STD

12. Amongst the given which is not a privilege instruction?

(a) CLTS

(b) LOOP

(c) HLT

(d) LLDT

13. Amongst the given which is a privilege instruction?

(a) AAA

(b) OR

(c) NOP

(d) LIDT

14. Amongst the given which is not a privilege instruction?

(a) STI

(b) RET

(c) HLT

(d) LLDT

15. Amongst the given which is a privilege instruction?

(a) AAA

(b) OR

(c) INVLPG

(d) SBB

16. Amongst the given which is not a privilege instruction?

(a) STI

(b) LGDT

(c) CMP

(d) LLDT

17. Amongst the given which is a privilege instruction?

(a) AAA

(b) OR

(c) CLD

(d) MOV DR3, AL

18. Amongst the given which is not a privilege instruction?

(a) STI

(b) LGDT

(c) MOV CR2, AH

(d) MOV AL, 05H

19. Amongst the given which is a privilege instruction?

(a) STD

(b) ROL

(c) MOV AL,CR2

(d) MOV AL, 05H

20. What is a size of individual page in protected mode of 80386?

(a) 1 KB

(b) 2 KB

(c) 4 KB

(d) 8 KB

21. What is the maximum memory accessing capacity of processor 80386 in protected mode?

(a) 1 MB

(b) 1 GB

(c) 4 GB

(d) 64 TB

22. What is the size of data bus of processor 80386 in protected mode?

(a) 8 bit

(b) 16 bit

(c) 20 bit

(d) 32 bit

23. What is the size of address bus of processor 80386 in protected mode?

(a) 8 bit

(b) 16 bit

(c) 20 bit

(d) 32 bit

24. Fragmentation is present in which operating mode of processor 80386?

(a) Real

(b) Protected

(c) Virtual

(d) None of these

25. Which control register enables the paging in protected mode?

(a) CR3

(b) CR1

(c) CR2

(d) CR0

26. Which control register is kept reserved by the INTEL manufacturer of the processor?

(a) CR3

(b) CR1

(c) CR2

(d) CR0

27. What is the size of all control registers of processor 80386?

(a) 8 bit

(b) 16 bit

(c) 32 bit

(d) 64 bit

28. What is the size of flag register in protected mode of processor 80386?

(a) 8 bit

(b) 16 bit

(c) 32 bit

(d) 64 bit

29. What is the long form of PDE?

(a) Page Directory Entry

(b) Page Directory Enable

(c) Public Directory Entry

(d) Private Directory Entry

30. What is the long form of PTE?

(a) Public Table Entry

(b) Private Table Entry

(c) Page Table Enable

(d) Page Table Entry

31. What is the long size of PDE?

(a) 8 bit

(b) 16 bit

(c) 32 bit

(d) 64 bit

32. What is the long size of PTE?

(a) 20 bit

(b) 16 bit

(c) 32 bit

(d) 64 bit

33. What is the size of directory field of linear address in protected mode?

(a) 8 bit

(b) 10 bit

(c) 12 bit

(d) 16 bit

34. What is the size of page field of linear address in protected mode?

(a) 8 bit

(b) 10 bit

(c) 12 bit

(d) 16 bit

35. What is the size of offset field of linear address in protected mode?

(a) 8 bit

(b) 10 bit

(c) 12 bit

(d) 16 bit

36. Each entry in page table of protected mode is how many bytes long?

(a) 2 byte

(b) 4 byte

(c) 6 byte

(d) 8 byte

37. What is the size of linear address in 80386?

(a) 8 bit

(b) 16 bit

(c) 20 bit

(d) 32 bit

38. What is the size of physical address in 80386 protected mode?

(a) 8 bit

(b) 16 bit

(c) 20 bit

(d) 32 bit

39. Which flag is a 2-bit flag in 80386?

(a) CY

(b) OF

(c) IOPL

(d) NT

40. What is the size of IP register in case of protected mode?

(a) 8 bit

(b) 16 bit

(c) 20 bit

(d) 32 bit

41. TLB cache holds how many entries of page table?

(a) 16

(b) 32

(c) 6

(d) 8

42. Machine status word is present in which control register?

(a) CRO

(b) CR1

(c) CR2

(d) CR3

43. Which control register is also called as PDBR?

(a) CRO

(b) CR1

(c) CR2

(d) CR3

44. What is the long form of TLB?

(a) Translation Lookaside Buffer

(b) Translation Lookup Buffer

(c) Test Lookaside Buffer

(d) Test Lookup Buffer

45. To flush out TLB cache which type of an instruction is used?

(a) MOV CR3, EAX

(b) MOV DX, 1000H

(c) LEA SI, ARRAY

(d) MOV AL,07H

46. To enable paging in protected mode which control registers need to be initialized?

(a) CR0 & CR1

(b) CR0 & CR2

(c) CR0 & CR3

(d) CR2 & CR1

47. What is the significance of setting R/W field of PDE in protected mode?

(a) Write privileges are allowed from PL3 code

(b) Write privileges are allowed from PL2 code

(c) Write privileges are allowed from PL1 code

(d) Write privileges are allowed from PL0 code

48. What is the significance of setting R/W field of PTE in protected mode?

(a) Write privileges are allowed from PL3 code

(b) Write privileges are allowed from PL2 code

(c) Write privileges are allowed from PL1 code

(d) Write privileges are allowed from PL0 code

49. What is the long form of D bit in page table entry?

(a) Dump

(b) Dividend

(c) Dirty

(d) Divisor

50. What size of paged memory is directly accessible using TLB?

(a) 80 KB

(b) 128 KB

(c) 256 KB

(d) 64 KB

51. Which instruction is used to invalidate the TLB entry?

(a) CLD

(b) CLTS

(c) WBINVD

(d) INVLPG

52. How much is the hit rate in TLB?

(a) About 20%

(b) About 50%

(c) About 76%

(d) About 98%

53. How many privilege levels are possible for each task?

(a) 1

(b) 2

(c) 3

(d) 4

54. Amongst given which is the most privilege level in protected mode?

(a) PL1

(b) PL0

(c) PL3

(d) PL2

55. Amongst given which is the least privilege level in protected mode?

(a) PL1

(b) PL0

(c) PL3

(d) PL2

56. What privilege level must be assigned to Kernel?

(a) PL1

(b) PL0

(c) PL3

(d) PL2

57. What privilege level must be assigned to system services like file accessing?

(a) PL1

(b) PL0

(c) PL3

(d) PL2

58. What privilege level must be assigned to Application program?

(a) PL1

(b) PL0

(c) PL3

(d) PL2

59. What condition must be satisfied to change the Interrupt flag bit?

(a) CPL<= IOPL

(b) DPL<= IOPL

(c) RPL<= IOPL

(d) CPL=> IOPL

60. What condition must be satisfied for successful control transfer using Call Gate mechanism?

(a) Target DPL=> Max(RPL, CPL) <= Gate DPL

(b) Target DPL<= Max(RPL, CPL) => Gate DPL

(c) Target DPL=> Max(RPL, CPL) => Gate DPL

(d) Target DPL<= Max(RPL, CPL) <= Gate DPL

61. For privilege instruction to be executed what must be the value of CPL?

(a) 0

(b) 1

(c) 2

(d) 3

62. For instruction HLT to be executed what must be the value of CPL?

(a) 2

(b) 1

(c) 0

(d) 3

63. To make an entry into protected mode which bit of CR0 must be set?

(a) PG

(b) ET

(c) MP

(d) PE

64. To enable paging mechanism which bit in CR0 needs to be set?

(a) PG

(b) ET

(c) MP

(d) PE

65. If ET bit of CR0 is in set condition then which coprocessor is selected by 80386?

(**a**) 8087

(**b**) 80287

(**c**) 80387

(**d**) 80187

66. If ET bit of CR0 is in reset condition then which coprocessor is selected by 80386?

(**a**) 8087

(**b**) 80287

(**c**) 80387

(**d**) 80187

67. What operation can be performed on control register 2?

(**a**) Write only

(**b**) Read only

(**c**) Read and write

(**d**) None of these

68. Which control register holds the base address of page directory?

(**a**) CR0

(**b**) CR1

(**c**) CR2

(**d**) CR3

69. Amongst given register which is known as debug status register?

(**a**) DR0

(**b**) DR2

(**c**) DR6

(**d**) DR7

70. Amongst given register which is known as debug control register?

(**a**) DR0

(**b**) DR2

(**c**) DR6

(**d**) DR7

71. Amongst given register who holds the linear address of the TLB?

   (a) DR7

   (b) TR6

   (c) DR6

   (d) TR7

72. Amongst given register who holds the physical address of the TLB?

   (a) DR7

   (b) TR6

   (c) DR6

   (d) TR7

Review Questions

1. What is the basic difference between segmentation and paging? How linear address produced by the segmentation process is handled in paging process to get an operand? Explain with the help of suitable diagram. Also explain the role of TLB in the process.
2. What is TLB? How is this useful while accessing physical memory? Draw the necessary diagram to explain your concepts.
3. What is the difference between real and protected mode of 80386? How will you switch from real mode to protected mode? Explain the steps in short.
4. Explain in detail address translation from logical to physical address in real mode as well as protected mode of 80386.
5. How does 80386 translate logical address to physical address, when paging is enabled in protected mode? Explain with the help of necessary formats of descriptors and diagrams.
6. Draw and explain the programmer's model of 80386 in protected mode.
7. What are privileged instructions in 80386 and the response if used?
8. What is the use of DPL field of conforming code segment descriptor? How does it differ from DPL field of non-conforming code segment?
9. Explain page translation process with diagram. Draw PTE and PDE formats.
10. How do we switch from protected mode to real mode? Explain the steps.
11. What are the different methods to call a function with higher privilege level? Explain with the help of suitable example.
12. What is use of DPL field of conforming code segment descriptor? How does it differ from DPL field of non-conforming code segment descriptor? Explain with suitable example.
13. How does I/O permission bit map helps in accessing the I/O Devices in processor 80386?
14. How many privilege levels that 80386 supports? Explain CPL, RPL and DPL concepts while accessing the code or data with protection mechanism of 80386. Also draw the data segment descriptor format and code segment descriptor format to demonstrate mechanism of privilege level checks.

15. What do you mean by privilege levels? What is the need? Explain any two privilege level instructions.
16. With neat diagrams explain process of address translation in protected mode of 80386 when paging is enabled?
17. Write difference between real and protected mode of 80386 with respect to
    (a) Memory segmentation
    (b) Physical address generation
    (c) Instruction set
18. What are DPL, RPL and CPL? Write privilege checks performed by 80386 while accessing code or data with protection mechanism?
19. CALL gate acts as an interface layer to a code with different privilege levels. Justify the statement with the help of CALL gate descriptor?
20. Write stack related steps performed by processor 80386 in executing an inter-level CALL?
21. What is conforming code segment?
22. Compare RM and PM modes of 80386.

Answers

Multiple-Choice Questions

1. (a)	**16.** (c)	**31.** (c)
2. (b)	**17.** (d)	**32.** (c)
3. (b)	**18.** (d)	**33.** (b)
4. (d)	**19.** (c)	**34.** (b)
5. (b)	**20.** (c)	**35.** (c)
6. (b)	**21.** (c)	**36.** (b)
7. (a)	**22.** (d)	**37.** (d)
8. (b)	**23.** (d)	**38.** (d)
9. (a)	**24.** (b)	**39.** (c)
10. (b)	**25.** (d)	**40.** (d)
11. (c)	**26.** (b)	**41.** (b)
12. (b)	**27.** (c)	**42.** (a)
13. (d)	**28.** (c)	**43.** (d)
14. (b)	**29.** (a)	**44.** (a)
15. (c)	**30.** (d)	**45.** (a)

46. (c)

47. (a)

48. (a)

49. (c)

50. (b)

51. (d)

52. (d)

53. (d)

54. (b)

55. (c)

56. (b)

57. (a)

58. (c)

59. (a)

60. (d)

61. (a)

62. (c)

63. (d)

64. (a)

65. (c)

66. (b)

67. (b)

68. (d)

69. (c)

70. (d)

71. (b)

72. (d)

6 Multitasking

LEARNING OBJECTIVES

After reading this chapter, you will be able to:

- Understand the multitasking feature of 80386 that is activated only when the processor is operated in the protected mode.
- Know the different supporting registers which are used in multitasking.
- Understand how the processor 80386 facilitates task switching.
- Understand the significance of some special system registers and descriptors needed for task switching.

6.1 Introduction

Using a uni-processor system such as PC, desktop or laptop, we keep on opening multiple windows whichmeans we run multiple application programs simultaneously. This is possible due to the concept of multitasking. In multitasking, even if only one CPU is involved, it switches from one program to another so quickly that it gives the appearance of executing all of the programs at the same time. Multitasking can be explained as follows:

1. Multitasking is basically a time-sharing method by which multiple tasks (processes) share common processing resources such as a microprocessor. Since multitasking system is based on time-sharing concept, only one task may be running at any instant of time, and other tasks keep waiting for their turn.
2. Multitasking refers to the ability of the operating system to run multiple tasks concurrently, that is, ability of running application program at the same time with on-chip hardware support.
3. Basic unit of work for a multitasking system is task. A task is a collection of program routines that perform a specific function. A processor can dispatch (submit), execute (run) and suspend (wait) a task. The task may have both global and local memory resources.
4. Multitasking needs software as well as hardware support too. Software support is required for switching from one task to another, that is, task switching.
5. Processor 80386 facilitates task switching with some special system registers and descriptors.

6.2 Task Structure

Each task uses register, data pointers, memory pointers, memory variables stack area, etc. This is referred to as environment or context of that task. When a task switch occurs, the environment or context of the interrupted task must be saved so that the task can be continued properly when it receives another time slice.

1. A task consists of the following two parts:
   - **Task execution space:** It is a portion of main memory where task (code) is loaded to run. All segments related to the task such as code segment, stack segment, one or multiple data segments form the task execution space.
   - **Task state segment (TSS):** TSS is a storage space used to store task state's vital information when that task is not running (task context). TSS also provides a mechanism for maintaining task link. Task link provides the information required to restart the task. Every task is assigned only one TSS. TSS is not accessible by any general user program, even at privilege level 0.
2. To provide efficient, protected multitasking, the 80386 employs several special descriptors. Various registers and descriptors required for multitasking are described in the following section.

6.3 Registers and Descriptors Associated with Multitasking

Registers and data structures that support multitasking are:

1. TSS.
2. TSS descriptor.
3. Task register (TR).
4. Task gate descriptor.

With these structures, the 80386 can rapidly switch execution from one task to another, saving the context of the original task so that the task can be restarted later. These registers and data structures will be discussed in the following subsections.

6.3.1 Task State Segment

As described earlier, TSS defines the state of execution environment for a task. The format of TSS is as shown in Fig. 1. Right-hand numbers in hexadecimal show the offset address of particular fields in the TSS. The fields of TSS can be categorised mainly as dynamic fields and static fields.

Dynamic fields are updated by processor 80386 prior to every task switch. The field contains state of eight general-purpose registers (32 bits each), six segment selectors (16 bits each), EFLAGS register and instruction pointer (32 bits each). All these registers are user accessible. It also contains previous task link field. This is used by the 80386 processor to keep track of a task chain.

The back link field contains the segment selector for the TSS of the previous task. As the name suggests, this allows a task switch back to the previous task by using the IRET instruction.

TSS also includes images of some system registers like control register 3 (CR3), that is page directory base register. Here, presence of image of CR3 indicates that the page directory and all other page related information is different per task.

The selector of the task's LDT changes whenever a task switch takes place. The static set includes pointers to the stacks for privilege levels 0–2. Use of separate stacks for each privilege level provides extra protection among tasks at different privilege levels. These stack pointers consist of a logical address made up of the segment selector for the stack segment (SS0, SS1 and SS2) and an offset into the stack (ESP0, ESP1 and ESP2).

The T-bit (task switch trap bit at byte 100, bit 0) causes the processor to enable or disable the task switch trap.

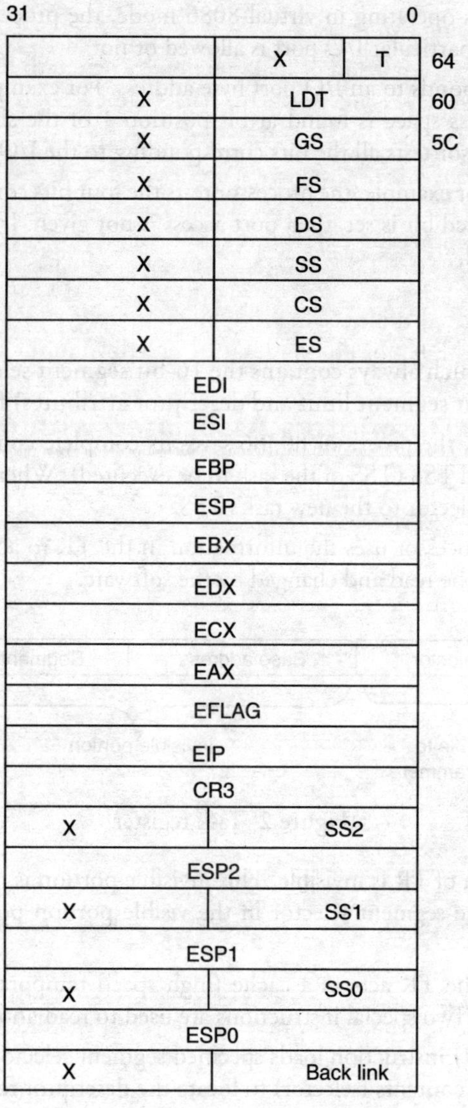

31	0	
X	T	64
X	LDT	60
X	GS	5C
X	FS	
X	DS	
X	SS	
X	CS	
X	ES	
EDI		
ESI		
EBP		
ESP		
EBX		
EDX		
ECX		
EAX		
EFLAG		
EIP		
CR3		
X	SS2	
ESP2		
X	SS1	
ESP1		
X	SS0	
ESP0		
X	Back link	

Figure 1 Task state segment.

6.3.2 I/O Map Base Address Field

It is a special input/output (I/O) protection mechanism for permitting limited access to I/O ports by less privileged programs or tasks and for tasks operating in virtual-8086 mode for the currently running task or program.

This field contains a 16-bit offset from the base of the TSS to the I/O permission bitmap and interrupts redirection bitmap. These maps may be stored in the TSS at higher addresses. The I/O map base address points to the beginning of the I/O permission bitmap and the end of the interrupt redirection bitmap.

Since every task has its own TSS, each task has its own I/O permission bitmap. This allows access to individual I/O ports which may be granted to individual tasks. In protected mode, the CPL is less than or equal to the current IOPL, the processor permits all I/O operations to proceed. If the CPL is greater than the IOPL or if the processor is operating in virtual-8086 mode, the processor checks the I/O permission bitmap to decide if access to a particular I/O port is allowed or not.

Each bit in the map corresponds to an I/O port byte address. For example, the control bit for I/O port address 30H in the I/O address space is found at bit position 1 of the sixth byte in the bitmap. Before granting I/O access, the processor tests all the bits corresponding to the I/O port being addressed.

For a double word access, for example, the processor tests the four bits corresponding to the four adjacent 8-bit port addresses. If any tested bit is set, then port access is not given. If all tested bits are clear, the I/O operation is allowed to proceed.

6.3.3 Task Register

The TR is a system register which always contains the 16-bit segment selector and the segment descriptor (32-bit base address, 16-bit segment limit and descriptor attributes) for the TSS of the current task.

When a task switch occurs, the processor 80386 saves its complete context in TSS. Then it loads new context from the newly selected TSS (TSS of the task to be executed). When new task is to be executed, the processor updates TR with a selector to the new task's TSS.

Figure 2 shows how the processor uses the information in the TR to access the TSS. The TR's selector part is a visible part which can be read and changed by the software.

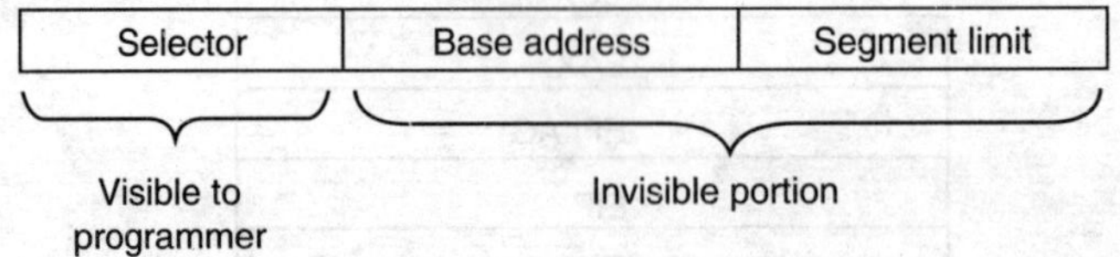

Figure 2 Task register.

Segment descriptor portion of TR is invisible. This invisible portion is maintained by the processor and is inaccessible by software. The segment selector in the visible portion points to a TSS descriptor in the global descriptor table.

The invisible portion of the TR acts as a cache (high speed temporary storage) so as to have more efficient execution of the task. Two special instructions are used to read and write the TR.

The load task register (LTR) instruction loads specified segment selector into visible portion of the TR. In turn, the processor uses TR contents (selector) to locate the descriptor for the TSS in the GDT.

LTR is a privileged instruction which can be executed only when the CPL is 0. LTR is used to initialize the TR. LTR instruction is commonly used in initialization code to establish the first task to be executed. Later, the contents of the TR are changed whenever a task switch occurs.

The STR (store task register) instruction stores the segment selector from the TR in the destination operand. The destination operand can be a general-purpose register or a memory location. The segment selector stored with this instruction points to the TSS for the currently running task. The STR instruction can only be used in protected mode, but it can be used at any privilege level.

6.3.4 TSS Descriptor

As the name suggests, TSS descriptor defines the memory area, that is segment, where the TSS is residing. The TSS may appear only in GDT and never in LDT or IDT. Figure 3 shows the format of a TSS descriptor.

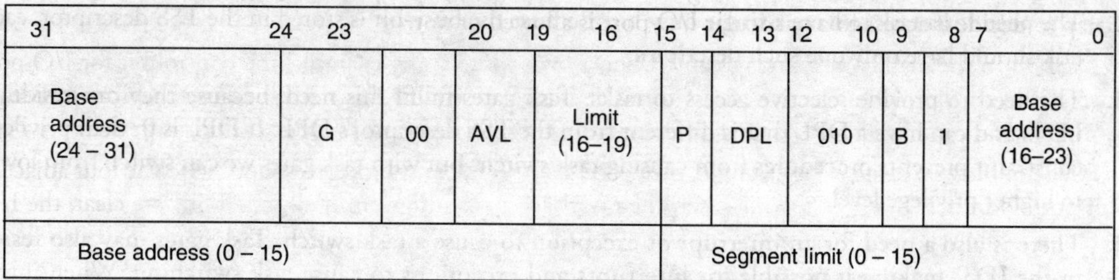

Figure 3 TSS descriptor.

The TSS descriptor is very much similar to any other segment descriptor. It contains base address, access right byte and limit fields. The base address determines the starting address of the TSS. It should point to writable memory segment. The limit field decides the size of the TSS. When the G flag is 0 in a TSS descriptor for a 32-bit TSS, minimum 104 bytes are required to save the state of a task. So the limit field must be greater than or equal to 67H value. Maximum value can be 4 GB.

An attempt to switch to a task whose TSS descriptor has a limit less than 67H generates an invalid TSS exception (#TS). Rests of the fields are as follows:

1. **AVL:** Available for use by system software.
2. **B (busy flag):** The busy flag in the type field indicates whether the task is busy. A busy task may be currently running or suspended. A type field containing a value of 1001B indicates that the task is inactive whereas a value of 1011B indicates a busy task. An attempt to call a task whose execution has been interrupted sets the busy flag. There is always only one busy flag associated with a task and so each TSS has only one TSS descriptor which points to it.
3. **DPL (descriptor privilege level):** Here DPL field does not directly indicate the privilege level of the TSS itself; rather TSS are not accessible to any programs. DPL field here determines what software can refer the task defined by the current TSS descriptor.

   A procedure that has access to a TSS descriptor can cause a task switch. In most systems, the DPL fields of TSS descriptors should be set to zero, so that only trusted software has the right to perform task switching.
4. **P (segment present):** Whenever P bit is high it indicates that the descriptor must be present.
5. **G** (Granularity bit).

6.3.5 Task Gate Descriptor

A task gate descriptor gives the information regarding the privilege level of the task through the 2 DPL bits. Figure 4 shows the format of a task gate. The task gate contains a selector to a TSS of new task and even the access right byte. The value of the RPL in this selector is not used by the processor.

The DPL field of a task gate controls the right to use the descriptor to cause a task switch. A procedure may not select a task gate descriptor unless the maximum of the selector's RPL and the CPL of the procedure is numerically less than or equal to the DPL of the descriptor. This constraint prevents untrusted procedures from causing a task switch. The 80386 has task gates in addition to TSS descriptors to satisfy the following three needs:

1. The need for a task to have a single busy bit. Because the busy-bit is stored in the TSS descriptor, each task should have only one such descriptor.
2. The need to provide selective access to tasks. Task gates fullfil this need, because they can reside in LDTs and can have a DPL that is different from the TSS descriptor's DPL. If DPL is 0, then privilege constraint prevents procedures from causing task switch. But with task gates we can switch from lower to higher privilege level.
3. There is also a need for an interrupt or exception to cause a task switch. Task gates may also reside in the IDT, making it possible for interrupts and exceptions to cause task switching. When interrupt or exception vectors to an IDT entry that contains a task gate, the 80386 switches to the indicated task.

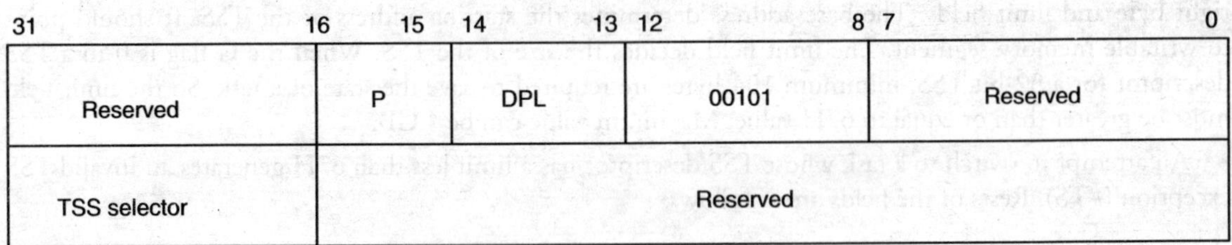

Figure 4 Task gate descriptor.

6.4 Task Switching

The 80386 switches from one task to another task in any of the following four different conditions:

1. The current task executes a JMP or CALL that refers to a TSS descriptor.
2. The current task executes a JMP or CALL that refers to a task gate.
3. An interrupt or exception vectors to a task gate in the IDT.
4. The current task executes an IRET when the NT flag is set.

Returning from a task is achieved by the IRET instruction. Control goes back to the interrupted task after the execution of IRET instruction. The state of current is saved in TSS and the old task state is restored from its TSS.

The NT (nested task) bit of EFLAG register controls the function of IRET instruction:

1. If NT = 0, IRET instruction performs regular return.
2. If NT = 1, IRET instruction performs a task switch operation back to the previous task.

Figure 5 shows a task switch operation without task gate. Following are the steps involved in task switching:

1. **Privilege check:** The current task status is verified to check whether it is permitted to switch to the designated task. Data-access privilege rules apply in the case of JMP or CALL instructions. It can be obtained if the DPL of the TSS descriptor or task gate is less than or equal to the maximum of CPL and the RPL of the gate selector [i.e., max(CPL, RPL) ≤ TSS descriptor DPL].
2. **Limit and present bit checking:** The TSS descriptor of the new task is marked presentand has a valid limit. Any errors up to this point occur in reference of the outgoing task.

3. **Saving the state of the current task:** The processor finds the base address of the current TSS cached in the TR. It then copies the registers into the current TSS (EAX, ECX, EDX, EBX, ESP, EBP, ESI, EDI, ES, CS, SS, DS, FS, GS, and the flag register):
   - The EIP field of the TSS points to the instruction after the instruction that caused the task switch.
   - The selector for the current task is saved as a back link selector in the new task.
4. **Loading the TR:** The visible portion of the TR is loaded with the selector of the designated task's TSS descriptor. The B bit in the new task descriptor is marked busy. An active task in indicated by setting the TS bit in the machine status word. The state information from the new task's TSS is loaded into the processor.
5. **Resuming execution:** While performing it, the selector of the old TSS is saved as the back link selector in the new TSS.

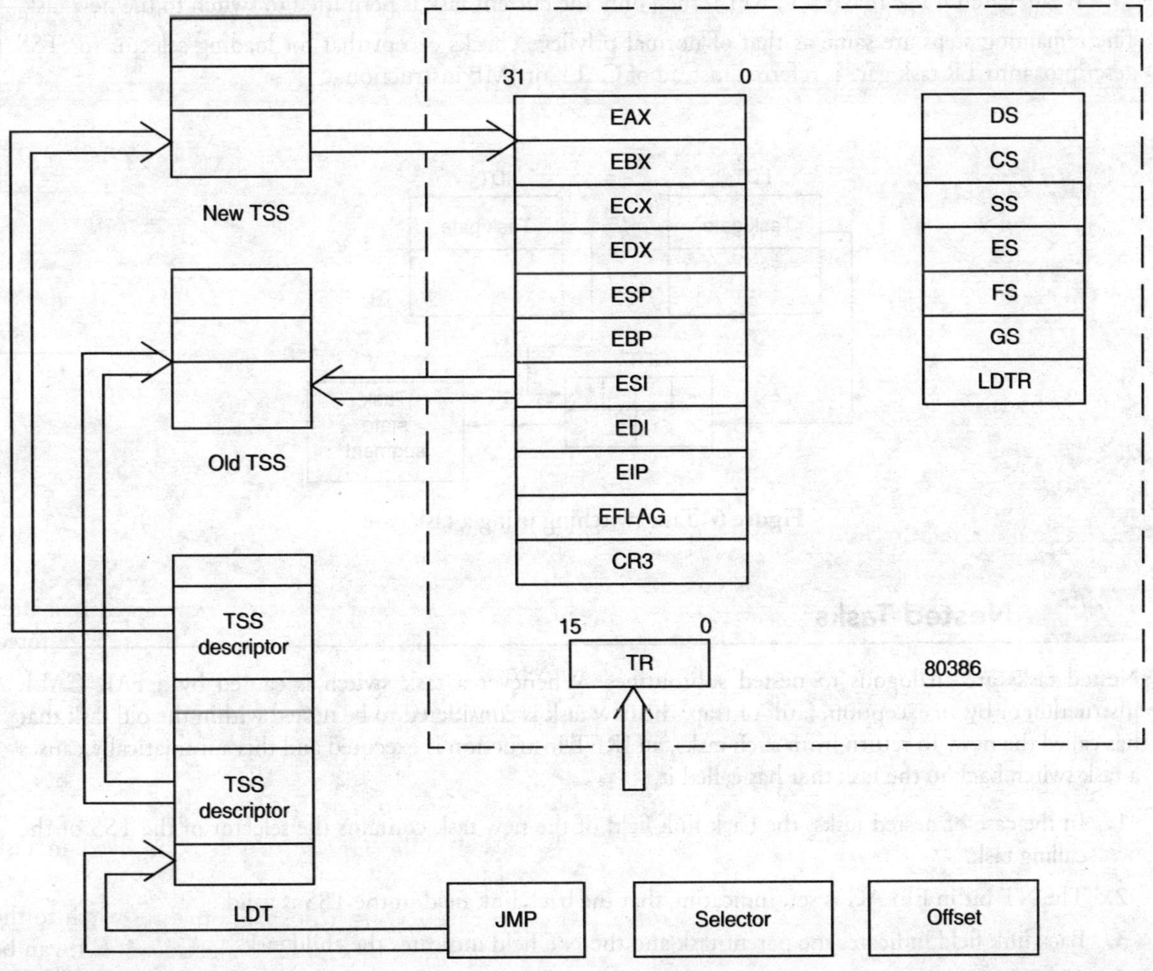

Figure 5 Task switching operation without task gate.

In this way, task switching operation takes place and execution resumes with the instruction identified by the new contents of the code segment selector and instruction pointer.

When return instruction is executed at the end of new task, the back link selector for the old TSS is automatically reloaded into the TR. This activates the old TSS and gets the prior conditions to resume the program at the point where it is left off in the old task. In this way the task switching and return operations take place.

6.4.1 Task Switching with Task Gate

Figure 6 shows task switching through a task gate. Here task switching is done through indirect method.

1. The DPL of new TSS descriptor is not used for privilege checking when a task is used.
2. The DPL of the task gate is compared with the CPL and RPL of the gate selector.
3. If task gate DPL ≥ max(CPL, RPL), then only the current task is permitted to switch to the new task.

The remaining steps are same as that of normal privilege checks except that for loading selector for TSS descriptor into TR task gate is referred instead of CALL or JMP instruction.

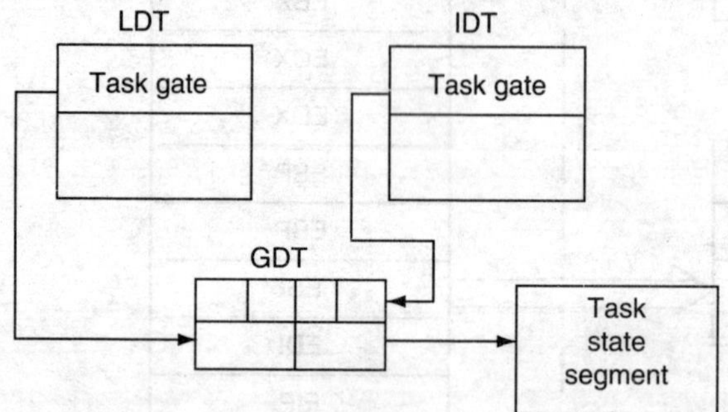

Figure 6 Task switching using a task gate.

6.5 Nested Tasks

Nested tasks are analogous to nested subroutines. Whenever a task switch is caused by a FAR CALL instruction or by an exception, fault or trap, the new task is considered to be nested within the old task that has called the new. To return from such tasks, an IRET instruction is executed and this automatically causes a task switch back to the task that has called it.

1. In the case of nested tasks, the back link field of the new task contains the selector of the TSS of the calling task.
2. The NT bit in EFLAG is set, indicating that the back link field in the TSS is valid.
3. Back link field indicates the parent task and the NT field indicates the child task.
4. To nest the tasks CALL instruction is used and not the JMP instruction.
5. IRET instruction is used to remove the nesting effect on the tasks.

6.6 I/O Permission Bitmap

There are two ways to achieve an I/O protection:

1. I/O privilege level.
2. I/O permission bitmap.

These will be discussed in the following subsections.

6.6.1 I/O Privilege Level

The IOPL field of flag register of 80386 is two-bit long.

1. The I/O instructions that directly refer to addresses in the processor's I/O space are IN, INS, OUT, OUTS.
2. These instructions are sensitive to IOPL field.
3. The condition necessary to execute these instructions is CPL <= IOPL.
4. Each task has its own EFLAG register and so can have its own IOPL. IOPL can be changed only if code is at PL0, else exception 13 is generated.

6.6.2 I/O Permission Bitmap

This method makes use of permission bits of I/O bitmap to provide I/O protection.

1. I/O permission bitmap is present on the top of the TSS. The size of the map and its location in the TSS is not fixed.
2. If the I/O permission check fails then the processor refers to the I/O permission bitmap which if 0 then the I/O instruction referring to I/O address is allowed and if 1 then it is not allowed.
3. If an instruction referring this address is executed, a general protection fault is generated.
4. The beginning of the I/O permission bitmap is identified by the 16-bit I/O map base offset.
5. The LIMIT field in the TSS descriptor sets the maximum length of the bitmap. The I/O permission bitmap is as shown in Fig. 7.
6. Each bit in the map corresponds to an I/O port address. The bit position of the I/O port 0 (I/O address: 0000H) is the LSB at the address given by the base offset. The base offset for I/O ports 0 to 31 are as shown in Fig. 7. The I/O ports address FFFFH indicates the last bit. This bit is the MSB of the double word located at offset equal to (1FFCH + BASE).
7. Restrictions can be put on I/O operations to each I/O port address of the 80386 processor with the help of bitmap.
8. In protected mode, the bit for the I/O port in the I/O permission bitmap is checked only if the CPL of the I/O instruction has less privileged than the IOPL. I/O operation can be performed to a particular port address only when the corresponding bit position of that port address in bitmap is zero. Logic one will not allow the I/O operation.
9. General protection exception will result if we try to perform any I/O operation using a port with 1 in I/O permission bitmap by a code having CPL less privileged than IOPL.

10. Any bitmap position that is located beyond the limit of the TSS is recognized at logic 1.
11. The bit positions that are located within the table are all made zero to permit I/O access to their corresponding ports.
12. I/O operations can be protected in the system by setting the bitmap base address value greater than the TSS limit.

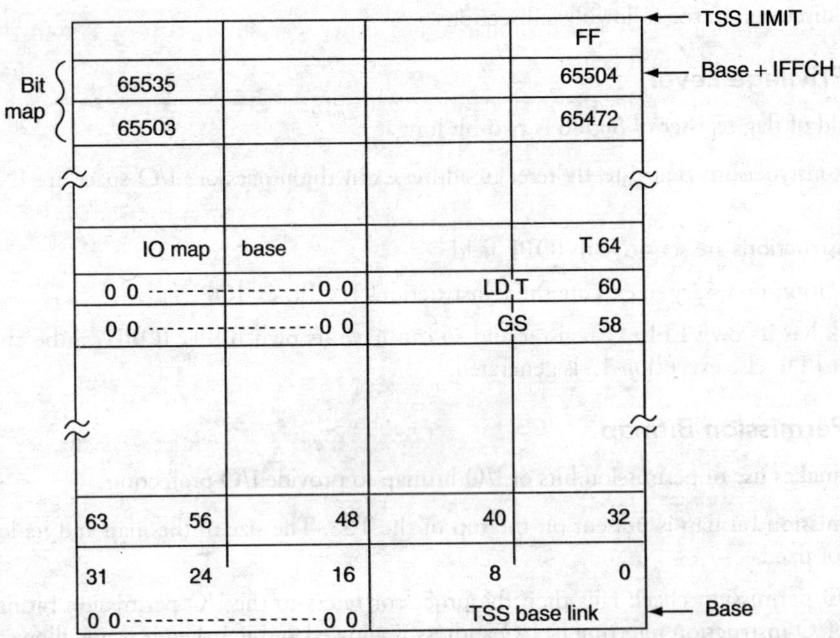

Figure 7 I/O permission bitmap.

Summary

- The processor 80386 activates multitasking feature only when it operates in protected mode.
- Multitasking is basically a timesharing method by which multiple tasks (processes) share common processing resources such as a microprocessor.
- Multitasking refers to the ability of the operating system to run multiple tasks concurrently.
- Basic unit of work for a multitasking system is task. A task is a collection of program routines that performs a specific function.
- A processor can dispatch (submit), execute (run) and suspend (wait) a task. The task may have both global and local memory resources.
- Multitasking needs software as well as hardware support too.
- Processor 80386 facilitates task switching with some special system registers and descriptors.
- The registers and data structures that support multitasking are:

  - TSS.
  - TSS descriptor.
  - Task register.
  - Task gate descriptor.
- TSS descriptor defines the memory area, that is, segment where the TSS is residing.
- The TSS descriptor is very much similar to any other segment descriptor. It contains base address, access right byte and limit fields.
- A task gate descriptor gives the information regarding the privilege level of the task through the 2 DPL bits.
- The task gate contains a selector to a TSS of new task and even the access right byte.
- There are two ways to achieve an I/O protection:
  - I/O privilege level.
  - I/O permission bitmap.

Multiple-Choice Questions

1. What is the long form of TR in multitasking?

(a) Task register

(b) Test register

(c) Task risk

(d) Test risk

2. What is the size of task register?

(a) 8 bit

(b) 16 bit

(c) 32 bit

(d) 64 bit

3. What is the long form of TSS in multitasking?

(a) TSS

(b) Task switch segment

(c) Task selector segment

(d) Test state segment

4. What is the size of T bit of TSS in multitasking?

(a) 1 bit

(b) 2 bit

(c) 3 bit

(d) 4 bit

5. What is the basic unit of work for a multitasking system?
   (a) Test
   (b) Task
   (c) Trap
   (d) Byte
6. Multitasking is activated in which mode of processor 80386?
   (a) Real
   (b) Protected
   (c) Virtual
   (d) VM86
7. In multitasking where I/O permission bitmap is located?
   (a) At the bottom of the Task gate descriptor
   (b) At the bottom of the TSS
   (c) On the top of the TSS
   (d) On the top of Task gate descriptor
8. What is the condition necessary to execute I/O privilege instructions?
   (a) CPL <= IOPL
   (b) CPL => IOPL
   (c) DPL <= IOPL
   (d) RPL => IOPL
9. What is the size IOPL field?
   (a) 1-bit
   (b) 2-bit
   (c) 8-bit
   (d) 4-bit
10. Amongst given which is the privilege instruction?
   (a) TEST
   (b) ADC
   (c) IN
   (d) XLAT
11. Which bit of EFLAG register indicates the validity of the back link field in the TSS?
   (a) IOPL
   (b) AC
   (c) PF
   (d) NTw

12. The parent task and child tasks are indicated by which fields of the TSS?

(a) Black link field and NT field
(b) NT field and Black link field
(c) ESP and Back link field
(d) NT field and ESP

13. Which instruction is used to nest the tasks?

(a) JMP
(b) CALL
(c) RET
(d) JBE

14. What condition is needed to permit the current task to switch to the new task?

(a) Task Gate DPL >= max(CPL, RPL)
(b) Task Gate DPL <= max(CPL, RPL)
(c) Task Gate RPL >= max(CPL, DPL)
(d) Task Gate CPL >= max(DPL, RPL)

15. TSS descriptor appears in which descriptor table?

(a) GDT and LDT
(b) GDT
(c) LDT
(d) IDT

16. Which portion of the task register is visible?

(a) Selector
(b) Segment descriptor
(c) Selector and base address
(d) Selector and segment limit

17. Which portion of the task register is invisible?

(a) Selector
(b) Segment descriptor
(c) Selector and base address
(d) Selector and segment limit

18. Which control register is present in task state segment?

(a) CR0
(b) CR1
(c) CR2
(d) CR3

19. Which descriptor table is present in task state segment?

(a) GDT

(b) IDT

(c) LDT

(d) None of these

20. What is the meaning of 'T' field in task state segment?

(a) Trap flag

(b) Task switch trap

(c) Task register

(d) Test register

21. What is the size of segment limit in task state segment descriptor?

(a) 8 bit

(b) 16 bit

(c) 20 bit

(d) 32 bit

22. What is the size of segment base address in task state segment descriptor?

(a) 8 bit

(b) 16 bit

(c) 20 bit

(d) 32 bit

23. Which instruction is used to load the new TSS selector to the task register?

(a) STR

(b) LTR

(c) STD

(d) CLD

24. Which instruction is used to read the visible portion of the task register into memory or general-purpose register?

(a) STR

(b) LTR

(c) STD

(d) CLD

25. Amongst given which is a privilege instruction?

(a) LOOP

(b) XLAT

(c) TEST

(d) LTR

26. What must be the CPL at the time of execution of LTR instruction?

(a) 0

(b) 1

(c) 2

(d) 3

27. Which of the following instruction is used in protected mode only?

(a) AAA

(b) LTR

(c) STD

(d) CLD

28. Amongst given which is not a privilege instruction?

(a) STR

(b) HLT

(c) OUT

(d) LTR

29. What condition is needed to change the IOPL of any task?

(a) If code is at PL3

(b) If code is at PL2

(c) If code is at PL1

(d) If code is at PL0

30. The maximum length of the bitmap is set by which field of the TSS descriptor.

(a) AVL

(b) DPL

(c) Base address

(d) Limit field

Review Questions

1. Explain the process of Task switching and highlights of TSS.
2. What are the different methods to switch from one task to another task? Explain task switch operation in detail with suitable diagram.
3. What is Nested task? Explain. Explain significance of Back link Field.
4. Write short note onTask State Segment (TSS).

5. Give significance of busy bit.
6. How does I/O permission bit-map helps in accessing I/O devices?
7. What is the use of TSS in task switching? Explain the details of TSS?
8. What is the functional difference between TSS Descriptor and Task Gate Descriptor? Explain with respect to Multitasking.
9. What is a Task State Segment (TSS) and how it supports task switching? How does it compare with code, data segment? What is its size and contents? How is TSS accessed? Explain clearly indicating checks and its usage by 80386.
10. What is back link field of TSS? What is its offset in TSS?
11. How does 80386 performs a task switch? Explain the significance and format of the TSS descriptor and the TSS. How tasks are nested?
12. With the help of neat diagram explain the process of Task Switching?
13. What is task? How it is invoked? With the help of suitable descriptor formats, explain the process of task switching.
14. Explain:
    (a) Task register
    (b) Busy bit
    (c) NT bit
    (d) TS bit

Answers

Multiple-Choice Questions

1. (a)	**11.** (a)	**21.** (c)
2. (b)	**12.** (a)	**22.** (d)
3. (a)	**13.** (b)	**23.** (b)
4. (a)	**14.** (a)	**24.** (a)
5. (b)	**15.** (b)	**25.** (d)
6. (b)	**16.** (a)	**26.** (a)
7. (c)	**17.** (b)	**27.** (b)
8. (a)	**18.** (d)	**28.** (a)
9. (b)	**19.** (c)	**29.** (d)
10. (c)	**20.** (b)	**30.** (d)

UNIT IV

Interrupts

7 Virtual Mode Operation

LEARNING OBJECTIVES

After reading this chapter, you will be able to understand:

- Features of virtual mode.
- Virtual 8086 tasks.
- Address generation and memory management in virtual 8086 mode.
- Virtual mode registers.
- Entering and leaving V86 mode.

7.1 Introduction

The 8086/8088 processor was commercially introduced in 1981. Since then they have been widely accepted and used in personal computers throughout the world. Consequently, a large amount of software have been developed to operate on 8086/8088-based machines running on MS-DOS or its variations. So after the release of 80286 in 1983, it was not possible to shift all the 8086-based applications to the new environment immediately. The 80286 lacked in providing complete compatibility with 8086 in its protected environment especially in the operating system software support required to support 8086-based applications. For this reason, the 80386 processor has a separate 8086 compatibility mode which is referred as virtual 8086 mode or VM86 or simply V86 mode.

The 80386 processor supports execution of one or more 8086/8088 programs in protected- mode environment. An 8086 program runs in this environment as a part of a V86 (virtual 8086) task. V86 tasks take the advantage of the hardware support for multitasking and multiprogramming offered by the protected mode. A V86 task forms a "virtual machine" with which it executes the 8086 program. A complete virtual machine consists of not only 80386 processor hardware but also the systems software. Thus, the emulation of an 8086 is the result of cooperation between hardware and software.

1. The hardware provides a virtual set of registers [via the Task State Segment (TSS)], a virtual memory space (the first megabyte of the linear address space of the task), and can directly execute all the instructions that handle these registers and this address space.
2. The software controls the external interfaces of the virtual machine, for example, input/output (I/O), interrupts, and exceptions. In the case of I/O, software can either emulate I/O instructions or the hardware directly executes them without any software intervention. The software that implements virtual 8086 machines is known as a V86 monitor.

7.2 Features of Virtual Mode

1. The 80386 processor can enter in virtual 8086 mode by setting VM bit in EFLAGS register.
2. Register architecture is the same as that of real mode.
3. In virtual 8086 mode, the segmentation hardware is practically turned OFF and the segment registers are treated in the same manner as in the real mode. Still paging can be available which makes multi-tasking support possible.
4. All segments are of fixed size, 64 KB.
5. Address calculation is similar to the real-mode addressing method. The contents of the segment register are shifted to left by 4 bits and added to the offset to form the segment base linear address.
6. The 80386 processor reserves the first 1 MB plus 64 KB (for monitor program) of each task's linear address space for the 8086 program. An 8086 processor task cannot generate addresses outside this range.
7. For handling interrupts and exceptions, the 80386 processor switches back to the protected mode environment.
8. In virtual mode, effective privilege level is always 3.
9. Only 8086 addressing modes are available.
10. The 80386 processor can return only to protected mode or RESET state and not to the real mode from virtual 8086 mode.

7.3 Virtual 8086 Tasks

As 80386 processor emulation of 8086 processor is task oriented, it is important to understand the structure of virtual 8086 mode task:

1. A virtual 8086 mode task consists of the following components:
   - A 32-bit TSS for the task.
   - The 8086 program.
   - A virtual 8086 monitor.
   - 8086 operating-system services.
2. Even though the 8086 program is a 16-bit structure, the TSS of the virtual 8086 mode must be a 32-bit TSS and not a 16-bit TSS. The reason is that the 16-bit TSS cannot task load the most significant word of the EFLAGS register, which contains the VM flag.
3. The processor enters virtual 8086 mode to run the 8086 program and returns to the protected mode to run the virtual 8086 monitor.
4. The virtual 8086 monitor is a 32-bit protected-mode program which runs at a privilege level 0. This monitor code consists of initialization, interrupt and exception handling, and I/O emulation procedures that emulate 8086-based system.
5. The code-segment descriptors for the virtual 8086 monitor must be existing in the global descriptor table (GDT) or in the task's local descriptor table (LDT) like any other protected mode task.

6. The linear addresses above 10FFEFH are available for the monitor, the operating system and other system software.
7. 8086 operating system services can be emulated in the virtual 8086 monitor.

7.4 Address Generation and Memory Management in Virtual 8086 Mode

As mentioned in Section 7.2, the address calculation is similar to the real mode addressing. Contents of the segment register are shifted 4 bits to the left and added to the offset to form the segment base linear address. Use of the paging mechanism permits one megabyte address space of the virtual mode task mapped to anywhere in the 4 GB linear address space of the 80386 processor. In virtual mode, segment registers are not treated as selector. All segments are 64 KB long. One can use two additional segments FS and GS by explicitly requesting use of segment overrides. Descriptors and descriptors tables are not used at all.

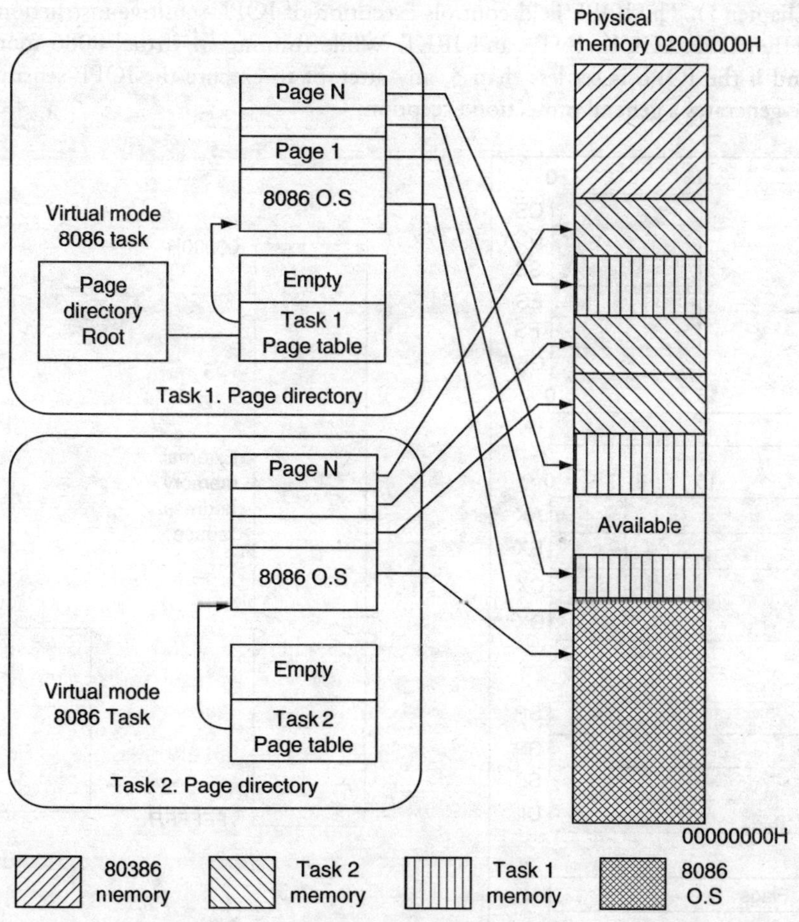

Figure 1 Memory management for virtual 8086 mode.

The concurrent running of multiple virtual mode tasks is possible due to the paging hardware. It also provides protection and operating system isolation. The paging allows the 20-bit linear address generated by a virtual mode program to be divided into 256 pages. Each one of the pages can be located anywhere within the maximum 4 GB physical address space of the 80386 processor. Figure 1 shows memory management for virtual 8086 mode.

7.5 Virtual 8086 Mode Registers

Figure 2 shows the registers available in virtual 8086 mode. Some of their features are as follows:

1. All general-purpose registers are available as 32-bit size giving both read and write access.
2. All segment registers are available. Since GS and FS are not default registers for 8086, they can be used with segment override prefixes.
3. The original 8086's flag register did not define bits 12, 13, 14, 15. For 80386 processor, EFLAG's bits 12 and 13 are IOPL field. Bit 14 is NT flag. Bit 15 is still undefined and holds 0 (refer to EFLAGS figure in Chapter 1). The IOPL field controls execution of IOPL-sensitive instructions such as CLI, STI, PUSHF, POPF, LOCK, INTn and IRET. While running in virtual 8086 mode, the CPL is always 3 and if the IOPL is set less than 3, any attempt to execute the IOPL-sensitive instructions listed above generates a general protection exception.

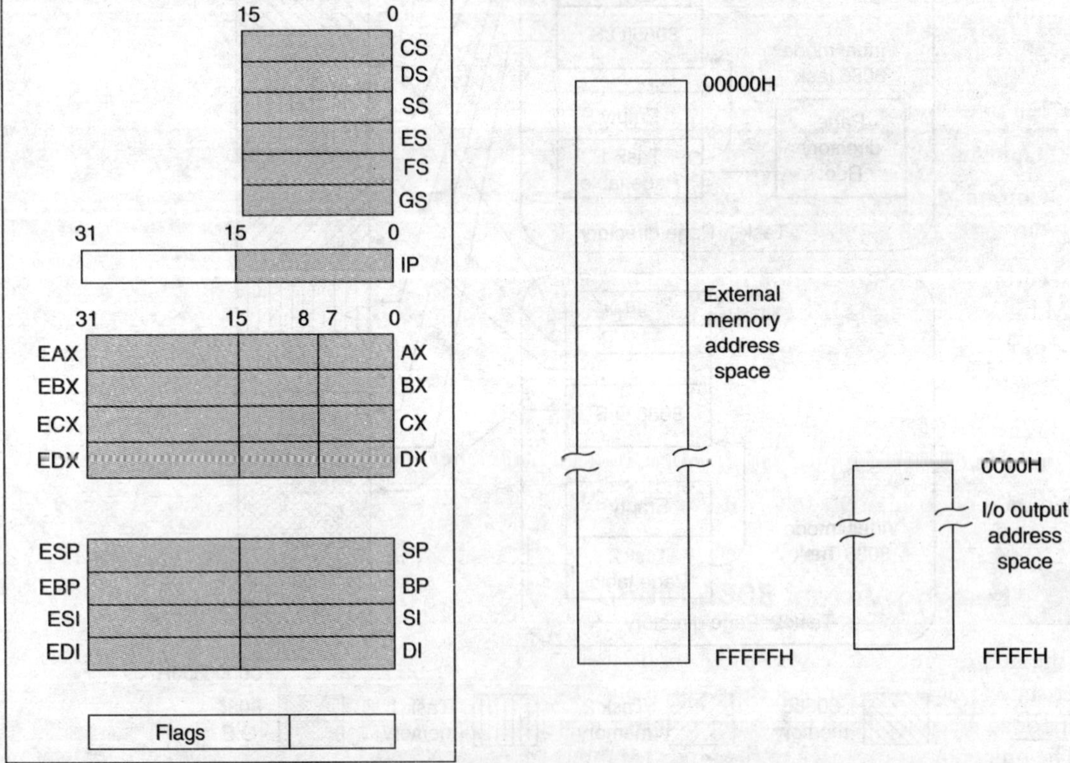

Figure 2 Programmer's model of 80386 in virtual mode.

4. GDTR, IDTR and control registers are available for store purpose and load access is not allowed.
5. Task register, LDTR, debug and rest registers are not accessible.

7.6 Entering in Virtual 8086 Mode

Basically, when the virtual mode (VM bit 17) bit in the EFLAGS register is set to 1 and the processor is executing a code at privilege level 0, the processor enters in virtual 8086 mode. But it is not that easy as it appears to be. A normal PUSHF followed by POPF cannot manipulate the VM flag even in the protected mode. There are two ways to alter VM flag – either a task switch or execution of IRET instruction. So 80386 processor can enter in virtual 8086 mode by means of two possible methods which are discussed as follows:

1. **Task switch method:** Task switch method is a preferred method since this can be done at any privilege level and is discussed as follows:
   - CALL or JMP instruction can be used for task switch.
   - Create a TSS such that VM bit in EFLAGS register's image (byte offset in TSS 36, bit offset 17) is set to 1.
   - Whenever the 80386 processor is switched to this task by means of CALL/JMP and it finds that the VM bit is set, it loads all segment registers from the image in the TSS, treats all addresses and instructions such as 8086 processor.
   - This should use a 32-bit 80386 TSS descriptor.
   - It uses all 32-bit registers as EAX-EDX, ESI-ESP.
   - ESP0 must point to the valid protected mode PL0 stack segment.
   - Though virtual 8086 mode task does not use descriptor table, still LDT is expected to be initialized.
   - Control register 3 (CR3) is loaded with the physical address of the base of the concerned page directory. This happens when the 80386 processor invokes a virtual 8086 mode task.
2. **Executing IRET instruction in protected mode task running at privilege level 0:** One way to set the VM bit is by executing IRET instruction at privilege level 0 and is discussed as follows:
   - EFLAGS contents with VM = 1 should be stored in a temporary register and then pushed on the stack.
   - When IRET is executed after return address, EFLAGS is immediately retrieved and if VM = 1, this may forcibly transit processor from the protected mode to virtual 8086 mode.

This method is not commonly followed but is suitable when multitasking is not used.

7.7 Leaving Virtual 8086 Mode

When the 80386 processor leaves virtual mode it has to either switch back in protected mode or enter in Reset state. The 80386 processor can come out of virtual 8086 mode only upon the occurrence of an interrupt or an exception. This may happen due to an attempt to execute IOPL-sensitive instruction such as HLT. The processor returns back to the protected mode to service the interrupt/exception.

When RESET pin is asserted, it is a special kind of interrupt. So the processor leaves virtual 8086 mode and enters real address mode.

Summary

- Virtual mode is used to execute 8086 based application programs in protected environment.
- Virtual 8086 mode works on tasks basis.
- Two methods are available for switching to and from virtual 8086 mode, which includes task switching and execution of IRET instruction.

Interrupt handling in virtual 8086 mode is discussed in Chapter 8.

Multiple-Choice Questions

1. Virtual mode of the 80386 is meant for executing task for the ______ processor.
(a) 8086
(b) 80186
(c) 80286
(d) 80386

2. Segment size in the virtual mode is ______.
(a) 64 MB
(b) 64 KB
(c) 1 MB
(d) 4 GB

3. A virtual task has surely a ______ descriptor.
(a) Task gate
(b) TSS
(c) Segment
(d) None of the given

4. The 80386 processor enters in the virtual mode from ______.
(a) Any mode
(b) Real mode only
(c) Protected mode only
(d) RESET state

5. A virtual mode task cannot execute ______ to a 32 bit 80386 procedure.
   (a) Far call
   (b) Near call
   (c) Far Jmp
   (d) All of the above
6. A POPF instruction cannot affect ______ bit of EFLAGS in virtual mode.
   (a) VM bit
   (b) RF bit
   (c) TF bit
   (d) DF bit
7. Which of the segments are available in virtual 8086 mode ?
   (a) CS, DS, SS, ES
   (b) CS, DS, SS
   (c) FS, GS
   (d) CS, DS, SS, ES, GS, FS
8. Virtual mode executes an 8086 task in the protected environment. (True/False)
   (a) True
   (b) False
9. In virtual mode, all segments created are equal. (True/False)
   (a) True
   (b) False
10. In virtual mode segment size is fixed.
    (a) True
    (b) False
11. In virtual mode descriptors and descriptor tables are used. (True/False)
    (a) True
    (b) False
12. In virtual mode segment registers hold selectors. (True/False)
    (a) True
    (b) False
13. Which of following registers are not available in virtual 8086 modes:
    (a) Task register
    (b) Debug registers
    (c) Test registers
    (d) All of the above

14. In virtual mode, general registers are of ______ size.

(a) 8 bits

(b) 16 bits

(c) 32 bits

(d) 64 bits

15. In virtual mode memory addresses are of ______ bits.

(a) 16 bits

(b) 20 bits

(c) 32 bits

(d) 64 bits

16. In virtual mode, memory address is of

(a) 64 KB

(b) 4 GB

(c) 1 MB

(d) 1 MB plus 64 KB

17. Total memory requirement in virtual mode by each task is

(a) 64 KB

(b) 4 GB

(c) 1 MB

(d) 1 MB plus 64 KB

18. In virtual 8086 task can reside ______ in total 4 GB memory.

(a) At the lower 1 MB

(b) Anywhere in 4 GB

(c) Anywhere in 4 GB but within 1 MB

(d) None of the above

19. Virtual mode programs are executed at privilege level

(a) 0

(b) 1

(c) 2

(d) 3

20. Virtual mode cannot avail which feature of the protected mode?

(a) Multitasking

(b) Segmentation

(c) Paging

(d) Use of 32 bit registers

21. Which of the instruction cannot be used to enter into virtual 8086 mode?
   (a) CALL
   (b) JMP
   (c) IRET
   (d) ENTER
22. Which of the following registers are not required to be initialized but still can be used in virtual mode?
   (a) CS, DS, SS,ES
   (b) GS , FS
   (c) LDTR
   (d) EIP
23. 80386 processor cannot switch to ______ from virtual mode.
   (a) Real Mode
   (b) Protected
   (c) RESET state
   (d) Another virtual mode task
24. Number of copies of MS DOS in virtual mode with n task is/are
   (a) 0
   (b) 1
   (c) 2
   (d) n
25. Interrupt generated in virtual 8086 mode has to be processed in
   (a) Real mode
   (b) Protected mode
   (c) Virtual 8086 mode
   (d) All of the given modes
26. Virtual mode cannot avail which of the following features of the protected mode?
   (a) Multitasking
   (b) Address pipelining
   (c) Paging
   (d) Use of 32 bit registers

Review Questions

1. What is V86 mode? Explain in detail.
2. The 80386 processor is operating in V86 mode. How does it react to an interrupt?

3. Explain the process by which 80386 processor can enter and leave V86 mode?
4. How to switch from real mode to V86 mode? Explain in detail.
5. Explain memory address calculations for virtual or V86 mode.
6. What are the registers available in virtual 8086 mode? Justify.

Answers

Multiple-Choice Questions

1. (a)	**10.** (a)	**19.** (d)
2. (b)	**11.** (b)	**20.** (b)
3. (d)	**12.** (b)	**21.** (d)
4. (c)	**13.** (d)	**22.** (b)
5. (d)	**14.** (c)	**23.** (a)
6. (a)	**15.** (c)	**24.** (d)
7. (d)	**16.** (c)	**25.** (b)
8. (a)	**17.** (d)	**26.** (b)
9. (a)	**18.** (c)	

8 Interrupt and Exception Processing

LEARNING OBJECTIVES

After reading this chapter, you will be able to:

- Classify interrupts and exceptions.
- Decide interrupt and exception priorities.
- Understand handling interrupts and exceptions in the real mode.
- Understand handling interrupts and exceptions in the protected mode.
- Understand handling interrupts and exceptions in the virtual 8086 mode.
- Compare all the three modes.
- Understand the working of Core Duo processors.

8.1 Introduction

Normal operation of a processor may be interrupted due to any of the following situations:

1. An application program requesting for I/O service.
2. Any critical condition occurring due to an external hardware.
3. The processor itself detects an emergency condition.

These situations are called *interrupts*. As a response to an interrupt, the processor suspends its current activity and services to the input/output (I/O) and sends a request to the external hardware in order to resolve the critical situation. For detecting external requests/critical situations (refer to Chapter 3, Section 3.1.1), 80386 has the ability to handle up to 256 different interrupts/exceptions. So, to service the interrupts, a table with up to 256 interrupt vectors is provided by 80386 processor. The interrupt vectors are nothing but pointers to the appropriate interrupt service routine (ISR). When an interrupt occurs, the address of the ISR is fetched from the interrupt vector table (IVT). Thus IVT acts as a link between the actual interrupt and the interrupt service routine. Figure 1 shows the interrupt vector table.

8.2 Processing Interrupts

When an interrupt occurs, the processor executes an interrupt acknowledgment sequence. At the same time, ISR vector address is fetched from the table and then the following steps are taken by the processor:

1. First, the current program address and the flags are saved on the stack. So, while resuming the interrupted program, return address becomes available.

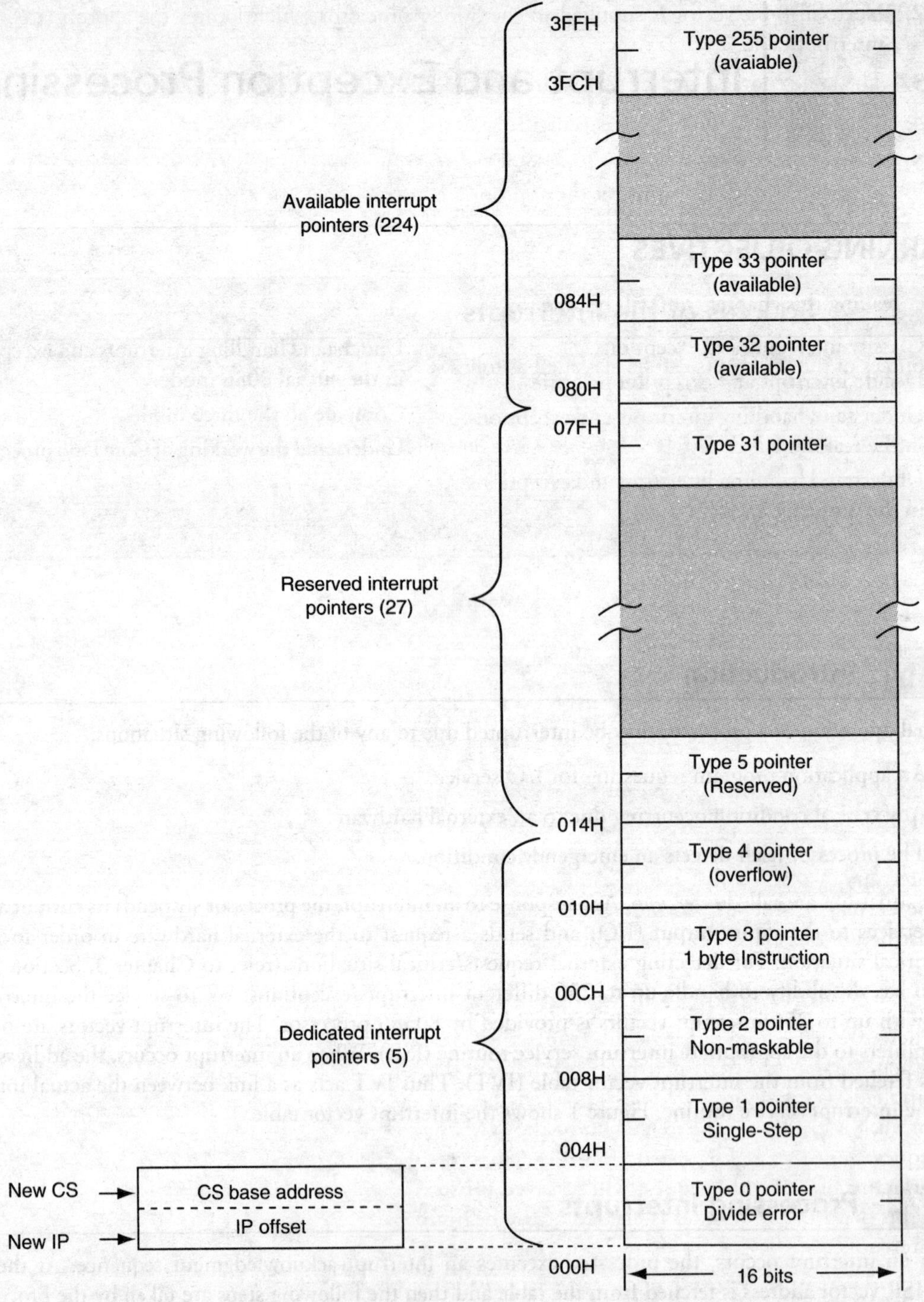

Figure 1 Interrupt vector table.

2. Next, an 8-bit vector is supplied to the 80386 processor which locates the appropriate entry in the interrupt table.
3. The table contains the starting address of the ISR. EIP points to this address.
4. Then, the concerned ISR is executed.
5. Finally, when an interrupt return (IRET) instruction is executed, the old processor state is restored and program execution resumes at the appropriate instruction.

8.3 Sources of the Interrupts

Sources of the interrupts can be classified as follows:

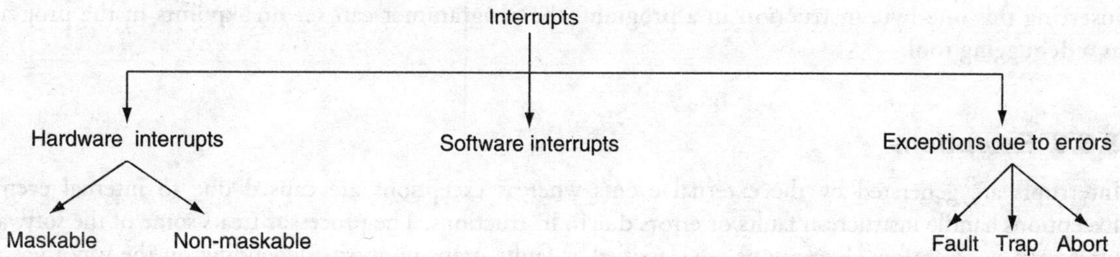

8.3.1 Hardware Interrupts

Hardware interrupt occurs as a result of an external event. As mentioned above, physical pins are provided on 80386 DX chip to detect the external asynchronous events. When certain logic level is detected on those pins, this indicates the occurrence of the interrupt. Two pins are available, INTR and non-maskable interrupt (NMI). When an interrupt occurs the control is transferred to the ISR after the execution of the current instruction, and after the servicing of the interrupt is over, execution is continued from the instruction immediately after the interrupted instruction.

8.3.1.1 Non-Maskable Interrupt

These are very high priority interrupts, for example, power failure, which just cannot be ignored. When NMI pin is activated high by the external hardware, it causes an interrupt with an internally supplied vector address of two. However, here, no interrupt acknowledgment sequence is performed for an NMI. During the execution of the NMI service routine, 80386 will not service any more NMI requests until an IRET instruction is executed or the processor is reset. If NMI occurs while currently servicing an NMI, the request will be saved for servicing after executing the first IRET instruction. The IF bit of EFLAGS register is cleared at the beginning of an NMI interrupt to hold back further INTR interrupts.

8.3.1.2 Maskable Interrupt

Hardware interrupt may also occur because of the events that are not much catastrophic. An example is, key pressed by the user. Such interrupts are maskable ones; this means that the response to this interrupt can be rejected. Maskable interrupts are the most common way used to respond to asynchronous external hardware events. When the INTR pin is pulled high, a hard ware interrupt is detected and the interrupt flag bit (IF) of EFLAGS register is enabled. When an interrupt occurs, the processor finds an 8-bit vector supplied by the hardware which identifies the source of the interrupt (one of 224 users defined interrupts). The IF bit in the EFLAG registers is reset when an ISR is being executed. This disables servicing any more interrupts during an ISR execution. Still, the IF bit can be set explicitly by the interrupt handler to allow the nesting of the interrupts. When an IRET instruction is executed, the original state of the IF is restored.

8.3.2 Software Interrupts

A program may generate a software interrupt using INT *n*, that is, a two-byte instruction. This leads the processor to execute the interrupt service routine pointed to by the *n*th vector in the interrupt table. A special case of this, INT 3, is the one-byte instruction which causes break-point interrupt. By inserting this one-byte instruction in a program, the programmer can set breakpoints in the program as a debugging tool.

8.3.3 Exceptions

Interrupts are generated by the external events whereas exceptions are caused due to internal events. Exceptions handle instruction faults or errors due to instructions. The processor treats some of the software interrupts as exceptions. Exceptions are classified as faults, traps or aborts depending on the way they are detected, and whether or not the restart of the instruction causing the exception is supported. Exceptions supply the interrupt vector internally.

1. Faults are exceptions that are detected and serviced before the execution of the faulting instruction. A fault may occur in a virtual memory system if the processor refers to a page or a segment which is not present in the main memory. The operating system may fetch the page or the segment from a secondary storage and then 80386 processor will restart the instruction.
2. Traps are exceptions which are reported immediately after the execution of the instruction which caused the problem. User-defined interrupts are examples of traps. Aborts are exceptions which do not permit the precise location of the instruction causing the exception to be determined. Typically, severe errors, such as a hardware error or illegal values in the system tables are reported by means of the aborts.

8.4 Exception and Interrupt Priorities

When NMI and maskable INTR are both detected at the same instruction boundary, first priority is given to the NMI service routine. Even after the NMI service routine has been invoked, if maskable interrupts are still enabled, then 80386 processor will invoke the appropriate ISR.

Assume that 80386 has just completed an instruction. It then performs the following checks before reaching the point where the next instruction is completed:

1. First check for exception 1: Traps from the instruction just completed (single-step via trap flag, or data breakpoints set in the debug registers).
2. Check for exception 1: Faults in the next instruction (instruction execution breakpoint set in the debug registers for the next instruction).
3. Check for external NMI and INTR.
4. Check for segmentation faults that prevented fetching the entire next instruction (exceptions 11 or 13).
5. Check for page faults that have prevented fetching the entire next instruction (exception 14).
6. Check for faults decoding the next instruction (exception 6) if illegal op code is in real mode or in virtual 8086 mode or attempt to execute an instruction for the protected mode only. Exception 13, in case instruction is longer than 15 bytes or privilege violation, is in the protected mode (i.e. not at IOPL or at CPL= 0).
7. If WAIT op code, check if TS =1 and MP =1 (exception 7 if both are 1).
8. If ESC op code for numeric co-processor, check if EM =1 or TS =1 (exception 7 if either is 1).
9. If WAIT op code or ESC op code for numeric co-processor, check ERROR #input signal (exception 16 if ERROR# input is asserted).
10. Check in the following order for each memory reference required by the instruction:
    - Check for segmentation faults that prevent transferring the entire memory quantity (exceptions 11, 12, 13).
    - Check for page faults that prevent transferring the entire memory quantity (exception 14).

This sequence of checking is repeated for every instruction being executed which means this checking is done in parallel with every instruction decoding and execution.

8.5 Handling Interrupts and Exceptions in Real Mode

80386 processor handles interrupts and exceptions in the same fashion as 8086 processor. It uses the IVT shown in Fig. 1 just like 8086. Handling of interrupts in real mode is discussed as follows:

1. The vector table contains 256 vector addresses of 4 byte each.
2. For real mode, the IVT occupies total 256 × 4 = 1024 bytes (1 KB) memory space starting from 0000 H to 03FF H.
3. The interrupts are identified by their types. The type value is multiplied by four to get the index address, that is, the location from where the processor gets the starting address of the ISR.
4. Each vector is of 4 bytes, that is, two words of 16-bit each. The higher word holds the segment base address of the ISR and lower word holds the offset in the segment.
5. Exception type 10, 11 and 14 from Table 1 are not supported in real mode.

Table 1 Types of Interrupts and Exceptions

Interrupt Number	*Function*	*Instruction Which May Cause Exception*	*Type*	*Whether Return Address Points to Instruction Causing Fault*	*Comments*
0	Divide error	DIV, IDIV	Fault	Yes	Generated if result of DIV/ IDIV instruction is too large to fit in the destination register.
1	Debug exception	Any instruction	Trap	Yes	Single-step interrupt occurs if Trap flag is set. Used for debugging.
2	Non-maskable interrupt	INT 2, NMI	NMI	No	Hardware interrupt cannot be disabled by any instruction.
3	Breakpoint interrupt	INT 3	Trap	No	Debugging tool, any number of break points can be inserted by the user.
4	Interrupt on overflow	INT 0	Trap	No	Checks overflow flag.
5	Array bounds check	Bound	Fault	Yes	Compares the contents of register with contents of memory location with specified range in the instruction.
6	Invalid op code	Any illegal instruction	Fault	Yes	Any illegal instruction can cause this interrupt.
7	Device not available	ESC, WAIT	Fault	Yes	EM/MP bit (in CR0) = 1 for any arithmetic co-processor instruction or TS BIT (in EFLAGS) = 1 for Task switch may raise this interrupt.

(Continued)

Table 1 (Continued)

Interrupt Number	*Function*	*Instruction Which May Cause Exception*	*Type*	*Whether Return Address Points to Instruction Causing Fault*	*Comments*
8	Double Fault	Any instruction that can generate exception	Abort	No	When the processor attempts to invoke an exception service routine for the segment exceptions, but at the same time detects an exception other than a page fault.
9	Co-processor segment over run				Not applicable for 80386.
10	Invalid TSS	JMP, CALL, INT, IRET	Fault	Yes	An attempt to access invalid TSS causes this exception.
11	Segment not present	Segment register instruction	Fault	Yes	If P bit in the descriptor = 0, then exception 11 is raised to indicate segment is not mapped in the main memory.
12	Stack fault	Any reference to stack	Fault	Yes	This fault occurs to indicate when stack operation causes limit violation.
13	General protection	Any reference to memory	Fault	Yes	Caused due to any one of the following reasons: 1. Violation of segment limit. 2. Write attempt to read only data segment. 3. Read attempt to execute only data segment. 4. Loading selector with system descriptor. 5. Switching to a busy task. 6. Violating privilege rules. 7. Leaving virtual mode with a wrong interrupt handler.

(Continued)

Table 1 (Continued)

Interrupt Number	*Function*	*Instruction Which May Cause Exception*	*Type*	*Whether Return Address Points to Instruction Causing Fault*	*Comments*
14	Page fault	Any memory access/code fetch	Fault	Yes	If PG bit (in CR0) = 1, and PDE contains 0 or incorrect PL.
15	Reserved by Intel			Yes	
16	Co-processor error	ESC, WAIT	Fault	Yes	Caused due to error from co-processor.
17–31	Reserved by Intel				
32–255	Two-byte interrupt	INT *n*	Trap	No	

8.6 Handling Interrupts and Exceptions in the Protected Mode

The protected mode uses the interrupt descriptor table (IDT) rather than the IVT (refer to Chapter 4, Section 4.2.3.3). Every interrupt is processed only through IDT. Handling of interrupts in the protected mode is discussed as follows:

1. The IDT consists of gate descriptors and not the interrupt vectors.
2. Each gate descriptor is of 8 bytes size.
3. IDT consists of 256 gate descriptors.
4. The table is relocatable.
5. The base address and size of the IDT is given by IDTR.
6. The process of retrieving the address of the segment containing ISR. is same as that of segmentation. Instead of GDT and GDTR, IDT and IDTR are used as shown in Fig. 2.

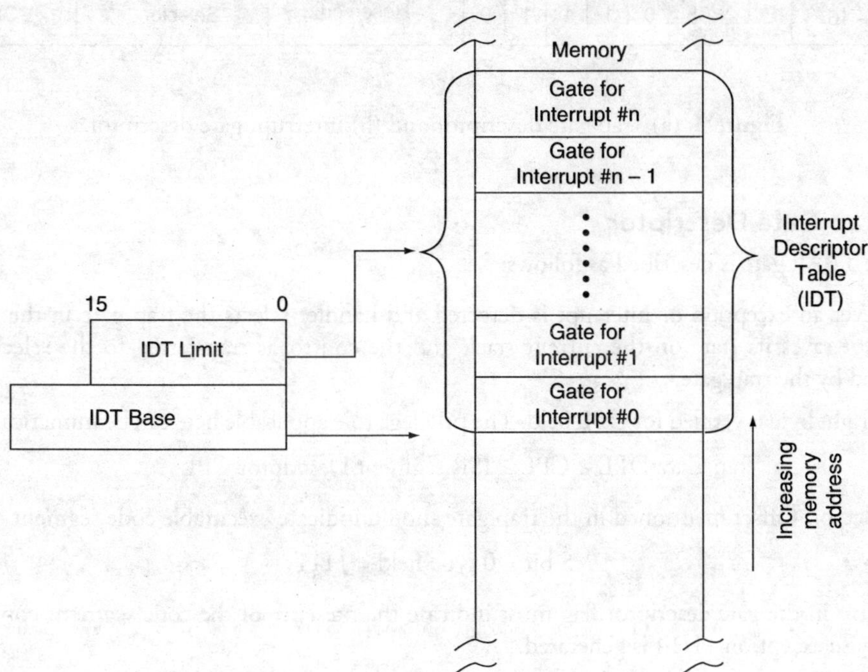

Figure 2 Use of IDTR for accessing IDT.

7. Whenever an exception or interrupt is detected, vector number is multiplied by eight and is added to the base address of the IDT, that is, to the contents of the IDTR. This result points to either the interrupt or trap fate descriptor.
8. In turn the gate descriptor supplies the 1-bit selector and 32-bit offset for the segment containing ISR.
9. The privileged instructions LIDT and SIDT are used to load and store contents to the IDTR. LIDT is executed only at privilege level 0, whereas SIDT is not a privileged instruction.

8.6.1 Gate Descriptors used for Interrupt Exception Handling in the Protected Mode

Two types of gate descriptors which can be used to access ISR via IDT are trap gate descriptor and interrupt gate descriptor. If any other descriptor is found in the IDT when an exception occurs, 80386 generates a general protection fault. Figure 3 shows the format of the interrupt and trap gate descriptors. Both descriptors are exactly same except the type field (refer to Table 4 in Chapter 4).

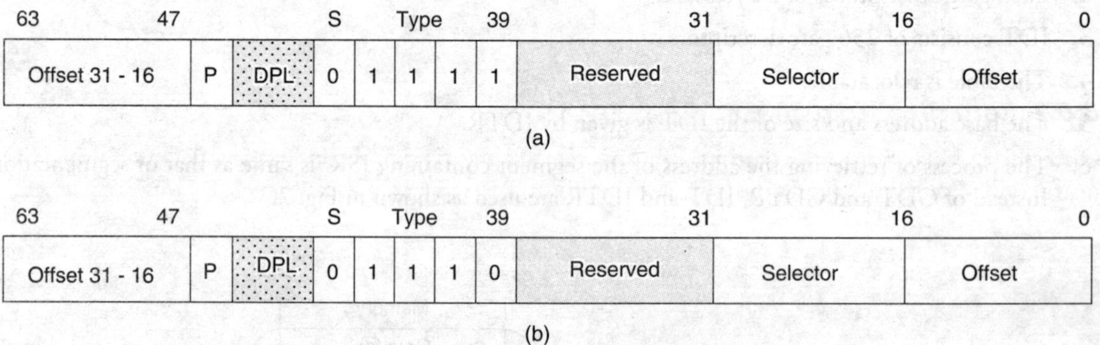

Figure 3 (a) Trap gate descriptor and (b) interrupt gate descriptor.

8.6.1.1 Trap Gate Descriptor

Usage of the TRAP gate is described as follows:

1. Whenever an exception or interrupt is detected and handler selects the trap gate in the IDT, 80386 processor saves its state on the current stack and the control is transferred to the selector; offset is specified by the trap gate.
2. Access right byte is verified for DPL field. The privilege rule applicable here can be numerically written as

   Trap Gate DPL ≥ CPL ≥ ISR segment Descriptor CPL

3. The selector: Offset mentioned in the trap gate should indicate executable code segment only.

   S bit = 0 type field = 1111

4. The P bit in the gate descriptor flag must indicate the presence of the code segment containing ISR. Otherwise exception 11/14 is generated.

8.6.1.2 Interrupt Gate Descriptor

The operation of the interrupt gate is described as follows:

1. Trap gate and interrupt gate operate almost similarly.
2. For interrupt gate, S bit = 0 but the type field = 1110.
3. One important point that distinguishes between trap gate and interrupt gate is that whenever an exception occurs and interrupt gate is selected, 80386 processor clears the interrupt flag (IF BIT of EFLAGS register) after it has pushed the return address and EFLAGS register on the stack.

4. This is done before the ISR is executed. Once the IF bit is cleared, 80386 processor ignores/masks all further hardware initiated interrupts.
5. Access right byte is verified for DPL field. The privilege rule applicable here can be numerically written as

$$\text{Interrupt gate DPL} \geq \text{CPL} \geq \text{ISR segment Descriptor CPL}$$

6. Upon execution of IRET at the end of ISR, the original image of EFLAGS is popped out of stack.

8.6.2 Returning from an ISR

Once the ISR has finished execution, it again transfers the control to the interrupted code using IRET instruction. The IRET restores the EFLAGS and returns to address (CS: EIP) and execution is resumed.

8.7 Handling Interrupts and Exceptions in Virtual 8086 Mode

This is not similar to the protected mode. First the processor examines VM bit in EFLAGS register to decide whether the interrupt/exception is to be processed like real mode (8086 style) or the protected mode style.

8.7.1 8086 Style ISR

Whenever any exception causes a task switch, 80386 sets the NT bit in EFLAGS register of a new task. But the NT bit is checked only when IRET is executed in the protected mode. NT bit is ignored in virtual 8086 mode. IRET is not able to clear the VM bit which means that there is no way to return back to its parent task with IRET instruction. So its difficult to invoke 8086 interrupt handlers. The only way to execute ISR is to go back to the protected mode. 80386 processor automatically switches to the protected mode if an interrupt/exception is detected in the virtual mode. Steps to process interrupt in virtual mode in 8086 pattern are given as follows:

1. When 8086 code passes control to the protected mode ISR at privilege level 0 and the state of the virtual 8086 mode program is saved on the PL0 (ISR) stack.
2. 16-bit IP, CS and flag register contents are copied from ISR stack to 8086 program stack so that ISR correctly interprets 8086 style segment reference.
3. ISR stack contents are preserved in more than one place for future use.
4. 32-bit EFLAGS image with VM BIT = 1, IOPL = 00 and CS:IP are also pushed.
5. Now IRET instruction is needed to be executed so as to terminate protected mode of ISR and pass the control to 8086 interrupt handler and not to the original 8086 program.
6. Again when IRET is executed, a general protection fault transfers control to the first ISR.
7. Whatever registers saved on 8086 stack (during step 2), are retrieved back.
8. Fetch parameters from ISR stack also and execute one more IRET instruction which will terminate protected mode ISR and pop the address of originally terminated program to resume execution.

8.7.2 The Protected Mode Style ISR

Steps taken by the processor for handling interrupt in the protected mode are as follows:

1. Whenever an interrupt is detected in the virtual 8086 mode, it switches from the virtual mode to the protected mode.
2. The processor locates current task's TSS from TR and finds out PL0 stack selector and pointer.
3. 8086 CS:EIP and EFLAGS are pushed on PL0 stack. Here, transition is from PL3 to PL0. 8086 SS:ESP are also pushed. Error code is also pushed.
4. All four data segment registers (DS, ES, FS, and GS) are also pushed and the registers are loaded with 0. This is required because 8086 segmentation treats these registers as simple 16-bit registers whereas in the protected mode, those hold selectors with INDEX, RPL and TI. 8086 segment register values are not meaningful in protected mode. Figure 4 shows this stack transition. Throughout rest of the procedure only PL0 stack is used.

Protected mode PL0 stack

31	15 0
xx	GS
xx	FS
xx	DS
xx	ES
xx	SS
ESP	
EFLAGS	
XX	CS
EIP	
SS : ESP (if Error code)	
Error Code (optional)	

Virtual mode stack

31 16	15 0
SS	ESP

Figure 4 Stack transition from 8086 stack to PL0 stack.

5. Once stack transition is over, 80386 follow the protected mode style interrupt handling process.
6. Once 80386 processor encounters IRET instruction at the end of ISR, it checks for VM bit in the EFLAGS register.
7. If VM = 1 then it retrieves 8086 CS:EIP and EFLAGS from PL0 stack and resumes the execution of virtual 8086 mode program.

8.8 Error Codes

With exceptions related to a specific segment, 80386 processor pushes an error code onto the stack of the exception handler. The error code format is shown in Fig. 5. The format of the error code is much similar to that of a selector, but instead of an RPL field. The error code contains the following two one-bit fields:

1. The processor sets the EXT bit if an event external to the program caused the exception.
2. The processor sets the I-bit (IDT-bit) if the index portion of the error code refers to a gate descriptor in the IDT.

If the I-bit is not set, the TI bit = 0 indicates whether the error code refers to the GDT or LDT (TI =1). The remaining 14 bits are the upper 14 bits of the segment selector involved. In some cases, the error code on the stack is null, that is, all bits in the low-order word are zero.

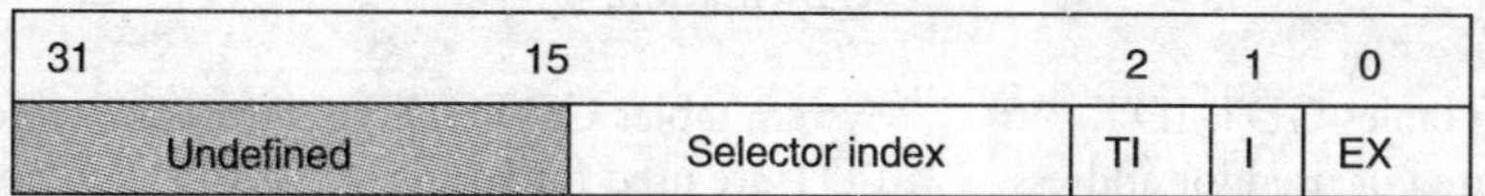

Figure 5 Error code format.

8.9 Comparison of Three Modes of 80386 Processor

We have studied operation of all three modes of the 80386 processor in detail. Table 2 summerises the comparison of those three modes.

Table 2 Comparison of Three Modes of 80386 Processor

S. No.	*Real Mode*	*Protected Mode*	*Virtual 8086/V86*
1	Upon RESET/Boot, the processor enters in the real mode.	The processor enters in the protected mode from real mode.	The processor enters in V86 mode from protected mode only.
2	The processor can switch to the protected mode only.	The processor can switch to any of the real mode or virtual 8086 mode from the protected mode.	The processor can switch to the protected mode only.
3	Not meant for executing application programs. Mainly used to set-up the processor for the protected mode operation.	Executes 80386 based application programs.	Executes 8086 based application programs.

(Continued)

Table 2 (Continued)

S. No.	*Real Mode*	*Protected Mode*	*Virtual 8086/V86*
4	16-bit mode.	32-bit mode.	16-bit mode.
5	Operand size 8/16-bit.	Operand size 8/16/32-bit.	Operand size 8/16–bit.
6	20-bit address bus.	32-bit address bus.	32-bit address bus.
7	1-MB address space wrap around.	4-GB address space.	1-MB + 64-KB address space, no wrap around
8	Address calculation mechanism similar to 8086.	Separate special address calculation mechanism for segmentation.	Address calculation mechanism similar to 8086.
9	System tables GDT, IDT, LDT are not used for address calculation.	System tables GDT, IDT, LDT are used for address calculation.	System tables GDT, IDT, LDT are not used for address calculation.
10	No usage of descriptors.	Full usage of descriptors.	No usage of descriptors once V 86 tasks are loaded.
12	No access to the LDTR.	Access to the LDTR is allowed.	No access to the LDTR.
13	Access to task, test and debug registers is available.	Access to task, test and debug registers is available only at PL = 0.	Access to task, test and debug Registers is not available.
14	Segmentation is not available.	Segmentation is fully explored and utilized.	Segmentation is not available.
15	Fixed segment length to 64 KB.	Variable segment length may be from 1 byte to 4 GB.	Fixed segment length to 64 KB.
16	Paging is not available.	Paging is optional.	Paging is optional.
17	Multi-tasking is not supported.	Multi-tasking is supported.	Multi-tasking is supported.
18	Interrupt processing is done via IVT in the same mode.	Interrupt processing is done via IDT in the same mode.	Interrupt processing is done via IVT/IDT in the protected mode.

(Continued)

Table 2 (Continued)

S. No.	*Real Mode*	*Protected Mode*	*Virtual 8086/V86*
19	Protection mechanism is not applicable hence no privilege levels.	Protection mechanism is Fully utilized with all 4 privilege levels.	Protection mechanism is not applicable still one can say PL is always 3.
20	Self test can be conducted.	Self test conduction is not possible.	Self test conduction is not possible.

8.10 Duo-Core Processors

With rapid growth in technology, there is steady continuous improvement in the execution performance of the microprocessors. Developers have observed saturation in performance for uni-processor systems. Increase in chip density, clock frequency, cache capacity for performance improvement has reached to the extent due to hardware performance issue. Software approaches such as pipelining, ILP and multi-threading are also not sufficient. So, designers have turned to a fundamentally new approach to improve performance, that is, placing multiple processors on the same chip with a large shared cache. The use of multiple processors on the same chip is also referred as multi-core which provides potential increase in the performance without increase in the clock rate. This meets to the latest high speed application demands.

In the stream of multi-core processors, Intel has introduced number of multi-core products. Here is the case study of Core Duo.

8.10.1 Features of Core Duo Processors

General structure and main features of the Core Duo are discussed as follows:

1. The intel Core Duo was introduced in 2006. As the name suggests, it consists of two X86 superscalar cores.
2. Each core has dedicated L1 split cache, 32-KB instruction cache and 32-KB data cache.
3. Two megabyte L2 cache is shared by both cores.
4. It has thermal control unit to ensure that the temperatures of all components in chip are maintained within their functional temperature range.
5. It has on-chip advance programmable interrupt controller (APIC).
6. It has on-chip power management logic.
7. It has front side bus (FSB) interface.

8.10.2 Organization of Core Duo

Figure 6 shows the block diagram of Core Duo processor. Each core has own individual dedicated L1 split cache. Both have 32-KB instruction cache and 32-KB data cache.

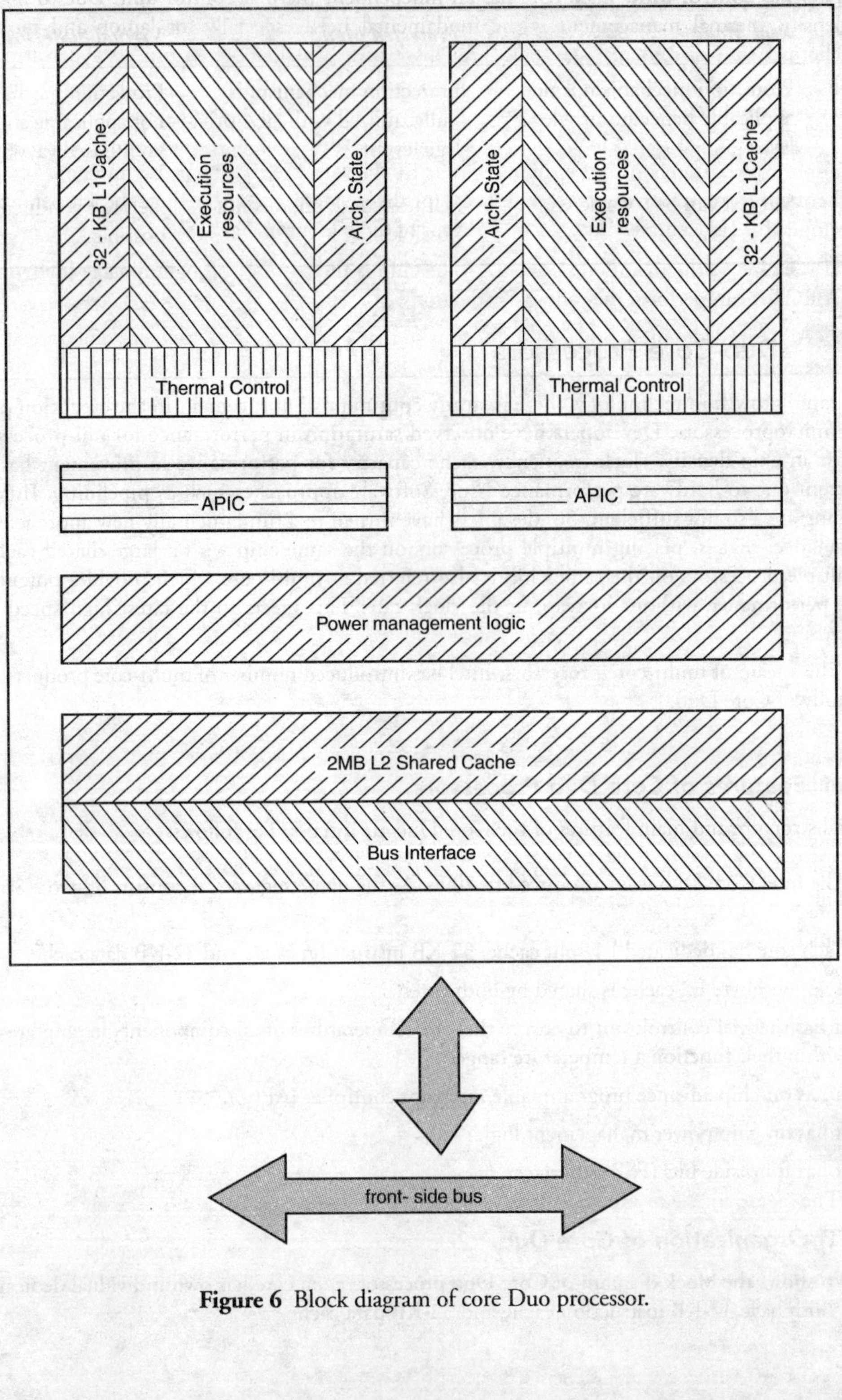

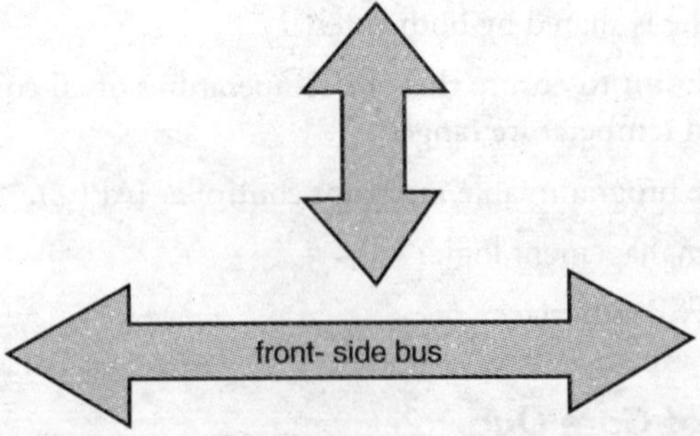

Figure 6 Block diagram of core Duo processor.

1. **Thermal control unit:** Each core has an independent thermal control unit. Due to high transistor density, thermal management is the fundamental need especially for laptop and mobile devices. Thermal control unit manages chip heat dissipation to enhance the processor performance within specified temperature range. It also helps to improve ergonomics with a cooling system and reduces fan acoustic noise too.

   Every core has individually defined temperature zone. The maximum temperature of each core is monitored separately using separate registers by the software. If any of the threshold is exceeded, the thermal control unit reduces the clock rate for the respective core to reduce the temperature. Chip die temperature is accurately measured by means of digital sensors.

2. **APIC:** One of the major component on the chip is the advanced programmable interrupt controller (APIC). It can perform the following functions:
   - APIC provides inter-processor interrupts so that any process can interrupt other processor too. For example, a thread in one core can generate an interrupt to the other core. Such interrupt requests are accepted by local APIC and then routed to the APIC of the other core.
   - APIC accepts I/O requests in common and then routes these to the appropriate core.
   - APIC contains an OS programmable timer to generate interrupt requests for the local core.

3. **Power management unit:** The battery life for mobile platforms such as laptop is increased with the help of power management unit which monitors thermal conditions, CPU activities and accordingly adjusts voltage levels and power consumption. It has a capability which allows fine-grained logic control such that it turns ON processor logic sub-systems as and when required for individual core. Division of buses and logic arrays is done such that the data required in some modes of operation can be put in low power state when not in use.

4. **L2 cache:** A shared L2 cache of 2 MB is included on the Core Duo chip. The cache control logic does dynamic allocation of the cache space depending upon the current core needs. So, one core may be assigned whole 100% L2 cache. L2 cache supports MESI protocol for maintaining cache coherency with local L1 cache.

   When a cache write is done at L1 level, the cache line is marked as M (modified) state. The line must not be in E (exclusive) or M state prior to writing to it. The cache sends read for ownership (RFO) request to ensure the existence of the line in L1 and is in I (Invalid) state in the other L1 cache. This protocol is modified for core duo processor for multiple cores also.

5. **Bus interface:** This interface connects to the external bus, FSB, that is, front side bus with frequency 667 MHz. The FSB is 64-bit wide with 5312 MB/s transfer rate. The FSB uses a split-transaction, deferred reply protocol. This FSB is used to connect with the main memory, I/O controllers and maybe other processor chips.

Summary

- The methodology for processing interrupts is different for all three modes of 80386 processor.
- The chapter also made the comparison among all three modes in all possible respects.
- An introduction to the all new concept, Core Duo processor, which is the current trend of the processors is also discussed.

Multiple-Choice Questions

1. Normal operation of the processor may be interrupted due to ________.
   (a) An application program requests for I/O service
   (b) Any critical condition occurrence due to an external hardware
   (c) The processor itself detects an emergency condition
   (d) All of the above

2. The 80386 has the ability to handle upto __________ different interrupts/exceptions.
   (a) 2
   (b) 224
   (c) 8
   (d) 256

3. Which of the following instruction is used to return from the interrupt service routine?
   (a) RETI
   (b) RET
   (c) IRET
   (d) ESC

4. Hardware interrupts are classified as __________ and __________ interrupts.
   (a) Trap, fault
   (b) Fault, abort
   (c) Maskable, non-maskable
   (d) Abort, trap

5. Exceptions are classified as
   (a) Trap, fault, abort
   (b) Maskable, non-maskable
   (c) Trap, fault
   (d) Hardware, software interrupts

6. 80386 processor supports ________ user-defined interrupts.
   (a) 2
   (b) 224
   (c) 27
   (d) 256

7. ________ is a one byte instruction which causes breakpoint interrupt.
   (a) INT 0
   (b) INT 3
   (c) INTO
   (d) ESC

8. Faults are exceptions that are detected and serviced
   (a) Before the execution of the faulting instruction
   (b) After the execution of the faulting instruction
   (c) During the execution of the faulting instruction
   (d) None of the above

9. Traps are exceptions that are reported immediately
   (a) Before the execution of the faulting instruction
   (b) After the execution of the faulting instruction
   (c) During the execution of the faulting instruction
   (d) None of the above

10. ________ are the exceptions which do not permit the precise location of the instruction causing the exception to be determined.
   (a) Trap
   (b) Fault
   (c) Abort
   (d) All of the above

11. ________ instruction compares the contents of register with contents of memory location with specified range in the instruction
   (a) BOUND
   (b) ESC
   (c) CMP
   (d) SUB

12. 'Device not available' fault is generated in the absence of ________ due to execution of ________ instruction.
   (a) Memory, WAIT
   (b) Keyboard, ESC
   (c) Co-processor, ESC
   (d) Printer, WAIT

13. General protection fault is generated due to

(a) Violation of segment limit

(b) Write attempt to read only data segment

(c) Violating privilege rules

(d) All of above

14. Which one has got the highest priority?

(a) NMI

(b) RESET

(c) INTR

(d) None of this

15. Checking for exception generation is done

(a) After every Instruction

(b) At the end of the segment

(c) At the end of the program

(d) As and when required

16. IDT cannot have _______ descriptors.

(a) Interrupt Gate Descriptors

(b) Task Gate Descriptors

(c) Segment descriptors

(d) System descriptors

17. LIDT instruction can be executed at privilege level.

(a) 0

(b) 1

(c) 3

(d) None of the above

18. In real mode for finding out location of interrupt vector in IVT interrupt number n is multiplied by

(a) 1

(b) 2

(c) 4

(d) 8

19. In Protected mode e for finding out location of interrupt Descriptor in IDT interrupt number n is multiplied by

(a) 1

(b) 2

(c) 4

(d) 8

20. In virtual mode, interrupt processing is doneat privilege level

(a) 1

(b) 2

(c) 0

(d) 3

21. Debugging tool single stepping trap is an

(a) Hardware interrupt

(b) Exception

(c) Software interrupt

(d) None of the above

22. When exception related to specific segment occurs the error code is saved in

(a) General purpose register

(b) Selector

(c) Stack

(d) None of the above

23. Core duo processor has _______ number of CPU on the same chip

(a) 1

(b) 2

(c) 3

(d) 4

24. The core duo has on chip L1 cache of size _______ code cache and _______ data cache

(a) 32 KB, 32 KB

(b) 8 KB, 8KB

(c) 512 KB, 512 KB

(d) None of the above

25. The core duo has on chip L2 cache of size

(a) 1 MB

(b) 2 MB

(c) 3 MB

(d) 4 MB

26. MESI stands for

(a) Modify, Exclusive, Shared, Invalid

(b) Modify, Error, Shared, Interrupted

(c) Modify, Exclusive, Shared, Interrupted

(d) Modify, Exclusive, Shared, Inaccurate

27. The FSB of the core duo is ________ wide.

(a) 16-bits

(b) 32-bits

(c) 64-bits

(d) 20-bits

28. The FSB is having ________ data transfer rate.

(a) 5212 MB/s

(b) 5312 MB/s

(c) 5312 MB/s

(d) None of the above

29. The FSB is used to connect

(a) Main memory

(b) I/O controllers

(c) Other processor chips

(d) All of the above

30. The error code generated for interrupt processing is of ________ bits.

(a) 16-bits

(b) 13-bits

(c) 15-bits

(d) None of the above

31. The type field of trap gate descriptor is

(a) 1111

(b) 1110

(c) 1101

(d) 1010

32. The type field of interrupt gate descriptor is

(a) 1111

(b) 1110

(c) 1101

(d) 1010

33. The type field of task gate descriptor is

(a) 1111

(b) 1110

(c) 1101

(d) 0101

34. The thermal control unit takes following action to reduce the temperature of core duo processor.

(a) Turns on the cooling fan

(b) reduce the clock rate

(c) Turn of the processor

(d) None of the above

35. Page Fault Type 14 exception occurs if

(a) PG bit 1

(b) Incorrect privilege level

(c) Invalid page table/Page dir entry

(d) All of the above

36. For real mode, the IVT occupies 1 KB memory space starting from

(a) 0000h to 03FF H

(b) 0000 to FFFF H

(c) 0000 to FFFF FFFF H

(d) FFFF to 3FFF H

37. In ______ mode(s), paging is not available but in ______ and ______ mode paging is optional.

(a) Real, protected, virtual 8086

(b) Protected, real, virtual 8086

(c) Virtual 8086, protected, real

(d) All, protected, virtual 8086

38. In ______, the address calculation mechanism is similar to 8086 processor

(a) real mode only

(b) protected

(c) real and virtual 8086 mode

(d) all of the three modes

39. System tables GDT, LDT and IDT can be used for address calculation in __ mode.

(a) real mode

(b) protected

(c) real and virtual 8086 mode

(d) all the three modes

State True or False

1. Protected mode uses IVT for interrupt processing.

2. Virtual mode switches to real mode for interrupt processing.

3. Virtual mode interrupt processing is done in virtual mode only.
4. Virtual mode switches to the protected mode for interrupt processing.
5. Real mode interrupts are processed in real mode only.
6. Real mode refers IDT for interrupt processing
7. Core duo has on chip L1 split cache.
8. Thermal control unit manages the power requirement of the core duo.
9. For core duo L2 cache usage for both cores is always 50 (%) each of the core.
10. The FSB is used to connect two cores with each other.

Review Questions

1. Explain the difference between IVT and IDT.
2. Differentiate between interrupt, fault, trap and abort.
3. How are interrupts and exceptions handled in the protected mode of 80386? Explain using various gate formats.
4. Explain 80386 operating in real mode. How does it respond to the interrupt?
5. Explain the following:
   (a) Trap gate descriptor.
   (b) Interrupt gate descriptor.
   (c) Task gate descriptor.
   Where are they located?
6. What is an IDTR? What are its contents upon RESET?
7. What is the difference between trap gate and interrupt gate descriptors? How do they differ from segment descriptors?
8. What is the use of DPL field of the trap gate and interrupt gate descriptors?
9 Compare and contrast real, protected mode and virtual 86 mode of 80386 processor.
10. Draw and explain block diagram of core duo processor.
11. Discuss the following terms with respect to core duo processor:
    (a) L1 and L2 cache.
    (b) Power management unit.
    (c) APIC.
    (d) Thermal control unit.
    (e) FSB.

Answers

Multiple-Choice Questions

1. (d)
2. (d)
3. (c)
4. (c)
5. (a)
6. (b)
7. (b)
8. (a)
9. (b)
10. (c)
11. (a)
12. (c)
13. (d)
14. (b)
15. (a)
16. (c)
17. (a)
18. (c)
19. (d)
20. (c)
21. (b)
22. (b)
23. (b)
24. (a)
25. (b)
26. (a)
27. (c)
28. (b)
29. (d)
30. (b)
31. (a)
32. (b)
33. (d)
34. (b)
35. (d)
36. (a)
37. (a)
38. (c)
39. (b)

State True or False

1. False
2. False
3. False
4. True
5. True
6. False
7. True
8. False
9. False
10. False

UNIT V

Microcontroller – I

9 Microcontroller 8051 Architecture

LEARNING OBJECTIVES:

After reading this chapter, you will be able to:

- Compare microprocessor and microcontroller.
- Describe features of microcontroller.
- Explain the concept of embedded system.
- Choose a microcontroller on the basis of functional requirements.
- Write program in assembly language.
- Understand the use of different addressing modes.
- Understand the use of power saving modes.
- Understand the use of security locks.
- Understand CPU timings and machine cycles.

9.1 Introduction

The previous chapters (1 to 8) are focused on the background of the architecture of the microprocessor. It is clear that the microprocessor alone cannot perform any task, and it needs the supporting hardware, software and interfacing with the peripheral devices. The microprocessor is mainly deployed to handle complex tasks with moderate or higher speed of operation.

There are number of real-time applications in which, the tasks to be handled do not require high speed and larger supporting hardware as compared to the microprocessors. These types of tasks can be performed in an efficient way with the help of compact hardware similar to the microprocessor system. The same is known as "*microcontroller*". The microprocessor system consists of a set of integrated circuit chips, whereas the microcontrollers have all necessary devices on the chip itself. This reduces the complexity of the microcontroller system.

The simplicity of the hardware, that is, its low cost and low power consumption, have made the microcontroller systems more popular in industries. Nowadays, microcontrollers have become the heart of most of the electronic gadgets which we use in our daily lives. There are a number of manufacturers who produce different types of microcontrollers. The proceeding chapters (10 to 14) will give us exposure to the Intel made microcontroller 8051.

Intel's 8051 core is a widely used and popular microcontroller among the beginners. The architecture, features and functionality of 8051 will be discussed in this chapter. 8051 based microcontrollers are offered in hundreds of variants from different silicon chips manufacturers. Before going into details of the chip, it is essential to understand what a microcontroller is, how it differs from a microprocessor and why it is necessary to learn about microcontrollers in general and 8051 in particular.

A microcontroller is a highly integrated chip with a processor, memory and peripherals. A microcontroller senses the happening of external events through signals received at input ports and responds to the events through output ports. Modern microcontrollers are found in almost every facet of modern life.

More and more consumers and commercial products, such as, but not limited to, household appliances, telecommunications devices, automobiles, security systems, thermostats, and the like are being controlled by these integrated circuit microcontrollers. The automotive market has been a major user of microcontrollers, many of which have been developed specially for automotive applications.

Generally, a microcontroller has a standard hardware design which is customized for a particular implementation by programming the firmware for a specific application. Microcontrollers combine relatively inexpensive, generic hardware with specialized firmware to provide cost-effective custom designs for different applications.

Almost all of us believe that 8051 is the first microcontroller by Intel, but it is not so. Intel 8048 microcontroller was Intel's first microcontroller. 8048 was inspired by, and was somewhat similar to, *the Fairchild F8* microprocessor. Intel introduced 8048 in 1976 and 8051 in 1980, which eventually replaced 8048. Architecturally, 8051 is an extension to 8048. Almost every feature and resource of 8048 is present in 8051 in the same or superior form. The 8051 has been licensed to various manufacturers worldwide. Some of the early adopters include Philips, Signetics and Siemens. Most of them manufacture one or more derivatives of 8051. The MCS-51 family is now made by dozens of companies with different features. Here is a small list of these companies – AMD, Atmel 89x, Dallas-Maxim, Infineon C500, SiLabs, and many others.

9.2 Features of 8051

8051 is the original member of the MCS-51 family and is the core for all MCS-51 based devices. Main characteristic of 8051 microcontroller are as follows:

1. Intel 8051 has **Harvard architecture** unlike Intel microprocessors (*Von Neuman Architecture*). The Harvard architecture is an architecture with physically separated storage and signal pathways for instructions and data.
2. It contains 8-bit arithematic and logic unit (ALU), accumulator and 8-bit registers. Hence it is an 8-bit Central Processing Unit (CPU) optimized for control applications, that is, maximum number of operations that can be performed are not more than 8-bits (1 byte) of data. So this is an 8-bit microcontroller.
3. Intel 8051 has extensive Boolean (single bit data) processing capabilities. So accordingly number of bitwise instructions is available. Bit-level boolean logic operations can be carried out directly and efficiently on internal registers and RAM. Due to this feature, 8051 has become popular in industrial control applications.

The 8051 microcontroller contains the following features:

1. **8-bit data bus:** It can access 8-bits of data in one operation.
2. **16-bit address bus:** It can access 2^{16} memory locations, that is, 64 KB (65536 locations) each of RAM (data memory) and ROM (program memory).
3. **On-chip hardware:** Data RAM – 128 bytes (data memory), ROM – 4 KB (program memory), clock oscillator – since clock oscillator circuit is also built on a chip, only crystal is required to be connected externally to the microcontroller 8051.
4. 32 bi-directional and individually addressable I/O lines (total four parallel ports of 8-bits each).
5. Two 16-bit timer/counters.

6. **Full duplex UART (one serial port):** 8051 Universal Asynchronoue Receiver-Transmitter (UART) makes it simple to use the chip as a serial communication interface. External pins can be configured to connect to the internal shift registers in a variety of ways and the internal timers can also be used allowing serial communications in a number of modes, both synchronous and asynchronous. Some modes allow communication with no external components.
7. Six sources for vector interrupt structure with two priority levels.
8. **Power saving modes:** For applications where power consumption is critical, the CMOS and CHMOS versions provide power-reduced modes of operation as a standard feature. Two types of power-saving modes can be used as per the requirement.

9.3 Functional Pin Description of the 8051

All the variants of 8051 family chips have 40 pins having various functions such as address, data, interrupts and input/output (I/O). Packaging for those variants may be dual in-line package (DIP), quadra flat package (QFP) or leadless chip carrier (LLC). Sometimes manufacturers supply 20-pin chips (e.g., Atmel 89c1051 or 89C2051) with a reduced number of I/O ports as per the application requirements.

Figure 1 shows the standard pin diagram of the 8051. However, for easy understanding, it is needed that the diagram should be studied according to the pin functionality rather than sequential pin numbers. It is clear that out of 40 pins, four parallel ports – P0, P1, P2 and P3 (each of 8-bits) – occupy 32 pins. Out of those 32 pins except 8 pins of port P1 others are having one or dual functions which are described subsequently.

The following describe the functions of the various pins of 8051:

1. **Power supply pins:**
   - Vcc (Pin 40) Input pin – The +5 Vdc of power supply is connected to this pin.
   - (Pin 20) Input pin – The ground (GND) terminal of the same power supply is connected to this pin.
2. **Clock pins:** XTAL1 and XTAL2 (Pin 19 and 18) – Though 8051 has chip oscillator circuit, it is necessary to connect only a quartz crystal to these pins. This oscillator drives the internal clock generator. The clock generator provides the internal clocking signals to the chip. Two capacitors (of approximately 30 pF) are required to be connected to get stable oscillations along with the crystal. Figure 2 shows the connection of crystal and capacitors and Fig. 3 shows an external oscillator connection with 8051. 8051 can work with variety of speed (frequency of the crystal) between the range 1 MHz and 16 MHz. One machine cycle lasts for 12 oscillator periods. Therefore, the crystal frequency (f) is internally divided by 12 to calculate the machine cycle period. The resulting frequency (fc) is the clock source for internal hardware of 8051.

   For example, consider crystal frequency f = 11.0592 MHz (typical value for 8051-based systems).

   Internal frequency

   $$fc = 11.0592\ \text{MHz}/12 = 921.6\ \text{kHz}$$

   Internal hardware will work at this speed. So machine cycle period is

   $$t = 1/921.6\ \text{kHz} = 1.085\ \mu\text{s}$$

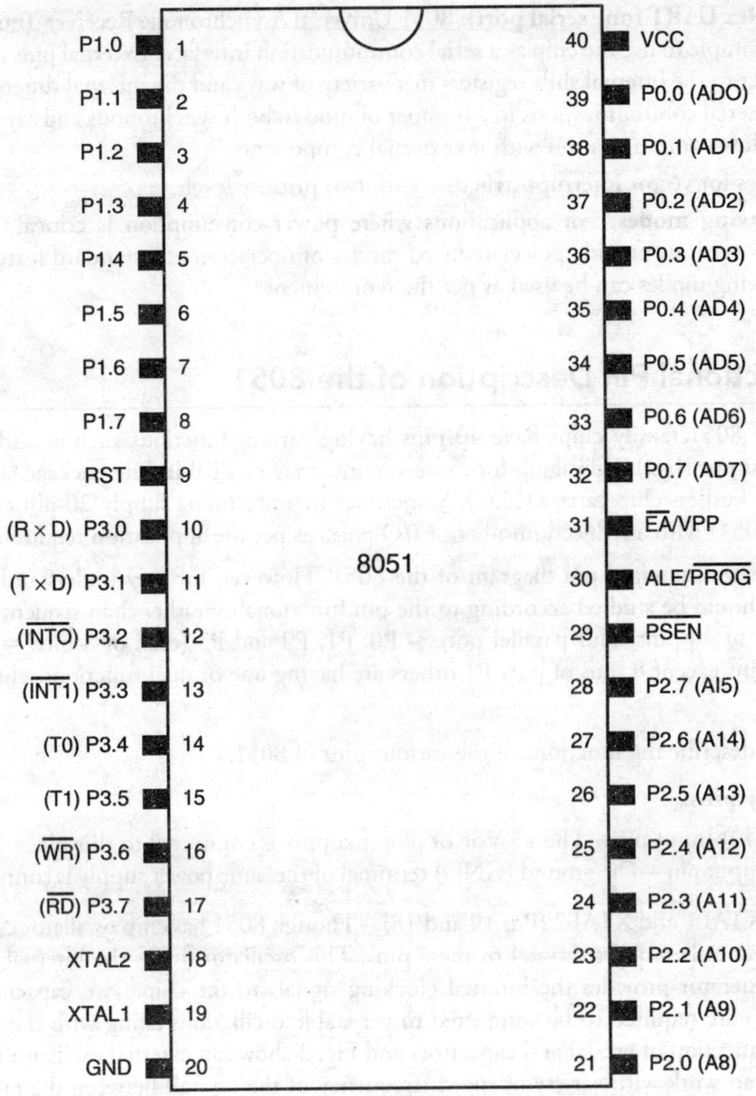

8051

P1.0	1	40	VCC
P1.1	2	39	P0.0 (ADO)
P1.2	3	38	P0.1 (AD1)
P1.3	4	37	P0.2 (AD2)
P1.4	5	36	P0.3 (AD3)
P1.5	6	35	P0.4 (AD4)
P1.6	7	34	P0.5 (AD5)
P1.7	8	33	P0.6 (AD6)
RST	9	32	P0.7 (AD7)
(R × D) P3.0	10	31	$\overline{\text{EA}}$/VPP
(T × D) P3.1	11	30	ALE/$\overline{\text{PROG}}$
($\overline{\text{INTO}}$) P3.2	12	29	PSEN
($\overline{\text{INT1}}$) P3.3	13	28	P2.7 (AI5)
(T0) P3.4	14	27	P2.6 (A14)
(T1) P3.5	15	26	P2.5 (A13)
($\overline{\text{WR}}$) P3.6	16	25	P2.4 (A12)
($\overline{\text{RD}}$) P3.7	17	24	P2.3 (A11)
XTAL2	18	23	P2.2 (A10)
XTAL1	19	22	P2.1 (A9)
GND	20	21	P2.0 (A8)

Figure 1 Pin diagram of 8051 microcontroller.

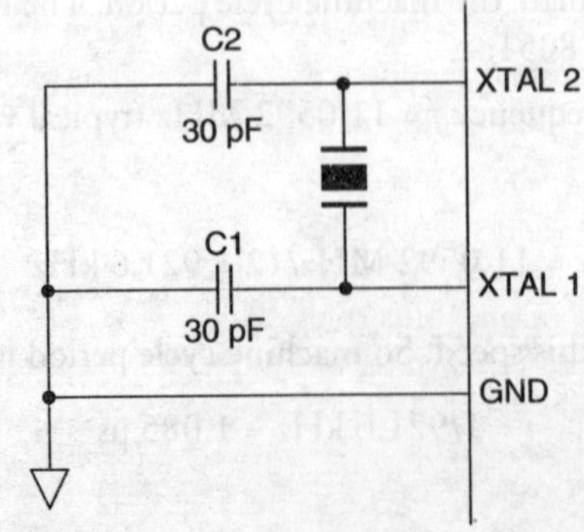

Figure 2 Crystal connection to 8051.

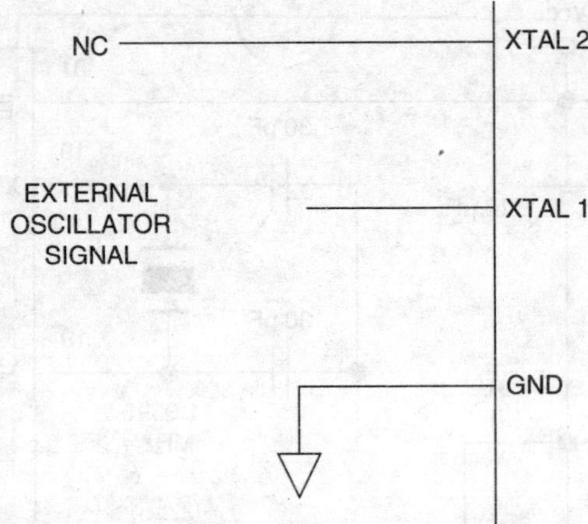

Figure 3 External source connection to 8051.

Table 1 Calculations of Instruction Execution Time

Instruction	*Number of Machine Cycles Required (say c)*	*Time Required to Execute = c × t μs*
MOV R0, # 10H	1	1 × 1.085 μs = 1.085 μs
SJMP LABEL	2	2 × 1.085 μs = 2.17 μs
DIV AB	4	4 × 1.085 μs = 4.34 μs

Now, it is needed to find out the time required for execution of one instruction. Time required for executing an instruction depends upon the number of machine cycles required for execution of the instruction.

Table 1 shows the calculations of instruction execution time with different machine cycles.

An RC resonator or TTL oscillators can be used in place of a crystal oscillator as a frequency source. An external frequency signal is applied to XTAL1. XTAL2 remains unconnected in CHMOS package as shown in Fig. 3 whereas in the HMOS versions, it uses at XTAL2 pin for external frequency source.

3. **Reset pin (Pin 9) input pin, active high:** A logic one on this pin terminates the microcontroller operation and clears the contents of most of the registers. In other words, the positive voltage for minimum two machine cycles (24 oscillator periods) on this pin resets the microcontroller. By applying logic zero to this pin, the program starts execution from the beginning. The external reset signal is asynchronous to the internal clock. Figure 4 shows power on reset circuit with reset key. Figures 5(a) and 5(b) show the power on reset network and the timing diagram, respectively. When the power is turned ON, an external *R-C* circuit holds the RST pin high for an amount of the time decided by the capacitor value. To ensure true reset state, capacitor value should be chosen as such that the "high" lasts at least for two machine cycles. After, the power ON reset contents of various registers are as following:

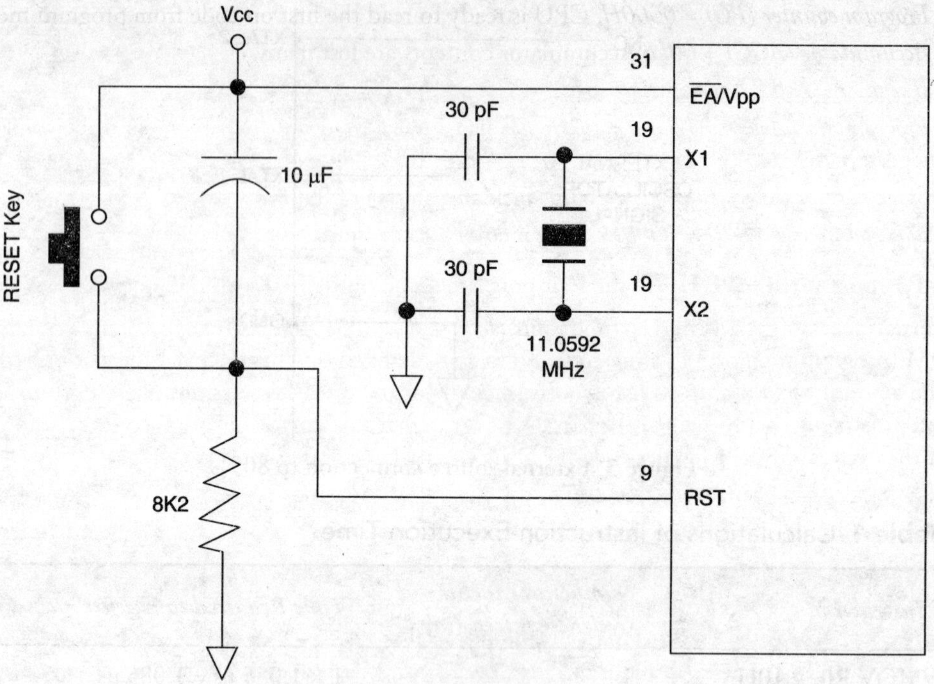

Figure 4 Power-on reset circuit with reset key.

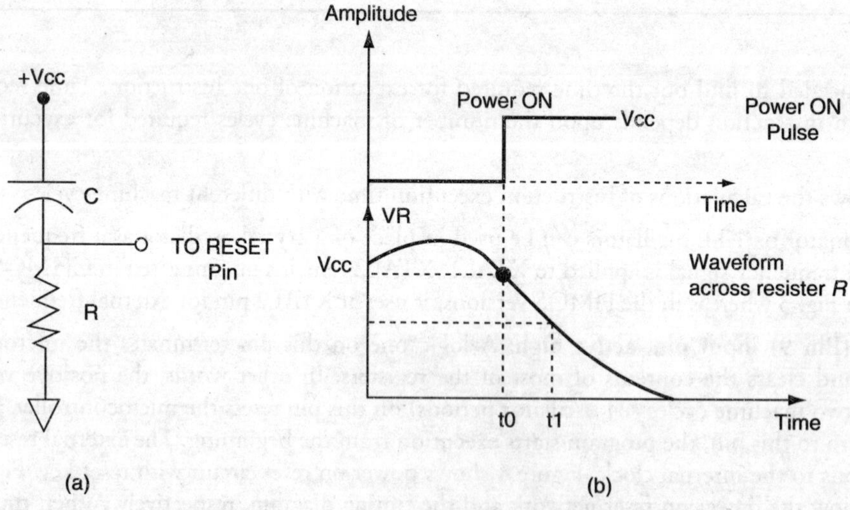

Figure 5 (a) Reset network and (b) timing diagram.

- *Program counter (PC) = 0000H.* CPU is ready to read the first op-code from program memory.
- *Accumulator (ACC) = 00H*: Accumulator contents are lost if any.
- *B register = 00H*: Contents are lost.
- *Program status word (PSW) = 00H*: All flags are cleared and the microcontroller will be using register bank 0.
- *Stack pointer (SP) = 0007H*: Default stack area starts at 0008H.
- *Data pointer (DPTR) = 0000H*: Data memory access starts from 00H address.

4. **P0–P3 (port pins) = FF H:** All the four port latches are initialized with the said value.
5. **External access (EA):** (Pin 31) Input pin, active low. 8051 and its many variants contain on-chip ROM (program memory) to store code. To fetch code from on-chip, ROM EA is connected to +Vcc. If the amount of ON-chip ROM is not sufficient (or in ROM-less versions like 8031), programs are stored on an external ROM (OFF-chip memory). In such cases, the EA pin is connected to ground so that the microcontroller fetches code from the external program memory.
6. **Program store enable (PSEN):** (Pin 30) output pin, active low. This pin is typically used in systems where external ROM (program memory) is used. When a byte is to be read from an external ROM, a low is essential on this pin which activates OE of the ROM. PSEN is discussed in detail in Chapter 10.
7. **Address latch enable (ALE):** (Pin 31) Input pin, active high. When any (data/code) external memory is to be read, the microcontroller puts the lower address byte (A0–A7) on P0 and activates the ALE output. After receiving the signal from the ALE pin, the external latch (probably 74LS373 chip) memorizes the state of P0 and uses it as a memory chip address. Immediately after that, the ALU pin is returned to its previous logic state and P0 is now used as a data bus. The port P0 is used for both data and address transmission.
8. **I/O port pins (P0–P3):** I/O pins Bidirectional. Total 32 pins are allotted for the four parallel ports (P0, P1, P2 and P3, respectively) of 8-bits each. All the four ports are configured as input port upon reset. Each port has a latch (P0–P3 special function register, respectively) associated with it. Each port also has an output driver and input buffer too. The port pins have dual or multiple functionalities such as Port 0 is acting as I/O port as well AD0–AD7 in the case of external memory interfacing along with Port 2. The alternate functionality of Port 3 pins will be discussed in Chapters 10,11,12, and 13.
9. **Port 0 (P0.0–P0.7) I/O or AD0–AD7:** Port 0 pins are denoted as I/O or AD0–AD7 because they can work as digital input/output or both, address bus and data bus. These pins are of "open drain type" for MOS integrated circuits which is same as "open collector" in the TTL integrated circuits. These pins are generally pulled up with resistors. These pins can be used as simple I/O such as P1 and P2 ports. They also serve as data bus and address bus for connecting an external memory to the microcontroller. The address and data information is separated by an external hardware latch (74LS373) with ALE signal generated by the microcontroller.
10. **Port 1 (P1.0–P1.7)I/O:** All the pins of Port 1 are internally pulled up with resisters. These port pins do not have dual functionality like other ports. These can only be used for simple I/O functions.
11. **Port 2 (P2.0–P2.7) I/O or A8–A15:** All the pins of Port 2 are internally pulled up with resisters. These port pins have dual functionality. They are used as a set of simple digital I/O in one mode and as a higher order address bus in the other mode. These pins are denoted as A8–A15. Port 2 pins provide

higher order address for externally connected memory. Combining Port 0 and Port 2 form a 16-bit address for addressing 64 KB memory.

12. **Port 3 (P3.0–P3.7) I/O or special functions:** Port 3 pins are internally pulled up with resisters. These pins can be used as simple digital I/O. These port pins are also used for special functions. Pin 3.0 (RxD) and pin 3.1 (TxD) are mainly used to communicate serially with external TTL devices such as slave displays, indicators, etc. These pins also facilitate to communicate with personal computers (PCs) and printers with the help of an external hardware chip (MAX232). Pins P3.2 (INT0) and P3.2 (INT1) are used to interface external interrupts. Pins P3.4 (T0) and P3.5 (T1) facilitate to count external events or timing functions. Pin 3.6 (WR) and Pin 3.7 (RD) provide timing signals for reading and writing operations of external memory. These pins are used in association with Ports 0 and 2 for interfacing external peripheral devices.

9.4 The Microcontroller 8051 Architecture

Figure 6 shows the internal architecture of 8051 core. Since the chip is designed for control applications, it provides the optimum number and types of components according to the average needs.

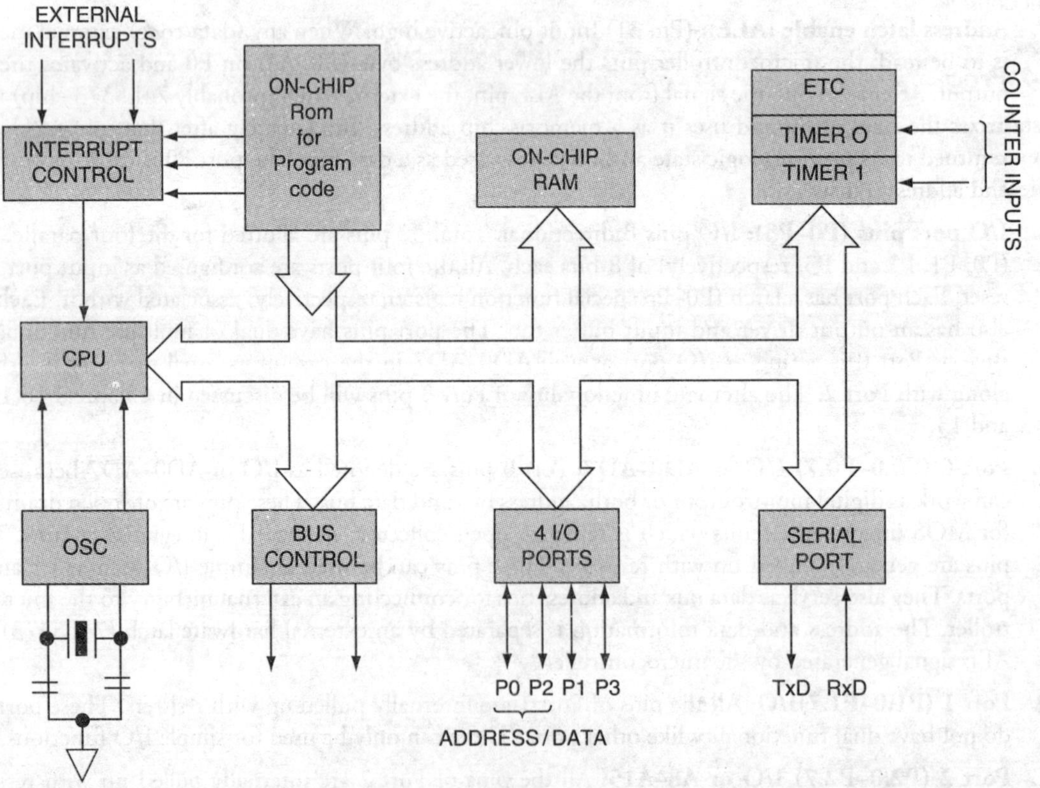

Figure 6 8051 internal architecture.

9.4.1 Accumulator (ACC)

ACC is the most important 8-bit register. 8051 can perform the basic four arithmetic operations namely addition, subtraction, multiplication and division. The source operand for these arithmetic operation is held in accumulator. The result of the arithmetic operation is returned to this register. It is also used for Boolean algebraic operations where it holds the operand and then the result. It is the source register for data transfer between external memory and I/O ports. The functions like, rotate and swap are possible only with this register.

9.4.2 Register B

The register B is always to be used with accumulator for multiplication and division operations. It is used as a general-purpose register for other instructions.

9.4.3 Arithmetic Logic Unit (ALU)

The name ALU of this unit suggests that it is used for arithmetic and logic operations. It performs basic arithmetic operations such as addition, subtraction, multiplication and division. The logical operations such as AND, OR, EX-OR, NOT (compliment) and rotate are done in the ALU. It also helps in branching instructions.

9.4.4 Program Status Word Register and Flags

The status of different flags is held in this register. A flag is like a single-bit memory which stores the result after execution of some of the instructions. The PSW is an 8-bit register. Seven bits out of eight bits are used to reflect different conditions. Table 2 shows the bit positions of PSW register.

Table 2 PSW Register and Map of Memory Bank – PSW Register

PSW.7	*PSW.6*	*PSW.5*	*PSW.4*	*PSW.3*	*PSW.2*	*PSW.1*	*PSW.0*
CY	AC	FO	RS1	RS0	OV	–	P

Map of Memory Bank

RS1	*RS0*	*Register Bank*	*Address*
0	0	0	00H–07H
0	1	1	08H–0FH
1	0	2	10H–17H
1	1	3	18H–1FH

The various bits are discussed as follows:

1. **PSW.0 (P) Parity:** The flag set or cleared by hardware for each instruction cycle indicates even or odd number of 1-bit in accumulator.
2. PSW.1 (–): User definable bit.
3. **PSW.2 (OV) Overflow:** The flag is set whenever the result of the operation is too large. It is affected by arithmetic operations. It is generally used to detect an error in signed arithmetic operations.
4. **PSW.3 (RS0), PSW.4 (RS1):** These two bits together are used to select register bank.
5. **PWS.5 (F0):** This bit is available to the users for general purpose.
6. **PSW.6 (AC) Auxiliary carry:** This bit is set when lower nibble of the accumulator overflows, that is, ACC.3 to ACC.4. It is used for BCD arithmetic operations.
7. **PSW.7 (CY) Carry:** This bit is set when there is an overflow from ACC.7. It is affected by addition and subtraction operations. The bit can be cleared or set by instruction "CLR C" or "SETB C".

9.4.5 Program Counter

It is a 16-bit register. It is used to address a location of an instruction in the memory. It keeps the track of execution of the program. It resets to 0000H whenever the power is turned ON. It increments automatically as the instruction is fetched from the memory. It gets modified according to the instructions like "Jump" or "Call".

9.4.6 Data Pointer

It is a 16-bit register which holds the address location of the data in the memory. It can be accessed as DPL (lower byte) and DPH (higher byte). It does not have an internal address. Both DPH and DPL have separate addresses, hence it helps to address a look-up table. It can be incremented by instruction "INC DPTR" but cannot be decremented.

9.4.7 Stack Pointer and Stack

It is a reserved RAM area of the microcontroller. It is used to store temporary information, that is, the data. It follows "Last In First Out" (LIFO) method. The stack operation is done by using "Stack Pointer" register. It is an 8-bit register. It is operated with "PUSH" and "POP" instructions. Writing data to stack is called PUSH. The data retrieval from stack is called POP. Upon reset, it is automatically initialized to 07H. The PUSH instruction first increments stack pointer to 08H and the data is copied. POP instruction decrements stack pointer during retrieval of the data. The stack always grows above 07H location in 8051 microcontroller.

9.4.8 Clock Signal Generator (Oscillator)

The microcontroller requires a clock signal for synchronization of all the internal operations. The clock generation circuit is on-chip hardware; only a quartz crystal needs to be connected. It is connected to XTAL1 and XTAL2 pins.

9.5 Memory Organization

The on-chip memory of all the MCS-51 family microcontrollers is partitioned as data memory and program memory. The data memory is readable/writable. It is accessed by 8-bit addresses, which can be quickly and easily read and written by an 8-bit microcontroller. If the data memory requires more than 8-bit address, then DPTR register is used to address the same.

The program memory is only readable to the microcontroller. The range of program memory can be 64 KB. Some of the microcontrollers similar to MCS51 provide ROM and external program memory (EPROM) versions with the range from 4 to 16 KB.

9.5.1 On-Chip Data Memory

Figure 7 shows the map of on-chip data memory, that is, RAM of the microcontroller. Each bank is of 8 RAM locations (registers) and is denoted as R0 to R7. Total 4 banks × 8 Registers become 32 locations. If the programmer does not want to use banks, then all 32 locations can be used as a scratch pad or general-purpose RAM.

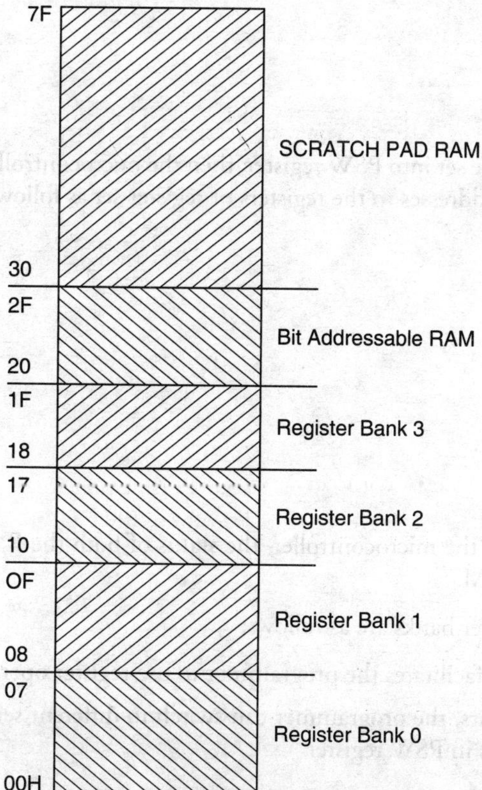

Figure 7 RAM allocation of 8051.

The first block ranges from 00H to 1FH. It is organized as follows:

1. **Register bank:** It is a group of four banks, namely, Bank 0, Bank 1, Bank 2 and Bank 3. The memory block of each bank is as follows:
   - Bank 0: 00H–07H
   - Bank 1: 08H–0FH
   - Bank 2: 10H–17H
   - Bank 3: 18H–1FH

   One out of four banks is selected by setting RS1 and RS0 bits in PSW resister as shown in Table 2. Each register bank is one set of eight registers. Every register is of 8 bits.
2. **Register set:** It is a group of eight registers, namely, R0, R1, R2, R3, R4, R5, R6 and R7. The addresses of the registers depend on the selection of register banks in PSW register. For example, if RS1 = 0 and RS0 = 0 are set into PSW register, then the microcontroller selects Bank 0 for operation. It automatically assigns address to each register of register set as:
   - Register 0 = 00H
   - Register 1 = 01H
   - Register 2 = 02H
   - Register 3 = 03H
   - Register 4 = 04H
   - Register 5 = 05H
   - Register 6 = 06H
   - Register 7 = 07H

   If RS1 = 0 and RS0 = 1 are set into PSW register, then the microcontroller selects Bank 1 for operation. It automatically assigns addresses to the registers of register set as follows:
   - Register 0 = 08H
   - Register 1 = 09H
   - Register 2 = 0AH
   - Register 3 = 0BH
   - Register 4 = 0CH
   - Register 5 = 0DH
   - Register 6 = 0EH
   - Register 7 = 0FH

   In the reset condition of the microcontroller, the status of both the RS0 and RS1 is set at 00H. This selects Bank 0 of the RAM.

The advantages of using register banks are as follows:

1. The use of register bank facilitates the programmer to use register operable instructions.
2. When the interrupt occurs, the programmer can switch to different set of registers (register banks) by setting RS0 and RS1 bits in PSW register.

3. This reduces the pushing and popping time (latency period) required during the execution of the interrupt subroutines.
4. This avoids overwriting of the data during register operations.

The RAM area 20H to 2FH is of 16 bytes. Each bit of these all byte locations is addressable. These bit addresses range from 00H to 7FH. The programmer can assign these bits for storing different program conditions as a flag.

The RAM area from 30H to 7FH is treated as general-purpose data RAM. The programmer can use it as a scratch pad. The programmer can also use it as a stack area if sufficient numbers of bytes are available.

It is not mandatory to use the RAM area as a scratch pad. Some instructions in the microcontroller allow using it as the data pointer. The registers R0 and R1 can be used to access internal as well as external RAM.

9.5.2 Special Function Registers

The RAM area from 80H to FFH is reserved for special function registers (SFRs). Table 3 shows the SFR structure and addresses. This area is a combination of bit and byte addressable registers. Some of the addresses within 80H to 7FH RAM area are not used, that is, from 84H to 86H. If the programmer writes or reads from these locations, then the result may be unpredictable. The data may be lost or any random data can be received from the reading operation.

Table 3 SFR Structure and Addresses

S. No.	*SFR*	*Address*	*Bit Addressable*
1	P0	80H	Yes
2	SP	81H	No
3	DPL	82H	No
4	DPH	83H	No
5	PCON	87H	No
6	TCON	88H	Yes
7	TMOD	89H	No
8	TL0	8AH	No
9	TL1	8BH	No
10	TH0	8CH	No
11	TH1	8DH	No
12	P1	90H	Yes

(Continued)

Table 3 (Continued)

S. No.	*SFR*	*Address*	*Bit Addressable*
13	SCON	98H	Yes
14	SBUF	99H	No
15	P2	A0H	Yes
16	IE	A8H	Yes
17	P3	B0H	Yes
18	IP	B8H	Yes
19	PSW	D0H	Yes
20	ACC.	E0H	Yes
21	B	F0H	Yes

9.5.3 Internal Program Memory

After reset, the program counter of the microcontroller CPU starts accessing the program memory from 0000H location. The vector address locations from 0003H, 0008H, 0013H and 001bH are reserved for the interrupts. The interrupts and their structure will be discussed in Chapter 13. The lowest 4 KB of program memory can either be on-chip or external ROM/EEROM. This selection is done by connecting EA pin to either Vcc or Gnd.

9.5.4 External Memory Interfacing

When the internal program memory and the data memory of the microcontroller is not sufficient, then these can be externally interfaced. This requires Port 0 and 2 pins for functioning as address bus and data bus for the external memory.

9.5.5 External Program Memory Interfacing

Figure 8 shows an interfacing scheme for external program memory. It must be noted that Ports 0 and 2 (16 I/O lines) are dedicated to bus operations during external program memory. Port 0 serves as multiplexed address/data bus. It outputs lower order byte of the program counter (PCL) and then it waits for the code byte. During the time ALE signal activates and latches the lower order address (A7–A0) to externally connected hardware latch. Meanwhile Port 2 pins (A15–A8) present the higher order address byte of program counter (PCH). Now the 16-bit address is ready for accessing the memory location in the EPROM with data bus ready for read operation. Then the PSEN strobes the EPROM and the code byte is read by the microcontroller.

The program memory addresses are always 16-bit wide. This clears that even if the external program memory is less than 64 KB, the unused address lines of Port 2 cannot be used as I/O lines.

9.5.6 External Data Memory Interfacing

Figure 9 shows hardware schematic for 2 KB of external RAM, that is, the data memory. The CPU executes from the internal ROM. Port 0 serves as multiplexed address/data bus for RAM. Three pins of Port 2 are used for addressing A8, A9 and A10 lines of RAM. This means that the RAM is divided in to 8 numbers

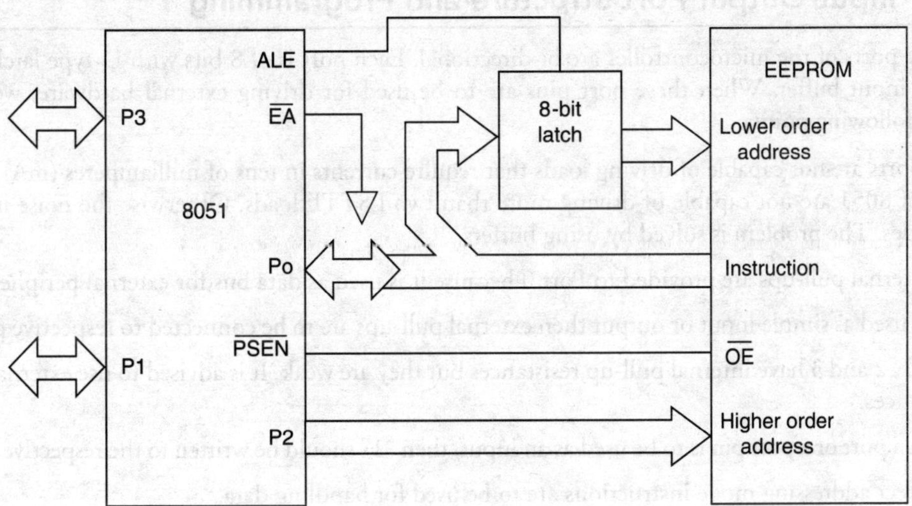

Figure 8 Program execution from external memory.

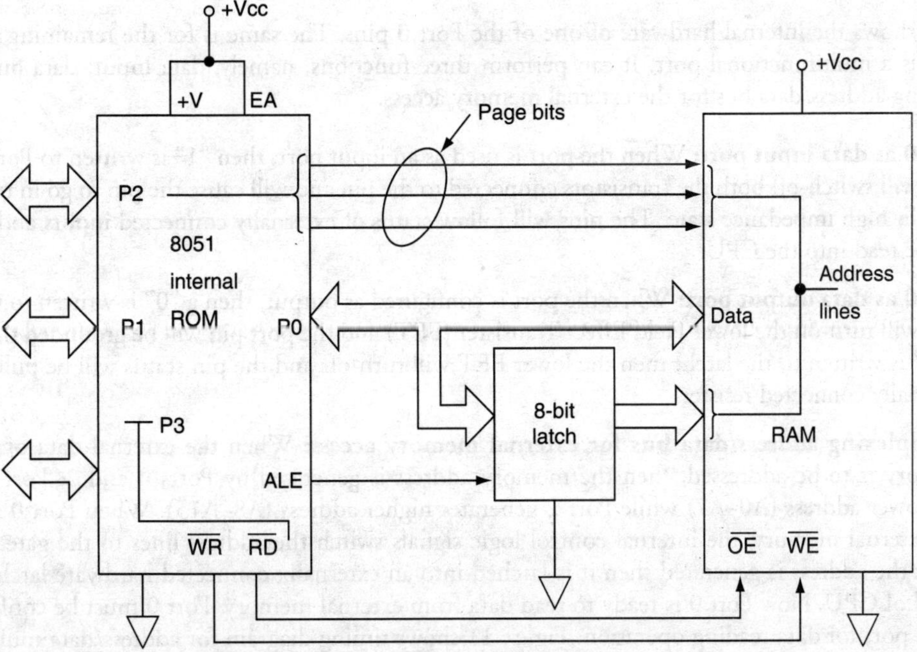

Figure 9 External data memory interface to 8051.

of pages ranging from 000H to 111H with 256 bytes per page. The CPU generates read (RD) and write (WR) signals required during external RAM access. The remaining 5 pins of Port 2 can be used as simple digital I/Os.

9.6 Input/Output Port Structure and Programming

All the four ports of the microcontroller are bi-directional. Each port is of 8 bits with D-type latch, output driver and input buffer. When these port pins are to be used for driving external hardware, we have to remember following points:

1. The ports are not capable of driving loads that require currents in tens of milliamperes (mA). The out pins of 8051 are not capable of driving more than two LSTTL loads. Otherwise the noise immunity degrades. The problem is solved by using buffers.
2. No internal pull-ups are provided to Port 0 because it is used as data bus for external peripherals.
3. If it is used as simple input or output then external pull-ups are to be connected to respective port pins.
4. Ports 1, 2 and 3 have internal pull-up resistances but they are weak. It is advised to use external pull-up resistances.
5. When a port or a port pin is to be used as an input, then "1" should be written to the respective port pin.
6. All direct addressing mode instructions are to be used for handling data.

9.6.1 *Port 0*

Figure 10 shows the internal hardware of one of the Port 0 pins. The same is for the remaining 7 pins of Port 0. It is a multifunctional port. It can perform three functions, namely, data input, data output and multiplexing address/data bus for the external memory access.

1. **Port 0 as data input port:** When the port is used as an input port, then "1" is written to Port 0 latch. This will switch-off both the transistors connected to the pin and will cause the pin to go in tri-state or float in high impedance state. The pins will follow status of externally connected inputs and the data can be read into the CPU.
2. **Port 0 as data output port:** When the port is configured as output, then a "0" is written to the latch. This will turn-on the lower Field Effect Transister (FET) and the port pin will be grounded through it. If "1" is written to the latch, then the lower FET will turn-off and the pin status will be pulled up by externally connected resister.
3. **Multiplexing address/data bus for external memory access:** When the external data or program memory is to be addressed, then the memory address is generated by Ports 0 and 2. Port 0 generates lower address (A0–A7) while Port 2 generates higher address (A8–A15). When Port 0 addresses the external memory, the internal control logic signals switch the address lines to the gate of FETs. Once the address is generated then it is latched into an externally connected hardware latch by ALE signal of CPU. Now Port 0 is ready to read data from external memory. Port 0 must be configured as input port for data reading operation. Figure 11 shows timing diagram for address/data multiplexing operation.

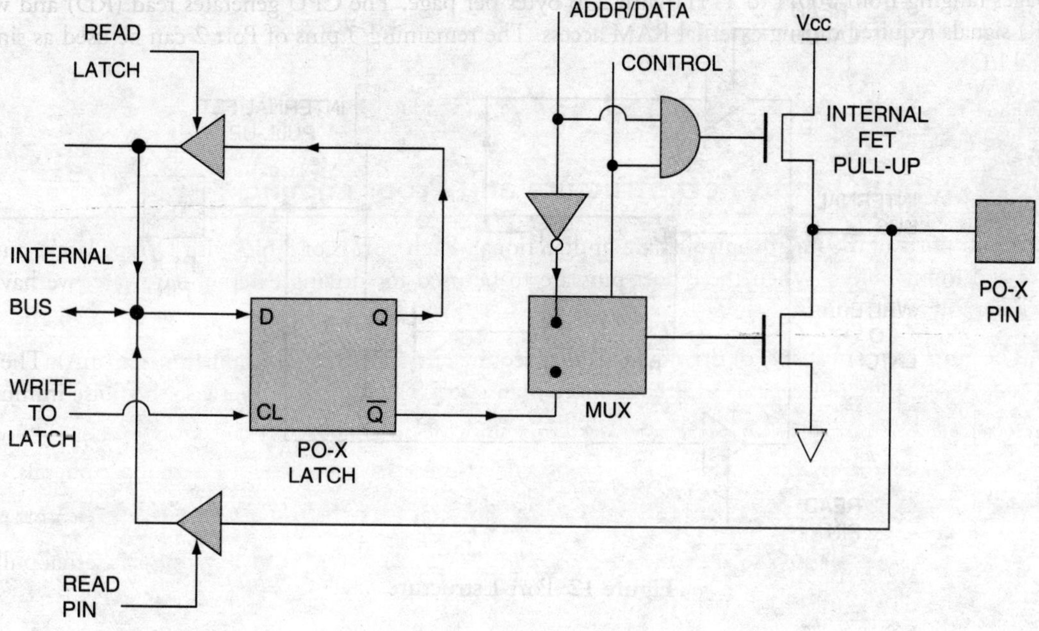

Figure 10 Port 0 structure.

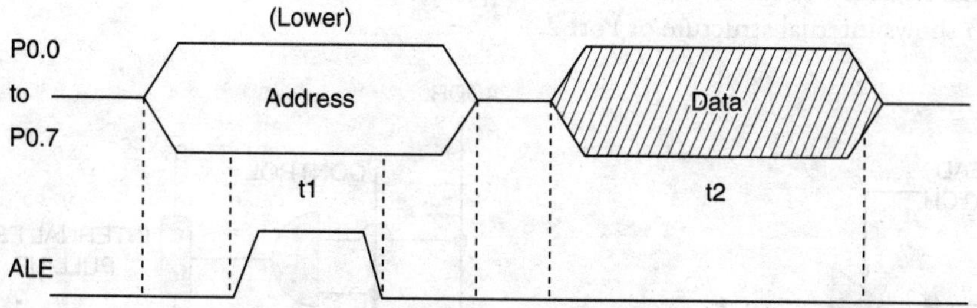

Figure 11 Multiplexed address/data bus.

9.6.2 Port 1

It is a simple I/O port of microcontroller. Figure 12 shows the internal circuit of Port 1. Port 1 is not multifunctional port, hence it is internally pulled up, discussed as follows:

1. **Port 1 as data input port:** Port 1 is initialized as data input port by writing "1" to the port latch bit. This turns OFF the internal FETs, hence the pin status is pulled up by the internal resister. Port 1 is called as "quasi-bidirectional port" because the port pins are pulled up by resister.
2. **Port 1 as data output port:** Port 1 is used as output port by programming latch pins to "0". This turns ON internal FETs and the port pin connected to the ground through FET. This will sink current from load to port pin. When the port pin status is set to "1", then the current is sourced to load.

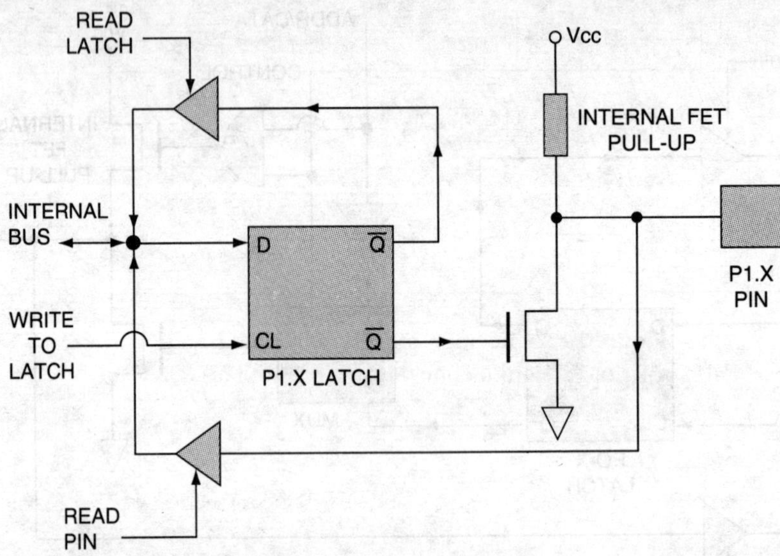

Figure 12 Port 1 structure.

9.6.3 Port 2

Port 2 is a malfunction port. It works as a simple I/O port as well as higher order address bus (A8–A15) for accessing external memory. It contains D-latch, multiplexer, pair of bi-directional buffer and FET output stage. Figure 13 shows internal structure of Port 2.

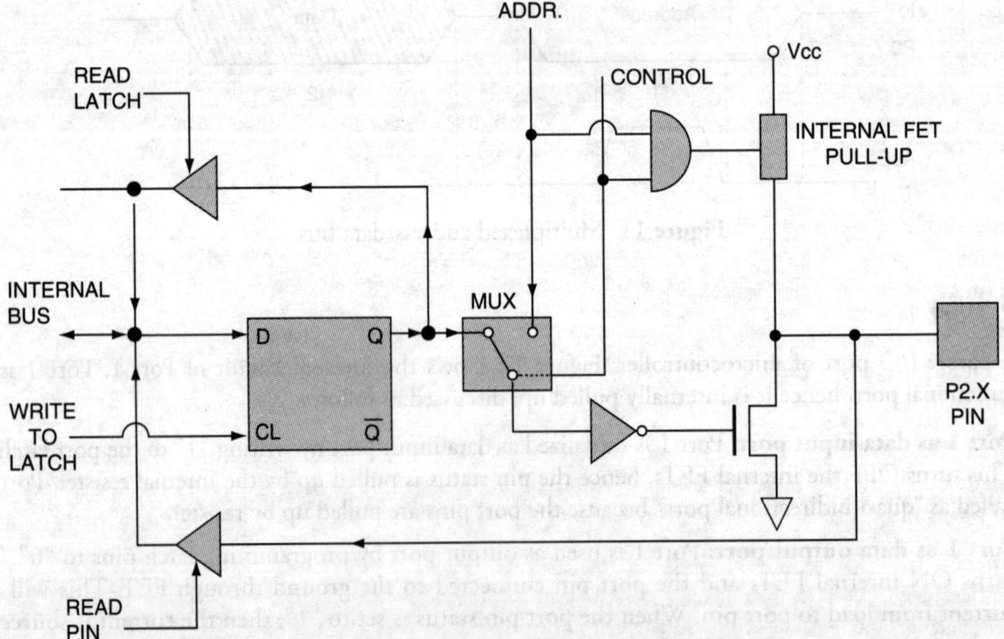

Figure 13 Port 2 structure.

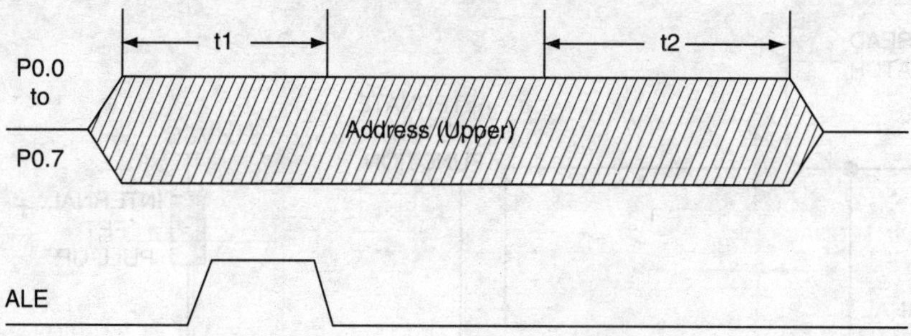

Figure 14 Generation of higher order address in conjunction with ALE from Port 2.

The functions of port 2 are as follows:

1. **Port 2 as data input port:** Writing "1" to corresponding Port 2 latch bit initializes Port 2 as simple input port. This will turn OFF the FET, and the port pin is pulled up by internal pull-up resister. It is also called as "quasi-bidirectional port" because the port pins are pulled up by resister.
2. **Port 2 as data output port:** When it is used as an output port, then the latch pins that are programmed to "0" will cause the internal FET to turn ON. This will turn OFF the internal pull up and the pin status will become 0. If "1" is written to port latch pin then it will drive the input of external hardware high through pull-up resister and the current is sourced to output. This turns OFF the internal FET.
3. **Port 2 for multiplexing address/data bus for external memory access:** Port 2 generates higher order address for external memory in conjunction with ALE signal. Figure 14 shows the timing diagram for the operation. It shows that Port 2 holds higher order address two times than that of Port 0. At the end of the t2 slot, the Port 2 address is ready for addressing the external memory.

9.6.4 Port 3

The internal structure of Port 3 is shown in Fig. 15. It is composed of D-latch, three uni-directional buffers and FET with internal pull-up resisters. It is also called as "quasi bi-directional port". It is a multiple function port which can work as simple I/O as well as some special functions. The functions of Port 3 are as follows. The special functions are listed in Table 4.

1. **Port 3 as data input port:** For using Port 3 as input port, "1" should be written to the respective Port 3 latch bit. This turns OFF the FET. The pin and the input to pin buffer are pulled to logic "1" by internal pull-up resister.
2. **Port 3 as data output port:** When the latch pins of Port 3 are programmed to "0", the internal FET turns ON with turning OFF internal pull up. This will set Port 3 as output port and the output status of port pin becomes "0".
3. **Special functions of Port 3:** Referring to Table 4, P3.0 and P3.1 are named as RxD and TxD, respectively. These pins are used for serial communication interface. It must be confirmed that P3.0 is set as input and P3.1 is set as output for communication. P3.2 and P3.3 are used as an external interrupts. The respective bits are to be set to input mode for this purpose. P3.4 and P3.5 can be used to

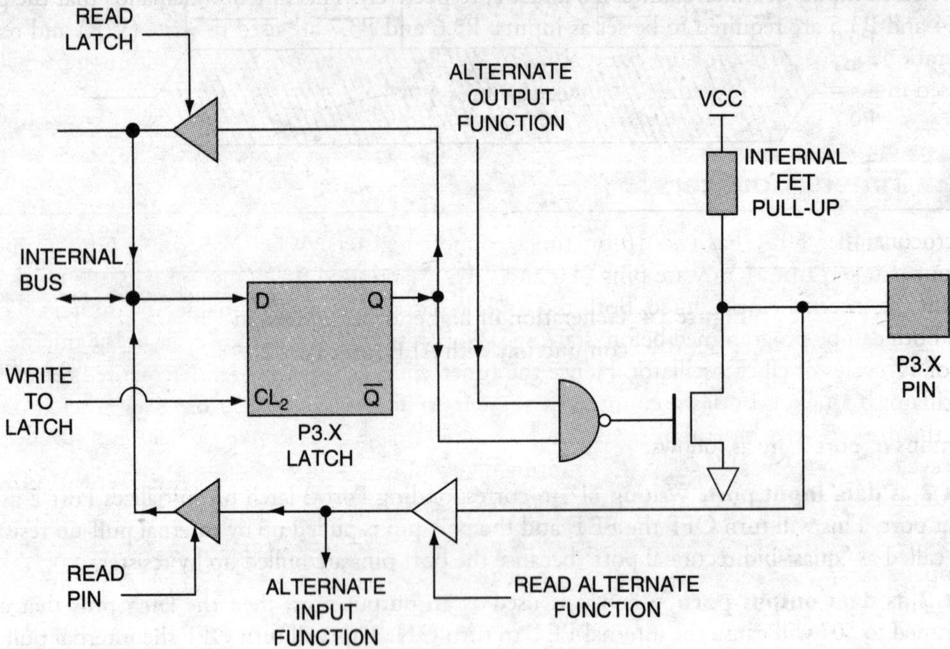

Figure 15 Port 3 structure.

Table 4 Special Functions of Port 3 Pins

Pin	*Symbol*	*SFR*	*Function*
P3.0	RxD	SBUF	Data receive pin for serial port in UART mode
P3.1	TxD	SBUF	Data transmit pin for serial port in UART mode
P3.2	INTO#	TCON.1	External hardware pin, level or edge triggered
P3.3	INT1#	TCON.3	External hardware pin, level or edge triggered
P3.4	T0	TL0	External input for timer/counter 0
P3.5	T1	TL1	External input for timer/counter 1
P3.6	WR#	–	External memory write signal pin
P3.7	RD#	–	External memory read signal pin

drive clock inputs of timer/counter T0 and T1, respectively. This function demands that the port pins P3.4 and P3.5 are required to be set as inputs. P3.6 and P3.7 are used to write (WR) and read (RD) operations, respectively, for the external memory. The above-mentioned special functions will be discussed in detail in the preceding chapters 10,11,12 and 13.

9.7 Timers/Counters

The microcontroller 8051 has two 16-bit timer/counter registers. When used in "Counter" mode, the clock input is taken from hardware pins (T0 and T1). When used in "Timer" mode, the clock signal is taken from the internal clock source. Both the timer counters are programmable up counters. The initial values in both can be programmed before starting the operation. The machine cycle of the microcontroller consists of 12 cycles of clock oscillator. Hence the timer/counter registers are incremented for 1/12 of the clock oscillator frequency. Both the counters increment on high-to-low transition, hence there is no limitations on the duty cycle of the input signals at T0 or T1. However, it should be held high for at least one machine cycle. Counter mode is used for counting continuous and discontinuous external events. It is also possible to measure pulse width and frequency of external signals by using combination of both the timer/counters.

The operation of both the timer/counter can be independently controlled by their respective control bits in SFRs, namely, TMOD and TCON. Tables 5 and 6 shows the Timer 0 and Timer 1 registers respectively.

Table 5 Timer 0 Register

Timer/Counter 0 Higher Byte								*Timer/Counter 0 Lower Byte*							
D15	D14	D13	D12	D11	D10	D9	D8	D7	D6	D5	D4	D3	D2	D1	D0

Table 6 Timer 1 Register

Timer/Counter 1 Higher Byte								*Timer/Counter 1 Lower Byte*							
D15	D14	D13	D12	D11	D10	D9	D8	D7	D6	D5	D4	D3	D2	D1	D0

9.7.1 TMOD Register

TMOD (timer mode) is an 8-bit register. It is divided into upper and lower 4 bits. Upper 4 bits and lower 4 bits are programmed to control operation of Timer 1 and Timer 0, respectively. The upper 2 bits of both are provided for operation and lower 2 bits specify timer mode. Table 7 shows the TMOD register.

Table 7 TMOD Register

MSB				*LSB*			
GATE	*C/T*	*M1*	*M0*	*GATE*	*C/T*	*M1*	*M0*
Timer/counter 1				Timer/counter 0			

The functions of the bits of TMOD register are as follows:

1. **C/T (clock/timer):** This bit in the TMOD register helps to set timers as delay generator or external event counter. If the timer is to be used as delay generator, then C/T is to be set at 0. This will enable timer to get clock signal from crystal oscillator of the microcontroller 8051. Setting C/T bits of TMOD to "1" by software enables both the timers to count external clock pulses from T0 and T1 pins. This will be discussed in Chapter 11.
2. **Clock source:** It is already learnt that the timer always needs a time base clock for its operation. The crystal oscillator frequency is the basic source for timers of 8051. It is internally divided by 12 and then it is applied to the timer. If we want to drive timer other than crystal oscillator, then an external clock source is to be connected to XTAL1 pin. If longer time delays are required, then it is always better to use low frequency source. This will considerably reduce power consumption. In addition to this, it will also decrease burden on software. Following example shows the scheme for timer calculations. When 8051 system has to communicate with IBM PC, it needs to have error-free baud rate generation. Hence, 11.0592 MHz crystal is popular.
3. **Gate:** The bit is provided for both Timer 0 and Timer 1. This bit of the TMOD register is used to control starting and stopping operation of the timers. It can be controlled by hardware as well as by software in 8051. The TR0 and TR1 (timer start) bits in TCON register are used to start the Timer 0 and Timer 1, respectively. It is programmed to "1" by software instructions SETB TR0 and SETB TR1 for starting both the timers and CLR TR0 and CLR TR1 for stopping the timers. These instructions can be used only when GATE = 0 in TMOD register. The hardware way of starting and stopping timers by external source is done by GATE = 1 in TMOD register.
4. **M0, M1:** These bits of TMOD register are used to operate the timers in different modes. The modes are shown in Table 8 and are discussed as follows:

Table 8 Mode Selection Table for Timer/Counter

M0	*M1*	*Mode*	*Function*
0	0	0	13-bit timer mode, 8-bit timer/counter THx with TLx of 5-bit prescaler
0	1	1	16-bit timer mode, both THx and TLx are cascaded, no prescaler
1	0	2	8-bit auto reload, the value in THx is loaded to TLx for each over flow
1	1	3	Split timer mode

- **Mode 0:** Figure 16 shows the steering logic for Mode 0 operation of timer/counter. This mode sets the timer as 13-bit register by cascading 5-bits from TL and 8-bits from TH. It means that the counter will count up to 1FFFH and overflows for next pulse. The lower 5-bits of TL work as 5-bit divider (i.e. divide by 32 pre-scalar) to the 8-bit counter (TH). It is enabled by setting GATE = 0, INTX = 1 and TR = 1. When GATE = 1, the timer is controlled by external input from INT pin. It is used for pulse width measurement when the counter and the modulus of TH counter can be shortened by presetting it

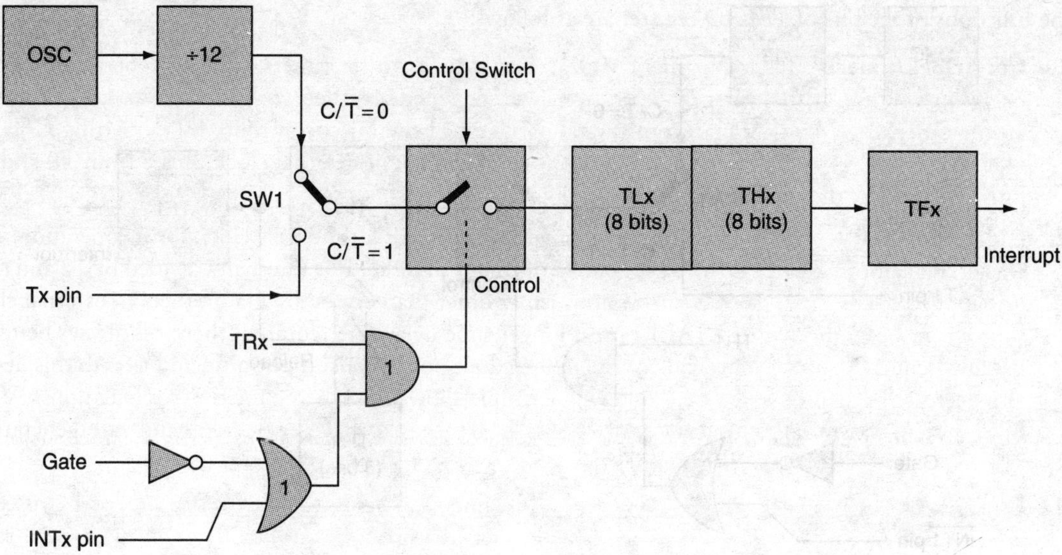

Figure 16 Timer/counter Mode 0, 13-bit counter.

to the desired value. It will start counting the incoming pulses from the same value and will reach to the highest value. The next clock pulse overflows the counter by resetting it to 0000H. The overflow condition sets the TF flag into the TCON register. The same can be used to generate an interrupt by enabling the respective bit in IE register. This makes the program to call Interrupt Service Routine (ISR).

- **Mode 1:** This mode is same as Mode 0. The only difference is in the length/modulus of the counter. It is 16-bit counter which ranges from 0000H to FFFFH. The TL and TH are cascaded together. It does not have presaler. The modulus of this 16-bit counter can be shortened by presetting it to the desired value in TH and TL. Setting the TR bit in TCON register will start counting the incoming pulses from the same value and will reach to the highest value. The next clock pulse overflows the counter by resetting it to 0000H. The overflow condition sets the TF flag into the TCON register. The same can be used to generate an interrupt by enabling the respective bit in IE register. This will vector to ISR.
- **Mode 2:** This mode configures timer/counter in 8-bit counter with auto-reload facility. Figure 17 shows timer/counter 1 in Mode 2. The TL1 works in a binary 8-bit counter. Setting TR1 bit in TCON register increments for every clock pulse till FFH. The next clock pulse sets TF1 flag in TCON register and reloads the contents of TH1 to TL1, then the counting processes continues. The TF1 flag can also be used to generate an interrupt by setting respective control bit in IE register. The count reloading process does not alter the contents of TH1 register. This mode can be used to generate a time base for certain applications, for example, baud rate generation.
- **Mode 3:** Figures 18(a) and 18(b) show the internal logic for Mode 3. Timer 1 is not used in this mode. Timer 0 is split into two separate 8-bit counters as TH0 and TL0. The TL0 register uses the control bits C/T#, GATE, TR0, INT0# and TF0 of Timer 0. TH0 uses the TR1 and TF1 bits from Timer 1. When Timer 0 is used in Mode 3, Timer 1 can be used in Modes 0, 1 and 2. As Timer 1 uses the TF1 flag, no interrupts will be generated. When Timer 0 is working in Mode 3, Timer 1 can be used for baud rate generation for serial communication.

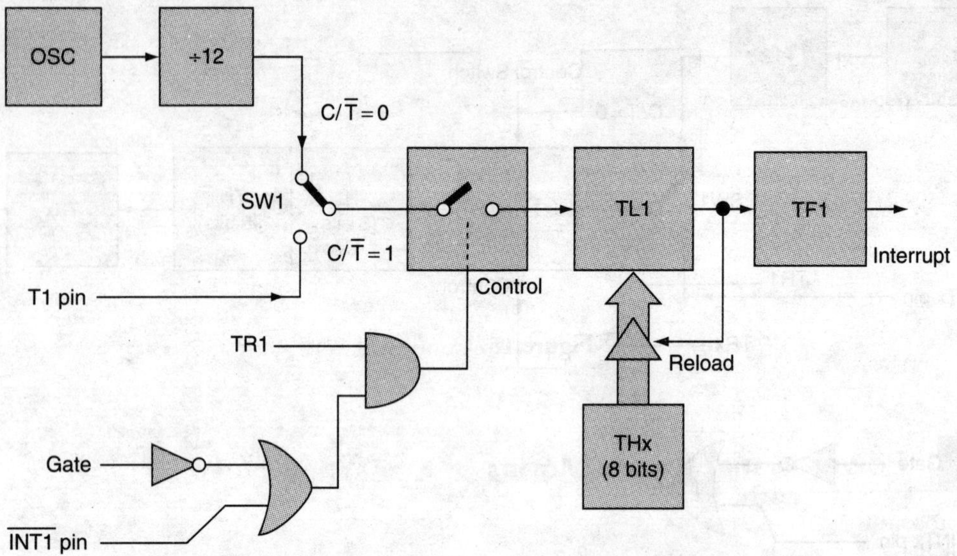

Figure 17 Timer/counter 1 Mode 2, 8-bit auto-reload.

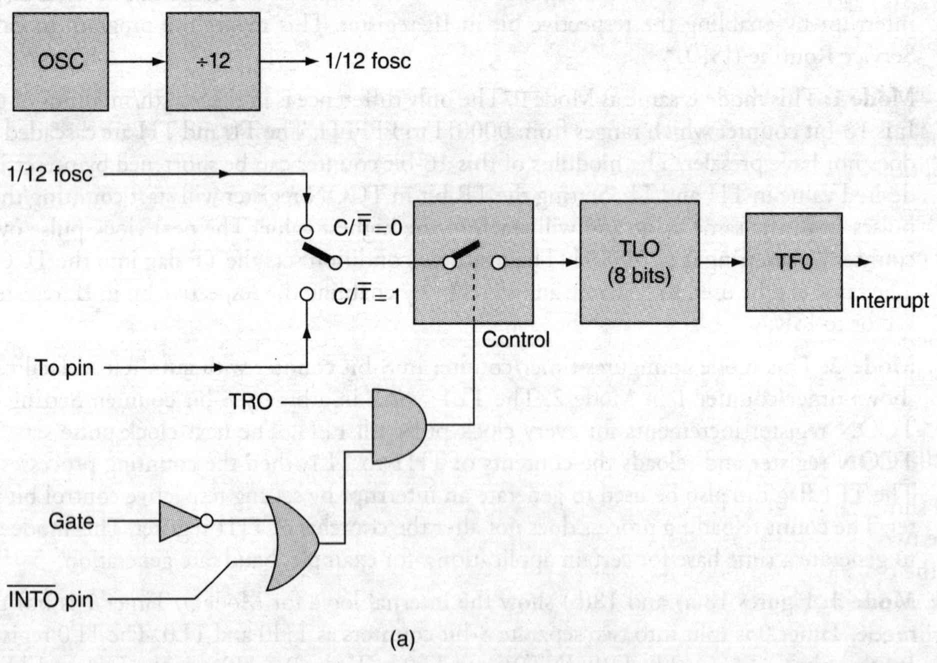

Figure 18 (a) TLO as timer or counter. (b) THO as timer.

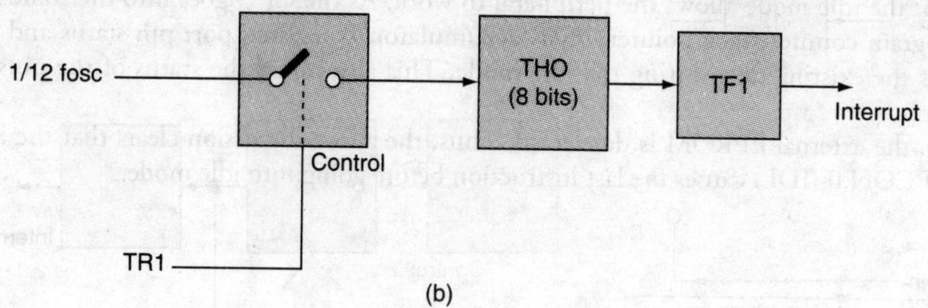

(b)

Figure 18 Continued.

9.8 Power Management Modes of Operation

The microcontroller requires nominal 5Vdc power supply. The power consumption of the microcontroller system is dependent on the current demand from the system. CHMOS versions of the microcontrollers have features of power-saving modes. The microcontroller has different sections. If some of them are kept in working conditions and some of them are held to previous status, then the power consumption can be reduced considerably. Generally, in the battery powered systems, the power consumption is critical. The CHMOS versions provide this facility as a standard feature. If the microcontroller system does not require high speed operation, then low frequency crystal oscillator can be used. This reduces power consumption as well as helps to optimize the length of the delay routines. Some of the advantages of the reduced power consumptions are listed as follows:

1. The microcontroller can be put into smaller space with optimized functionality.
2. Generally, batteries contribute lot of weight to the microcontroller system. Reduction in power consumption allows using lighter batteries/power supplies.
3. This reduces heat generation and increases packing density.
4. The expensive cooling fans and noisy blowers can be avoided.

There are different power-saving and efficient modes available in microcontrollers. These are application-specific modes. These are implemented by setting bits in PCON register. Following discussion will help us to understand the mechanism and function of power-saving modes.

9.8.1 Idle Mode

Figure 19 shows the hardware implementing idle and power down modes. The IDL# and clock generator signals are two inputs of the AND gate. The output of the AND gate drives the CPU clock. If the IDL# = 1 then the clock generator signal passes to CPU. If the IDL# = 0, it disables the AND gate which will stop clock signal to CPU. This ultimately stops the program execution process of the CPU and it will go in standstill condition. The figure shows that the clock signal to the on-chip peripherals, that is, timers, interrupts, RAM, serial port, etc., is not stopped, hence it will continue to work in normal condition.

This means that the idle mode allows the peripheral to work. As the CPU goes into the standstill mode, the data in program counter stack pointer, PSW, accumulator, B register, port pin status and other registers maintains the existing data during the idle mode. This also forces the status of the pins ALE and PSEN# to "1".

Due to this, the external EPROM is deselected. Thus, the above discussion clears that the instruction which sets the PCON.0 (IDL) causes the last instruction before going into idle mode.

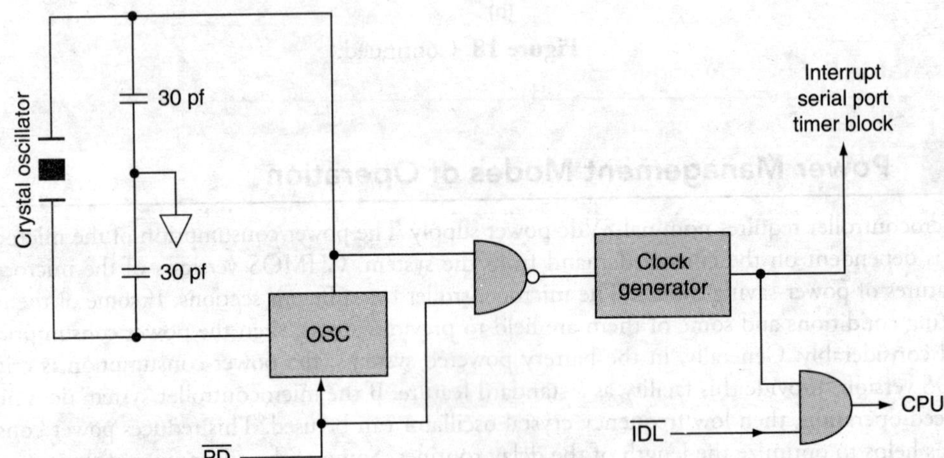

Figure 19 Hardware diagram for idle mode and power down mode.

9.8.2 Exit from Idle Mode

The idle mode is invoked by setting IDL# = 1. It is done in two ways:

1. Activation of any enabled interrupt will clear the PCON.0. This will execute the ISR and after RETI instruction, the CPU will start execution from the instruction just next to the idle mode entry.
2. The activation of RST pin clears the IDL bit directly and CPU resumes the program execution from where it was left.

9.8.3 Power Down Mode

This mode of activation is done by setting PCON.1 bit = 1 in the PCON register. This will stop the oscillator. If the microcontroller is driven with an external oscillator, it gets off the path to the internal phase generator. This will stop the clock and, hence, all the functions of the microcontroller. If the power supply voltage, that is, +Vdc is maintained, then the contents of the SFRs and RAM are held. This mode holds ALE and PSEN# pins at low logic level. The contents of the SFRs and the I/O port status are held unchanged. The instruction sets the PCON.1 bit = 1 and causes the last instruction executed before the action of power down mode. Table 9 summarizes the pin status in power down mode.

9.8.4 Exit from Power Down Mode

The power down mode can be terminated by following steps:

1. The power down mode stops the clock generation. Hence, the hardware reset is the only way to come out of the mode.
2. This needs to activate the RST pin for long time, so as to start the oscillator and stabilize.
3. The SFRs are initialized to their reset values and the program execution starts from 0000H. This will not change the contents of the RAM. The contents of RAM are retained.

Table 9 Power Down Mode

Pin	*Internal Execution*		*External Execution*	
	Idle	Power down	Idle	Power down
ALE	1	0	1	0
PSEN#	1	0	1	0
P0	SFR data	SFR data	High impedance	High impedance
P1	SFR data	SFR data	SFR data	SFR data
P2	SFR data	SFR data	PCH	SFR data
P3	SFR data	SFR data	SFR data	SFR data

SFR data: Internal register data
PCH: Higher byte of program counter

9.8.5 Use of Power-Saving Modes

The above discussion shows that power saving is done by using two modes. It is mainly advantageous for the battery powered system. Power down mode consumes less power than the idle mode. Following are the examples that explain the use of power-saving modes:

1. **Idle mode:** Figure 20 shows scheme for the idle mode. The mode can be used for campus lighting control system. The ambient light can be sensed by a light sensing hardware connected to INTx pin. The pin status will follow the condition as INTx pin = 0 (low intensity), INTx = 1 (high intensity). A program can be written to set the idle mode ON when the light intensity is high. When the intensity falls to low, the high-to-low transition on INTx pin activates the interrupt and invokes the system from the idle mode. This will switch ON the campus lights. As it goes high, the program will again go back to the idle mode by setting PCON.0 = 0.

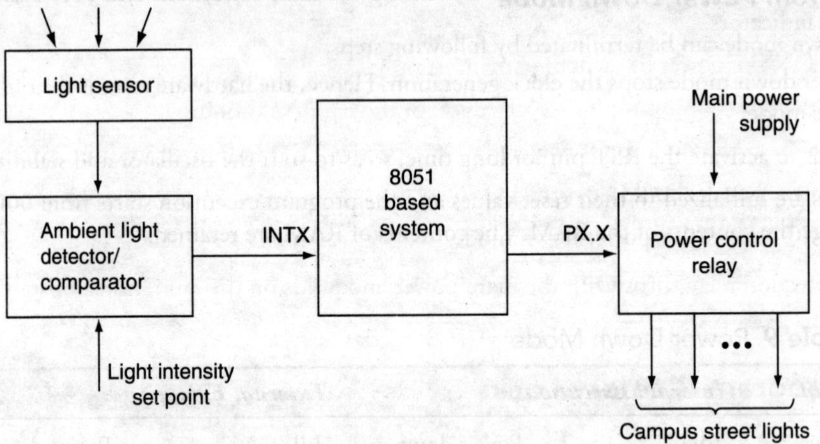

Figure 20 Campus street light control system.

2. **Power down mode:** Figure 21 shows scheme for power down mode. This mode can be used in home protection relay system. The hardware can be designed to activate an input pin of the microcontroller for the fault conditions such as low voltage, high voltage, over load, short circuit and earth leakage. A program can be written to follow the steps as:

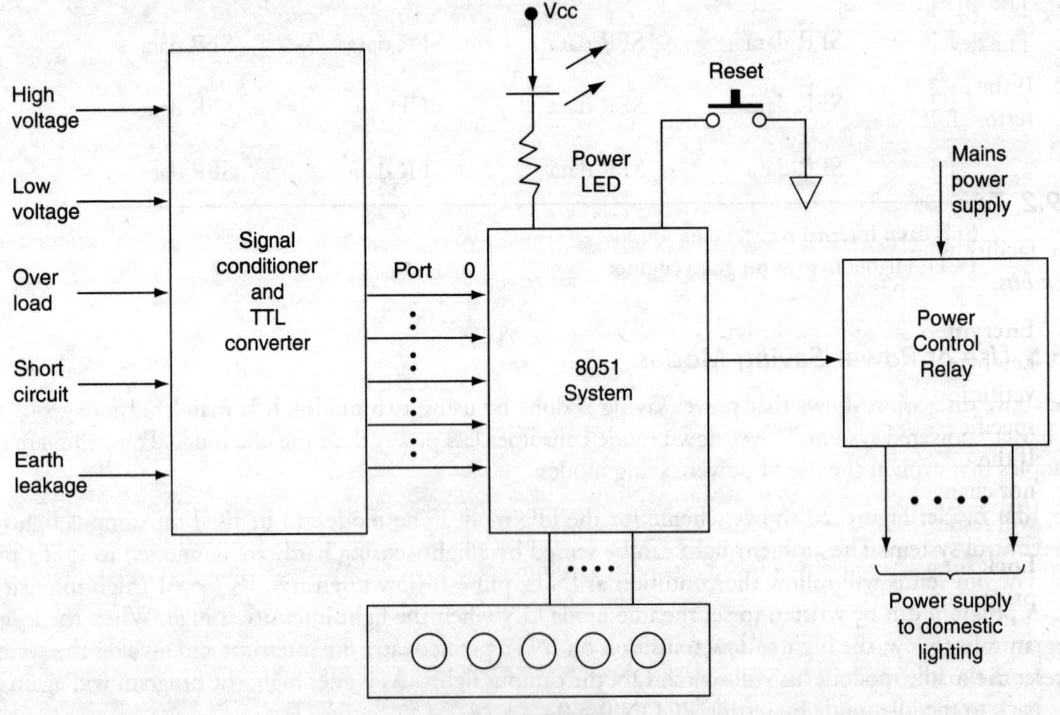

Figure 21 Home protection relay system.

- Initialize the system as Port 0 input for sensing the fault conditions and Port 1 as the output for LED indicators.
- Turn ON the power by switching mains supply.
- Scan the status of input pins for detection of the fault condition.
- When the fault condition is detected, the respective LED indicators must be switched ON.
- The main power should be turned OFF.
- Set PCON.1 = 1 for power down mode.

The home protection relay turns OFF the main power and holds on the fault indicator status.

9.9 Program Memory Locks

It is always desirable that the monitor program of the microcontroller system should be secured from piracy. 8051 microcontroller has software security lock facility which protects the program software from illegal reading or copying. The scheme in 8051 provides multilevel locking facility.

9.9.1 One Bit Lock

Th facility is provided in 8051H. It is only bit lock. The results of programming this bit are as follows:

1. The on-chip program memory-read operation is denied.
2. The device cannot be programmed further.
3. If the program memory is erased, the lock bit will be deactivated and full functionality of the device is restored. It means that the device can be re-programmed.

9.9.2 Two-Level Program Memory Lock

The facility is supported in 87C51 and 8752BH. It provides two schemes namely *Encrypted verify* and *Lock bits*.

1. **Encrypted verify:** It is mixing-up of some known information. Here the user has to program 32 key-byte EPROM array. The array is used to encrypt the program code bytes during EPROM data verification. Each byte of EPROM is X-NORed with one of the 32 key bytes. The key bytes are sent in specific sequence. The ROM code-reading process requires the same 32 key bytes in a proper sequence. If these 32 key bytes are not programmed then un-programmed bytes will contain FFH data. This will not change code bytes even if it is X-NORed. It means that leaving encryption array un-programmed will result in bypassing the encryption feature.
2. **Lock bits:** There are two lock bits. Table 10 shows the features. If the bits are un-programmed (U) or programmed (P), different features are possible.

Programming bit 1 samples the logic level of EA# at EA pin and latched during reset. It is always required to reset the microcontroller when powered ON otherwise the latch will hold any random value.

Table 10 Features of Lock Bits

Bit 2	*Bit 1*	*Additional features*
U	U	None
U	P	Externally fetched code cannot access internal program memory. Further programming is disabled.
P	U	Reserved
P	P	Externally fetched code cannot access internal program memory, further programming and verification disabled.

9.9.3 ROM Protection

8051 AHP and 8051 BHP are ROM protected versions of 8051 AH and 8051 BH, respectively. If this feature is used then program verification is disabled and external memory access is limited to 4 KB.

9.9.4 ONCE Mode

This mode, that is, on-circuit emulation, is very much useful for testing and debugging the system without removing the device from the circuit. The ONCE mode is invoked by the following steps:

1. Pull ALE pin low while the device is in reset and PSEN# in high.
2. Hold ALE low as RST is de-activated.
3. When the device is in ONCE mode, the Port 0 pins will go in tri-state and ALE, PSEN# and other port pins will be weakly pulled up. The oscillator stays in the active mode. While the device is in this mode, an emulator or test CPU can be used to drive the circuit. Normal operation is restored when normal reset is applied.

9.10 CPU Timing and Machine Cycle

The crystal oscillator signal internally generates different timing signals. These timing signals are used for synchronization of different operations like reading op-codes, moving data from source to destination, and addressing external memory etc. Following steps are useful for understanding the timing operations of CPU:

1. Figure 22 shows the state sequence in MCS 8051. The top most clock signal shows the waveform of the oscillator clock. A machine cycle consists of six states (s1–s6). Each state is of two clock periods, hence one machine cycle takes 12 clock periods.
2. The machine cycle states are numbered as S1P1 (state 1, period 2), S2P2 (state 1, period 2), …, S6P2 (state 6, period 2).
3. Typically arithmetic and logic operations occur during period one and register to register data transfer occurs during period two. The timing diagram in Fig. 22 shows the execution sequence in states and phases for different instructions.
4. One-byte two-cycle instruction, for example, MOVX instruction, accesses external data memory. Two fetches are skipped while the external data memory is being addressed and strobed.

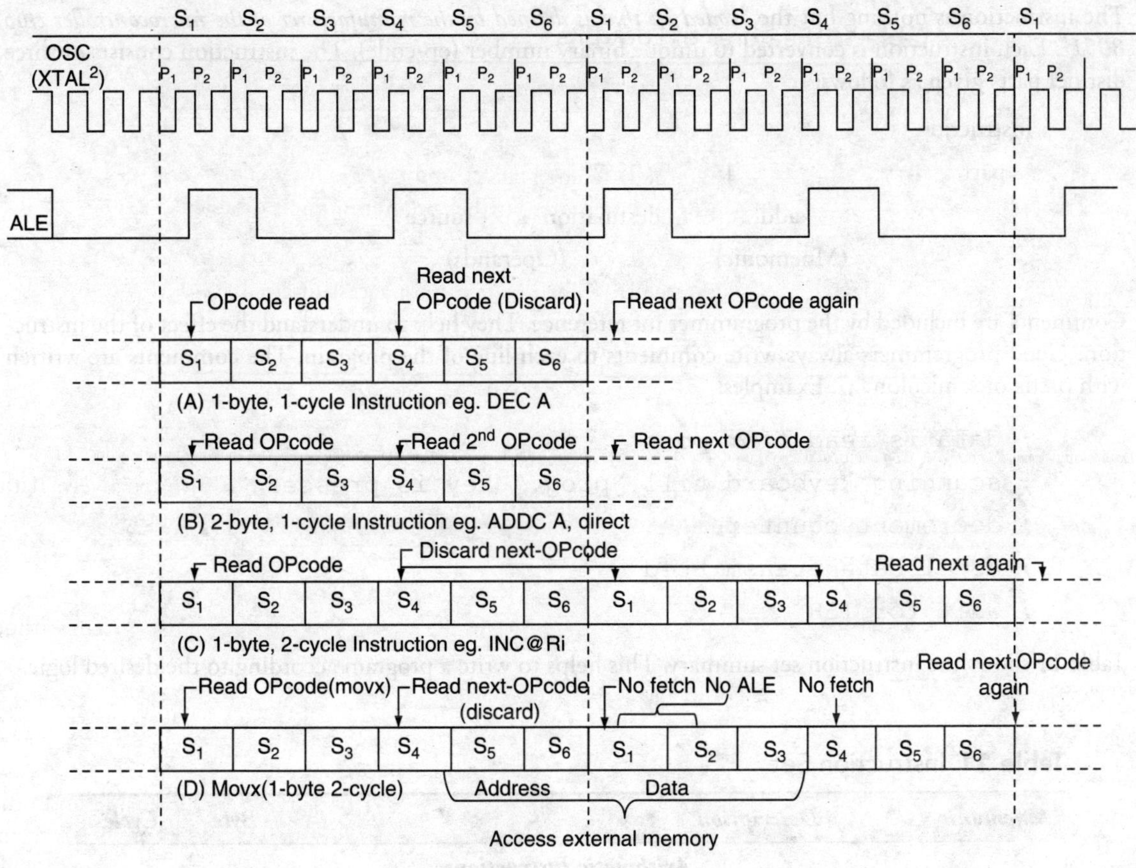

Figure 22 Timing diagram of CPU and machine cycles.

9.11 Instruction Set Summary and Format

The 8051 microcontroller needs to follow the steps, that is, instructions, for performing task desired by the programmer. The programmer has to enter the same task, that is, program into the microcontroller in a specific manner (i.e., syntax) known as the format of the instruction. The syntax for the program code of 8051 microcontroller is as follows:

```
Label: Instruction ; Comment(s)
```

Label is a combination of up to eight letters (A to Z), numbers (0 to 9) and (.). It must begin with a letter or "." . It should not begin with decimal number. Examples:

```
Delay:
Start:
Scan:
Routine3:
ISR4:
```

The instruction is nothing but the "*coded set that is defined by the manufacturer of the microcontroller chip 8051*". Each instruction is converted to unique binary number (op-code). The instruction consists of three distinct parts given as follows:

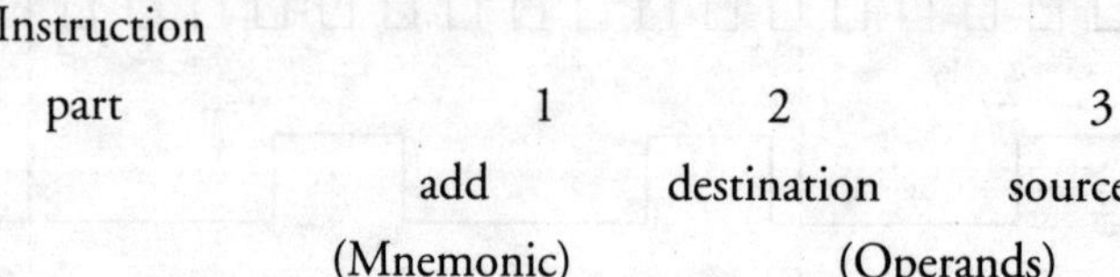

Comments are included by the programmer for reference. They help to understand the effect of the instruction. Good programmers always write comments to each line of the program. The comments are written with prefix of semicolon ";". Examples:

```
; data is read from port
; scanning keyboard till "prog." key is pressed
; decrement counter
; ASCII data transmitted
; wait for ISR
```

Table 11 shows the instruction set summary. This helps to write a program according to the desired logic.

Table 11 Instruction Set

Mnemonic	*Description*	*Byte*	*Cycle*
	Arithmetic Instructions		
ADD A,Rn	Adds the contents of register to the accumulator	1	1
ADD A,direct	Adds the direct data to the accumulator	2	2
ADD A,@Ri	Adds the indirect RAM data by the register data to the accumulator	1	2
ADD A,#data	Adds the immediate data to the accumulator	2	2
ADDC A,Rn	Adds the register to the accumulator with a carry flag	1	1
ADDC A,direct	Adds the direct byte to the accumulator with a carry flag	2	2
ADDC A,@Ri	Adds the indirect RAM data to the accumulator with a carry flag	1	2
ADDC A,#data	Adds the immediate data to the accumulator with a carry flag	2	2

(*Continued*)

Table 11 (Continued)

Mnemonic	*Description*	*Byte*	*Cycle*
SUBB A,Rn	Subtracts the register from the accumulator with a borrow	1	1
SUBB A,direct	Subtracts the direct byte from the accumulator with a borrow	2	2
SUBB A,@Ri	Subtracts the indirect RAM data from the accumulator with a borrow	1	2
SUBB A,#data	Subtracts the immediate data from the accumulator with a borrow	2	2
INC A	Increments the accumulator by 1	1	1
INC Rn	Increments the register by 1	1	2
INC Rx	Increments the direct byte by 1	2	3
INC @Ri	Increments the indirect RAM data by 1	1	3
DEC A	Decrements the accumulator by 1	1	1
DEC Rn	Decrements the register by 1	1	1
DEC Rx	Decrements the direct byte by 1	1	2
DEC @Ri	Decrements the indirect RAM data by 1	2	3
INC DPTR	Increments the Data Pointer by 1	1	3
MUL AB	Multiplies A and B	1	5
DIV AB	Divides A by B	1	5
DA A	Decimal adjustment of the accumulator according to BCD code	1	1
	Branch Instructions		
ACALL addr11	Absolute subroutine call	2	6
LCALL addr16	Long subroutine call	3	6
RET	Returns from subroutine	1	4
RETI	Returns from interrupt subroutine	1	4
AJMP addr11	Absolute jump	2	3
LJMP addr16	Long jump	3	4
SJMP rel	Short jump (from –128 to +127 locations relative to the following instruction)	2	3

(Continued)

Table 11 (Continued)

Mnemonic	*Description*	*Byte*	*Cycle*
JC rel	Jump if carry flag is set. Short jump.	2	3
JNC rel	Jump if carry flag is not set. Short jump.	2	3
JB bit,rel	Jump if direct bit is set. Short jump.	3	4
JBC bit,rel	Jump if direct bit is set and clears bit. Short jump.	3	4
JMP @A+DPTR	Jump indirect relative to the DPTR	1	2
JZ rel	Jump if the accumulator is zero. Short jump.	2	3
JNZ rel	Jump if the accumulator is not zero. Short jump.	2	3
CJNE A,direct,rel	Compares direct byte to the accumulator and jumps if not equal. Short jump.	3	4
CJNE A,#data,rel	Compares immediate data to the accumulator and jumps if not equal. Short jump.	3	4
CJNE Rn,#data,rel	Compares immediate data to the register and jumps if not equal. Short jump.	3	4
CJNE @ Ri,#data,rel	Compares immediate data to indirect register and jumps if not equal. Short jump.	3	4
DJNZ Rn,rel	Decrements register and jumps if not 0. Short jump.	2	3
DJNZ Rx,rel	Decrements direct byte and jump if not 0. Short jump.	3	4
NOP	No operation	1	1
	Data Transfer Instructions		
MOV A,Rn	Moves the register to the accumulator	1	1
MOV A,direct	Moves the direct byte to the accumulator	2	2
MOV A,@Ri	Moves the indirect RAM data to the accumulator	1	2
MOV A,#data	Moves the immediate data to the accumulator	2	2
MOV Rn,A	Moves the accumulator to the register	1	2
MOV Rn,direct	Moves the direct byte to the register	2	4
MOV Rn,#data	Moves the immediate data to the register	2	2
MOV direct,A	Moves the accumulator to the direct byte	2	3
MOV direct,Rn	Moves the register to the direct byte	2	3
MOV direct,direct	Moves the direct byte to the direct byte	3	4

(Continued)

Table 11 (Continued)

Mnemonic	*Description*	*Byte*	*Cycle*
MOV direct,@Ri	Moves the indirect RAM data to the direct byte	2	4
MOV direct,#data	Moves the immediate data to the direct byte	3	3
MOV @Ri,A	Moves the accumulator to the indirect RAM location	1	3
MOV @Ri,direct	Moves the direct byte to the indirect RAM location	2	5
MOV @Ri,#data	Moves the immediate data to the indirect RAM location	2	3
MOV DPTR,#data	Moves a 16-bit data to the data pointer	3	3
MOVC A,@ A+DPTR	Moves the code byte relative to the DPTR to the accumulator (address = A+DPTR)	1	3
MOVC A,@A+PC	Moves the code byte relative to the PC to the accumulator (address = A+PC)	1	3
MOVX A,@Ri	Moves the external RAM (8-bit address) to the accumulator	1	3-10
MOVX A,@DPTR	Moves the external RAM (16-bit address) to the accumulator	1	3-10
MOVX @Ri,A	Moves the accumulator to the external RAM (8-bit address)	1	4-11
MOVX @DPTR,A	Moves the accumulator to the external RAM (16-bit address)	1	4-11
PUSH direct	Pushes the direct byte onto the stack	2	4
POP direct	Pops the direct byte from the stack/td>	2	3
XCH A,Rn	Exchanges the register with the accumulator	1	2
XCH A,direct	Exchanges the direct byte with the accumulator	2	3
XCH A,@Ri	Exchanges the indirect RAM data with the accumulator	1	3
XCHD A,@Ri	Exchanges the low-order nibble indirect RAM with the accumulator	1	3
	Logic Instructions		
ANL A,Rn	AND register to accumulator	1	1
ANL A,direct	AND direct byte to accumulator	2	2
ANL A,@Ri	AND indirect RAM Data to accumulator	1	2

(Continued)

Table 11 (Continued)

Mnemonic	*Description*	*Byte*	*Cycle*
ANL A, #data	AND immediate data to accumulator	2	2
ANL direct,A	AND accumulator to direct byte	2	3
ANL direct, #data	AND immediae data to direct register	3	4
ORL A,Rn	OR register to accumulator	1	1
ORL A,direct	OR direct byte to accumulator	2	2
ORL A, @Ri	OR indirect RAM data to accumulator	1	2
ORL direct,A	OR accumulator to direct byte	2	3
ORL direct, #data	OR immediate data to direct byte	3	4
XRL A,Rn	Exclusive OR register to accumulator	1	1
XRL A,direct	Exclusive OR direct byte to accumulator	2	2
XRL A,@Ri	Exclusive OR indirect RAM data to accumulator	1	2
XRL A,#data	Exclusive OR immediate data to accumulator	2	2
XRL direct,A	Exclusive OR accumulator to direct byte	2	3
XORL direct,#data	Exclusive OR immediate data to direct byte	3	4
CLR A	Clears the accumulator	1	1
CPL A	Complements the accumulator (1=0, 0=1)	1	1
SWAP A	Swaps nibbles within the accumulator	1	1
RL A	Rotates bits in the accumulator left	1	1
RLC A	Rotates bits in the accumulator left through carry	1	1
RR A	Rotates bits in the accumulator right	1	1
RRC A	Rotates bits in the accumulator right through carry	1	1
	Bit-Oriented Instructions		
CLR C	Clears the carry flag	1	1
CLR bit	Clears the direct bit	2	3
SETB C	Sets the carry flag	1	1
SETB bit	Sets the direct bit	2	3
CPL C	Complements the carry flag	1	1
CPL bit	Complements the direct bit	2	3
ANL C,bit	AND direct bit to the carry flag	2	2

(Continued)

Table 11 (Continued)

Mnemonic	*Description*	*Byte*	*Cycle*
ANL C,/bit	AND complements of direct bit to the carry flag	2	2
ORL C,bit	OR direct bit to the carry flag	2	2
ORL C,/bit	OR complements of direct bit to the carry flag	2	2
MOV C,bit	Moves the direct bit to the carry flag	2	2
MOV bit,C	Moves the carry flag to the direct bit	2	3

The list of the operands and their meanings is as follows:

1. **A** – accumulator.
2. **Rn** – It is one of the working registers (R0-R7) in the currently active RAM memory bank.
3. **Direct** – It is any 8-bit address register of RAM. It can be any general-purpose register or the Special Function Register SFR (I/O port, control register, etc.).
4. **@Ri** – It is indirect internal or external RAM location addressed by register R0 or R1.
5. **#data** – It is an 8-bit constant included in instruction (0-255).
6. **#data16** – It is a 16-bit constant included as bytes two and three in instruction (0-65535).
7. **addr16** – It is a 16-bit address. It may be anywhere within 64 KB of program memory.
8. **addr11** – It is an 11-bit address. It may be within the same 2 KB page of program memory as the first byte of the following instruction.
9. **rel** – It is the address of a close memory location (from –128 to +127 relative to the first byte of the following instruction). On the basis of it, assembler computes the value to add or subtract from the number currently stored in the program counter.
10. **bit** – It is any bit addressable I/O pin, control or status bit.
11. **C** – It is carry flag of the status register (register PSW).

9.12 Addressing Modes for Data Transfer

8051 has eight addressing modes applicable. They are as follows:

1. Direct.
2. Indirect.
3. Immediate.
4. Register.
5. Relative.
6. Absolute.
7. Long.
8. Indexed.

These addressing modes will be discussed in the following subsections.

9.12.1 Direct Addressing Mode

This mode consists of two bytes, namely, op-code and address. The instructions are used to access hardware register or on-chip data/variables. This addressing mode can be used to access only on-chip RAM addresses ranging from 00H to 7FH. Example: MOV P2, A. The data in the accumulator is transferred to Port 2. The port address of Port 2 is A0. It is automatically inserted by assembler as a second byte of instruction.

9.12.2 Indirect Addressing Mode

The instruction operates on data pointed by the contents of the register R0 or R1. These are single-byte instructions. Example: SUBB A, @R1. The instruction subtracts data pointed by the contents of the register R1 from accumulator with carry.

9.12.3 Immediate Addressing Mode

The instructions with this mode are two byte instructions. The first byte is an op-code instruction and second byte is an operand. The operand can be numeric constant, arithmetic expression or a symbolic variable. It is denoted with "#" symbol. Example: ANL a, #56. The contents of accumulator are logically ANDed with immediate data 56H and the result is stored in the accumulator.

9.12.4 Register Addressing Mode

The instruction with this mode operates on the data in one of the specified eight (R0–R7) registers. There are four register banks. One out of four banks is selected by setting RS0 and RS1 bit in the PSW register. The power-on reset makes RS0 = RS1 = 0 and by default bank 0 become active. Example: ORL A, R4. The data in the accumulator is logically ORed with contents of register R4 and the result is kept in accumulator.

9.12.5 Relative Addressing Mode

This mode belongs to some of the JUMP instructions. An 8-bit signed value (offset) is added to the current value of program counter and the execution starts from the new formed address. The range of such JUMP instruction is −128 to +127 locations from existing address in the program counter. Example: JNZ rel. The contents of the accumulator are checked for 0. If it is not 0, then program counter will jump to address labeled "rel", otherwise it continues the execution from the next instruction.

9.12.6 Absolute Addressing Mode

The two instructions namely ACALL (absolute call) and AJMP (absolute jump) belong to this addressing mode. The branching is limited to the current 2 KB page of the program memory.

9.12.7 Long Addressing Mode

The two instructions, namely LCALL and LJMP, belong to this addressing mode. These are 3-byte instructions. The first byte is an op-code of the instruction and the next two bytes form 16-bit address which gets loaded in program counter for further execution. This enables to branch any where in full 64 KB of program memory address space.

9.12.8 Indexed Addressing Mode

The instructions JMP @A+DPTR, MOVC A, @A+DPTR and MOVC A, @A+PC support this addressing mode. The base register containing 16-bit address is added with an offset of 8-bit positive value to form new effective address. The contents of the accumulator are treated as an offset value in these instructions.

Summary

- The chapter has described the pin connections and their functions. Ports 0, 2 and 3 have multiple functions.
- 8051 has working registers and the SFRs.
- 8051 has program and data memory, timers/counters, serial communication module.
- 8051 also has the facility for power management and handling interrupts.
- 8051 can be used for embedded systems.

Chapter number 10 is devoted for interfacing an external memory to the 8051 microcontroller.

Multiple-Choice Questions

1. The DPTR of 8051 is _____ bit wide.

(a) 8

(b) 16

(c) 4

(d) 32

2. At power on the reset, the _____ register bank is set.

(a) bank 1

(b) bank 3

(c) bank 0

(d) bank 2

3. The content at 0000H location of 8051 is _____.

(a) data

(b) instruction

(c) flag

(d) none

4. Indirect addressing mode of 8051 uses _____ register.

(a) R0

(b) R4

(c) R3

(d) R2

5. 8051 does not have instruction for _____.

(a) addition

(b) subtraction

(c) multiplication

(d) integration

6. 8051 can execute _____ byte instructions.

(a) 3

(b) 4

(c) 5

(d) 6

7. The machine cycle of 8051 takes _____ clock cycles

(a) 8

(b) 16

(c) 12

(d) 32

8. 8051 controller consumes more power for _____ crystal oscillator

(a) 1 MHz

(b) 2 MHz

(c) 11.0592 MHz

(d) 16 MHz

9. The _____ instruction has 64 KB range of address.

(a) JNC

(b) LJMP

(c) DJNZ

(d) SJMP

10. The _____ register of 8051 cannot be decremented by an instruction.

(a) R0

(b) DPTR

(c) R1

(d) R2

Review Questions

1. Differentiate between microprocessors and the microcontrollers.
2. Explain the working of reset circuit of 8051 microcontroller.
3. What are the bits provided in PSW register?
4. What is the function of ALE pin in 8051 microcontroller?
5. Explain stack operation of 8051.
6. Explain the steps to change a bit of non-bit addressable register.
7. Which conditions set carry and auxiliary flag?
8. What is the use of register banks?
9. What are the different addressing modes in 8051 microcontroller?
10. Elaborate on the use of instructions used with DPTR.
11. Compare JUMP and CALL instructions.
12. Why does Port 0 not have internal pull-up resistances?
13. Explain the working of Port 1 as an input and output.
14. Which instructions are used to access RAM of 8051?
15. What actions can be taken to reduce power consumption of 8051?
16. What operations are done in ALU of the 8051?
17. What are the security facilities provided in 8051?
18. Explain lock bit scheme for program security in 8051?
19. What is the encrypted verification for program security in 8051?
20. What are the power management modes provided in 8051?
21. Explain the idle mode for power management in 0851.
22. Explain power down mode in 8051.
23. What is the function of pull-up resisters in 8051 ports?
24. Explain the use of TxD and RxD pins of 8051.
25. What is the function of CY flag? Explain with an example.
26. What is function of parity flag?
27. Explain the use of indirect addressing.
28. What is direct addressing?
29. What are the different addressing modes supported in 8051?
30. What are the conditions where zero flag is activated?
31. In which case OV flag activates?
32. What are the logical instructions in 8051?
33. What are the methods to clear accumulator?

34. Explain DA A instruction.
35. Explain RRC A instruction with an example.
36. Explain SWAP A instruction.
37. Explain execution sequence for 1 byte instruction in 8051.
38. Explain execution sequence for 2 byte instruction in 8051
39. Explain execution sequence for 3 byte instruction in 8051
40. Draw and explain block diagram of 8051 microcontroller.

Answers

Multiple Choice Questions

1. (b)
2. (c)
3. (b)
4. (a)
5. (d)
6. (a)
7. (c)
8. (d)
9. (b)
10. (b)

10 Interfacing External Data Memory and Program Memory to 8051

LEARNING OBJECTIVES

After reading this chapter, you will be able to:

- Compare the types of various memories.
- Describe the relation between capacity and address lines.
- Define data memory, program memory and describe their use in 8051.
- Explain how to use on-chip and external memory.
- Explain the steps followed by 8051 to address a memory location.
- Describe mechanism of multiplexed data and address bus.
- Use different combinations of RAM and ROM for 8051 system.

10.1 Introduction

In Chapter 9, we have seen the memory section of microcontroller 8051. It has on-chip memory. The whole memory is divided into two parts: (a) Program memory and (b) data memory. Some of the 8051 derivatives have various on-chip memory capacities. Following points show the utility of on-chip memory of 8051 microcontroller:

1. **Program memory:** The program memory contains the monitor program of the system. 8051 reads instructions from this program memory and performs operations accordingly. The program memory of 8051 is a ROM. Some of the variants of 8051 have EEPROM for program memory.
2. **Data memory:** The data memory of 8051 is a RAM. The data stored in this memory is volatile. It will remain in the RAM till the power supply of 8051 is ON.

Sometimes the monitor program of the system needs more space than the capacity of 8051, hence it is necessary to expand the program memory. This is done by connecting an external program memory by using EA and PSEN pins of 8051 microcontroller . The maximum addressable capacity of memory for 8051 is 128 KB.

The 128 KB memory can be divided into 64 KB program memory and 64 KB data memory. The program memory space is accessed by program counter, but the data memory space is accessed by DPTR register and MOVX instruction.

All memories have three types of busses, namely, address bus, data bus and control bus for interfacing with 8051. In addition to that, EA and PSEN pins of controller are needed.

10.2 Address Decoding for External Memory

The CPU of the microcontroller provides the address for accessing an external memory location. The external memory can be a ROM or RAM. These memories are physically separate integrated circuit (IC) chips. These are required to be addressed by using a decoding logic, and the same is known as chip select (CS) logic. CS is a hardware pin of the memory chip. CS pin is used along with EA and PSEN pins of microcontroller.

10.2.1 CS Pin

The CS pin is activated by using chip enable (CE) logic circuit. This logic helps to access a desired location in the memory. The following points are to be considered for connecting CPU to memory chip:

1. Data pins of memory chip and CPU should be directly connected together.
2. The control signals WR (write) and RD (read) of CPU should be connected to write enable (WE) and output enable (OE) pins of memory chip, respectively.
3. If lower address lines of CPU are connected to memory chip, then the higher address lines of CPU should be used to activate the CS pin of memory chip. The CS pin along with WR/RD pins of CPU controls the flow of data to and from memory chip. The read and write operation cannot be performed to memory unless the CS pin is activated.

The CS signal is normally active low and activated by output of decoder circuit. The TTL devices treat input as logic "1" if it is kept open or floating. If there is a disconnection of CS pin by mistake, this will not cause bus contention. Normally, the memories are divided into blocks and the output of decoder activates the selected block of the memory. Decoder logic can be generated by using the following devices:

1. Simple logic gates.
2. A decoder 74138 IC.
3. A programmable logic gate (PAL/GAL).

Figure 1 shows a decoder logic circuit using simple logic gates.

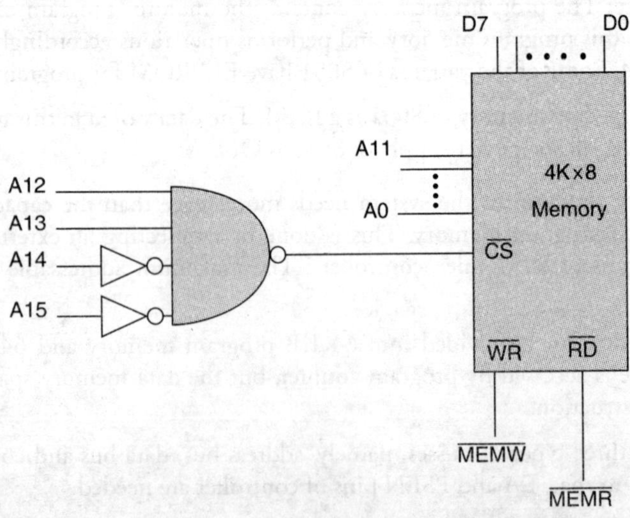

Figure 1 Logic gate as decoder.

Figure 2 shows a pin diagram and Table 1 shows the truth table of 74138 IC. The decoder IC eliminates the complexity of hardware and offers flexibility for CS logic.

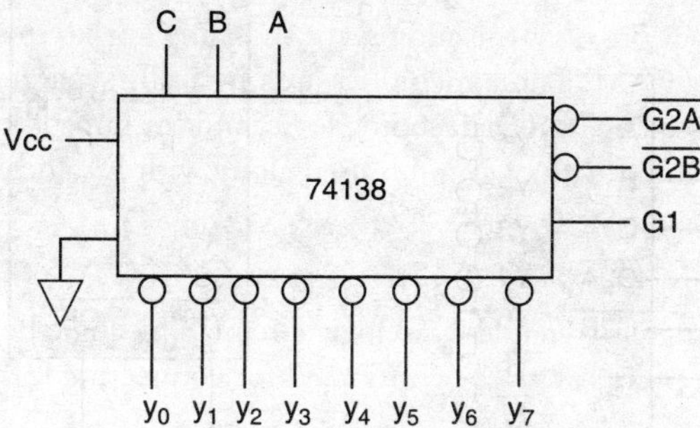

Figure 2 74138 pin-outs.

Table 1 Truth Table of Decoder

Inputs					*Outputs of 74138*							
Enable		*Select*										
G1	G2	C	B	A	Y0	Y1	Y2	Y3	Y4	Y5	Y6	Y7
X	1	X	X	X	1	1	1	1	1	1	1	1
0	X	X	X	X	1	1	1	1	1	1	1	1
1	0	0	0	0	0	1	1	1	1	1	1	1
1	0	0	0	1	1	0	1	1	1	1	1	1
1	0	0	1	0	1	1	0	1	1	1	1	1
1	0	0	1	1	1	1	1	0	1	1	1	1
1	0	1	0	0	1	1	1	1	0	1	1	1
1	0	1	0	1	1	1	1	1	1	0	1	1
1	0	1	1	0	1	1	1	1	1	1	0	1
1	0	1	1	1	1	1	1	1	1	1	1	0

Figure 3 shows an example where chip selection is done using decoder 74138. The lower address lines from A0 to A11 are connected to memory chip and remaining higher address lines are connected to input of decoder 74138. The Y4 output is activated for a unique combination of A15–A12, that is, 0100. This circuit can address memory locations ranging from 4000H to 4FFFH.

The PAL/GAL ICs have programming facility for setting desired CS logic. It requires a programming software and programming adaptor. This can have 10 or more input lines (74138 has only six input lines). They can have a capacity of thousands of addresses.

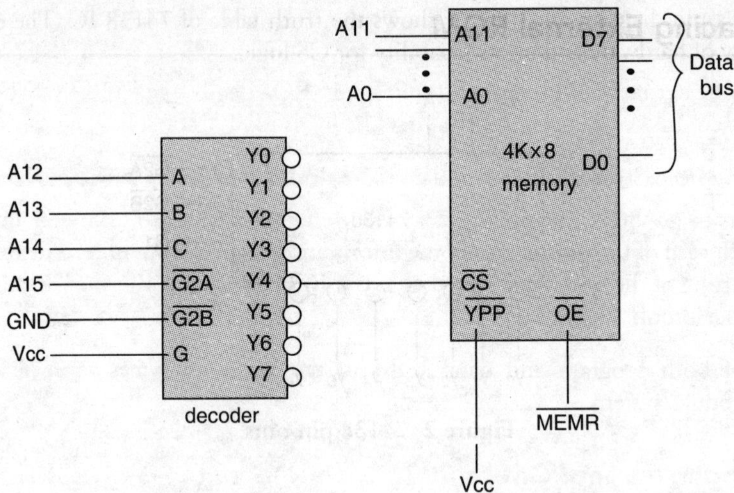

Figure 3 Chip select using decoder 74138.

10.2.2 EA Pin

It is an input signal to 8051 microcontroller. If 8051 is using an on-chip ROM, then this pin is connected to Vcc. If the monitor program is stored in external ROM, then the pin is connected to GND.

10.2.3 PSEN Pin

It is an output pin of 8051 microcontroller. This should be connected to OE pin of ROM containing monitor program code. It is always used with EA pin. If EA pin is grounded, then 8051 fetches op-code from external ROM. Figure 4 shows address, data and control bus for 8051.

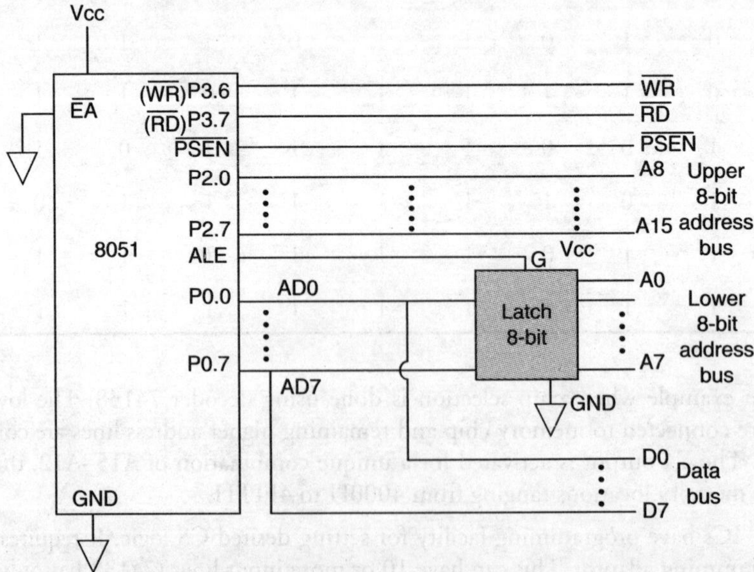

Figure 4 Address, data and control buses for 8051.

10.3 Interfacing External ROM

There are two types of external ROM for 8051: (a) Program ROM and (b) data ROM. The program ROM is always used to store monitor program code but data ROM is used in the following cases:

1. When the system needs a large amount of data to be read, for example, look-up tables.
2. If the user wants to use 8051 microcontroller in a product and wants to secure the information of the same in the birth card of the product, then the information like serial number, date of manufacture, or security code setting of the system are stored in a data ROM. The data ROM is "Read Only Memory"; hence it is tamper-proof.

The combination of both program and data ROM in the system provides more flexibility for mass production of the product/system.

10.3.1 Interfacing Program ROM to 8051

Figure 5 shows the connection for external program ROM. It shows that the 8-KB ROM is connected to 8051. The 8-KB ROM needs A0 to A12 address lines; hence, the address lines A13–A15 are not connected.

The EA pin is grounded for enabling 8051 to fetch program from external ROM; hence, PSEN pin is never activated. It is, therefore, used to activate CE# pin of the program ROM.

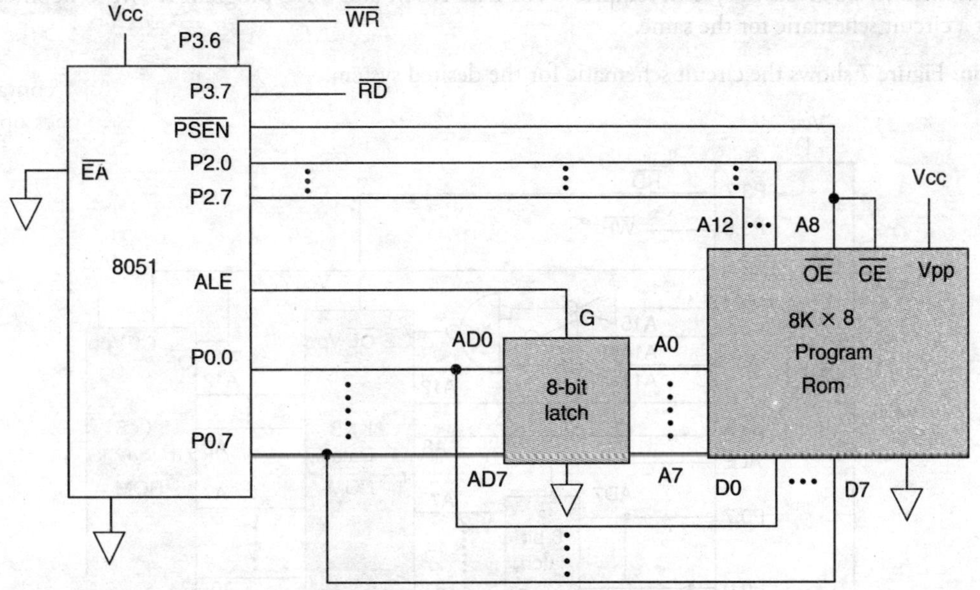

Figure 5 External program ROM connection to 8051.

10.3.2 Interfacing Data ROM to 8051

When an external data ROM is to be used, then the RD (pin P3.7) is to be connected to OE pin of the ROM chip. The data ROM is accessed by using MOVX instruction. This instruction is used along with DPTR. Figure 6 shows the connection diagram for external data ROM.

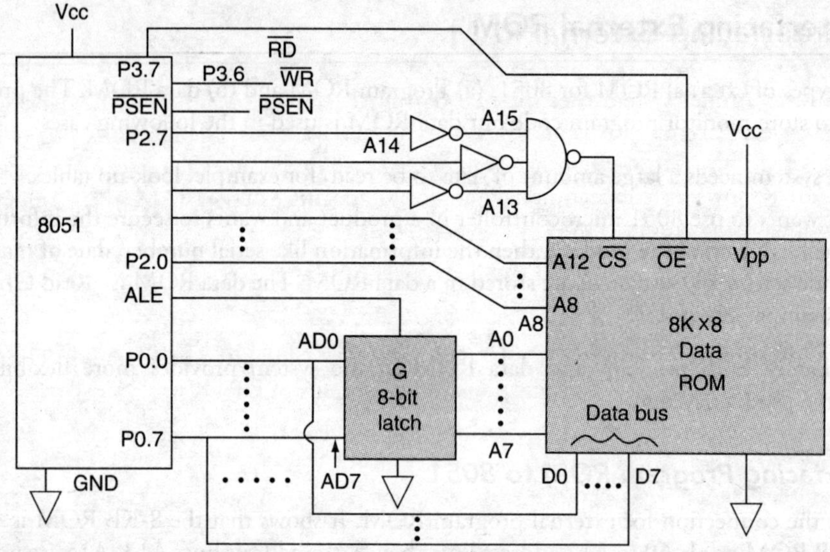

Figure 6 External data ROM connection to 8051.

Example 1

A microcontroller 8051-based system requires 8 KB data ROM and 8 KB program ROM to be interfaced. Suggest a circuit schematic for the same.

Solution: Figure 7 shows the circuit schematic for the desired system.

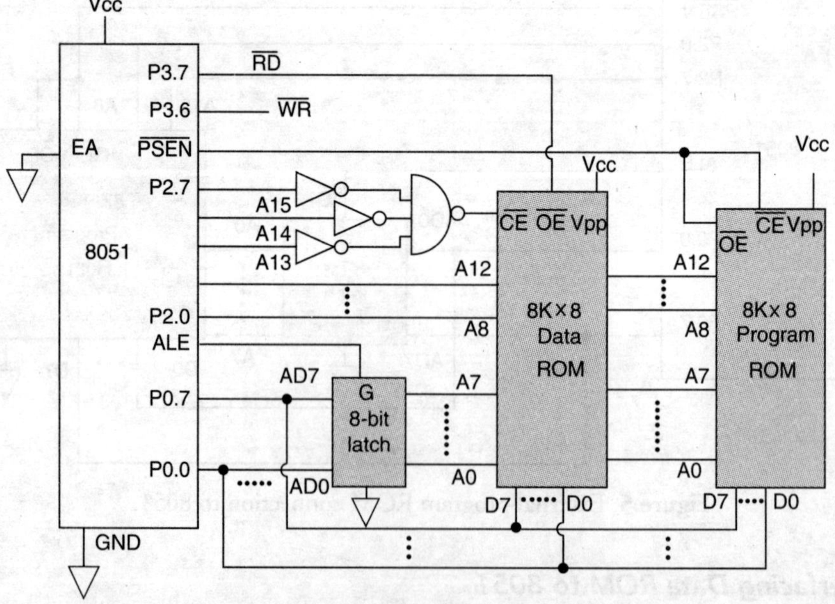

Figure 7 External data ROM and program connection to 8051.

10.4 Interfacing External RAM

The 8051 microcontroller system uses internal data RAM for its operations. The data RAM is nothing but SRAM. The capacity of SRAM in 8051 is only of 128 bytes. Some of the 8051 derivatives have kilobytes of SRAM, but, if the system needs more capacity of SRAM, then it is required to be interfaced externally. Figure 8 shows the connection diagram for interfacing external RAM to 8051 microcontroller for performing following operations:

1. The data from SRAM can be read or written to it; hence, it is required to connect both control signals, namely, WR (P3.6) and RD (P3.7).
2. The data is written to external SRAM by using MOVX @ DPTR, an instruction. The instruction will write accumulator data to the address pointed by contents of DPTR.
3. This has many applications in industries for logging data over a longer period of time. The SRAM can be replaced with an NV-RAM (non-Volatile RAM) which holds logged data even in case of power failure.

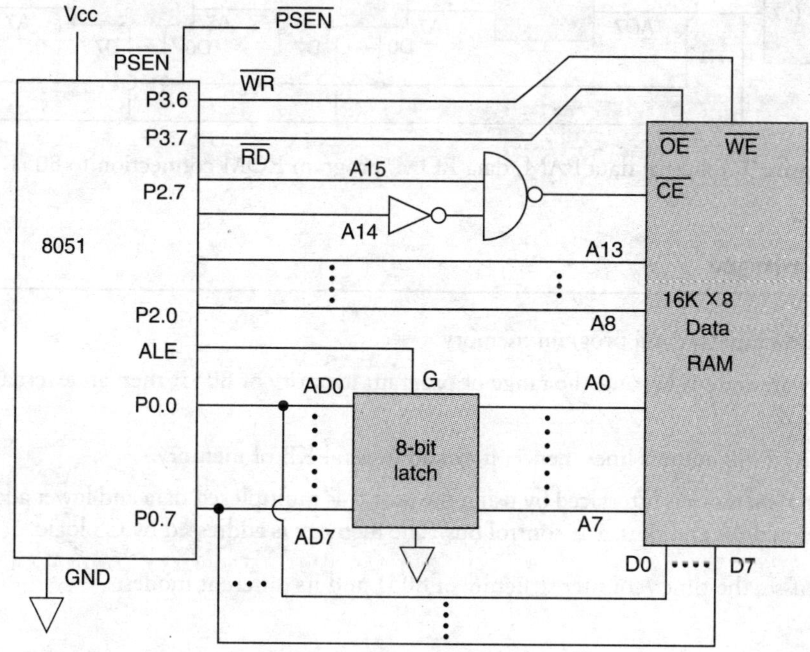

Figure 8 External data RAM connection to 8051.

Example 2

Show the design of 8051 microcontroller based system with 16-KB-data RAM, 16-KB-data ROM and 16-KB-program ROM.

Solution: Figure 9 shows the circuit schematic for desired system.

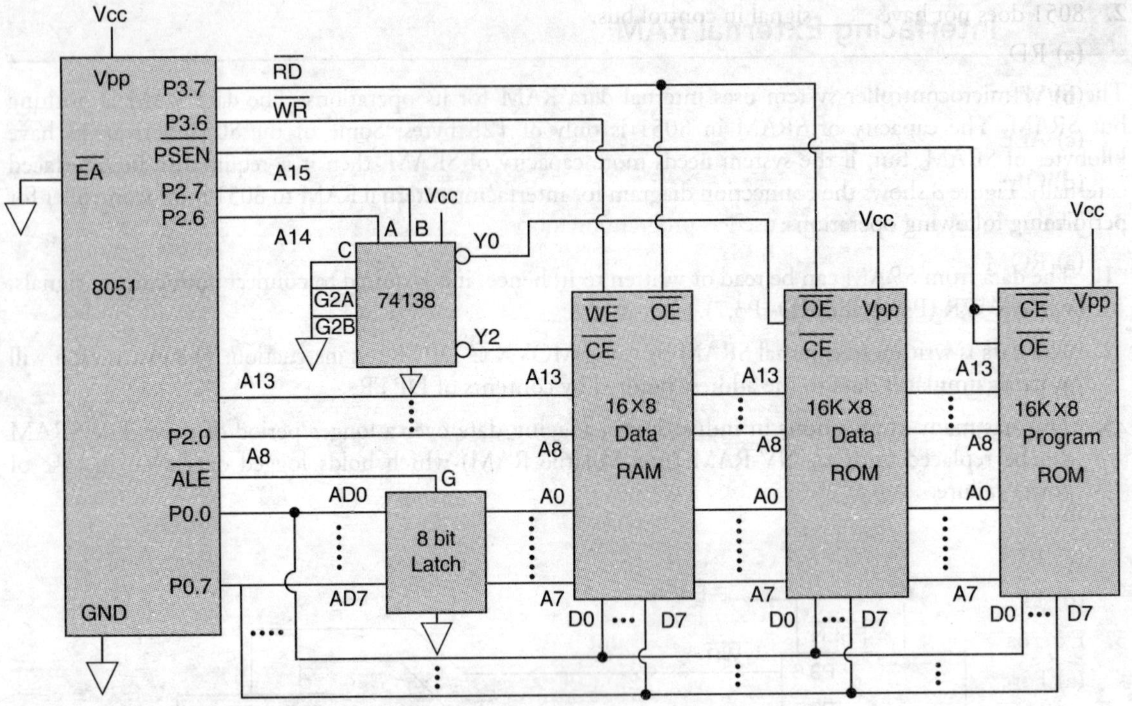

Figure 9 External data RAM, data ROM, program ROM connection to 8051.

Summary

- 8051 has on-chip data and program memory.
- If the software code is beyond the range of program memory of 8051, then an external memory can be interfaced.
- 8051 has A15–A0 address lines; hence, it can address 64 KB of memory.
- The external memory is interfaced by using the port 0 as multiplexed data and lower address bus, port 2 as higher address and port 3 as control bus. The memory is addressed by CS logic.

Chapter 11 discusses the timer/counter structure of 8051 and its different modes.

Multiple-Choice Questions

1. The program code of 8051 is always in

(a) ROM
(b) RAM
(c) NV-RAM
(d) data memory

2. 8051 does not have ____ signal in control bus.
   (a) RD
   (b) WR
   (c) ALE
   (d) OE
3. The ____ type of memory is used as program memory.
   (a) ROM
   (b) RAM
   (c) NV-RAM
   (d) EEPROM
4. For accessing 2-KB memory, ____ address lines are required.
   (a) 8
   (b) 9
   (c) 10
   (d) 11
5. External memory interfacing for 8051 does not need
   (a) Port 0
   (b) Port 1
   (c) Port 2
   (d) Port 3
6. For accessing 1000 memory locations, ____ address lines are required.
   (a) 8
   (b) 9
   (c) 10
   (d) 11
7. Externally connected ROM does not have ____ pin.
   (a) WR
   (b) RD
   (c) Vcc
   (d) CS
8. The ____ flip flops are used in address latching ICs.
   (a) RS type
   (b) JK type
   (c) Toggle type
   (d) D type

9. SRAM is considered as ____ memory.
(a) non-volatile
(b) pre-programmed
(c) volatile
(d) ROM

10. A memory having 20 address lines can access ____ locations.
(a) 1 MB
(b) 2 MB
(c) 3 MB
(d) 4 MB

Review Questions

1. Explain the address decoding for 8-KB RAM using simple logic gates.
2. What is the role of ALE pin for addressing external memory?
3. Explain the sequence of operation for accessing external ROM.
4. What is the role of PSEN pin in interfacing memory?
5. What is the role of CS and OE in interfacing memory?
6. Show chip selection logic for 4-KB RAM and 8-KB ROM using simple logic gates.
7. Explain MOVX instruction for accessing memory.
8. Design CS logic for addressing memory from 7000H to 7FFFH.
9. What are the advantages of using decoder IC instead of logic gates for CS logic?
10. Why chip select (CS) pin is generally active low?
11. Give an example where external RAM is required.
12. What are the advantages of using external ROM in 8051 system?
13. Compare the simple logic-gate-based and decoder-IC-based chip select circuit.
14. Show chip selection logic for 4-KB RAM and 4-KB ROM using the decoder chip.
15. Enlist and explain the signals required for interfacing data and program memory to 8051 microcontroller.

Answers

Multiple-Choice Questions

1. (a)
2. (d)
3. (a)
4. (d)
5. (b)
6. (c)
7. (a)
8. (d)
9. (c)
10. (a)

UNIT VI

Microcontroller – II

11 Programming Timers/Counters of 8051

LEARNING OBJECTIVES

After reading this chapter, you will be able to:

- Use the special function register (SFRs) of 8051.
- Use different modes of 8051 timers.
- Program 8051 timers in assembly language to generate time delays.
- Program 8051 counters in assembly language to work as an event counter and a frequency counter.

11.1 Introduction

Chapter 10 has given insight into microcontroller 8051. Now, we will see the different modes of timer/counter and the programming steps and procedure. Microcontroller 8051 has two 16-bit timers. The timers can be used for different applications. Both the timers can be used as a counter. The timers can be programmed according to the function requirement. The following sections will help us to understand different modes of timer/counter.

11.2 Timer Programming in Mode 0

Mode 0 of timer/counter has the following characteristics:

1. Mode 0 of timer/counter is the same as Mode 1, except for the modulus of the counter.
2. It is an 8-bit counter with divide-by-32 prescaler with a counting range from 0000H to 01FFFH.
3. It uses lower 5 bits of the TL for prescaler and ignores the upper 3 bits.
4. The timer is started by setting TR0 for Timer 0 and TR1 for Timer 1.
5. The timer counts up to the limit 1FFFH. As it overflows, it sets TF flag bit (Timer 0 = TF0 and Timer 1 = TF1). The timer flag can be monitored to stop the timer. It is done by clearing TR0 for Timer 0 and TR1 for Timer 1.
6. If the timer is not stopped after overflow, then it starts counting from 0000H towards 1FFFH.

11.3 Timer Programming in Mode 1

Mode 1 of timer/counter has the following characteristics:

1. It is a 16-bit timer with the range of counting from 0000H to FFFFH.

2. The initial value is loaded in TH and TL registers to count from the initial value to the FFFFH value.
3. The timer is started by setting TR0 for Timer 0 and TR1 for Timer 1.
4. The timer counts up to the limit FFFFH. As it overflows, it sets TF flag bit (Timer 0 = TF0 and Timer 1 = TF1). The timer flag can be monitored to stop the timer. It is done by clearing TR0 for Timer 0 and TR1 for Timer 1.
5. If the timer is not stopped after overflow, then it starts counting from 0000H towards FFFFH.
6. If it is required to start the counting process by presetting TH and TL, then the process should be followed from step 2.

The following steps are to be used to program timer in Mode 1 to generate a time delay:

1. Load the TMOD register with the desired value for setting which timer (Timer 0 or Timer 1) is to be used and which timer mode (0 or 1) is selected.
2. Load registers TL and TH with the calculated count value by referring to the clock frequency.
3. Start the desired timer (0 or 1) by setting TR bit in TCON register.
4. Keep monitoring the timer flag (TFx) with proper software instruction, for example JNB TFx, to check if it is set.
5. Stop the timer clearing TRx bit in TCON register.
6. Reset the TF flag to "0" for the next round.
7. Go back to follow from step 2 where the TH and TL are loaded again.

Example 1

The following program shows how to generate square wave of 50% duty cycle on the P1.7 bit. Timer 0 is used to generate the time delay. What are the steps involved in the program?

```
      MOV TMOD, #01     ;Timer 0, mode 1(16-bit mode)
WAIT: MOV TL0, #0F2H    ;TL0=F2H, the low byte
      MOV TH0, #0FFH    ;TH0=FFH, the high byte
      CPL P1.7          ;toggle P1.7
      ACALL DELAY
      SJMP WAIT
DELAY:
      SETB TR0          ;start the Timer 0
AGAIN:
      JNB TF0, AGAIN    ;monitor timer flag 0 until it rolls
                        over
      CLR TR0           ;stop Timer 0
      CLR TF0           ;clear Timer 0 flag
      RET
```

Solution: The above program shows the following steps:

1. TMOD is loaded to set Timer 0 in Mode 1 (16-bit timer).
2. FFF0H is loaded into TH0–TL0 (TH0 = FFH and TL0 = F0H).
3. P1.7 is toggled for getting square wave output (on time = off time).
4. The DELAY subroutine is called for Timer 0.
5. DELAY subroutine sets TR0 bit to start Timer 0.
6. Timer 0 counts up the clock pulses coming from the one-twelfth of crystal frequency divider.

Example 2

Find the delay generated by Timer 0 in the following code using hex as well as decimal method. Do not include the overhead due to instruction. Assume crystal frequency as 12 MHz.

```
        CLR P2.3            ;Clear P2.3
        MOV TMOD,#01        ;Timer 0, 16-bit mode
LOOP:   MOV TL0,#3AH        ;TL0=3Eh, the low byte
        MOV TH0,#0B8H       ;TH0=B8H, the high byte
        SETB P2.3           ;Set port pin P2.3
        SETB TR0            ;Start the Timer 0
AGAIN:JNB TF0,AGAIN         ;Monitor timer flag 0
        CLR TR0             ;Stop the Timer 0
        CLR TF0             ;Clear TF0 for next round
        CLR P2.3            ;Reset port pin P2.3
        SJMP LOOP
```

Solution: Consider the following steps:

1. (FFFFH – B83A + 1) = 47C6H = 18374 in decimal and 18374 × 1 μs = 18.374 ms.
2. Since TH – TL – B83AH – 47162 (in decimal), we have 65536   47162 = 18374. This means that the timer counts from B38AH to FFFF. This plus rolling over to 0 goes through a total of 18374 clock cycles, where each clock is 1 μs in duration.

Therefore, we have 18374 × 1 μs = 18.374 ms as the width of the pulse at P2.3.

The following steps show the calculation of the values to be loaded into the TL and TH registers, assuming crystal frequency as 12 MHz:

1. Divide the desired time delay by 1 μs. The result denoted by '*n*'.
2. Perform 65536 – *n*, where *n* is the decimal value we got in step 1.

3. Convert the result of step 2 to hex, where *xxyy* is the initial hex value to be loaded into the timer's register.
4. Set TL = *yy* and TH = *xx*.

Example 3

Calculate the values to be loaded to generate delay of 5 ms. Show the program for Timer 0 to create a pulse width of 5 ms on P2.6. Assume crystal frequency as 11.0592 MHz.

Solution: Since crystal frequency is 11.0592 MHz, the counter counts up every 1.085 μs. This means that out of many 1.085 μs intervals, we must make a 5 ms pulse. So, we need 5 ms/1.085 μs = 4608 clock pulses. To implement this, we need to load TL and TH registers with the value 65536 – 4608 = EE00H. It means that TH = EE and TL = 00. The program is as follows:

```
       CLR P2.6            ;Clear P2.6
       MOV TMOD,#01        ;Timer 0, 16-bitmode
LOOP:  MOV TL0,#0          ;TL0=0, the low byte
       MOV TH0,#0EEH       ;TH0=EE, the high byte
       SETB P2.6           ;SET high P2.6
       SETB TR0            ;Start Timer 0
AGAIN:JNB TF0,AGAIN        ;Monitor timer flag 0
       CLR TR0             ;Stop the Timer 0
       CLR TF0             ;Clear Timer 0 flag
       CLR P2.6            ;Clear P2.6
       SJMP LOOP
```

Example 4

Write a program to generate a square wave with a frequency of 2 KHz on pin P1.6. Assume crystal frequency as 11.0592 MHz.

Solution: The square wave is generated by toggling the port pin P1.6. The following steps show the process:

1. $T = 1/f = 1/2$ kHz = 500 μs the period of square wave.
2. It means that P1.6 should be made high for 250 μs and low for 250 μs.
3. 250 μs/1.085 μs = 230 and 65536 – 230 = 65306, that is, FF1AH.
4. TL = 1AH and TH = FFH.

The program is as follows:

```
       MOV TMOD,#01       ;Timer 0, 16-bit mode
AGAIN:MOV TL1,#1AH        ;TL1=1A, low byte of timer
       MOV TH1,#0FFH      ;TH1=FF, the high byte
```

```
         SETB TR1              ;Start Timer 1
         SETB P1.6             ;set pin P1.6
    WAIT:JNB TF1,WAIT          ;wait until timer rolls over
         CLR TR1               ;Stop the Timer 1
         CLR P1.6              ;Clear pin P1.6
         CLR TF1               ;Clear Timer 1 flag
         SJMP AGAIN            ;Reload timer
```

11.4 Timer Programming in Mode 2

Mode 2 of timer provides the following characteristics and operations:

1. It separates the 16-bit timer register into a pair of 8-bit registers where TL is an 8-bit timer and TH acts as a preset register, where any value between 00H and FFH can be loaded into it.
2. An 8-bit value is loaded into TH, and 8051 copies the same into the TL timer register. Timer 0 is started by instruction SETB TR0 and Timer 1 with SETB TR1.
3. As the timer is started, it counts up by incrementing the TL register and reaches its limit of FFH. As it rolls over from FFH to 00H, it sets the TF (timer flag) to "1".
4. As TF is set to 1, TL gets reloaded automatically with the preset value in TH register. The process can be repeated by only clearing the TF flag. This makes Mode 2 an auto-reload.

Example 5

Write a program to generate a square wave using Timer 1 with 25 kHz frequency on pin P2.4. Assume crystal frequency as 12 MHz.

Solution: The following steps show the process:

1. The period of the square wave is calculated as $T = 1/25 = 40$ µs.
2. It means that P2.4 should be made high for 20 µs and low for 20 µs.
3. 20 µs/1 µs = 20 and 256 – 20 = 236 in decimal, that is, ECH.
4. TH – ECH.

The program is as follows:

```
         MOV TMOD,#20H         ;Set Timer 1 in mode 2 (Auto reload)
         MOV TH1,#0ECH         ;Set TH1=ECH
         SETB TR1              ;Start Timer 1
    WAIT:JNB TF1,WAIT          ;Wait until Timer 1 rolls over
         CPL P2.4              ;Compliment port pin P2.4
         CLR TF1               ;Clear TF1
         SJMP WAIT             ;Mode 2 is auto reloaded
```

11.5 Applications of Timer/Counter

The basic timer/counter provided in 8051 is mainly a clock/pulse counter and signal waveform generation like pulse and square wave. It can also be used for applications like event counting, frequency measurement and pulse width measurement. The preceding discussion gives an idea about applications.

11.5.1 Event Counter

Figure 1 shows the circuit schematic for an event counter. This application can be used for counting the number of bottles passing over a conveyor and for giving alarm at the end of desired batch size. Generally, the bottles are detected by using a through beam type optical proximity sensor operating on 12 Vdc. The detected signal is then converted into TTL signal level to become compatible with 8051 controller. Once it is converted to TTL level, then the following steps will guide to use 8051 as an event counter using Timer/Counter 1.

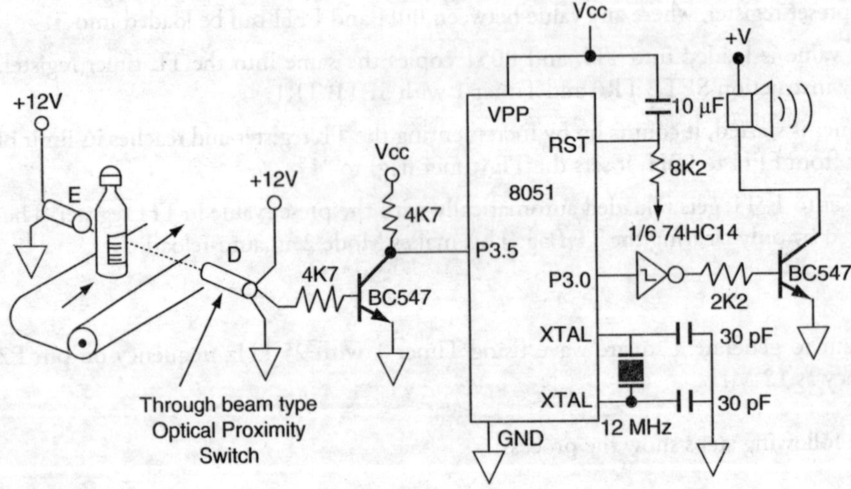

Figure 1 Event counter.

1. Initialize Timer 1 by setting TMOD register as follows:
   - TMOD.0 – TMOD.3 = 0.
   - TMOD.4 = 1, TMOD.5 = 0 –>Mode 1.
   - TMOD.6 = 1 –> Timer 1 as a 16 bit counter to take signal from port pin P3.5.
   - Connect optical proximity sensor to P3.5.
   - TMOD.7 = 0 –> Gate is not used for controlling counting process.
   - Connect P3.0 to Buzzer/alarm driver.
2. Preset TH1 and TL1 = 65536-batch size.
3. Set bit P3.0 to switch off alarm.
4. Set TR1 = 1 to enable counting process.
5. Keep on scanning TF1 flag.

6. If flag is not set, then jump to step 5.
7. If TF1 is set, then switch on alarm by clearing P3.0 = 0.
8. Jump to step 2.

11.5.2 Frequency Measurement

There are a number of measurements where the information is in the form of frequency. Examples include the mains frequency and angular speed of a rotor. Figure 2 shows a circuit schematic for an application of 8051 as mains frequency metre. Mains frequency is specified in Hertz. It is measured as the number of cycles per second. Generally, it is 50 Hz or 60 Hz. The mains signal is converted into TTL compatible signal by using simple Schmitt trigger integrated circuit (IC) so as to match with the 8051 signal standard. This will require the following:

1. 1 second delay routine.
2. An 8-bit counter.
3. An 8-bit output port for displaying measured frequency data in hexadecimal form.
4. An input port pin for getting frequency signal into 8051 controller.

The following steps discuss an application of 8051 as frequency metre.

1. Initialize Timer 1 by setting TMOD register as follows:
   - TMOD.0 – TMOD.3 = 0.
   - TMOD.4 = 1, TMOD.5 = 0 –>Mode 1.
   - TMOD.6 = 1 –> Timer 1 as a 16-bit counter to take mains frequency signal from port pin P3.5.
   - TMOD.7 = 0 –> Gate is not used for controlling counting process.
   - Port 1 as an output port for displaying measured frequency.

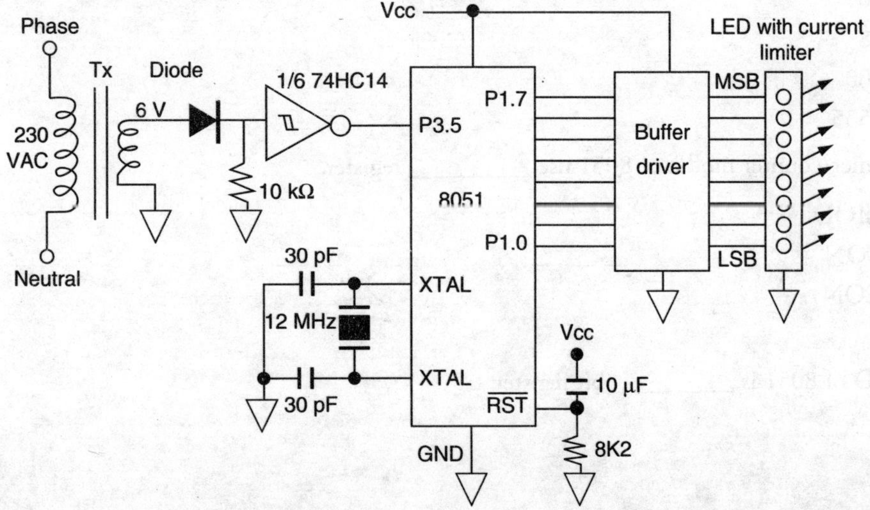

Figure 2 Mains frequency metre.

2. Clear TH1 and TL1 = 00H.
3. Out put data of TL1 to Port 1.
4. Set TR1 = 1 to start counting process.
5. Call 1 second delay routine.
6. Clear TR1 = 0 to stop counting process.
7. Out put the contents of TL1 on Port 1.
8. Jump to step 2.

Summary

- 8051 has a pair of timer/counter. They are used as timers to generate time delays. When the clock source is disconnected, then they can be used as event counters.
- The 16-bit timers can be programmed for various modes. They are accessed as lower byte and higher byte, namely, TLx and THx.
- Both timer operations are programmed by setting the TMOD register.
- The timers can be programmed in 4 modes; Mode 0, 1, 2 and 3. Mode 3 is rarely used.
- When the timer/counter is clocked by crystal oscillator, then it is called timer and when clocked by external pins (T0 or T1), then it is called counter. Both the counters are pre-settable up counters.

Chapter 12 is devoted for understanding the serial communication section of 8051.

Multiple-Choice Questions

1. 8051 with 12-MHz crystal can generate maximum delay of __________ μs.

   (a) 256
   (b) 128
   (c) 1000
   (d) 65535

2. The timer/counter modes of 8051 use _________ register.

   (a) TMOD
   (b) SCON
   (c) PCON
   (d) IP

3. TMOD of 8051 is _________ bit register.

   (a) 4
   (b) 8
   (c) 16
   (d) 32

4. Mode 0 of timer with 12-MHz crystal generates a delay of ________ µs.

   (a) 8191
   (b) 1000
   (c) 2048
   (d) 8000

5. The Mode 2 of Timer 1 can count a maximum of ________ clock pulses.

   (a) 8
   (b) 16
   (c) 255
   (d) 512

6. Timer overflow flag is in ________ register.

   (a) TCON
   (b) TMOD
   (c) IE
   (d) IP

7. In Mode 0 of timers, TL is of ________ bits.

   (a) 4
   (b) 5
   (c) 6
   (d) 8

8. TL in Mode 0 overflows after ________ clock pulses.

   (a) 8
   (b) 16
   (c) 32
   (d) 64

9. Timer 1 in Mode 1 acts as ________ counter.

   (a) 8-bit
   (b) bi-directional
   (c) down
   (d) up

10. The upper 3 bits of TL in Mode 0 are

    (a) not used
    (b) used as flags
    (c) used as I/O
    (d) used as a decoder

Review Questions

1. What is the function of TMOD register?
2. Is it possible to use Timers 0 and 1 interrupts in place of INT0 and INT1?
3. Explain the scheme for pulse-width measurement using timers of 8051.
4. Design MOD-60 counter using Timer 0 of 8051.
5. How can external frequencies be measured with 8051.
6. Explain the use of TCON register of 8051.
7. Generate 1 sec. time base signal using 8051 timer. Comment on the selection of oscillator frequency.
8. What is the function of C/T# bit of TMOD register?
9. Explain the function of GATE bit in TMOD register.
10. Write a program to generate 2 KHz square wave using Mode 0 of Timer 0.
11. Write a program to generate 1 KHz pulse waveform with 25% duty cycle using Mode 1 of Timer 1.
12. Explain with hardware diagram Timer 1 in auto-reload mode.
13. Explain the function of TCON register.
14. What is the use of external hardware interrupts in timers of 8051?
15. Explain the working of timers of 8051 in Mode 3.

Answers

Multiple-Choice Questions

1. (d)
2. (a)
3. (b)
4. (a)
5. (c)
6. (a)
7. (b)
8. (c)
9. (d)
10. (a)

12 Serial Port Structure of 8051 and Programming

LEARNING OBJECTIVES

After reading this chapter, you will be able to:

- Describe similarities in parallel and serial communication.
- Use protocol for serial communication.
- Compare and contrast asynchronous and synchronous communication.
- Describe advantages of serial communication.
- Compare and contrast full- and half-duplex communication.
- Explain data framing process.
- Use different baud rates.
- Define RS232 standard for communication.
- Use MAX 232 chip to Interface 8051 with computer with RS232 connector.
- Describe features of serial communication process of 8051.
- Write program for serial communication using 8051.

12.1 Introduction

Data transfer between two points is known as communication. The data may be analog or digital. As the microcontroller is a digital device, we will consider digital data communication. There are two possible ways of data transfer between two points:

1. **Parallel data transfer:** It requires an 8-bit wide port at both transmitting and receiving ends. This requires one common electrical ground line in between two points. Sometimes additional lines are used as handshake between the points for faithful data transfer.
2. **Serial data transfer:** It requires one line for data and the other line as a common ground between two points. It uses shift registers. Data sending point is known as transmitter and receiving point is known as receiver. The transmitter uses parallel-in-serial-out and receiver uses serial-in-parallel-out shift register. Figure 1 shows the connection between the two points.

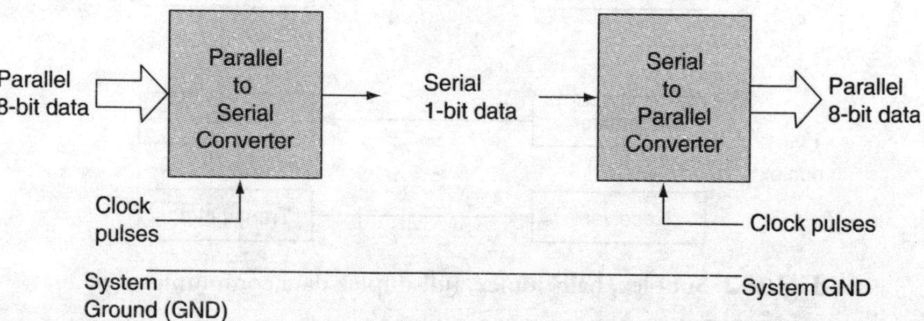

Figure 1 Serial input/output connection.

The comparative study of both types of data transfer is given in Table 1.

Table 1 A Comparison of Serial and Parallel Data Transfers

Serial Data Transfer	*Parallel Data Transfer*
At a time, 1-bit data is transferred	At a time, 8 bits of data is transferred
Data transfer is slow	Data transfer is fast
Useful for short and long distance	Useful only for short distance
Low-cabling cost	High-cabling cost
No possibility of crosstalk	Possibility of crosstalk
Multi-point data transfer is possible	Multi-point data transfer is not possible
Wireless data transfer is possible	Wireless data transfer is not possible

12.2 Basic Types of Communication System

The classification of communication system is based on the transmission method. It is as follows. Figure 2 gives the connection diagrams for all the different types of communication system.

1. **Simplex:** It is one-way communication. At any instance of time, the data transfer is only in one direction. It means that point *A* is the transmitter and point *B* is the receiver.

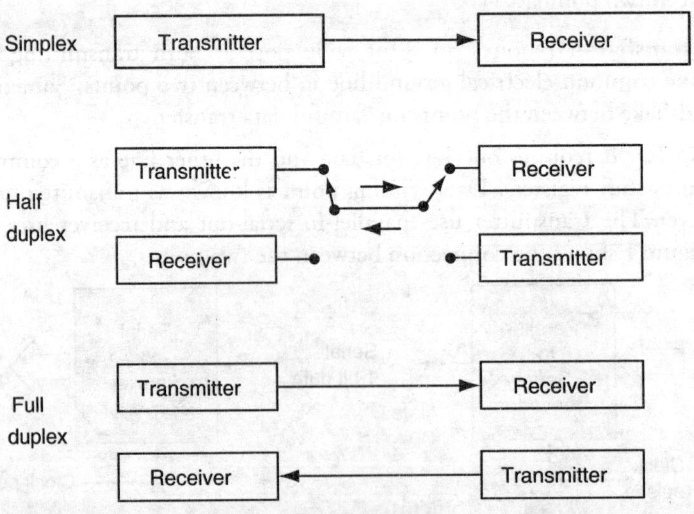

Figure 2 Simplex, half-duplex, full-duplex data communication.

2. **Duplex:** It is two-way data transfer type communication further divided as half duplex and full duplex.

   - **Half duplex:** The data transfer is two way. The two points are connected in such a manner that the data transfer is only in one direction at a time.
   - **Full duplex:** There are two independent connections between both the points *A* and *B*, so the data transfer is possible in both directions simultaneously.

12.3 Data Transmission Formats

There are two types of data transfer in serial communication, namely, asynchronous and synchronous.

12.3.1 Asynchronous Data Transfer

Asynchronous data transfer uses independent physical clocks for the transmitter and the receiver, hence the name. 8051 has built-in Universal Asynchronous Receiver-Transmitter (UART). Some of the peculiarities of asynchronous data transfer are as follows:

1. It is used for less amount of data transfer, typically "character"-oriented data transfer.
2. The synchronization between the transmitter and the receiver is done by a start bit, then the data is transferred bit-by-bit with the least significant bit first.
3. The data bits are followed by stop bits. Sometimes more number of stop bits are used. Table 2 shows the asynchronous data format for communication.
4. Before receiving the data, the receiver detects a low level on data line for one bit time and then it is treated as valid start bit.
5. After receiving the start bit, the receiver accepts data bits from D0 to D7. It checks for a stop bit and then goes back to the initial status. The same process is followed for the next data byte.
6. The communication speed is synchronized between the transmitter and the receiver by maintaining predefined baud rate (bit period).

Figure 3 shows the format for asynchronous communication.

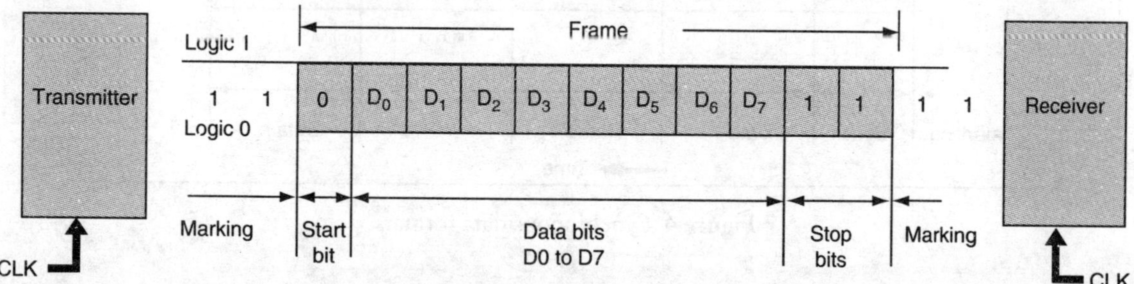

Figure 3 Asynchronous data format.

Table 2 Asynchronous Data Format

Specification	*Typical Values*
Data bits/character	5,6,7 or 8
Stop bits	1,1.5 or 2
Parity	Odd or even parity
Baud rates	1200,2400,4800,9600,19200

12.3.2 Synchronous Data Transfer

Synchronous data transfer uses common clock source for transmitter and the receiver for synchronization, hence the name. Some of the peculiarities of synchronous data transfer are as follows:

1. Both the transmitter and the receiver physically use the same clock source.
2. It is a "data-block"-oriented data transfer. It transfers a block of data serially.
3. The synchronization between the transmitter and the receiver is achieved by using a special character which is known as sync. character, for example, @, #, $, %, etc.
4. The transmitter sends sync. character to start the communication.
5. The receiver keeps on checking input line status.
6. When the receiver detects matching between sync. character, it considers that it has been synchronized with the transmitter.

Figure 4 shows the format for a synchronous data communication.

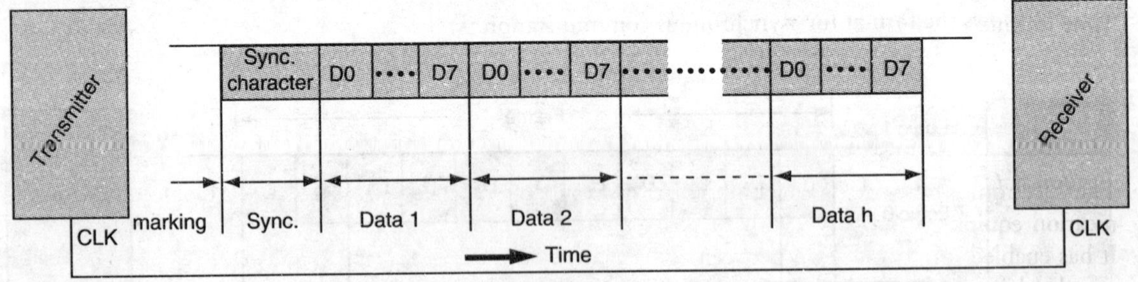

Figure 4 Synchronous data formats.

12.3.3 Comparison of Asynchronous and Synchronous Formats

Table 3 shows a comparison between synchronous and asynchronous data transfer.

Table 3 Comparison of Synchronous and Asynchronous Data Transfer

Synchronous Data Transfer	*Asynchronous Data Transfer*
It transfers block of character at a time	It transfers one character at a time
Data transfer rate is ≥ 20 kilobits/second	Data transfer rate is ≤ 20 kilobits/second
It uses sync. character	It does not use sync. character
Start and stop bit is not used	Start and stop bit is used with every character
Common clock is used by both the transmitter and the receiver	Independent clocks are used by both the transmitter and the receiver
Synchronization is mandatory, hence implemented only with hardware	No synchronization is required, hence can be implemented by both software and hardware
Speed of communication is high because overheads are distributed over a block of data bytes	Every byte of data has start and stop bits which increases overheads, hence communication speed is low

12.3.4 Baud Rate Generation

The rate at which the data bits are transmitted in serial communication is termed as baud rate. Baud rate is defined as bit per second (b/s) or the number of changes in voltage levels on transmission line per second. Some typical baud rates are 2400, 4800, 9600, etc. The following is an example which illustrates the concept.

Transmission rate = 9600 Baud = 9600 bits/s

Time for one bit = 1/9600 = 104.1 μs

12.4 RS232 Standard

The Electronic Industries Association (EIA) developed a common standard for interfacing data communication equipment in early 1960s. It is a serial data bus standard used for transmission and reception. It has enabled interconnection between equipment produced by different manufacturers. RS232 specifies signal voltages, signal function, signal timing and a protocol for exchanging information and mechanical connectors.

12.4.1 RS232 Signals

The format of RS232 specifies the format for communication signals and handshake signals. Table 4 shows the pin details of RS232 DB-9 connector and Fig. 5 shows the physical connector.

12.4.1.1 Hardware Specifications

1. Logic level 0 = +3 V to +25 V, Logic level 1= –3 V to +25 V.
2. –3 V to +3 V regions are undefined.
3. Communication cable is a twisted pair of wire with 300 pf to 2500 pf acceptable capacitance.
4. Maximum length of cable is 16 metres.
5. The interfacing circuit should be single-ended and bi-polar.

Table 4 Pin Details of RS232 DB-9 Connector

Pin	*Description*
1	Data carrier detect (DCE)#
2	Received data (RxD)
3	Transmitted data (TxD)
4	Data terminal ready (DTR)
5	Signal ground (GND)
6	Data set ready (DSR)#
7	Request to send (RTS)#
8	Clear to send (CTS)#
9	Ring indicator (RI)

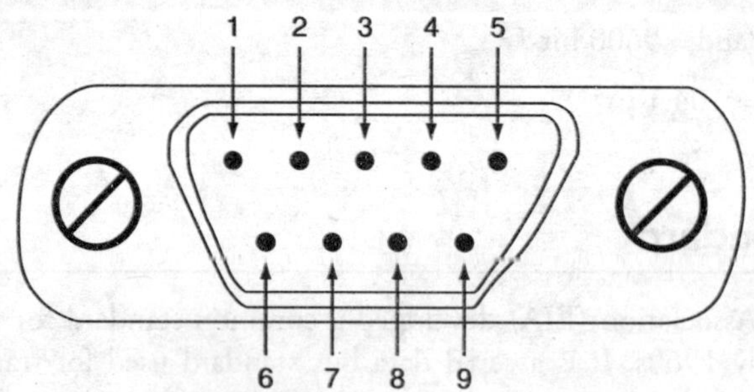

Figure 5 RS232 DB-9 connector.

12.4.1.2 Signal Specifications

1. **DTR# (data terminal ready):** When communication equipment becomes ready after self test, it sends out this DTR# signal to indicate that it is ready for communication.
2. **DSR# (data set ready):** When DCE (modem) is powered ON, it goes through the self test and asserts DSR to indicate that it is ready to communicate.

3. **RTS# (ready to send):** When a DTE device (such as a PC) has a byte to transmit, it activates this signal to indicate modem that it has a data byte to transmit.
4. **CTS# (clear to send):** This signal is in response to RTS. If a receiving equipment is ready to accept data, then it activates the signal. This begins the communication process.
5. **DCD# (data carrier detect):** The signal is asserted by modem to inform the DTE (PC) that it has detected valid carrier.
6. **RI (ring indicator):** The signal is mainly used by modem and PC to indicate that the telephone is ringing. It switches ON and OFF according to ringing sound. The signal is used very rarely.

12.4.2 MAX 232

As we know RS232 signals are not compatible with 8051 signal levels (TTL), hence it needs to have a signal converter. It is done with MAX 232 integrated circuit. It consists of TTL to RS232 and RS232 to TTL both packaged in a single chip. Figure 6 shows the connection diagram for interfacing 8051 UART with RS232 compatible device.

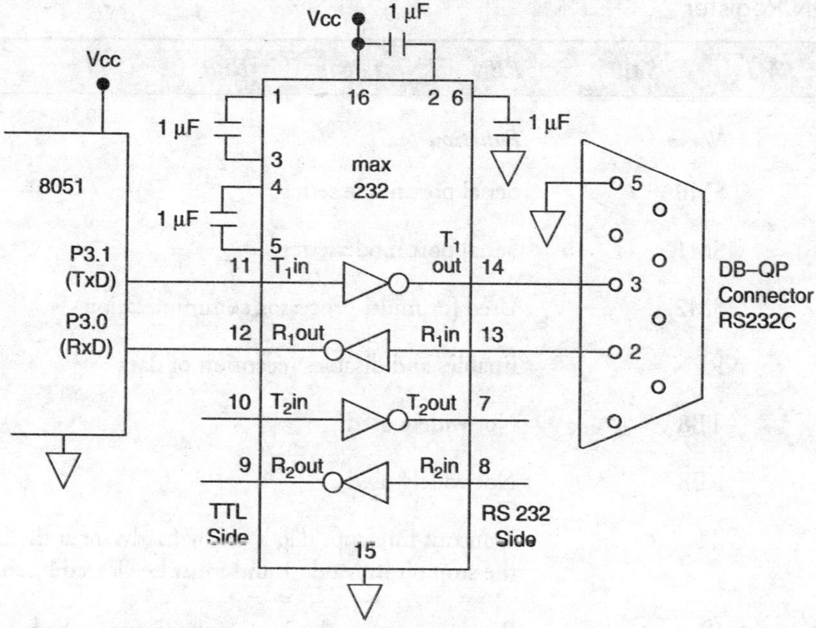

Figure 6 RS232 connection to 8051 UART.

12.5 Serial Communication Programming with 8051

The concept of serial communication is already discussed in Section 12.4. The communication between two computers can be done by using serial communication link. 8051 microcontroller can also communicate with computers by using same serial link. It has in-built data communication circuit block. It uses

Special Function Registers (SFRs), namely, SBUF, SCON and PCON. The SBUF register holds data for communication, the SCON register controls the data communication process and the PCON register sets the data rates for communication.

The SBUF register internally consists of two registers. The data to be transmitted is held in one register (write only register). The transmitted data is routed through TxD pin towards PC. The data received from PC is routed from RxD pin to the other register of SBUF (read only register).

8051 can be used for full-duplex asynchronous serial communication. The receiver of 8051 is double buffered. This facilitates to receive second byte, while the first one is in intermediate register. The chance of an overrun and complexity is reduced greatly because of double buffering scheme in 8051. 8051 provides four modes of serial communication which can be set by using SCON register.

Table 5 shows the details of SCON register. Modes 2 and 3 are useful for multiprocessor communication which facilitates to have master–slave configuration. The baud rate is generated by using on-chip hardware and the crystal oscillator. Mode 0 has fixed baud rate, while other modes can be used for variable baud rates. The over flow of Timer 1 is used to generate variable baud rates.

Table 5 SCON Register

SM0 (MSB)	*SM1*	*SM2*	*REN*	*TB8*	*RB8*	*TI*	*RI (LSB)*

SFR Bit	*Name*	*Function*
SCON.7	SM0	Serial port mode setter
SCON.6	SM1	Serial port mode setter
SCON.5	SM2	Used for multi-processor communication
SCON.4	REN	Enables and disables reception of data
SCON.3	TB8	Not widely used
SCON.2	RB8	Not widely used
SCON.1	TI	Transmit interrupt flag is set by hardware at the beginning of the stop bit in Mode 1 and must be cleared by software
SCON.0	RI	Receive interrupt flag is set by hardware at the beginning of the stop bit in Mode 1 and must be cleared by software

Note: Make SM2, TB8 and RB8 = 0

The serial port has four settable modes. The modes are set by referring to Table 6 which shows the SCON. 7 (SM0) and SCON.6 (SM1) bits used for mode setting of serial communication.

Table 6 Mode Setting of Serial Communication

SM0	*SM1*	*Mode*	*Description*	*Baud Rate*
0	0	0	Shift register	$f_{osc}/12$
0	1	1	8-bit UART	Variable
1	0	2	9-bit UART	$f_{osc}/64$ or $f_{osc}/32$
1	1	3	9-bit UART	Variable

12.5.1 Mode 0

It is a half-duplex mode of serial communication. It is also known as shift register mode. It can perform both right- and left-shifting operations. The shift register accepts both data and clock signals. The data can be transmitted or received via RxD pin. The shift clock is generated by TxD pin. Following are the characteristics of Mode 0:

1. Mode 0 does not need start and stop bits. All the 8 data bits are transmitted at a time. The D0 bit of data is transmitted and received first.
2. The baud rate is defined as

$$\text{Baud rate} = \frac{\text{Crystal frequency}}{12}$$

3. This mode can be used to increase I/O ports by using 8-bit shift registers externally.

12.5.2 Mode 1

It is a full-duplex mode. The data transmission and reception are done independently. Following are the characteristics of Mode 1:

1. The 8-bit asynchronous communication is done with this mode. It transmits "1" only when there is a change in the data bit, otherwise it transmits "0".
2. It uses 2 extra bits (start bit and stop bit) in addition to 8 bits of data. During the transmission of data, the start bit and stop bit are automatically appended to 8 data bits by the internal hardware.
3. The baud rate is generated by using Timer 1 in Mode 2 (auto-reload). The desired baud rate can be generated by referring to the following equation:

$$\text{Baud rate} = \frac{2^{\text{SMOD}}}{32} \times \frac{\text{Crystal frequency}}{12(256-(\text{TH1}))}$$

   SMOD is a control bit in PCON register. It can be 0 or 1.

4. From the above equation, it is clear that the baud rate can be doubled by using SMOD bit in PCON register. When it is set to 1, then it is doubled. Table 7 shows the setting required to generate popular baud rates.

Timer 1 = Mode 2 (TH1 holds the auto reload value).
Crystal frequency = 11.0592 MHz.

Table 7 TH1 Setting for some Populas Baud Rates

TH1 (Decimal)	*TH1 (Hex)*	*SMOD = 0*	*SMOD = 1*
–3	FD	9600	19200
–6	FA	4800	9600
–12	F4	2400	4800
–24	E8	1200	2400

12.5.3 Mode 2

This mode can be used for communication only when the microcontroller has two independent blocks for communication, namely, transmission block and reception block. Following are the characteristics of Mode 2:

1. This mode supports full-duplex, 11-bit asynchronous data communication. It provides NRZ (non-return to zero) format. It means that it transmits "1" when there is a change in the data, otherwise it transmits "0".
2. It supports 11-bit format for communication, that is, 1 start bit, 9 data bits and 1 stop bit. TB8 bit of SCON register is copied as 9th bit of data. It is stored in RB8 bit of SCON register when the data is received. The start and stop bits are discarded.
3. The baud rate can be set by following equation:

$$\text{Baud rate} = \frac{2^{\text{SMOD}}}{64} \times \text{Crystal frequency}$$

Mode 2 provides higher baud rates which are demanded for high-speed data communication in multiprocessor systems.

12.5.4 Mode 3

The baud rate in Mode 3 is determined as in Mode 1 using Timer 1. Otherwise it is similar to Mode 2.

12.6 Programming 8051 for Serial Communication

The above discussion has given the internal structure of UART in the 8051 microcontroller. It is mainly used to communicate with an external standard device like personal computer (PC). Following examples will help to program 8051 for data communication.

Example 1

Write a program to transmit a letter "P" serially with baud rate of 9600 continuously.

Solution: The data byte is transmitted serially through pin 11 (P3.1), that is, TxD pin. The program is as follows:

```
        MOV TMOD, #20H   ; Timer 1, Mode 2, (Auto reload)
        MOV TH1, #-3     ; Baud rate 9600
        MOV SCON, #50H   ; 8-bit data, 1 stop, REN enabled
        SETB TR1         ; Start Timer 1
REDO:   MOV SBUF, #'P'   ; Transmit 'P' serially
WAIT:   JNB TI, WAIT     ; Wait till transmission is over
        CLR TI           ; Clear TI bit for next transmission
        SJMP REDO        ; go to repeat the process
```

Example 2

Write a program to receive data serially which has been transmitted by a PC with 4800 baud rate output to Port 1.

Solution: The data byte is to be received serially from pin 10 (P3.0), that is, RxD pin. The program is as follows:

```
        MOV TMOD, #20H   ; Timer 1, Mode 2, (Auto reload)
        MOV TH1, #0FAH   ; Baud rate 4800
        MOV SCON, #50H   ; 8-bit data, 1 stop, REN enabled
        SETB TR1         ; Start Timer 1
        CLR RI           ; Clear RI flag
WAIT:   JNB RI, WAIT     ; Wait for data to come in SBUF
        MOV A, SBUF      ; Move received data to Acc.
        MOV P1,A         ; Move data to Port 1
        END
```

Summary

- Serial communication means the data is sent bit-by-bit. The data can be transmitted to a longer distance.
- In parallel communication, the data is transmitted byte-by-byte, which is faster than serial communication.
- Serial communication can be done over telephone lines.
- The serial communication supports asynchronous and synchronous methods.
- Byte-by-byte data is sent in asynchronous communication, whereas block-by-block is sent in synchronous communication.
- The data communication can be simplex, half duplex and full duplex. RS232 is a standard connector for serial communication.

Chapter 13 discusses the interrupt structure and response.

Multiple-Choice Questions

1. The crystal of ___ MHz causes minimum errors in communication.
   (a) 11.059
   (b) 1.000
   (c) 12.000
   (d) 2.000
2. The baud rate can be doubled by using ___ register setting.
   (a) SCON
   (b) PCON
   (c) IE
   (d) IP
3. The ___ stop bits can be used for serial communication.
   (a) 5
   (b) 4
   (c) 3
   (d) 2
4. Serial communication can be used for ___ metres.
   (a) 1000
   (b) 500
   (c) 200
   (d) 50
5. Minimum of ___ lines are required for full-duplex communication.
   (a) 2
   (b) 3
   (c) 4
   (d) 5
6. Mode 0 of serial port can perform ___ communication.
   (a) full duplex
   (b) half duplex
   (c) simplex
   (d) parallel
7. Baud rate is dependent on
   (a) SBUF data
   (b) number of bytes

(c) length of program

(d) oscillator frequency

8. Start and stop bits are in ___ register.

(a) PSW

(b) SBUF

(c) none

(d) SCON

9. Baud rate is set by using ___ register.

(a) PCON

(b) IE

(c) DPTR

(d) PSW

10. The ___ bit = 1, then data can be received on RxD pin of 8051.

(a) TI

(b) REN

(c) RI

(d) SMOD

Review Questions

1. Compare serial and parallel communication techniques.
2. What is the importance of MAX 232 chip in serial communication?
3. Explain the calculations for setting 4800 baud rate using Timer 1.
4. What is a function of SBUF register in serial communication?
5. Distinguish between asynchronous and synchronous data transfer.
6. What is the role of SMOD bit in serial communication?
7. What settings are required for full-duplex serial communication?
8. Explain the importance of start bit and stop bit in serial communication.
9. What are the sources of error in serial communication?
10. Explain the use of Mode 0 of serial communication.
11. Is it possible to use Mode 0 for extending ports of 8051?
12. Write a program to transmit 6 bytes of data over serial port with 4800 baud rate (Crystal freq. 11.0592 MHz).
13. Write a program to receive data coming with baud rate of 9600, 1 start bit , 1 stop bit and no parity. Assume crystal frequency as 11.0592 MHz.
14. A data is coming over Port 0, write the program to transmit the same data using Mode 0.
15. What is parity? Explain its significance in serial communication.

Answers

Multiple-Choice Questions

1. (a)
2. (b)
3. (d)
4. (d)
5. (b)
6. (c)
7. (d)
8. (c)
9. (a)
10. (b)

13 8051 Interrupt Structure and Programming

LEARNING OBJECTIVES

After reading this chapter, you will be able to:

- Explain the utility of Interrupt Service Routine (ISR).
- List interrupts of 8051.
- Describe significance of interrupt vector table.
- Compare and contrast polling versus interrupt.
- Define priority of interrupts in 8051.
- Differentiate and compare edge-triggered and level-triggered interrupts.
- Describe the use of external hardware interrupts.

13.1 Introduction

The basic task of a microcontroller is to execute program according to user-defined sequence of instructions. Sometime if it is desired to change the sequence of execution, then an interrupt facility is used. Microcontroller has internal as well as external sources of interrupt. It is an asynchronous input to microcontroller. Following are steps taken by microcontroller to respond to interrupts:

1. When an interrupt is activated, the microcontroller completes the execution of current instruction and then it fetches *interrupt service routine*.
2. Once the interrupt request is served, it resumes to the main operation. The interrupt handling routine has predefined fixed address in the program memory.
3. Microcontroller 8051 has six interrupt sources. Reset, INT0 and INT1 are generated by external sources. The other three are internally generated interrupts, namely, Timer 0 (TF0), Timer 1 (TF1) and serial port (TI or RI).
4. The functions of all the interrupts are under control of the program. The desired interrupt can be enabled or disabled by setting respective bit to "1" or "0" in interrupt enable (IE) register, interrupt priority (IP) register and timer control register (TCON).

Figure 1 shows the interrupt structure and control system.

13.2 Interrupt Enable Register

Table 1 shows the structure of IE register. The interrupts are enabled or disabled by setting or clearing the bit in this register.

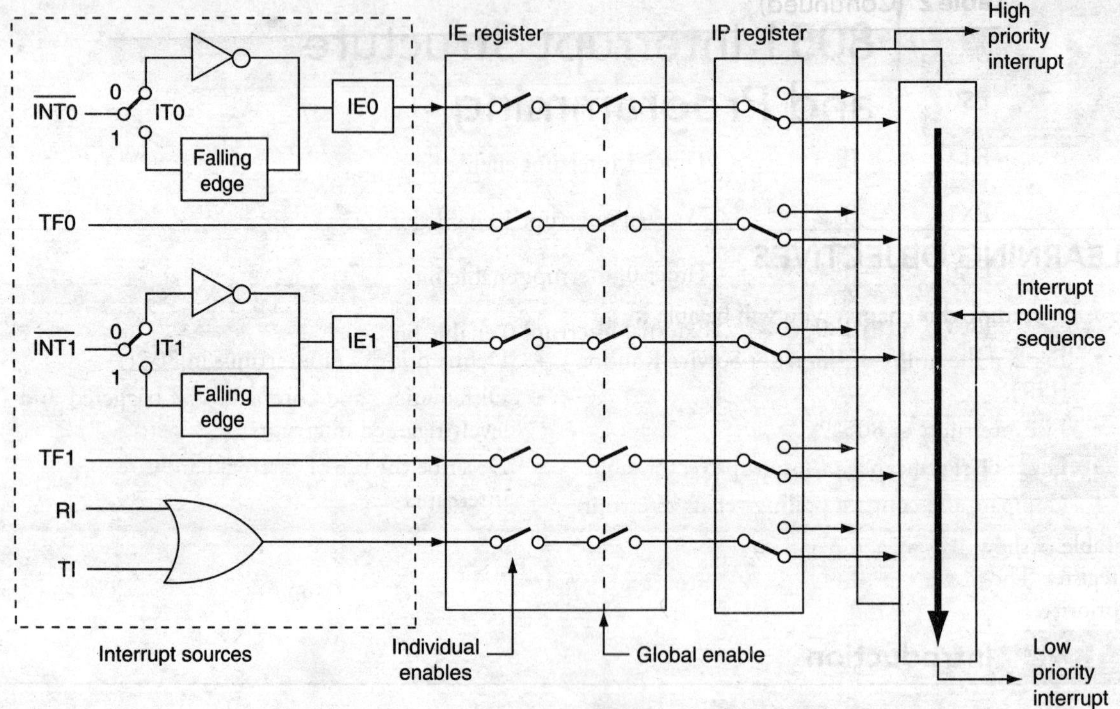

Figure 1 Interrupt structure and control system of 8051.

Table 1 Structure of IE Register

MSB							*LSB*
EA	–	–	*ES*	*ET1*	*EX1*	*ET0*	*EX0*

EA = 1 enables interrupt; EA = 0 disables interrupt

Table 2 shows the functions of IE register bits. The table will help us to understand and use the setting of the required interrupts in the system.

Table 2 IE Register Bit Functions

Symbol	*Position*	*Function*
EA	IE.7	Disables all interrupts If EA = 0, interrupt will be acknowledged. If EA = 1, each interrupt is individually enabled or disabled by setting or clearing its enable bit
–	IE.6	Reserved
–	IE.5	Reserved

(Continued)

Table 2 (Continued)

Symbol	*Position*	*Function*
ES	IE.4	Serial port interrupt enable bit
ET1	IE.3	Timer 1 interrupt enable bit
EX1	IE.2	External interrupt 1 enable bit
ET0	IE.1	Timer 0 interrupt enable bit
EX0	IE.0	External interrupt 0 enable bit

13.3 Interrupt Priority Register

Table 3 shows the structure of IP register. The priority of the interrupts is decided by setting bits in IP register. The highest priority is set by setting the respective bit to "1". Clearing the bit to "0" assigns lowest priority.

Table 3 Structure of IP Register

IP.7	*IP.6*	*IP.5*	*IP.4*	*IP.3*	*IP.2*	*IP.1*	*IP.0*
–	–	–	*PS*	*PT1*	*PX1*	*PT0*	*PX0*

Symbol	*Position*	*Function*
–	IP.7	Reserved
–	IP.6	Reserved
–	IP.5	Reserved
PS	IP.4	Serial port interrupt priority bit
PT1	IP.3	Timer 1 interrupt priority bit
PX1	IP.2	External interrupt 1 priority bit
PT0	IP.1	Timer 0 interrupt priority bit
PX0	IP.0	External interrupt 0 priority bit

EA = 1 assigns high priority; EA = 0 assigns low priority.

If simultaneously two interrupts are received then the interrupt having the highest priority will be served first. If two interrupts are set for the highest priority and the same are activated simultaneously then the microcontroller follows default priority.

If no priority is set for the interrupts, then the controller follows default priority as shown in Table 4. When the microcontroller is in reset condition Then, also the same priorities are followed as in Table 4.

Table 4 Default Priorities of Interrupts

Number	*Source*	*Priority*
1	Reset	Highest
2	IE0	–
3	TF0	–
4	IE1	–
5	TF1	–
6	RI or TI	Lowest

13.4 Interrupt Vector Addresses

Table 5 shows the interrupt vector table. For example, if TF1 interrupt is generated by Timer 1, then the microcontroller PUSHes the address of the next instruction on the stack and jumps to 001BH location by loading program counter = 001BH. It executes the program till RETI instruction. After RETI instruction, the program counter POPs the last PUSHed address and then continues to execute the program from the POPed location.

Table 5 Interrupt Vector Table

Interrupt	*ROM Location*	*Pin*	*Flag Clearing*
Reset	0000H	9	Auto
External hardware interrupt 0 (INT0)	0003H	P3.2(12)	Auto
Timer 0 interrupt (TF0)	000BH		Auto
External hardware interrupt 1 (INT1)	0013H	P3.3(13)	Auto
Timer 1 interrupt (TF1)	001BH		Auto
Serial communication interrupt (TI and RI)	0023H		Manually cleared

13.5 Interrupt Programming

The interrupts are to be handled by using program code known as Interrupt Service Routine (ISR). The 8051 has five interrupts. The activation of the interrupt diverts the execution pointer of the 8051 to ISR. The ISR is always to be written at the respective vector address of that interrupt. The following discussion helps to get idea of programming the 8051 for interrupts.

13.5.1 Serial Port Interrupt

The 8051 microcontroller has two serial interrupts, namely, receive interrupt (RI) and transmit interrupt (TI) but both interrupts have common vector address. Following steps help to resolve the situation:

1. When the controller receives a data byte serially from RxD pin 3.0, the RI bit is set and when transmits a data byte serially through TxD pin3.1, the TI bit is set. Both the bits RI and TI are in Serial CONtrol (SCON) register.
2. The TI and RI bits are logically ORed to provide single interrupt to the controller.
3. The TI and RI bits in SCON register are set by transmission and reception of data. These bits are not cleared automatically but are cleared in the program by writing instruction CLR TI or CLR RI.

Example 1

Write a program to read from P0 and write the same to P1 continuously while transmitting the same data over the serial port at 9600 baud rate. Assume crystal frequency as 11.0592 MHz.

Solution: The microcontroller has to keep on taking data from Port 0 and output it on Port 1. The task will be interrupted by the serial interrupt. Hence the main program will be executed continuously and the data transmission program should be in ISR of the microcontroller. The same is shown in the following program:

```
      .ORG 0
      LJMP INIT
      .ORG 0023H
      LJMP SERL                      ;jump serial ISR
      .ORG 0030H
INIT:MOV P0,#FFH                     ;set P0=input
      MOV TMOD, #20H                 ;Timer1, Mode 2,
      MOV TH1, #0FDH                 ;9600 baud rate
      MOV SCON, #50H                 ;8bit,1stop, REN enable
      MOV IE, #10010000B             ;enable serial interrupt
      SETB TR1                       ;start timer
LOOP:MOV A,P0                        ;read data from port0
      MOV SBUF,A                     ;copy to SBUF
      MOV P1,A                       ;send it to port1
      SJMP LOOP                      ;be in loop for ever
                                     ;------------------ Serial ISR
```

```
      .ORG 100H
      SERL:JB TI,TRNS          ;jump if TI = 1
      MOV A,SBUF               ;otherwise receive
      CLR RI                   ;clr RI
      RETI                     ;return from ISR
TRNS:CLR TI                    ;clear TI
      RETI                     ;return from ISR

      .END
```

13.5.2 Timer Interrupts

8051 microcontroller has two timers; hence, there are two interrupts. The overflow condition of Timer 0 sets TF0 flag and Timer 1 sets TF1 flag. If we want to go to a subroutine as the timer overflows, then we have to poll the status of TF flag and wait until TF flag sets to "1". This ties down the microcontroller while waiting.

The TF flag is always set to "1" as the timer overflows. But the interrupt will be generated only when the respective bit is set into IE register.

When the timer generates interrupt, the microcontroller jumps to specific address in program memory from which the ISR is called.

Example 2

Write a program to generate 5 kHz on square wave on pin P1.5. Assume crystal frequency as 22 MHz.

Solution: Figure 2 shows the hardware connection for the solution of Example 2.

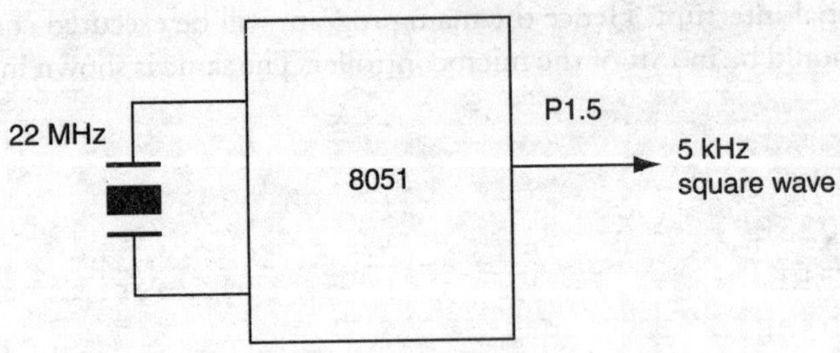

Figure 2 8051-based square wave generator.

The following program has two routines: One is the main program for handling the Timer 0 and the other is the ISR which updates the status of Port pin P1.5.

```
.ORG 0
LJMP INIT                      ;
                               ;------ISR for Timer 0-----
.ORG 000BH                     ;Interrupt vector Timer 0
CPL P1.5                       ;complement bit P1.5
RETI                           ;
                               ;----Main program------
```

```
      .ORG 30H
      MOV TMOD,#02H          ;initialise Timer 0 in Mode 2
      MOV IE,#82H            ;enable Timer 0 interrupt
      MOV TH0,#48H           ;count va vmer 0
   DO:SJMP DO                ;wait till Timer 0 over flows
      .END
```

13.5.3 External Hardware Interrupts

There are three external hardware interrupts provided for microcontroller 8051, namely, Reset, INT0# and INT1#. Reset has a separate pin whereas INT0 and INT1 are provided on P3.2 and P3.3, respectively.

The interrupts INT0# and INT1# can be set to level triggered or edge triggered.

Example 3

Write a program to work 8051 as a toggle flip-flop by using INT0 as an input clock pin and port 1 as output. Assume crystal frequency as 12 MHz.

Solution: Figure 3(a) shows the hardware scheme and Fig. 3(b) shows the waveforms for solution of Example 3. The timing diagram shows the output status of the Port pin 1.x. (The whole port 1 is toggled hence the status can be checked on any of the pins of port 1.)

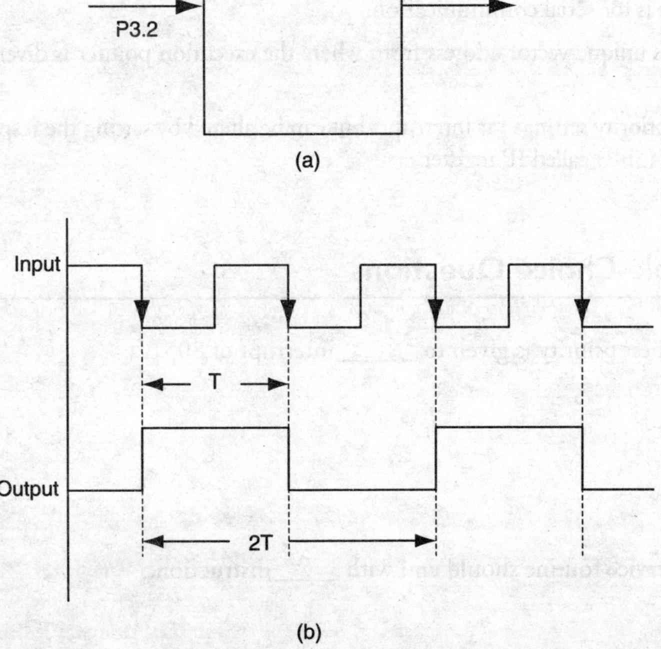

Figure 3 (a) 8051-based toggle flip-flop and (b) the waveforms.

The microcontroller performs the task with the help of two program segments. The main program segment initializes the TCON register by setting INT0 as edge-triggered interrupt and the other handles an ISR for interrupt INT0. The microcontroller stays in active halt condition (Wait). As the external input at pin 3.2 activates the interrupt, the ISR is executed. The following program shows the sequence of operation:

```
         .ORG 0
         LJMP INIT                 ;
                                   ;------ISR for INT0-------
         .ORG 0003H                ;
         CPL P1                    ;Complement Port 1
         RETI                      ;
         .ORG 0030H
   INIT:SETB TCON.0                ;make INT0 = edge triggered
         MOV IE,#81H               ;enable INT0
   DO:   SJMP DO                   ;
         .END
```

Summary

- The interrupt is nothing but a task request coming externally or internally to the microcontroller 8051.
- The microcontroller 8051 supports five interrupts out of which two are for timers, two are for external hardware and one is for serial communication.
- Each interrupt has unique vector address from where the execution pointer is diverted to Interrupt Service Routine (ISR).
- 8051 has default priority settings for interrupts but can be altered by setting the respective bits in the Special Function Register (SFR) called IP register.

Multiple-Choice Questions

1. The default highest priority is given to ______interrupt of 8051.

(a) TI

(b) INT0

(c) Reset

(d) T0

2. The interrupt service routine should end with _____instruction.

(a) JUMP

(b) RETI

(c) RET
(d) END

3. The ______ interrupt of 8051 has two sources but one vector address.
(a) INT0
(b) INT1
(c) T1
(d) Serial

4. The _____ register of 8051 is used for changing the priority of interrupt.
(a) IE
(b) IP
(c) T0
(d) T1

5. The ISR in the interrupt vector table must not be more than ____ bytes.
(a) 8
(b) 16
(c) 32
(d) 64

6. At the end of ISR, 8051 takes next address from _____ register.
(a) IE
(b) SBUF
(c) PSW
(d) Stack

Review Questions

1. What step is taken by 8051 in the case of activated interrupt?
2. Explain the interrupt structure of 8051 microcontroller.
3. Write a program to read port 0 and write the same to port 1 while Timer 1 is generating 2 kHz square wave.
4. What care is to be taken for connecting external signal to interrupt pins of 8051?
5. What is the necessity of setting priority for interrupts of 8051? Explain with an example.
6. What is IE register and what is the function of each bit of it?
7. What action is taken by the controller on the activation of an interrupt?
8. What is the importance of interrupts in 8051-based system?
9. Explain the use of level-triggered and edge-triggered interrupt with the help of an example.

10. What are the disadvantages of polling method?
11. Explain interrupt structure of 8051.
12. What is the use of level-triggered and edge-triggered interrupts in 8051?
13. Explain EA.

Answers

Multiple-Choice Questions

1. (c)	**3.** (d)	**5.** (a)
2. (b)	**4.** (b)	**6.** (d)

14 Design of Minimum System Using 8051

LEARNING OBJECTIVES

After reading this chapter, you will be able to:

- Explain the use of peripherals in 8051 base system.
- Describe the methods of interfacing light emitting diode (LED) display.
- Explain the advantages of multiplexed display technique.
- Explain the drawbacks of mechanical switch.
- Use the software technique for key de-bouncing.
- Describe the interfacing method of ADC0809, DAC0808 and stepper motor.
- Describe the procedure for designing embedded system.

14.1 Introduction

8051 microcontroller has 32 input/output (I/O) pins which are divided into four ports, namely, Port 0, Port 1, Port 2 and Port 3. These entire pins can be used as input/output or in combination. We can find the microcontrollers in many of the electronic gadgets, domestic appliances such as washing machine, water purifiers, cameras, microwaves, ovens, etc.

14.2 Peripheral Interfaces

Now we will explore some of the real-time applications using 8051 microcontroller. It is needed for us to see how to interface 8051 with different devices such as LED display, keyboard, analog to digital converter (ADC), digital to analog converter (DAC), stepper motor, etc.

14.2.1 LED 7-Segment Display Interfacing

Display is an output device that is used to show the result or operand. There are many display devices such as cathode ray tube (CRT), LED, liquid crystal display (LCD). The displays are used according to size of the data. CRT is used to show large amount of data. It is also used to show graphs, trends and alphanumeric information. LCDs are used for low-power portable instruments. They are delicate and are rarely used for industrial applications. LED displays are bright and rugged. These are widely used in industrial displays.

LED displays are mainly used to display numbers only. The display consists of seven LEDs arranged in eight-figured form along with an additional LED for decimal point. There are two types of LED displays, that is, common cathode (CC) and common anode (CA). The CC display has cathode terminal of all the LEDs in common and CA has all anodes of the LEDs connected in common.

Figure 1 shows the pin-outs of displays and Fig. 2 shows the connections to 8051 port. Figure 3 shows seven-segment LED display connection using Binary Coded Decimal (BCD) to 7-segment decoder.

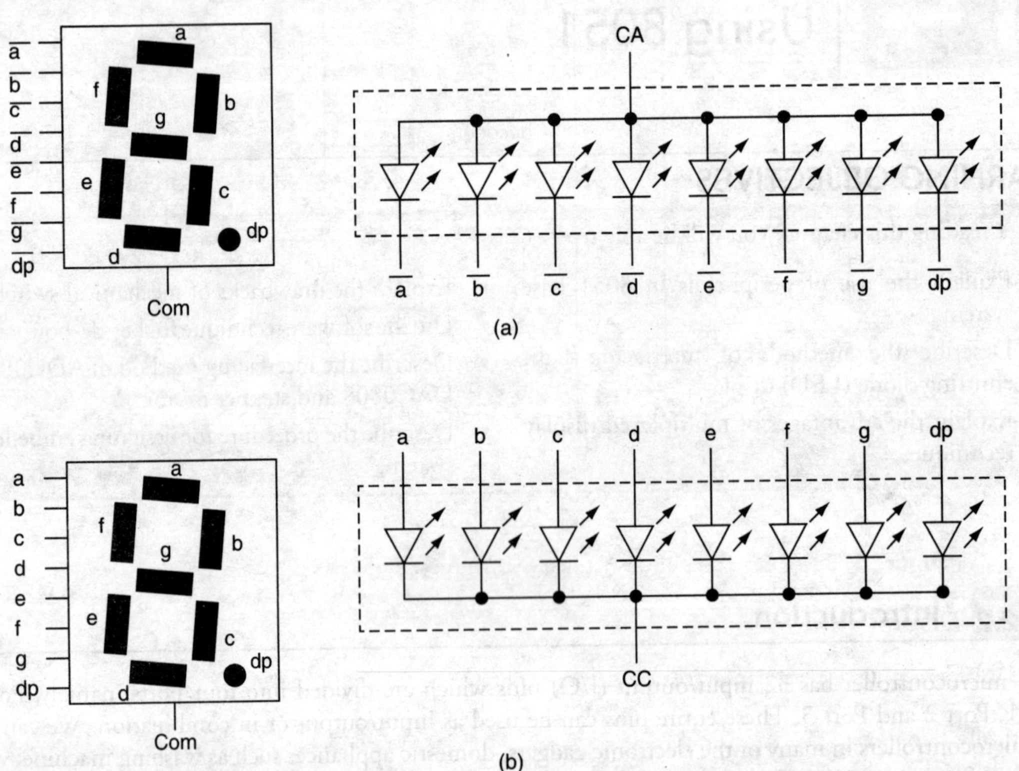

Figure 1 (a) Pin-points of common anode (CA) LED display.
(b) Pin-points of common cathod (CC) LED display.

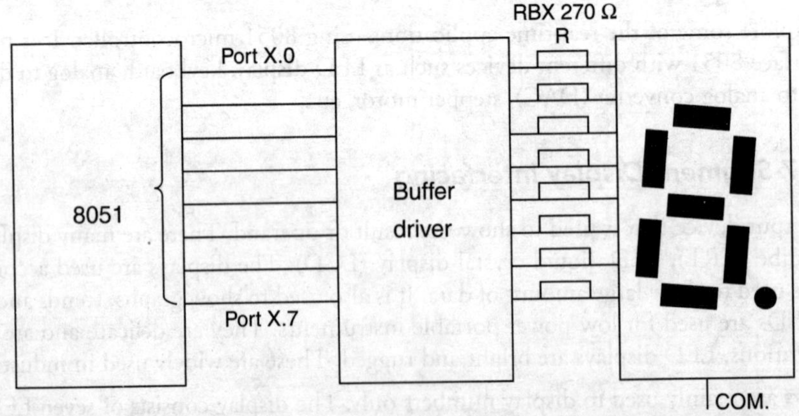

Figure 2 Seven-segment LED display with buffer connection to 8051.

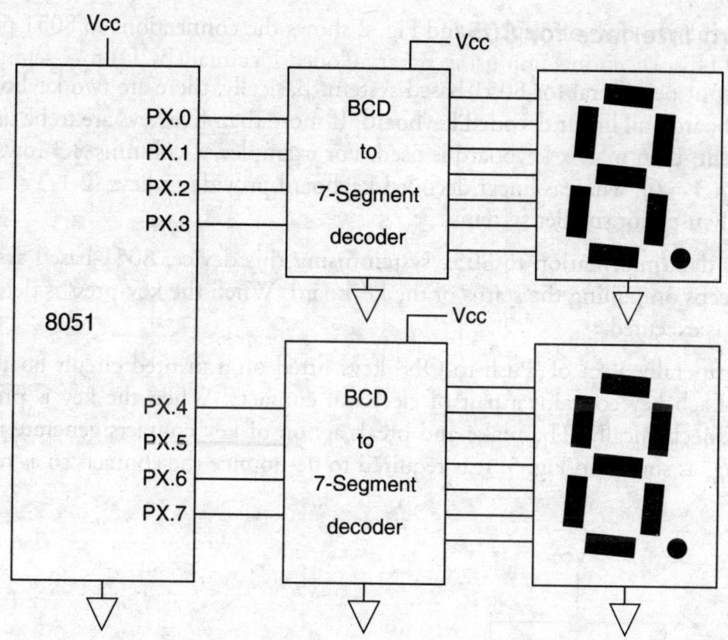

Figure 3 Seven-segment LED display connection using BCD to 7-segment decoder.

14.2.2 Display Multiplexing

Each LED of the display takes around 12 mA current. The total current drawn by one display will be $8 \times 12\,\text{mA} = 96$ mA per display. As the number of digits increases, the demand of the current increases drastically. This increases the overall power consumption of the system. This problem is solved by the use of multiplexing technique. This reduces the over-all power consumption of the system to a greater extent. This technique adds some burden on the software but decreases the hardware cost considerably. Figure 4 shows the hardware scheme for multiplexing displays.

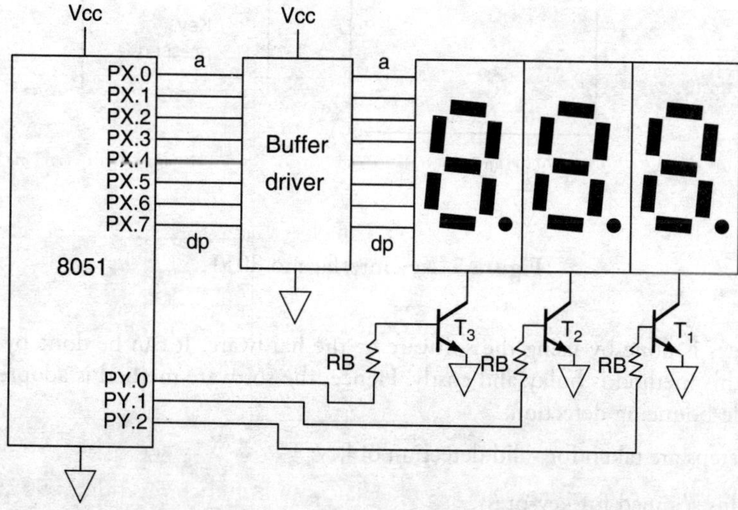

Figure 4 Seven-segment LED display connection using multiplexing technique.

14.2.3 Keyboard Interface for 8051

A keyboard is an input peripheral for 8051 based system. Basically, there are two keyboard configurations namely, matrix keyboard and linear decoded keyboard. If more than five keys are to be used and input port pins are not sufficient, then matrix keyboard is used. For examples, 2 columns × 3 rows matrix key board provides 6 keys (2 × 3 = 6), whereas linear decoded keyboard provides 5 keys (2 + 3 = 5). Linear decoded keyboard is generally used for smaller systems.

The user enters data/information to 8051 system using this device. 8051-based system initializes the ports and then it keeps on polling the status of the keyboard. When the key-press is detected, the function assigned to the key is executed.

A keyboard is generally a set of 'Push-to-ON' keys fitted on a printed circuit board (PCB) pad with proper connector. Each key contains a pair of electrical contacts. When the key is pressed, the contacts are short circuited mechanically. The make and break action of key contacts generate a typical waveform known as 'bouncing' as shown in Fig. 5. It is required to de-bounce the contacts so as to avoid false detection of key.

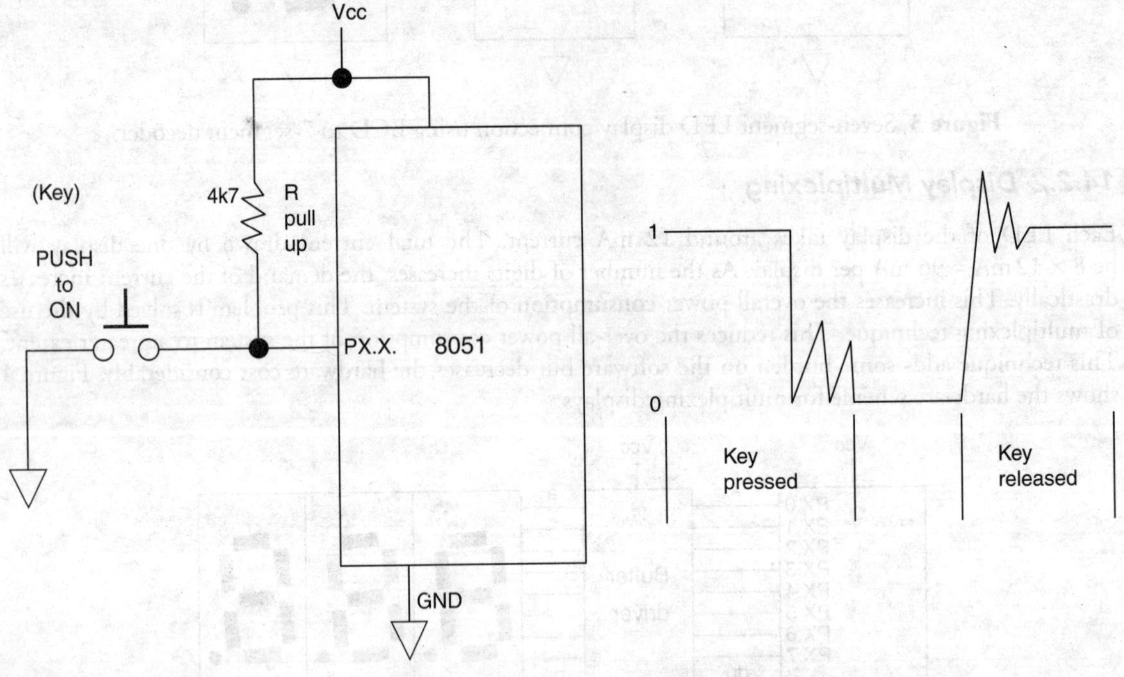

Figure 5 Key interface to 8051.

De-bouncing of keys is done by using the software or the hardware. It can be done by using an RS flip-flop or latch. But this method is bulky and costly. Hence, the software method is adopted. Figure 6 shows flowchart for key de-bouncing detection.

The following steps are taken for valid detection of key:

1. The keyboard is scanned for key-press.
2. When the key-press is detected, the program calls delay routine of 20 ms.

3. After waiting for 20 ms, key status is checked again. If it is found to be pressed then step 4 is followed otherwise go back to step 1.
4. The key entry is accepted and the function of the same key is executed.

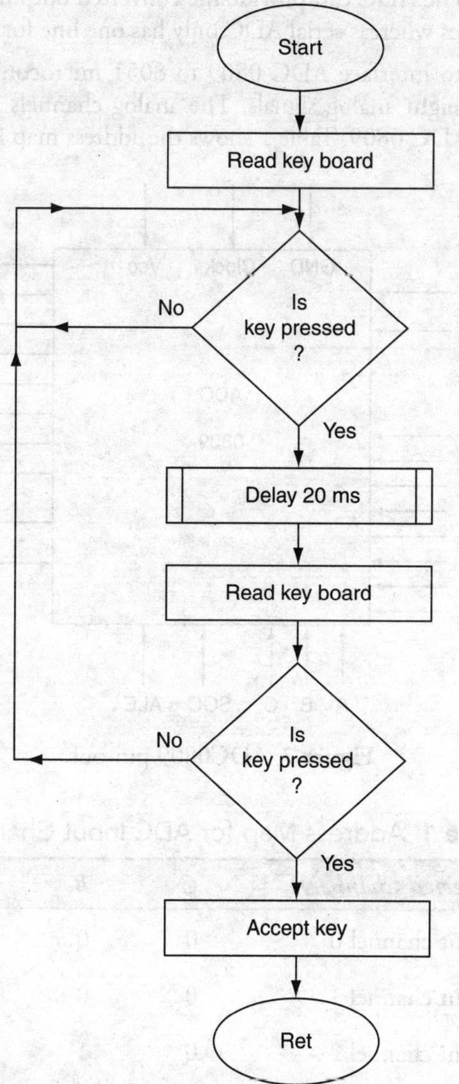

Figure 6 Flow chart for key detection.

14.2.4 Analog to Digital Converter (ADC) 0809 Interface for 8051

The ADC is a widely used device for data acquisition. The digital computers work on binary (discrete) values. The physical world is of analog values (continuous). The process parameters such as temperature, pressure, velocity, humidity, level, etc. are converted to electrical signal by using suitable transducers.

The ADC converts an analog signal in to a digital number. The ADC has *n*-bit resolution where *n* can be 8, 10, 12, 16 or 24 bits. The ADC with higher resolution provides smaller step size of the analog signal. Step size is the smallest change that ADC can detect. ADC requires a clock signal for its conversion process. The ADC takes finite time to convert the analog signal to the digital number. The time is known as 'conversion time' of an ADC. The ADC can provide the converted output in parallel or serial format. The parallel ADC has *n*-bit data lines whereas serial ADC only has one line for data out.

We will now discuss how to interface ADC 0809 to 8051 microcontroller. It is an 8-bit ADC with parallel output. It can handle eight analog signals. The analog channels are multiplexed for digitization. Figure 7 shows the pin out of ADC 0809. Table 1 shows the address map for ADC input channel.

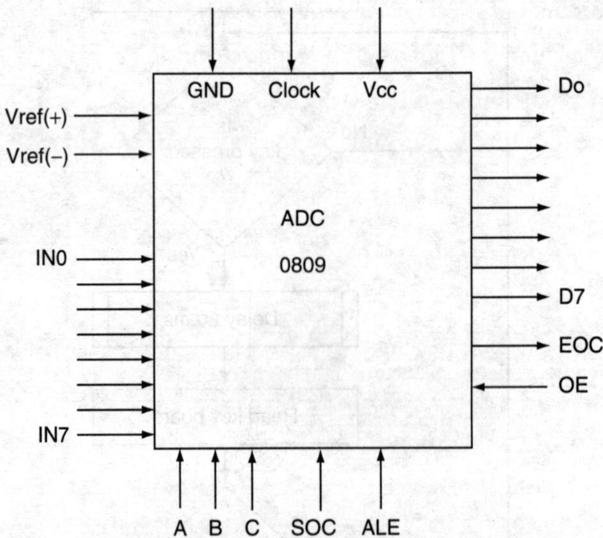

Figure 7 ADC0809 pin-out.

Table 1 Address Map for ADC Input Channel

Selected Channel	*C*	*B*	*A*
Input channel 0	0	0	0
Input channel 1	0	0	1
Input channel 2	0	1	0
Input channel 3	0	1	1
Input channel 4	1	0	0
Input channel 5	1	0	1
Input channel 6	1	1	0
Input channel 7	1	1	1

The ADC requires 5 Vdc supply. The reference voltage to the ADC decides the range of analog input voltage to be digitized. The *A*, *B* and *C* pins are the address pins used to select one channel out of IN0–IN7. The internal blocks of ADC are synchronized with the help of externally connected clock oscillator. The conversion is started by activating "Start of Conversion" (SOC) signal. This samples the analog input signal and held till the conversion is complete. The "End of Conversion" (EOC) signal is activated by ADC after the conversion is complete. The "Out Enable" (OE) pin is controlled by 8051 microcontroller. The OE pin is activated by the microcontroller for getting the data into 8051. De-activation of OE pin will force all the data output lines of ADC to tri-state (high impedance state) condition.

The following are the software steps to be followed to get the digitized data from ADC:

1. Set A, B and C address lines to select analog input channel.
2. Activate ALE pin for latching the address of the input channel.
3. Activate SOC signal to start conversion process.
4. Keep on polling the status of EOC pin. Wait for the status of EOC pin to change from low to high.
5. Activate OE pin to read the converted data from ADC.

Figure 8 shows the connection diagram for interfacing ADC0809 to Microcontroller 8051.

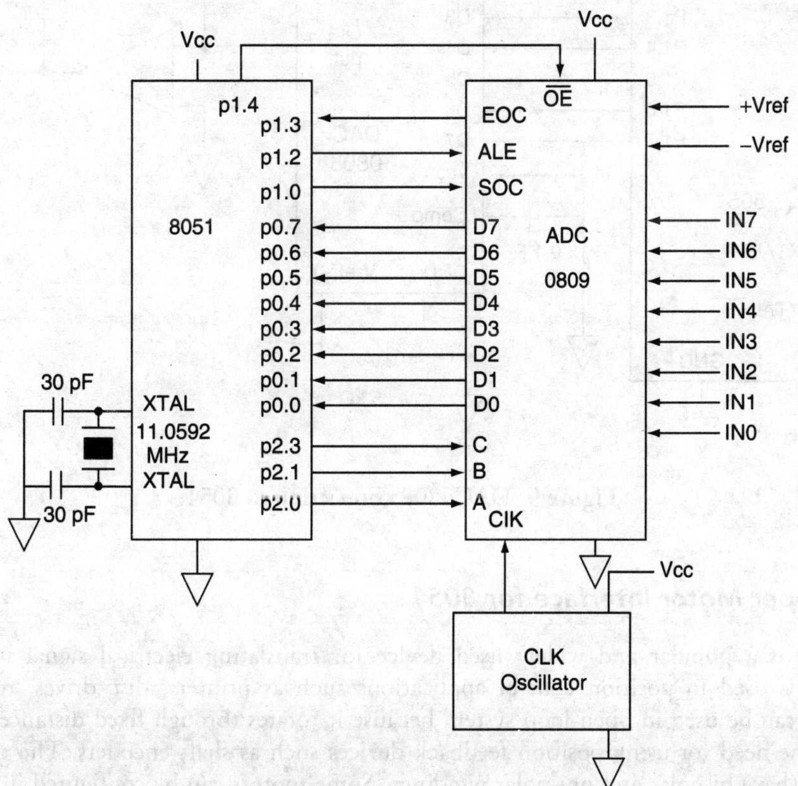

Figure 8 Interfacing ADC0809 to 8051.

14.2.5 Digital to Analog Converter 0808 Interface for 8051

The DAC is a widely used device to convert digital number into proportional analog voltage signal. There are different techniques used for the DAC. The DAC can accept digital input ranging from 8,10,12,16 bits, etc., in both parallel and serial form.

We will now discuss how to connect DAC 0808 to 8051 microcontroller. The interfacing scheme is very simple for this DAC. One of the 8051 port has to be initialized as an output port. The Px.0 to Px.7 pins of the output are to be connected directly to the digital input pins of DAC 0808.

The DAC 0808 converts digital input signal into proportional output current. The same current signal is converted to voltage by using simple current to voltage (*I/V*) converter. An operational amplifier (Op-Amp) can be used as *I/V* converter. Figure 9 shows interfacing DAC 0808 with 8051 microcontroller.

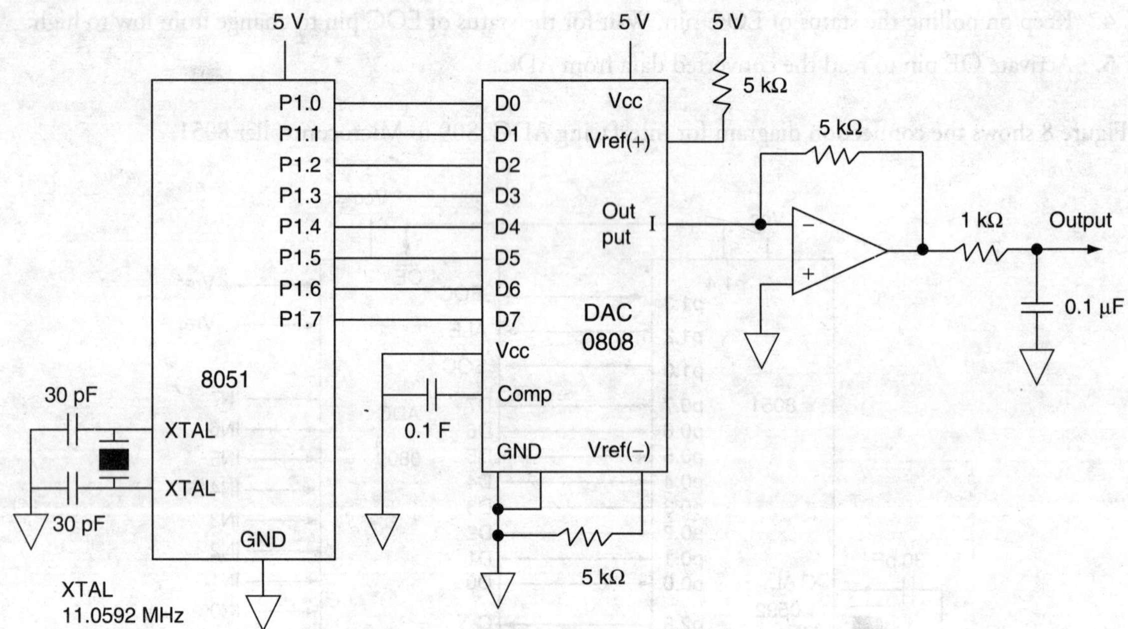

Figure 9 DAC0808 connection to 8051.

14.2.6 Stepper Motor Interface for 8051

Stepper motor is a popular and widely used device for translating electrical signal into mechanical movement. It is used in position control applications such as printers, disc drives, robots, etc. The stepper motor can be used in open-loop system because it rotates through fixed distance for every step. It eliminates the need for using position feedback devices such as shaft encoders. The commonly used stepper motors have bi-polar and uni-polar windings. Some motors can be configured in both uni-polar and bi-polar. Most of the motors have angular position resolution 1.8° per step. Uni-polar stepper motors have five wires and bi-polar have four wires. Bipolar motors provide better torque than uni-polar motors. Most of the stepper motors use 4-bit sequences to control four-phase signal for motion control applications. The motor can be driven in half-step or full-step mode. Table 2 shows the full-step sequence, Table 3 shows the half-step sequence and Table 4 shows wave-drive four-step sequence for stepper motor. The arrows show the sequence of steps to be followed for driving stepper motor in clockwise (CW) or counter clockwise (CCW).

Table 2 Full-Step Sequence for Stepper Motor

Clockwise (CW) ↓				*Counter Clockwise (CCW)* ↑
Steps	*Phase A*	*Phase B*	*Phase C*	*Phase D*
1	1	0	0	1
2	1	1	0	0
3	0	1	1	0
4	0	0	1	1

Table 3 Half-Step Sequence for Stepper Motor

Clockwise (CW) ↓				*Counter Clockwise(CCW)* ↑
Steps	*Phase A*	*Phase B*	*Phase C*	*Phase D*
1	1	0	0	1
2	1	0	0	0
3	1	1	0	0
4	0	1	0	0
5	0	1	1	0
6	0	0	1	0
7	0	0	1	1
8	0	0	0	1

Table 4 Wave Drive Four-Step Sequence for Stepper Motor

Clockwise (CW) ↓				*Counter Clockwise(CCW)* ↑
Steps	***Phase A***	***Phase B***	***Phase C***	***Phase D***
1	1	0	0	0
2	0	1	0	0
3	0	0	1	0
4	0	0	0	1

Stepper motor draws considerably high current, e.g., 500 mA, 1 A, 2 A and 3.5 A per phase. The microcontroller 8051 cannot source the current demanded by stepper motors. This problem can be solved by using power transistors or a buffer/driver. Figure 10 shows an interfacing scheme for connecting stepper motor to 8051.

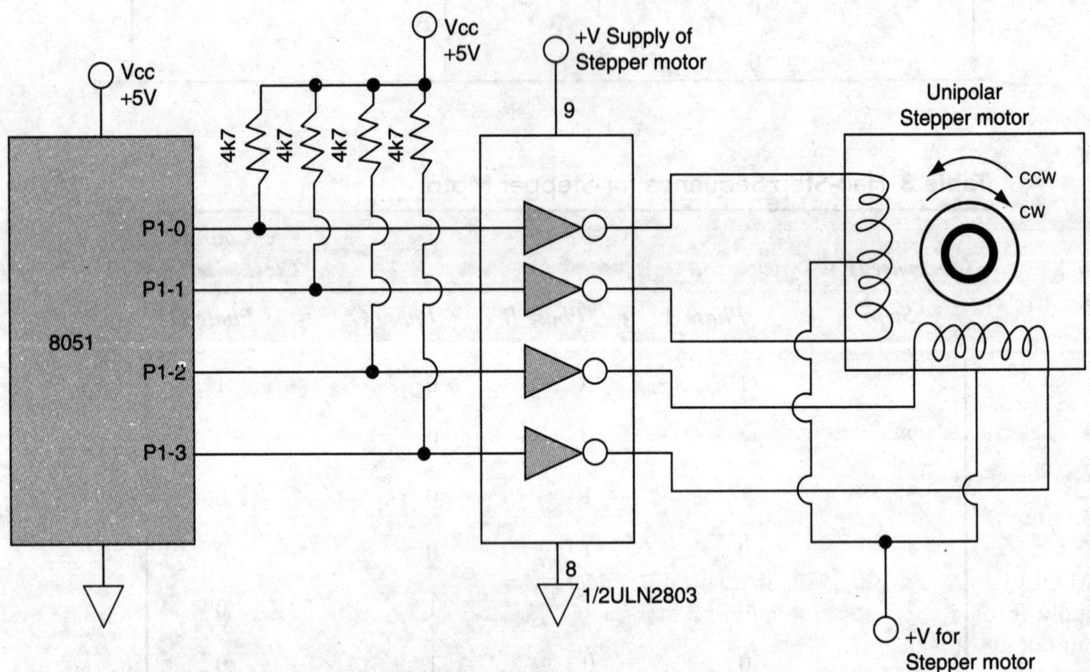

Figure 10 Unipolar stepper motor interface to 8051.

The following program is used to drive unipolar stepper motor for the circuit shown in Fig. 10:

```
        MOV A,#99H       ; Load step sequence
LOOP:   MOV P1,A         ; Output the sequence to motor
        RR A             ; Rotate Acc. Right for clockwise motion
        ACALL DELAY      ; Wait
        SJMP LOOP        ; Go back to loop

DELAY:  MOV R4,#100
OUT:    MOV R5,#250
IN:     DJNZ R5,IN
        DJNZ R4,OUT
        RET
```

The same program can be used to rotate the motor in counter clockwise direction. It is done by replacing the instruction RR A with RL A. the speed of the motor can be varied by changing the contents of R4 and R5 in delay routine. The following relation will help to set speed of the motor:

$$\text{Steps per second} = \frac{\text{rpm} \times \text{steps per revolution}}{60}$$

14.3 Microcontroller 8051-Based System Design and Application

We have already seen the schemes for interfacing different peripherals to 8051 microcontroller in Sections 14.2.1 to 14.2.6. Now we will put all the things together to develop an 8051 based system.

The application discusses design of an electronic thermometer. The following steps are required for the design:

1. Selection of temperature sensor.
2. Signal conditioning scheme.
3. Interfacing ADC and display.

LM35D semiconductor sensor is used as a temperature sensor. It can directly operate on 5 Vdc power supply. It follows the output trend of 10 mV per °C. The range of sensor is from 0°C to 100°C. The least count of measurement is 1°C; hence, the maximum count for the desired temperature range is 100.

This will need an ADC of 8-bit resolution. The Analog to Digital Converter ADC 0809 is used for interfacing with 8051. It is successive approximation register (SAR) type ADC. The reference voltage of ADC will be set to 10 mV □ 256 = 2.56 V.

The measured temperature is to be displayed on the indicator. The temperature range is up to 100°C. This means that three 7-segment displays will be required. The display can be interfaced with 3 ICs of 7-segment decoder driver such as CD4511/ CD4543.

Figure 11 shows the connection diagram of the temperature indicator system. The pin assignment for microcontroller 8051 is as follows:

1. P0.0–P0.7 = ADC output pins D0–D7.
2. P1.0–P0.3 = LSD display (Unit's digit).
3. P1.4–P1.7 = Middle display (Ten's digit).
4. P2.0–P2.3 = MSD display (Hundred's digit).

The temperature indicator uses only one analog input channel (IN0) of ADC 0809. The channel IN0 is permanently selected by grounding the address lines A, B and C. Also there is no need of a handshake in between 8051 and ADC. Connecting SOC, ALE and EOC pins together keeps ADC in continuous conversion mode. The output data bus of ADC0809 is not used anywhere other than 8051; hence, OE pin is permanently activated.

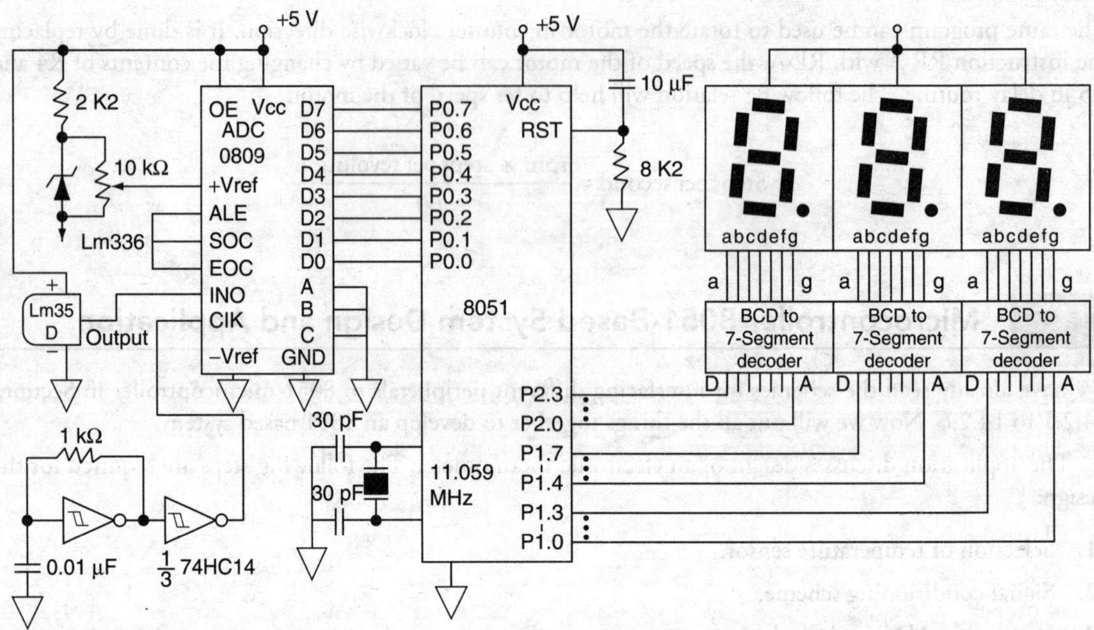

Figure 11 0–100°C temperature indicator using 8051. Note that the common pins of all the 7-segment displays are to be connected to GND in the case of CC-type display driver and + 5V in the case of CA-type display driver.

The software program for the system is as follows:

```
MOV R7, #00H      ;Clear R7 register
MOV R6, #00H      ;Clear R6 register
MOV A, #00H       ;Clear Acc.
MOV P1, A         ;Set port P1 as output
```

```
          MOV P2, A        ;Set port P2 as output
          MOV A, #FFH      ;
          MOV P0, A        ;Set port P0 as input
LOOP:     MOV A,P0         ;Read ADC
          ACALL CONV       ;Hex to BCD conversion
          ACALL DISPLAY    ;Display data to ports
          SJMP LOOP        ;Go back read ADC
CONV:     MOV B,#100       ;
          DIV AB           ;
          MOV R7, A        ;Unpacked MSD in R7
          MOV A, B         ;
          MOV B, #10       ;
          DIV AB           ;
          SWAP A           ;
          ADD A, B         ;
          MOV R6, A        ;Packed BCD in R6
          RET              ;
DISPLAY:  MOV P1, R6       ;Display LSD and Middle digit
          MOV P2, R7       ;Display MSD
          RET              ;
```

Summary

- The digital display can be interfaced directly with 8051 or by using display decoder devices.
- The power consumption is reduced by multiplexing the displays.
- Keyboard is interfaced with software de-bouncing technique.
- Matrix keyboard optimizes the keys and I/O port lines.
- ADC is interfaced with a temperature sensor but can be connected to any type of sensor with the help of proper signal conditioner.
- The DAC interface does not require any handshake with microcontroller 8051.
- Stepper motor is controlled in half and full step. It is driven with power devices such as buffer arrays.
- An embedded system for temperature indicator is designed by choosing necessary peripheral devices. The system can be enhanced further by adding software program modules.

Review Questions

1. What are the other ways to interface LED display to 8051 based system?
2. What are the ways possible to decrease power consumption of 8051 based system?

3. Design a digital clock using 8051 microcontroller.
4. Explain a scheme for logging a temperature data on a personal computer (PC). What components will be required to implement the same?
5. Design a sawtooth wave form generator using 8051 and DAC0808.